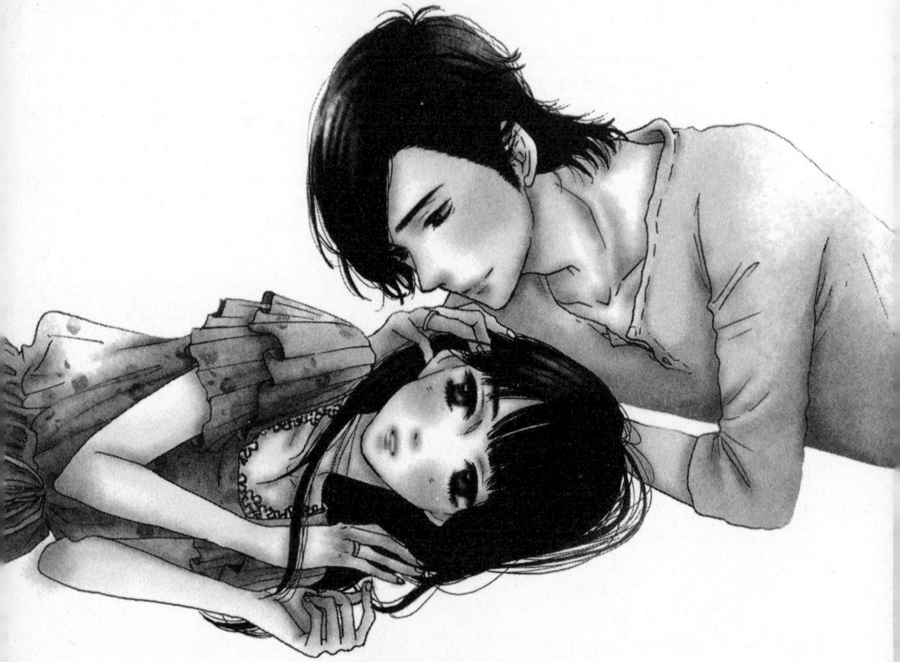

Say I Love You.

17

by
Kanae
Hazuki

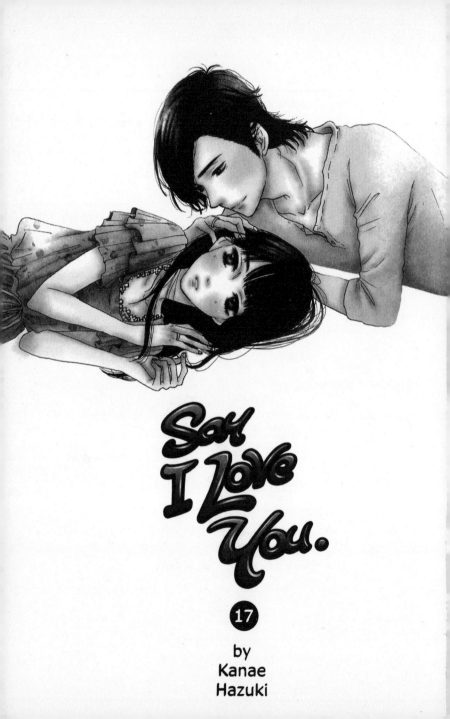

Kanae Hazuki
presents

Chapter 65

Chapter 66

Chapter 67

Chapter 68

CHARACTER

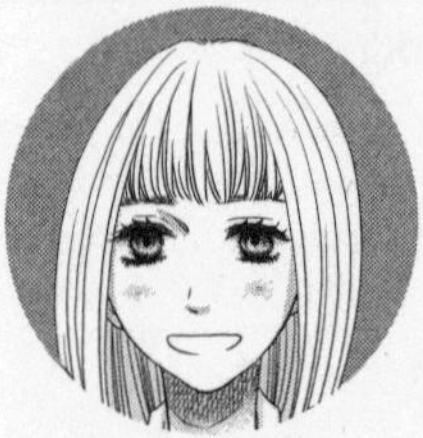

Mei Tachibana
A girl who hadn't had a single friend, let alone boyfriend, for sixteen years. She started dating Yamato, the most popular boy in school, and is now growing as a woman. She's going to vocational school to become a preschool teacher.

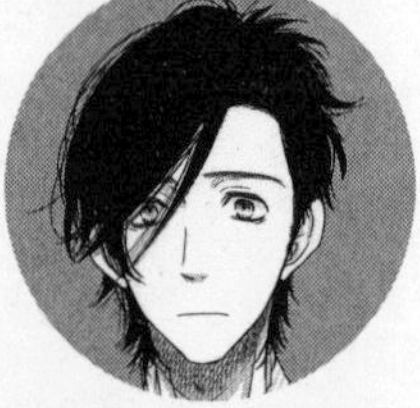

Yamato Kurosawa
The most popular boy at school. He was taken in by the charms of the brooding weirdo Mei, and they are now dating. He chose to go to college as he pursues a career in photography.

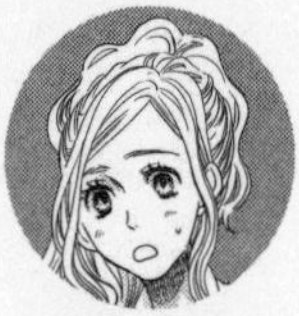

Asami Oikawa
An amiable girl, and Mei's first friend. She currently dates Yamato's friend Nakanishi. Like Mei, she aspires to be a preschool teacher.

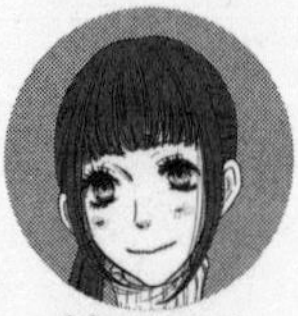

Megumi Kitagawa
A popular amateur model who was once extremely aggressive in her pursuit of Yamato. After he dumped her, she got serious about her career. After graduating high school, she is now fighting to make it in Paris.

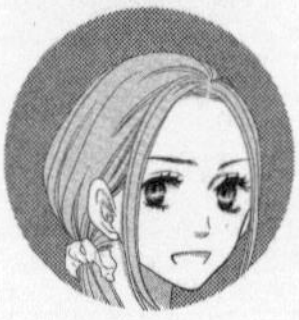

Natsuki
A fellow freshman at Yamato's college. She dropped out of high school and resumed her education later, so she is actually older than he is. She joined Yamato's photography club, but...

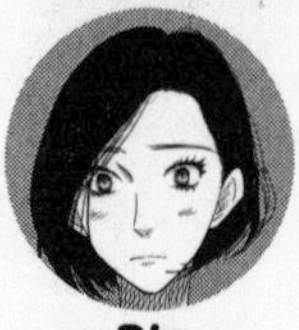

Rin Aoi
A student at Mei's old high school. She's a popular model going by the name RIN, and has been given the opportunity to walk in Paris Fashion Week. She aspires to be like Megumi.

STORY

Mei graduates from the high school that holds so many memories for her, and moves on to a vocational school for childcare. Meanwhile, Yamato decides to attend college as he pursues a career in photography. They must go to different schools to achieve their individual goals, and their new lives give them fewer and fewer opportunities to see each other. Then one day, Asami reveals to Mei that her relationship with Nakanishi might be over, and Mei gets a message from Aiko about Yamato walking around with another girl...?!

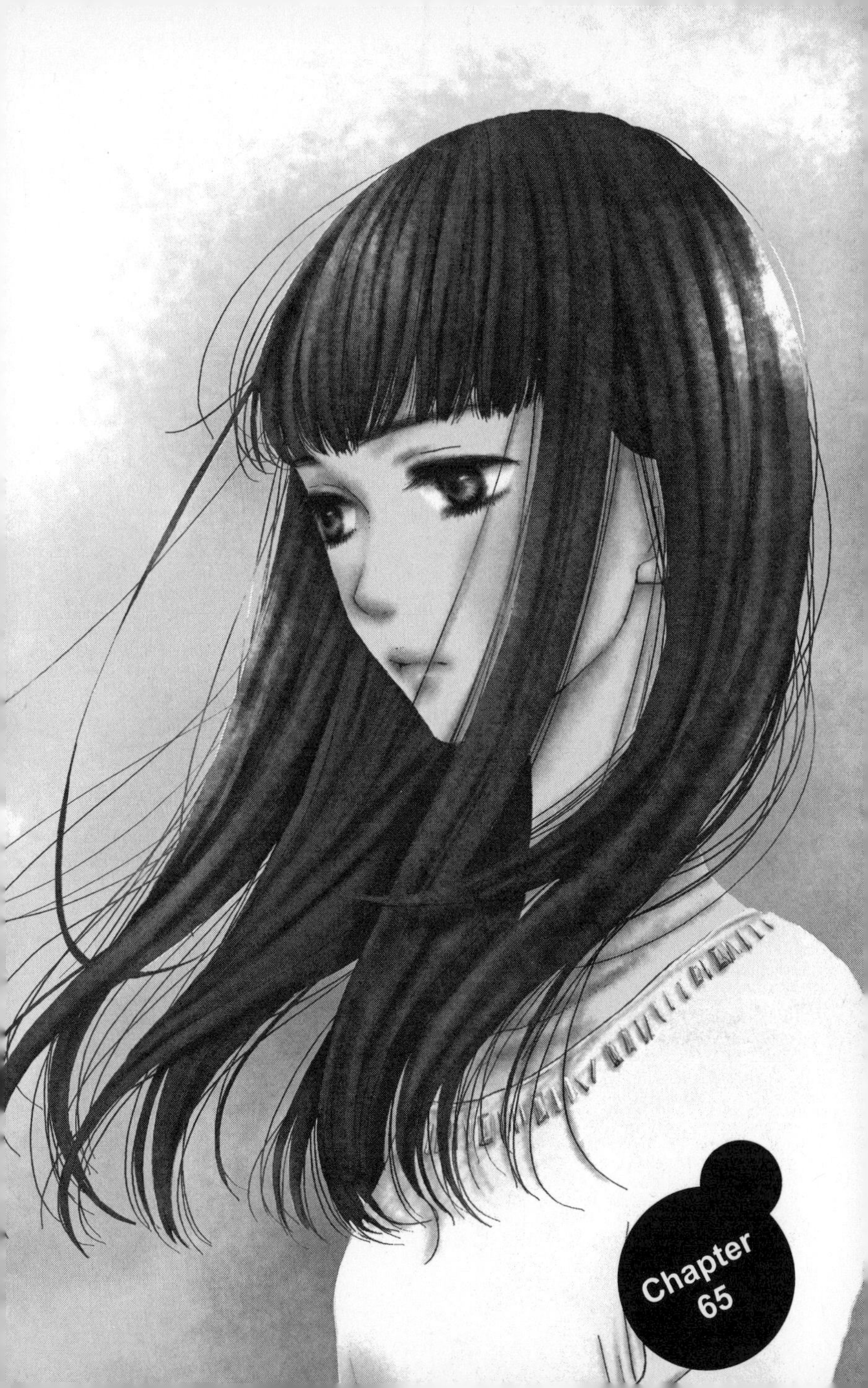
Chapter
65

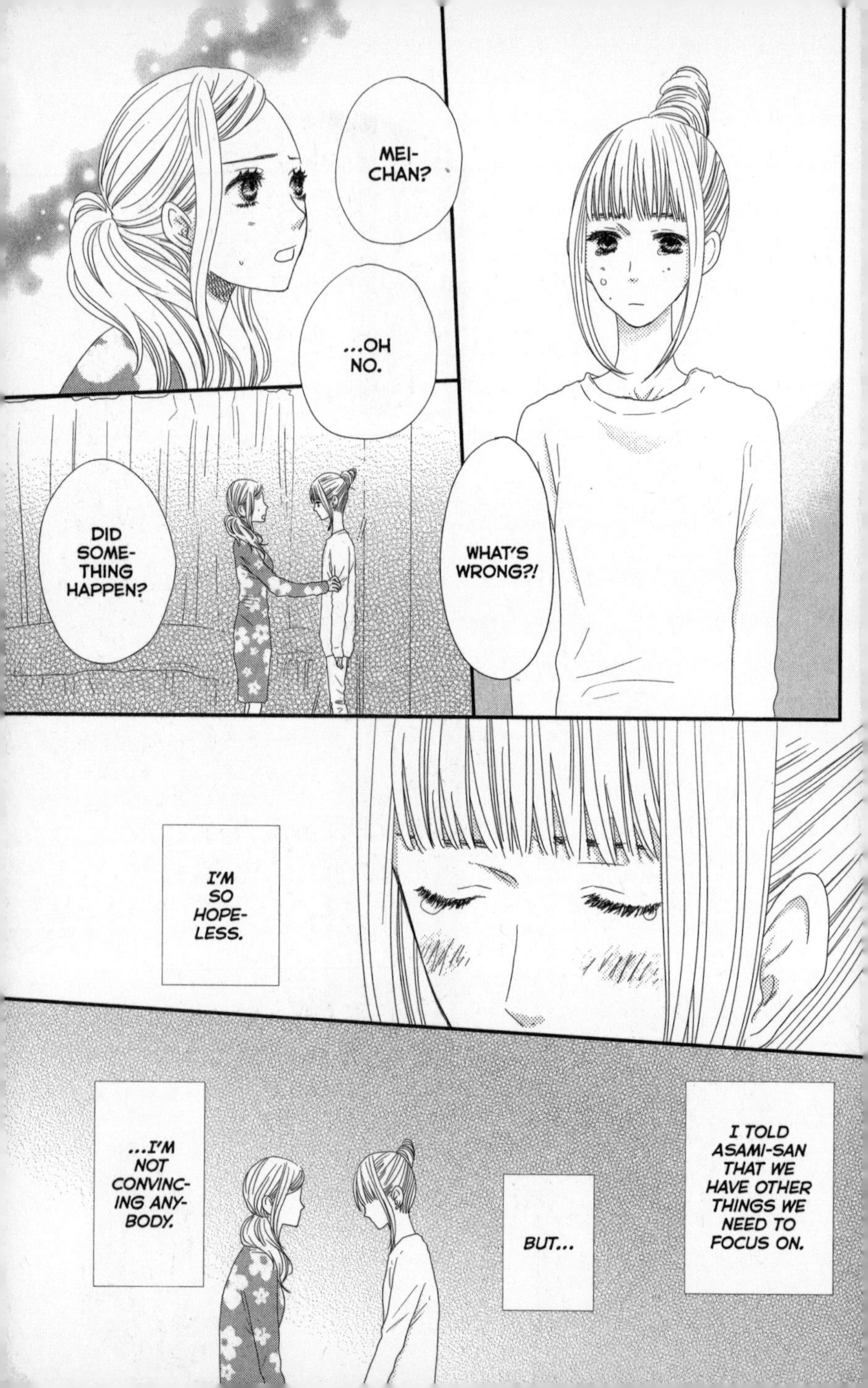
WHAT'S WRONG?!
MEI-CHAN?
...OH NO.
DID SOMETHING HAPPEN?
I'M SO HOPELESS.
I TOLD ASAMI-SAN THAT WE HAVE OTHER THINGS WE NEED TO FOCUS ON.
BUT...
...I'M NOT CONVINCING ANYBODY.

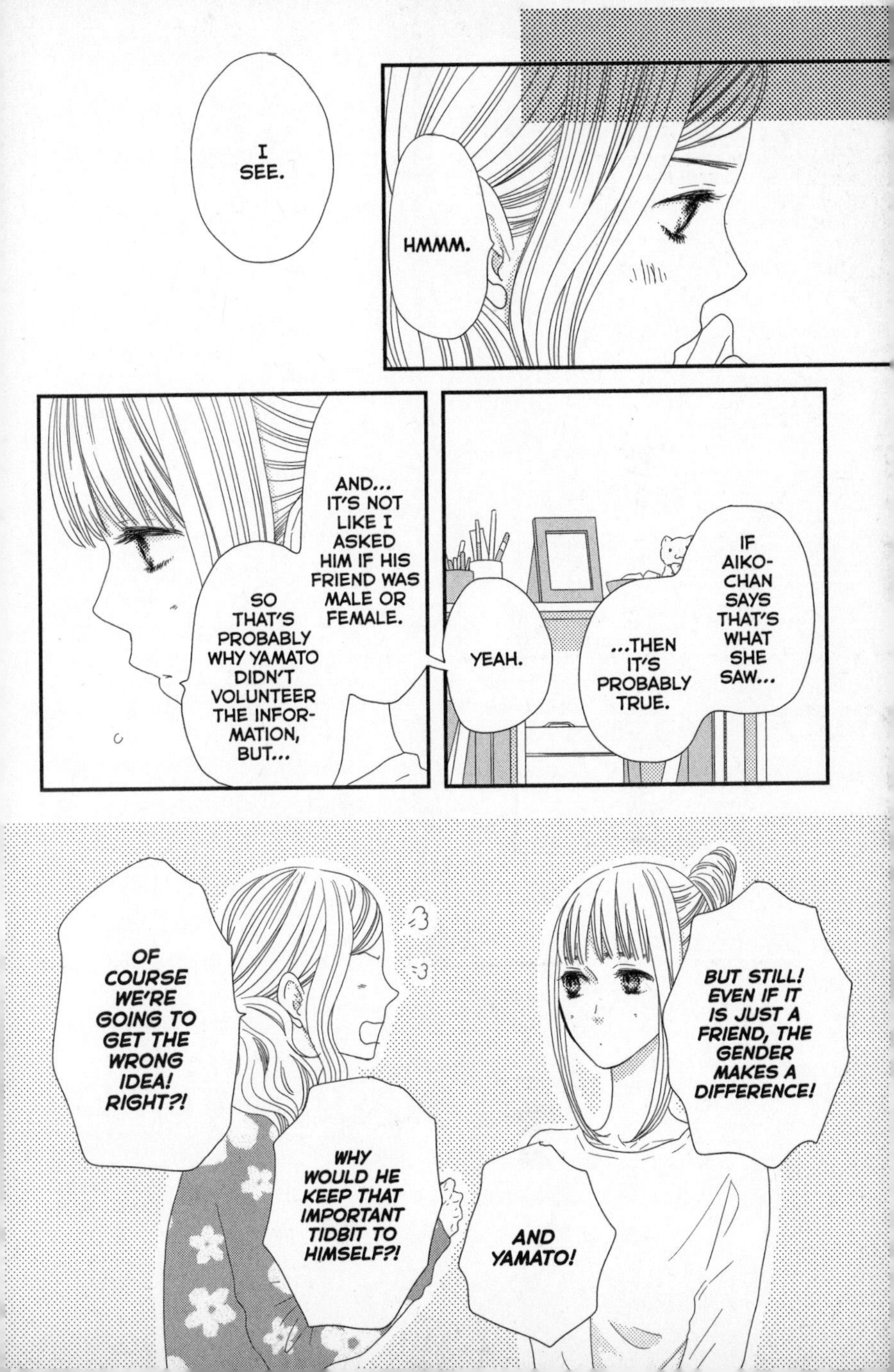
HMMM.
I SEE.
IF AIKO-CHAN SAYS THAT'S WHAT SHE SAW...
...THEN IT'S PROBABLY TRUE.
YEAH.
AND... IT'S NOT LIKE I ASKED HIM IF HIS FRIEND WAS MALE OR FEMALE.
SO THAT'S PROBABLY WHY YAMATO DIDN'T VOLUNTEER THE INFOR-MATION, BUT...
BUT STILL! EVEN IF IT IS JUST A FRIEND, THE GENDER MAKES A DIFFERENCE!
AND YAMATO!
WHY WOULD HE KEEP THAT IMPORTANT TIDBIT TO HIMSELF?!
OF COURSE WE'RE GOING TO GET THE WRONG IDEA! RIGHT?!

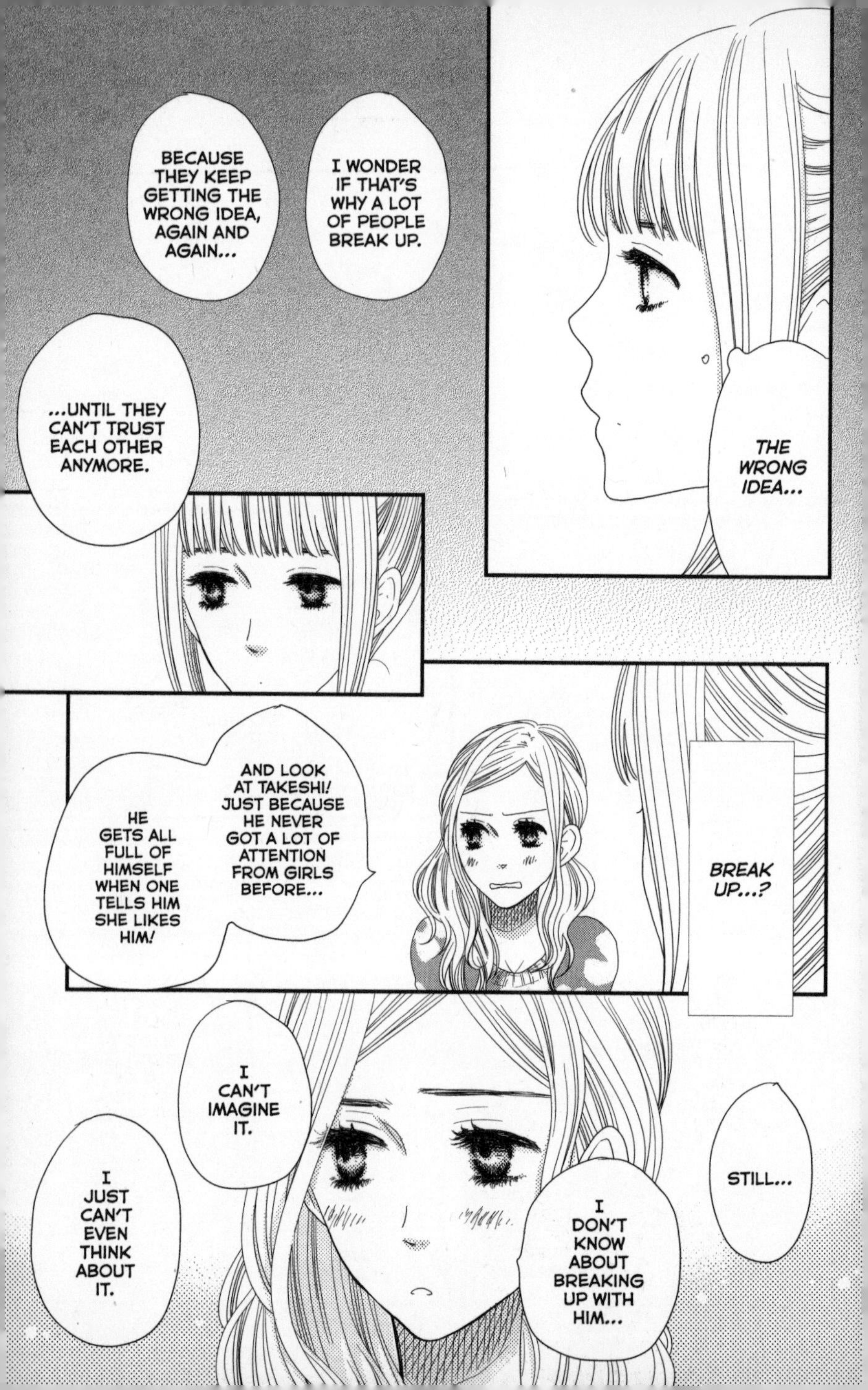
I WONDER IF THAT'S WHY A LOT OF PEOPLE BREAK UP.
BECAUSE THEY KEEP GETTING THE WRONG IDEA, AGAIN AND AGAIN...
...UNTIL THEY CAN'T TRUST EACH OTHER ANYMORE.
THE WRONG IDEA...
BREAK UP...?
AND LOOK AT TAKESHI! JUST BECAUSE HE NEVER GOT A LOT OF ATTENTION FROM GIRLS BEFORE...
HE GETS ALL FULL OF HIMSELF WHEN ONE TELLS HIM SHE LIKES HIM!
STILL...
I DON'T KNOW ABOUT BREAKING UP WITH HIM...
I CAN'T IMAGINE IT.
I JUST CAN'T EVEN THINK ABOUT IT.

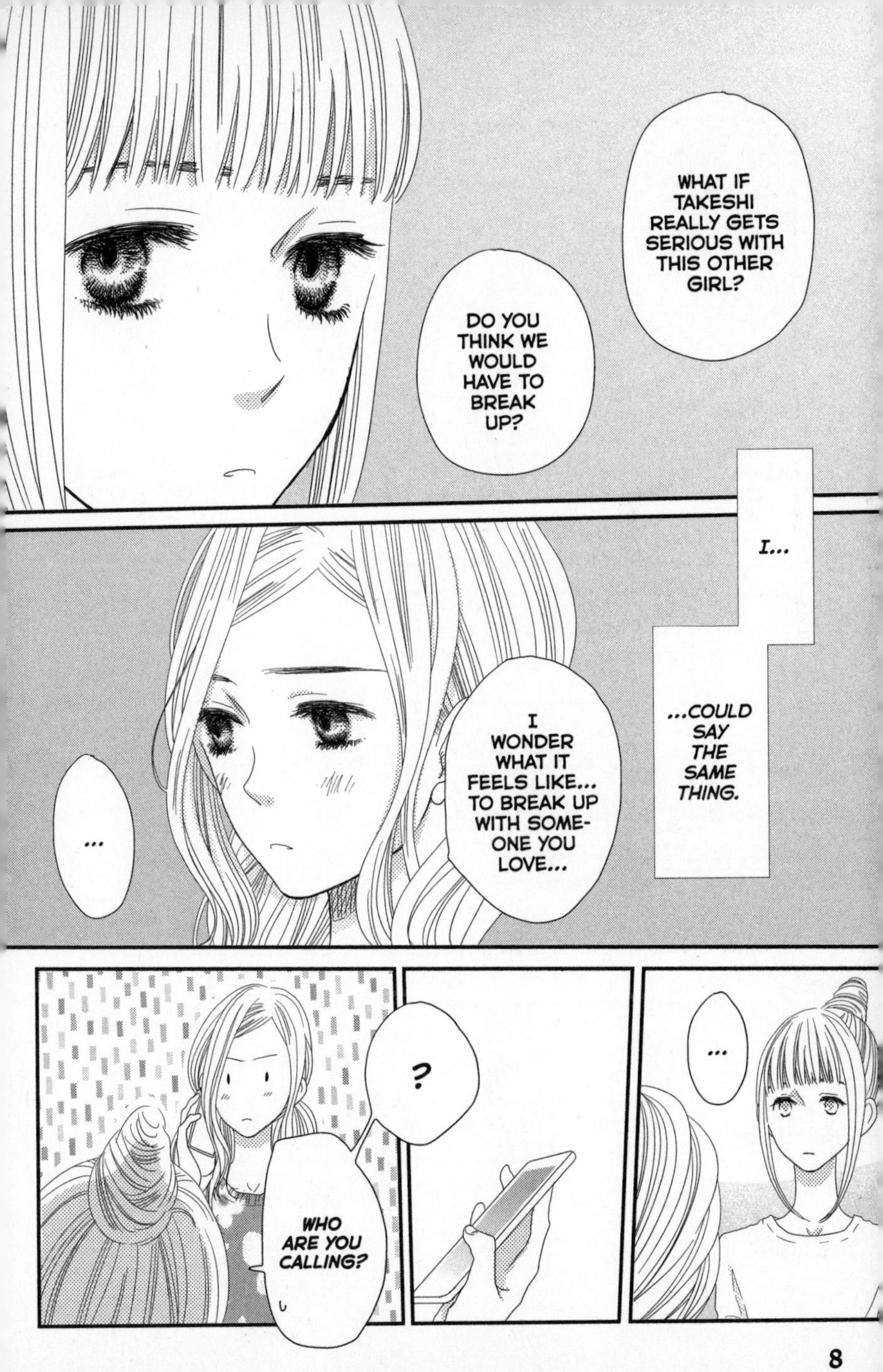
WHAT IF TAKESHI REALLY GETS SERIOUS WITH THIS OTHER GIRL?
DO YOU THINK WE WOULD HAVE TO BREAK UP?
I...
...COULD SAY THE SAME THING.
I WONDER WHAT IT FEELS LIKE... TO BREAK UP WITH SOME-ONE YOU LOVE...
...
...
?
WHO ARE YOU CALLING?

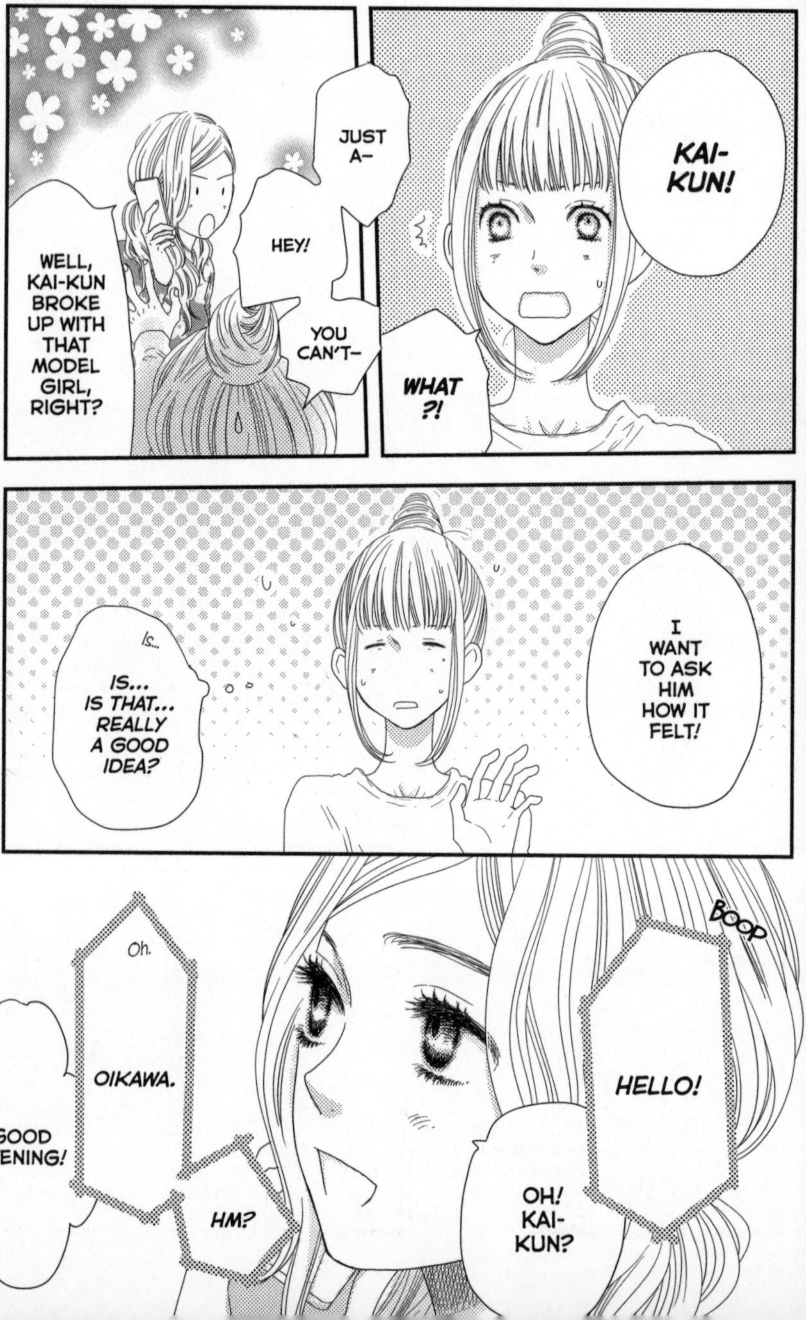
KAI-KUN!
WHAT?!
JUST A–
HEY!
YOU CAN'T–
WELL, KAI-KUN BROKE UP WITH THAT MODEL GIRL, RIGHT?
I WANT TO ASK HIM HOW IT FELT!
Is...
IS... IS THAT... REALLY A GOOD IDEA?
BOOP
HELLO!
OH! KAI-KUN?
Oh.
OIKAWA.
HM?
GOOD EVENING!

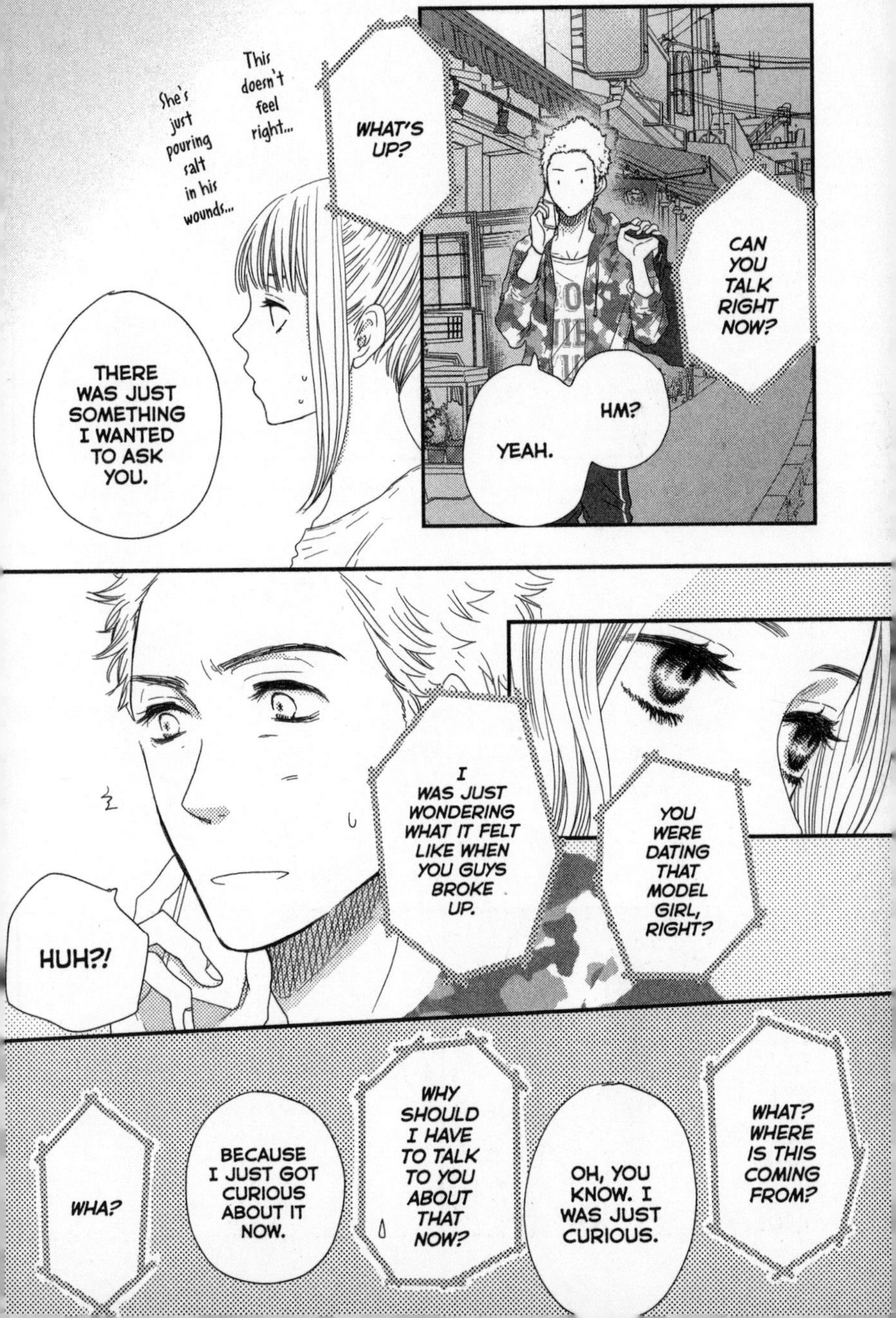
CAN YOU TALK RIGHT NOW?
HM? YEAH.
WHAT'S UP?
This doesn't feel right...
She's just pouring salt in his wounds...
THERE WAS JUST SOMETHING I WANTED TO ASK YOU.
YOU WERE DATING THAT MODEL GIRL, RIGHT?
I WAS JUST WONDERING WHAT IT FELT LIKE WHEN YOU GUYS BROKE UP.
HUH?!
WHAT? WHERE IS THIS COMING FROM?
OH, YOU KNOW. I WAS JUST CURIOUS.
WHY SHOULD I HAVE TO TALK TO YOU ABOUT THAT NOW?
BECAUSE I JUST GOT CURIOUS ABOUT IT NOW.
WHA?

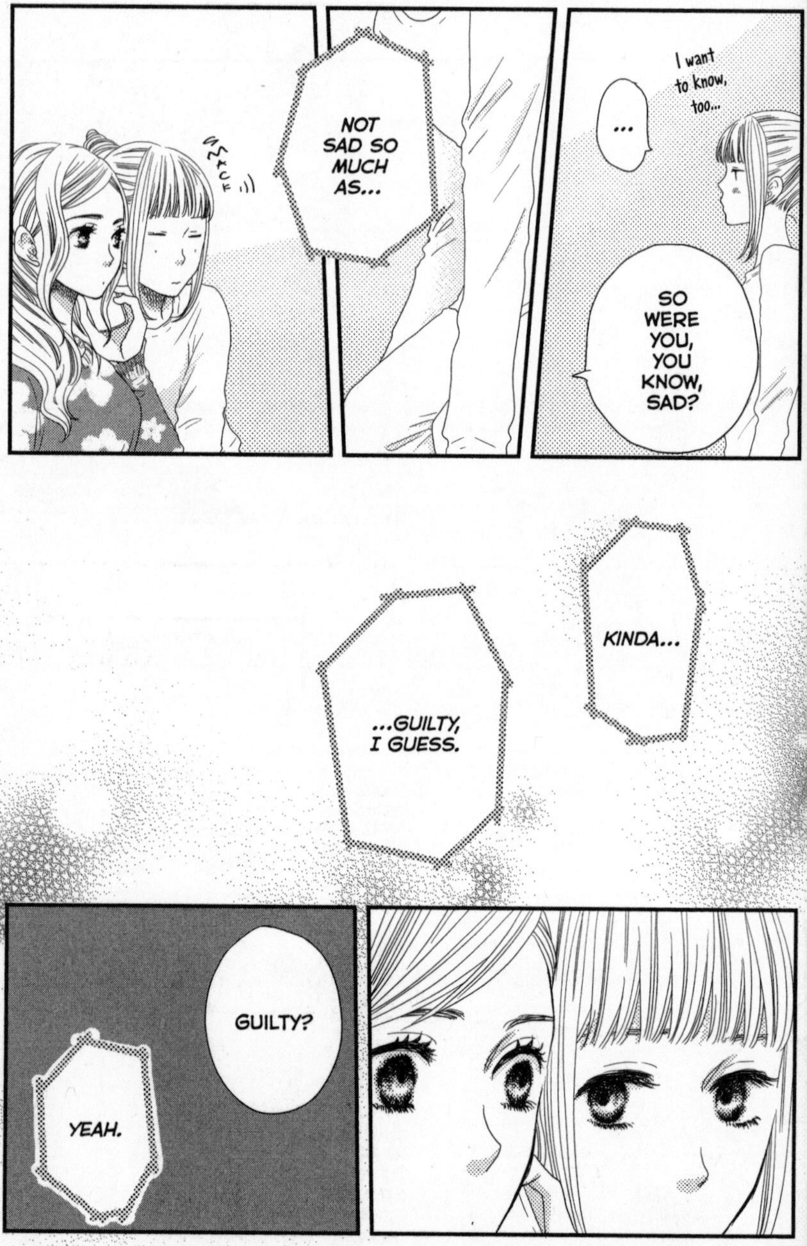
I want to know, too...
...
SO WERE YOU, YOU KNOW, SAD?
NOT SAD SO MUCH AS...
KINDA...
...GUILTY, I GUESS.
GUILTY?
YEAH.

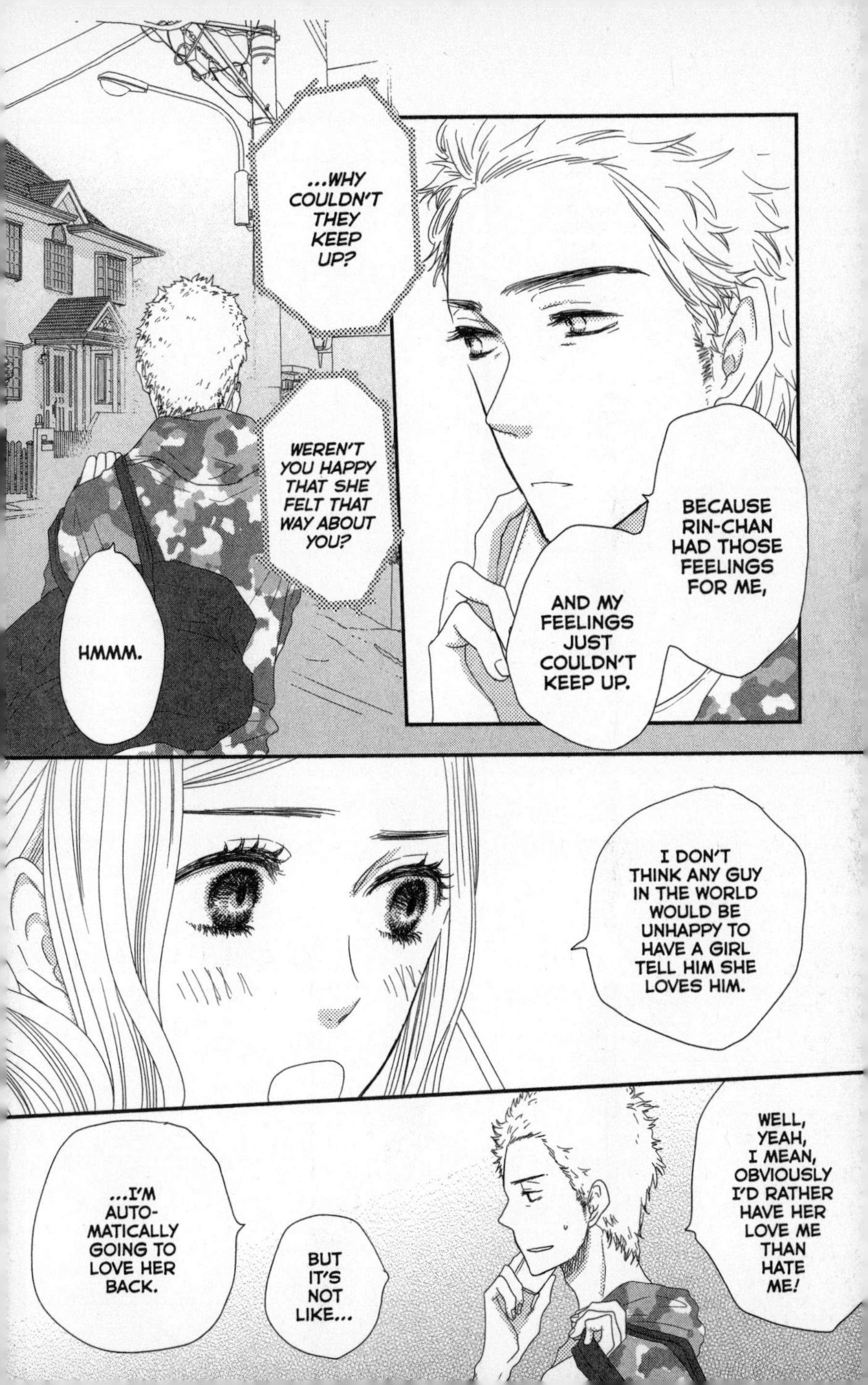
BECAUSE RIN-CHAN HAD THOSE FEELINGS FOR ME,
AND MY FEELINGS JUST COULDN'T KEEP UP.
...WHY COULDN'T THEY KEEP UP?
WEREN'T YOU HAPPY THAT SHE FELT THAT WAY ABOUT YOU?
HMMM.
I DON'T THINK ANY GUY IN THE WORLD WOULD BE UNHAPPY TO HAVE A GIRL TELL HIM SHE LOVES HIM.
WELL, YEAH, I MEAN, OBVIOUSLY I'D RATHER HAVE HER LOVE ME THAN HATE ME!
BUT IT'S NOT LIKE...
...I'M AUTO-MATICALLY GOING TO LOVE HER BACK.

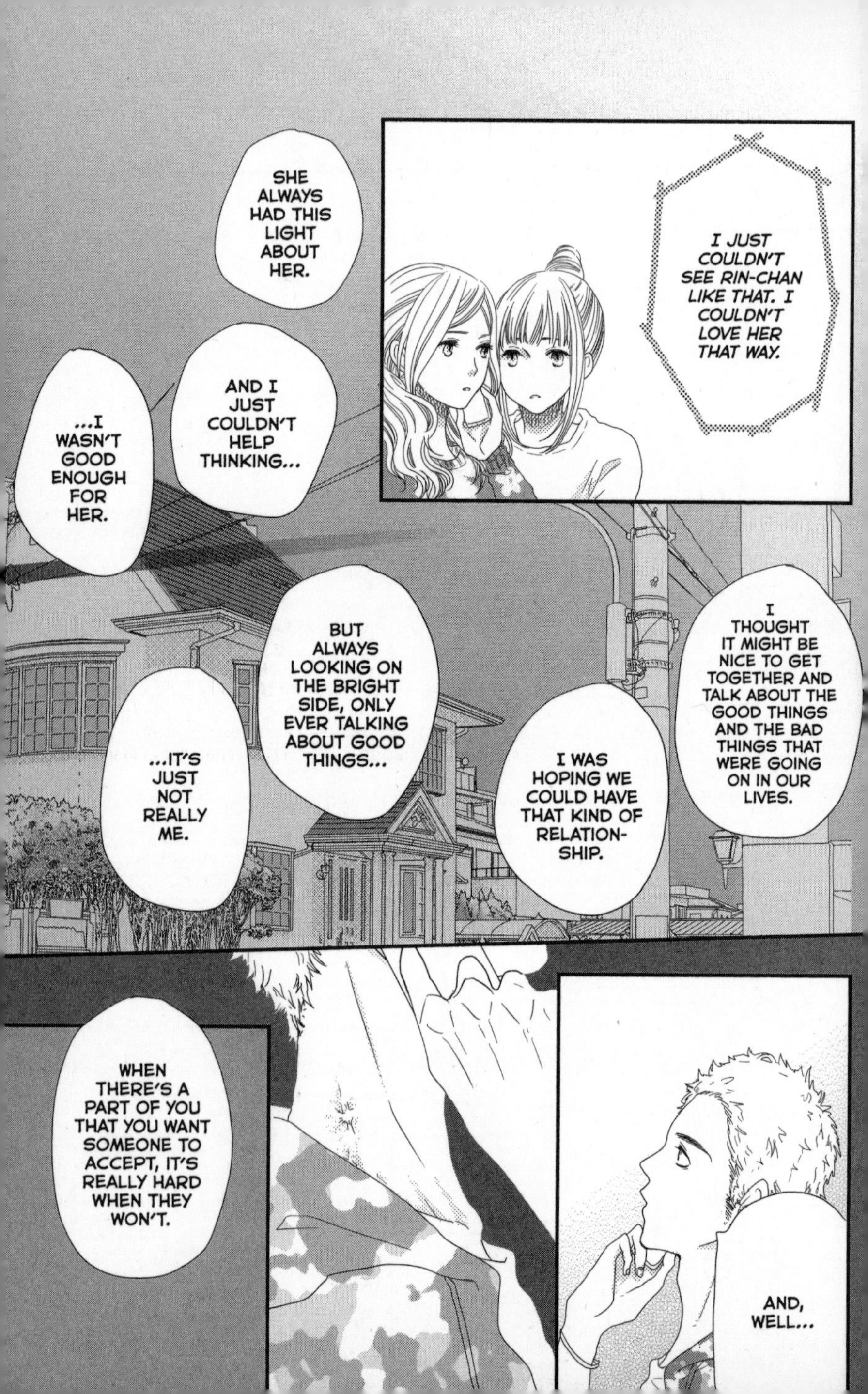
I JUST COULDN'T SEE RIN-CHAN LIKE THAT. I COULDN'T LOVE HER THAT WAY.
SHE ALWAYS HAD THIS LIGHT ABOUT HER.
AND I JUST COULDN'T HELP THINKING...
...I WASN'T GOOD ENOUGH FOR HER.
I THOUGHT IT MIGHT BE NICE TO GET TOGETHER AND TALK ABOUT THE GOOD THINGS AND THE BAD THINGS THAT WERE GOING ON IN OUR LIVES.
I WAS HOPING WE COULD HAVE THAT KIND OF RELATION-SHIP.
BUT ALWAYS LOOKING ON THE BRIGHT SIDE, ONLY EVER TALKING ABOUT GOOD THINGS...
...IT'S JUST NOT REALLY ME.
AND, WELL...
WHEN THERE'S A PART OF YOU THAT YOU WANT SOMEONE TO ACCEPT, IT'S REALLY HARD WHEN THEY WON'T.

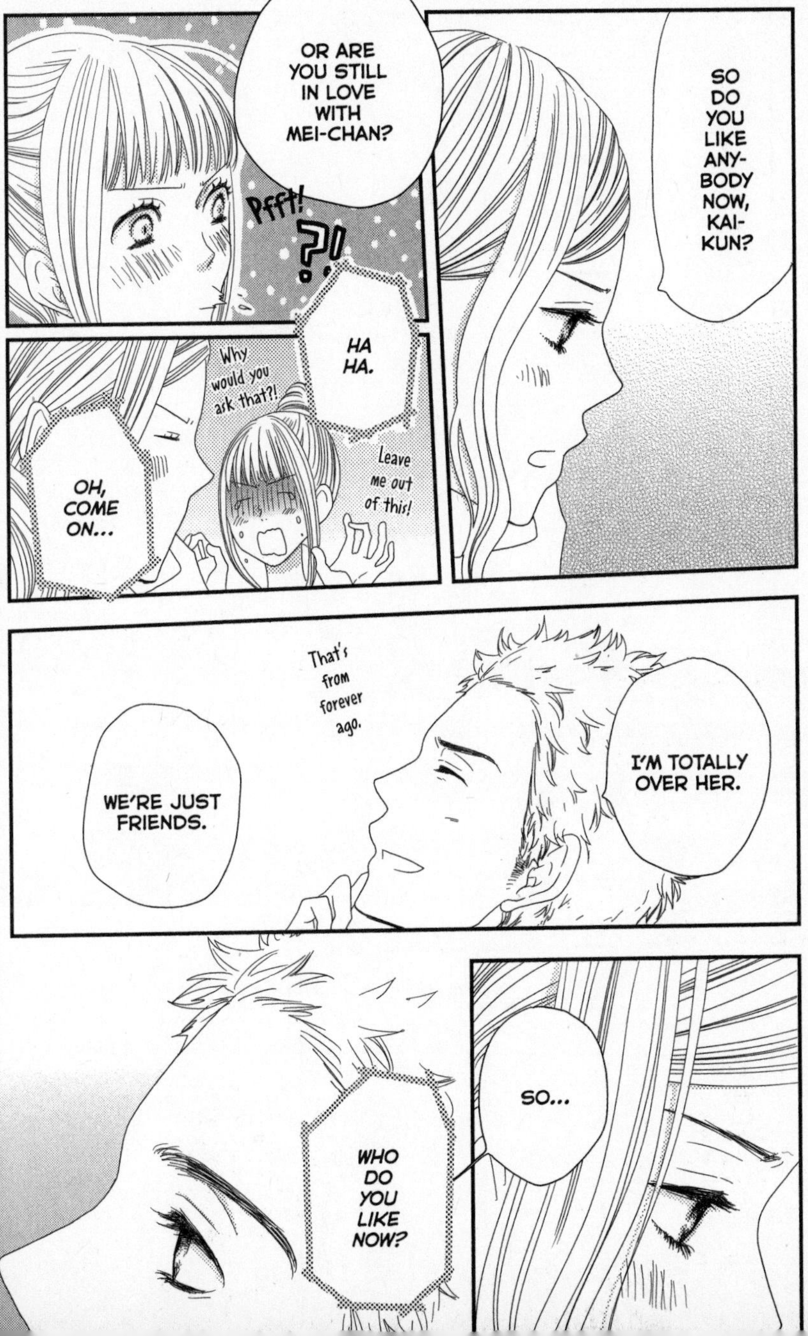
SO DO YOU LIKE ANYBODY NOW, KAI-KUN?
OR ARE YOU STILL IN LOVE WITH MEI-CHAN?
Pfft!
?!
HA HA.
Why would you ask that?!
Leave me out of this!
OH, COME ON...
I'M TOTALLY OVER HER.
That's from forever ago.
WE'RE JUST FRIENDS.
SO...
WHO DO YOU LIKE NOW?

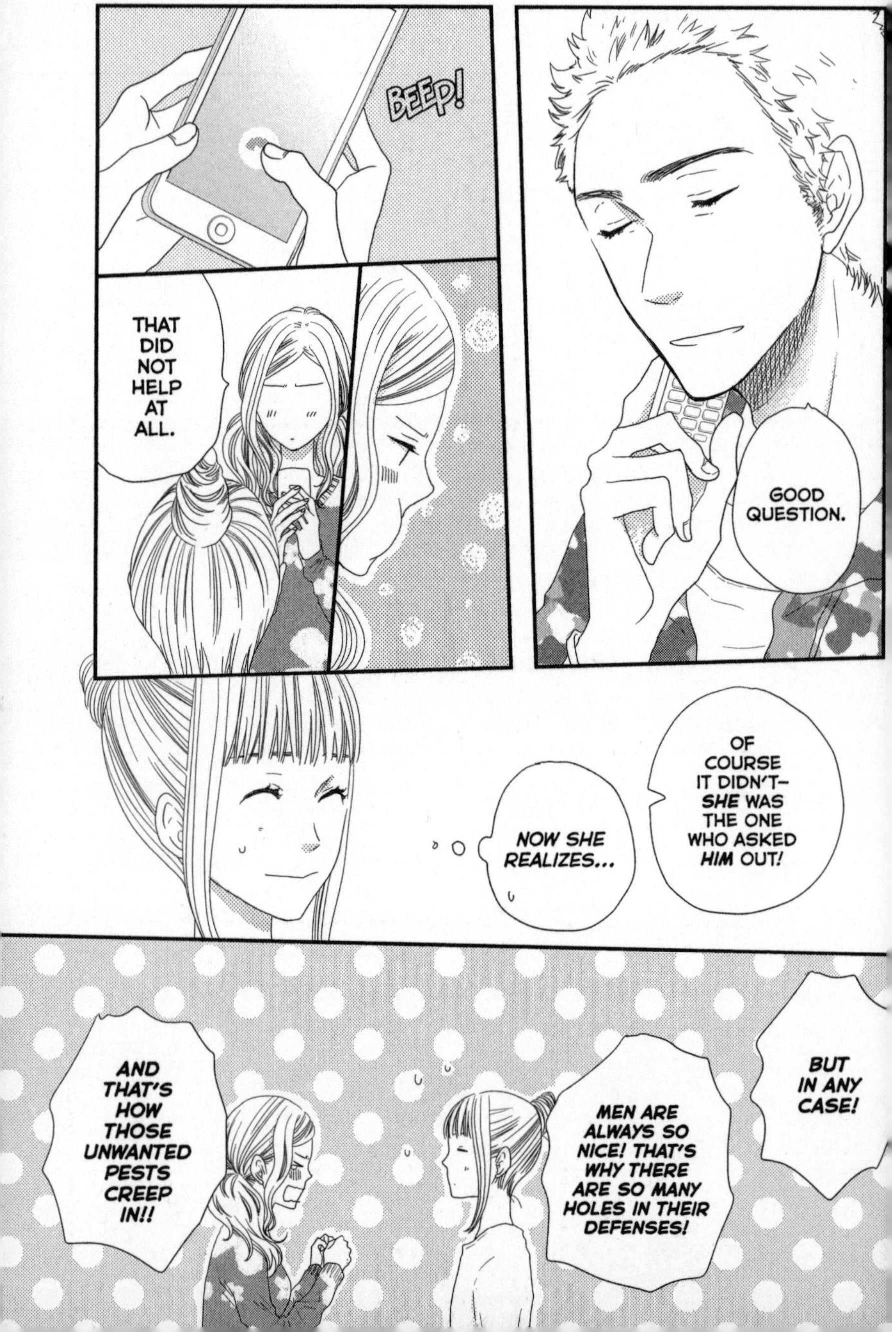
GOOD QUESTION.
BEEP!
THAT DID NOT HELP AT ALL.
OF COURSE IT DIDN'T— *SHE* WAS THE ONE WHO ASKED *HIM* OUT!
NOW SHE REALIZES...
BUT IN ANY CASE!
MEN ARE ALWAYS SO NICE! THAT'S WHY THERE ARE SO MANY HOLES IN THEIR DEFENSES!
AND THAT'S HOW THOSE UNWANTED PESTS CREEP IN!!

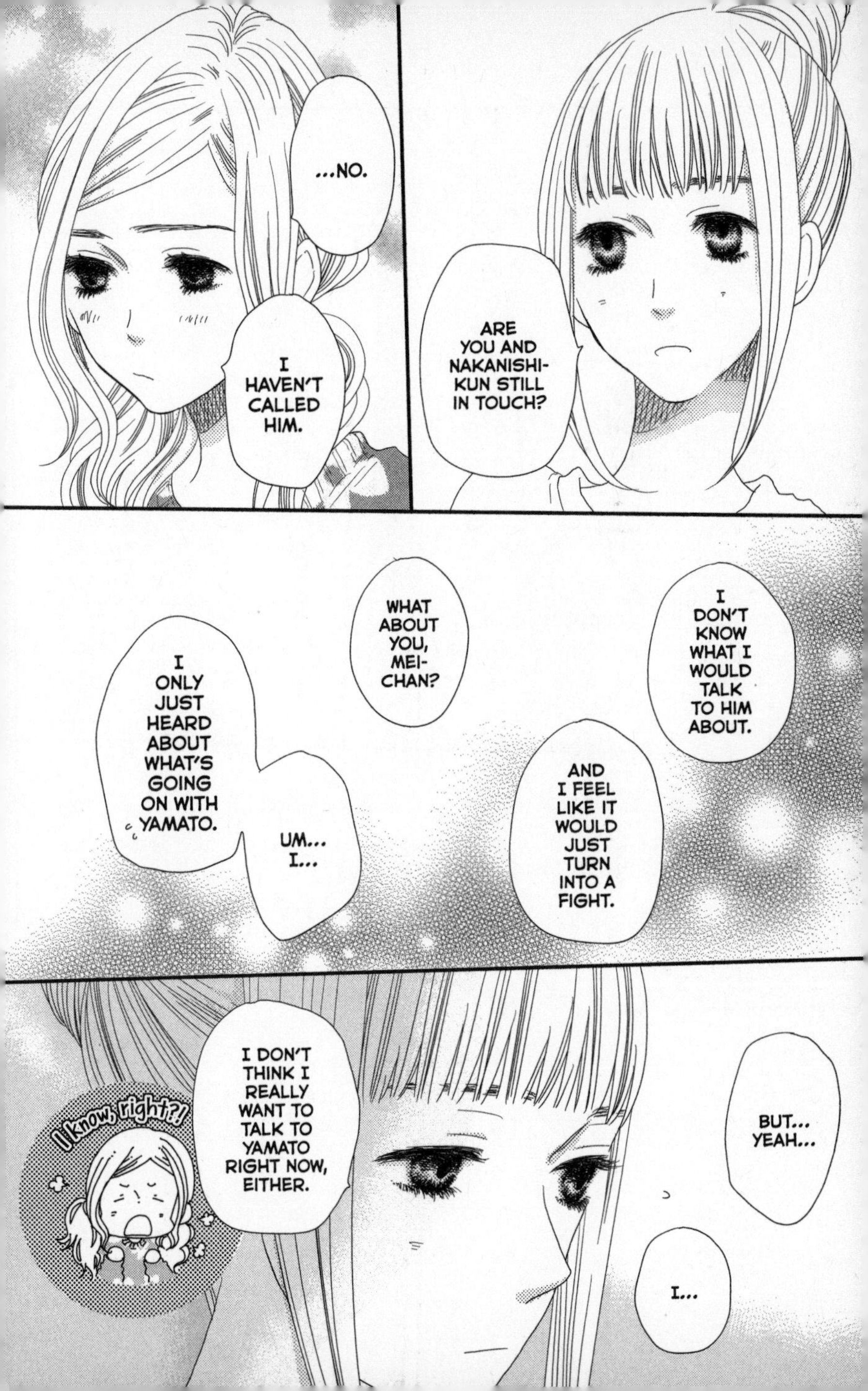
ARE YOU AND NAKANISHI-KUN STILL IN TOUCH?
...NO.
I HAVEN'T CALLED HIM.
I DON'T KNOW WHAT I WOULD TALK TO HIM ABOUT.
AND I FEEL LIKE IT WOULD JUST TURN INTO A FIGHT.
WHAT ABOUT YOU, MEI-CHAN?
UM... I...
I ONLY JUST HEARD ABOUT WHAT'S GOING ON WITH YAMATO.
BUT... YEAH...
I...
I DON'T THINK I REALLY WANT TO TALK TO YAMATO RIGHT NOW, EITHER.
I know, right?!

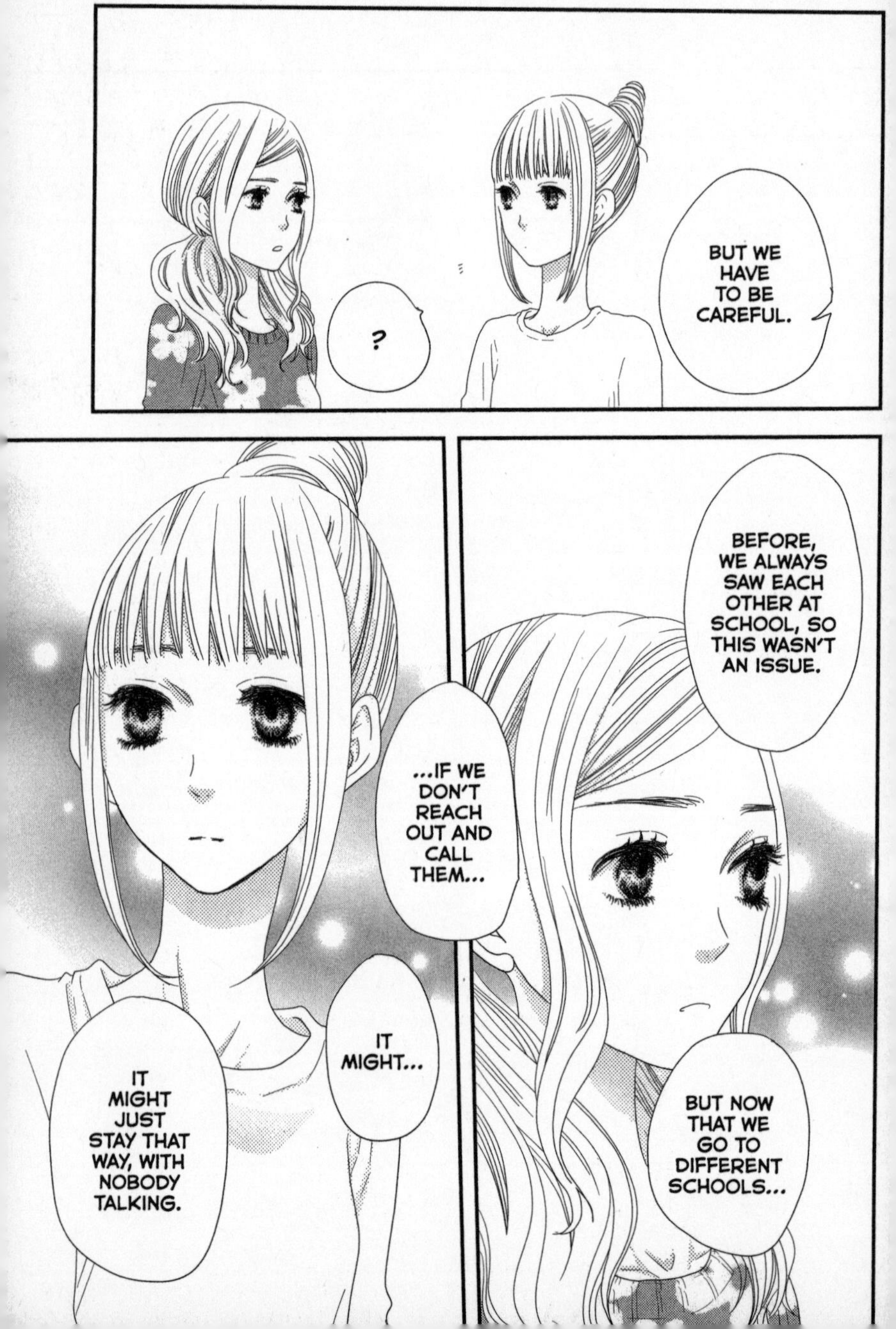
BUT WE HAVE TO BE CAREFUL.
?
BEFORE, WE ALWAYS SAW EACH OTHER AT SCHOOL, SO THIS WASN'T AN ISSUE.
BUT NOW THAT WE GO TO DIFFERENT SCHOOLS...
...IF WE DON'T REACH OUT AND CALL THEM...
IT MIGHT...
IT MIGHT JUST STAY THAT WAY, WITH NOBODY TALKING.

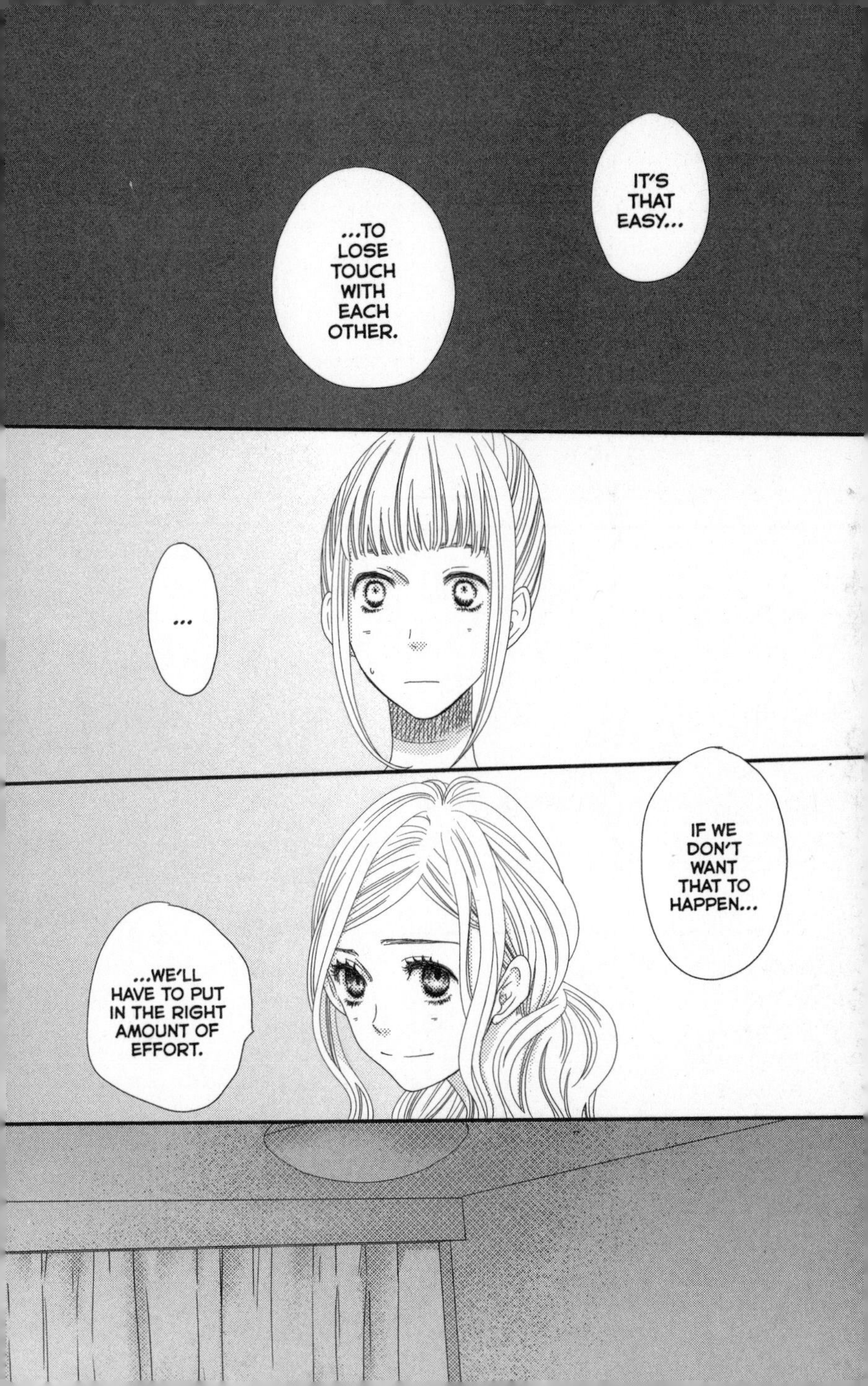
IT'S THAT EASY...
...TO LOSE TOUCH WITH EACH OTHER.
...
IF WE DON'T WANT THAT TO HAPPEN...
...WE'LL HAVE TO PUT IN THE RIGHT AMOUNT OF EFFORT.

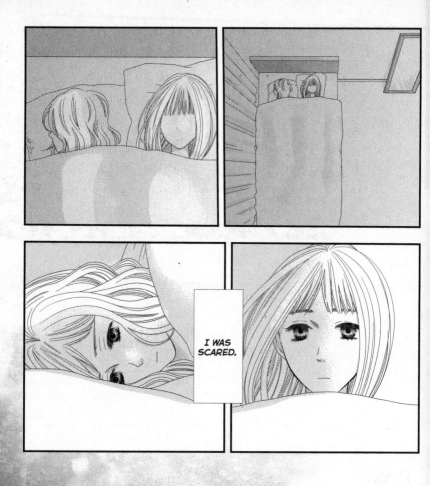

I WAS SCARED.

LIKE BEING IN THE SAME BED...

...BUT SLEEPING MILES APART.

THAT'S...

...WHAT IT FELT LIKE.

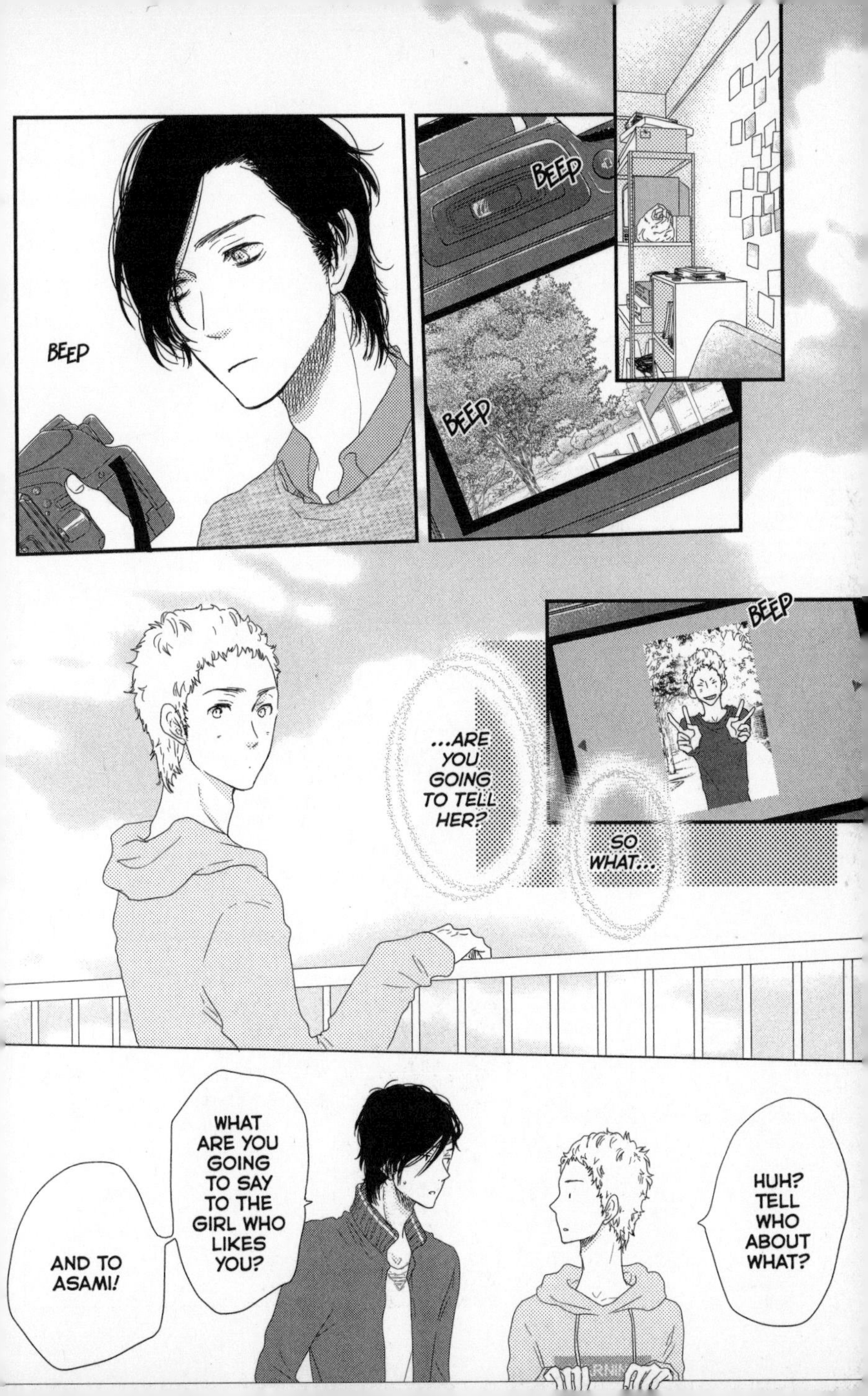
BEEP
BEEP
BEEP
BEEP
SO WHAT...
...ARE YOU GOING TO TELL HER?
HUH? TELL WHO ABOUT WHAT?
WHAT ARE YOU GOING TO SAY TO THE GIRL WHO LIKES YOU?
AND TO ASAMI!

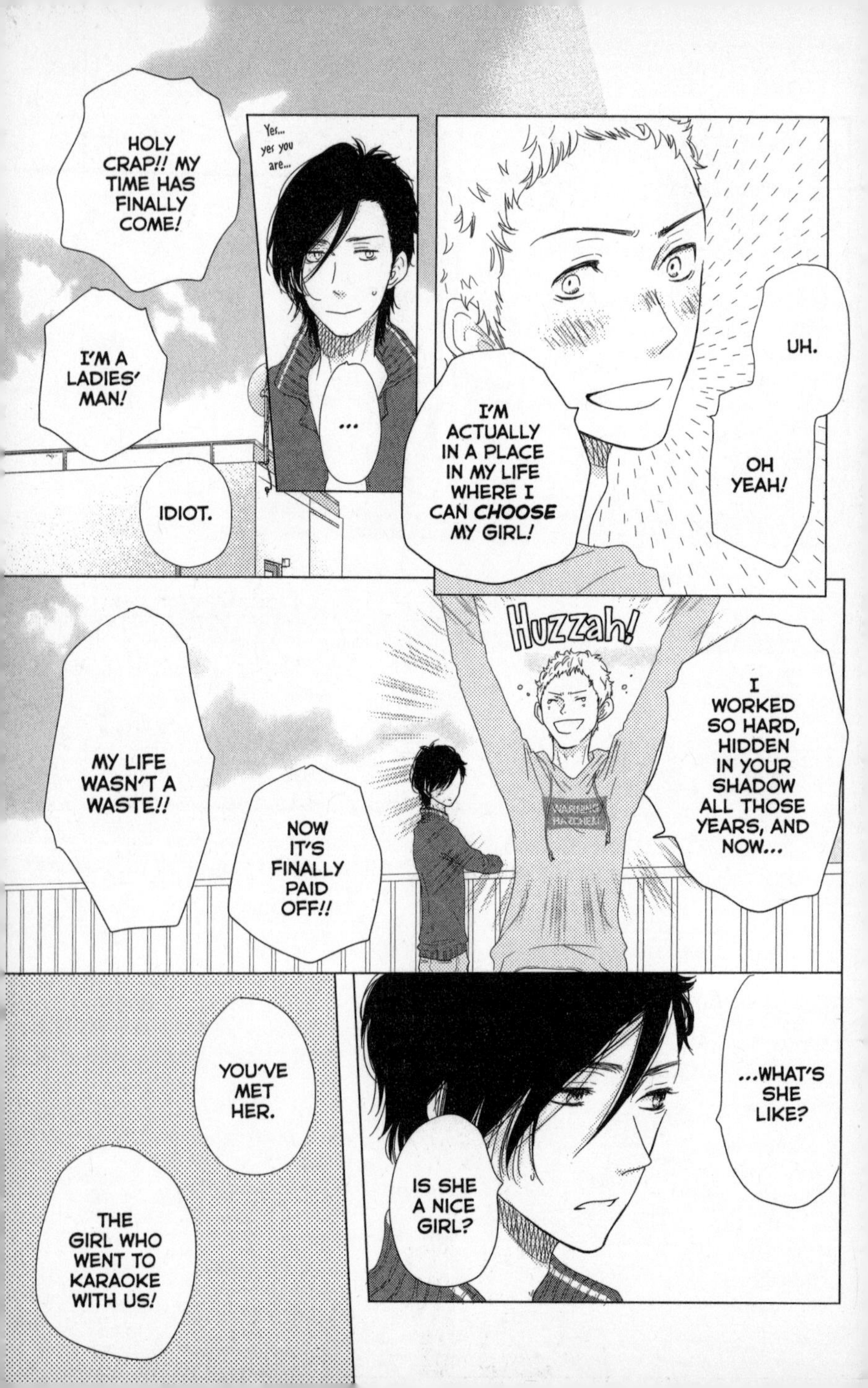
UH.
OH YEAH!
I'M ACTUALLY IN A PLACE IN MY LIFE WHERE I CAN *CHOOSE* MY GIRL!
Yes... yes you are...
...
HOLY CRAP!! MY TIME HAS FINALLY COME!
I'M A LADIES' MAN!
IDIOT.
Huzzah!
I WORKED SO HARD, HIDDEN IN YOUR SHADOW ALL THOSE YEARS, AND NOW...
NOW IT'S FINALLY PAID OFF!!
MY LIFE WASN'T A WASTE!!
...WHAT'S SHE LIKE?
IS SHE A NICE GIRL?
YOU'VE MET HER.
THE GIRL WHO WENT TO KARAOKE WITH US!

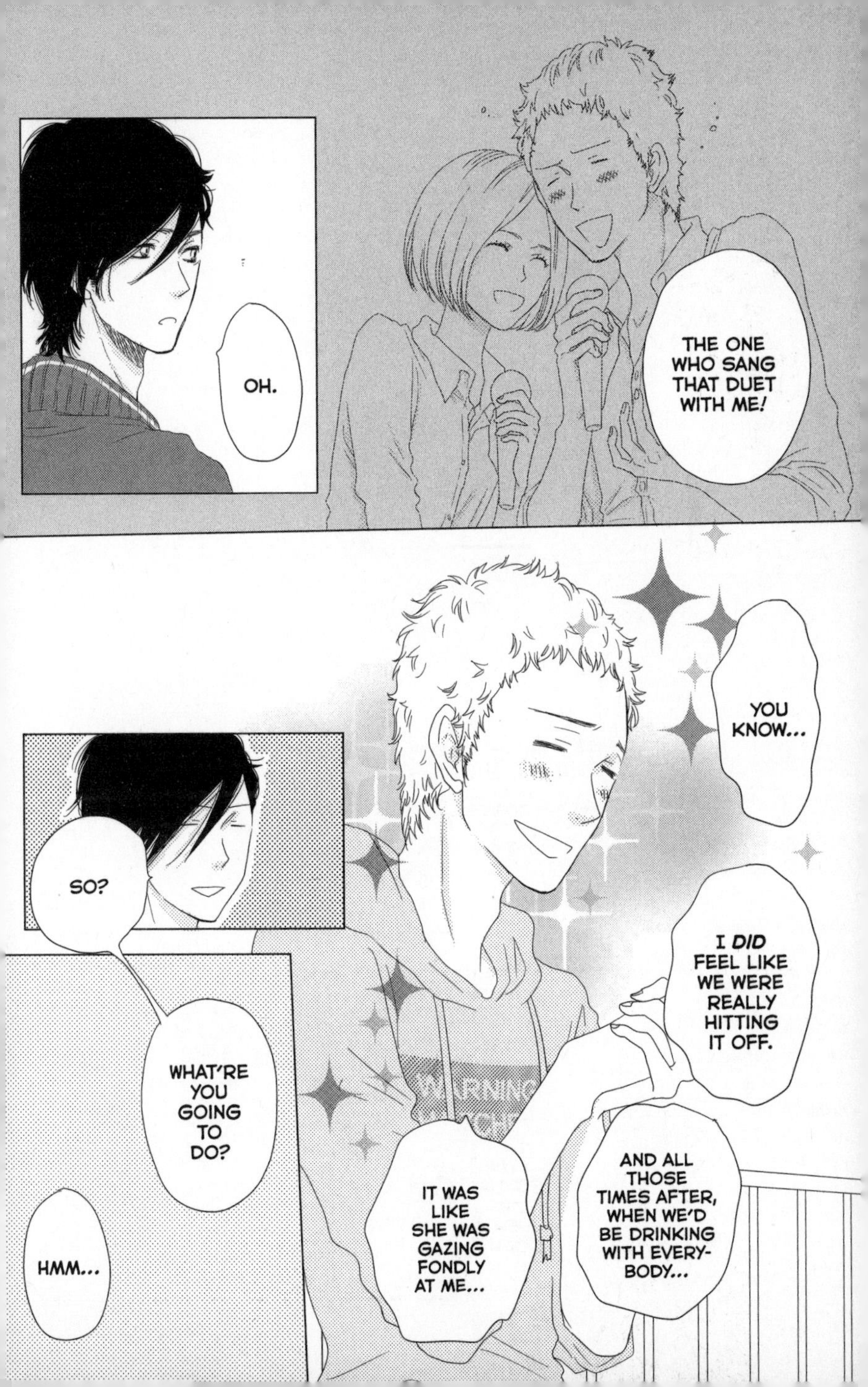
THE ONE WHO SANG THAT DUET WITH ME!
OH.
YOU KNOW...
I *DID* FEEL LIKE WE WERE REALLY HITTING IT OFF.
AND ALL THOSE TIMES AFTER, WHEN WE'D BE DRINKING WITH EVERY-BODY...
IT WAS LIKE SHE WAS GAZING FONDLY AT ME...
SO?
WHAT'RE YOU GOING TO DO?
HMM...

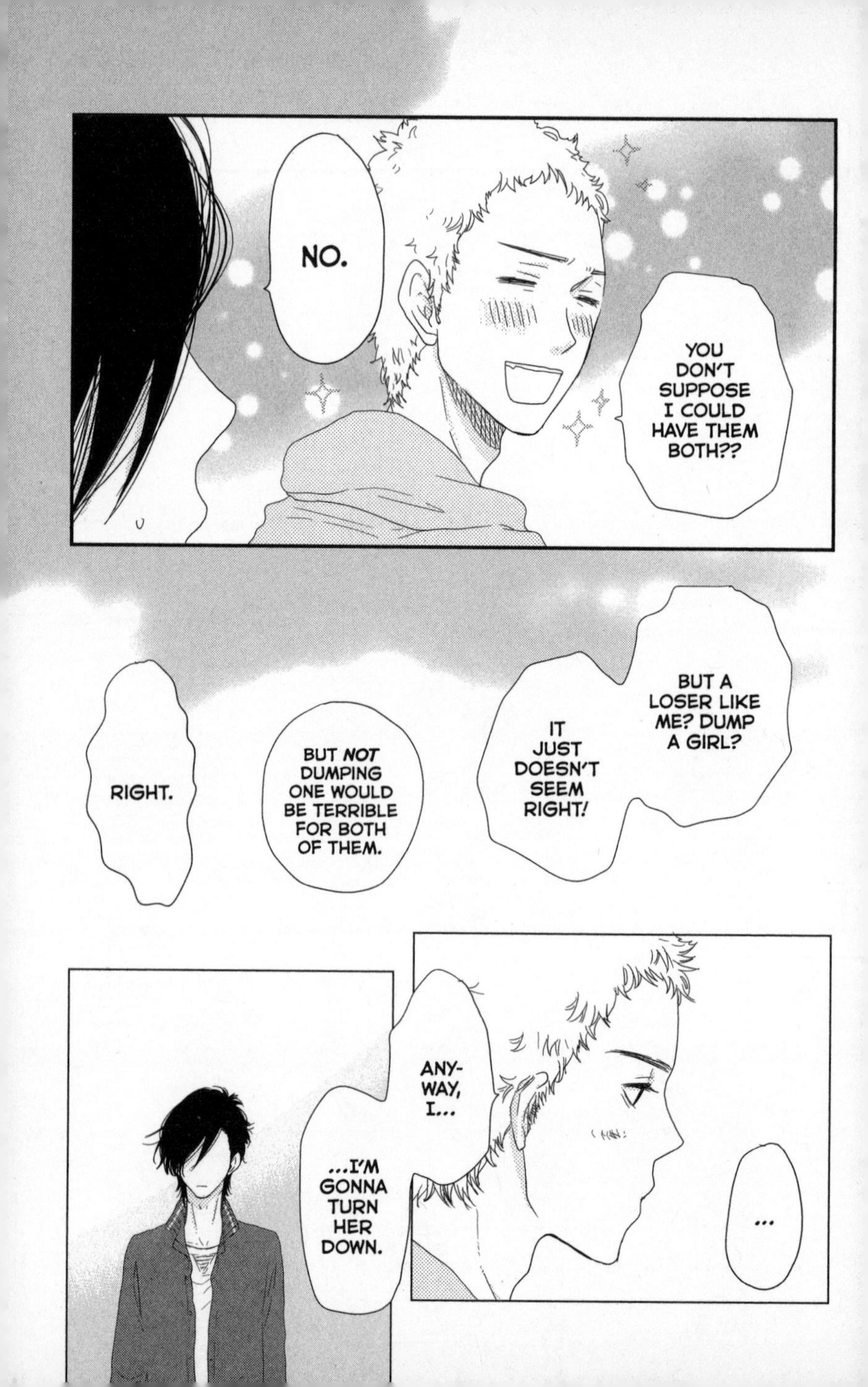
YOU DON'T SUPPOSE I COULD HAVE THEM BOTH??
NO.
BUT A LOSER LIKE ME? DUMP A GIRL?
IT JUST DOESN'T SEEM RIGHT!
BUT *NOT* DUMPING ONE WOULD BE TERRIBLE FOR BOTH OF THEM.
RIGHT.
...
ANY-WAY, I...
...I'M GONNA TURN HER DOWN.

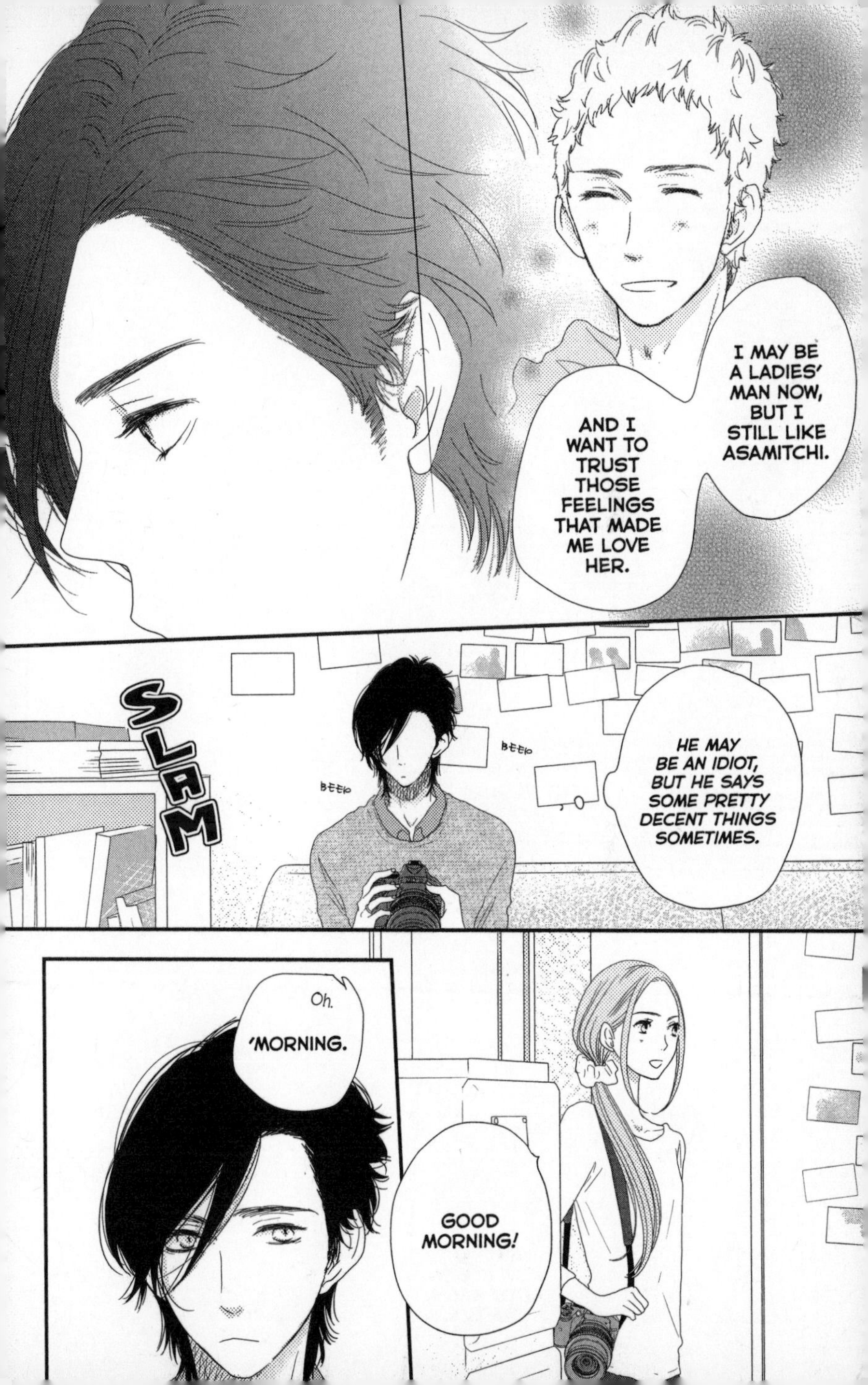
I MAY BE A LADIES' MAN NOW, BUT I STILL LIKE ASAMITCHI.
AND I WANT TO TRUST THOSE FEELINGS THAT MADE ME LOVE HER.
HE MAY BE AN IDIOT, BUT HE SAYS SOME PRETTY DECENT THINGS SOMETIMES.
BEEP
BEEP
SLAM
GOOD MORNING!
Oh.
'MORNING.

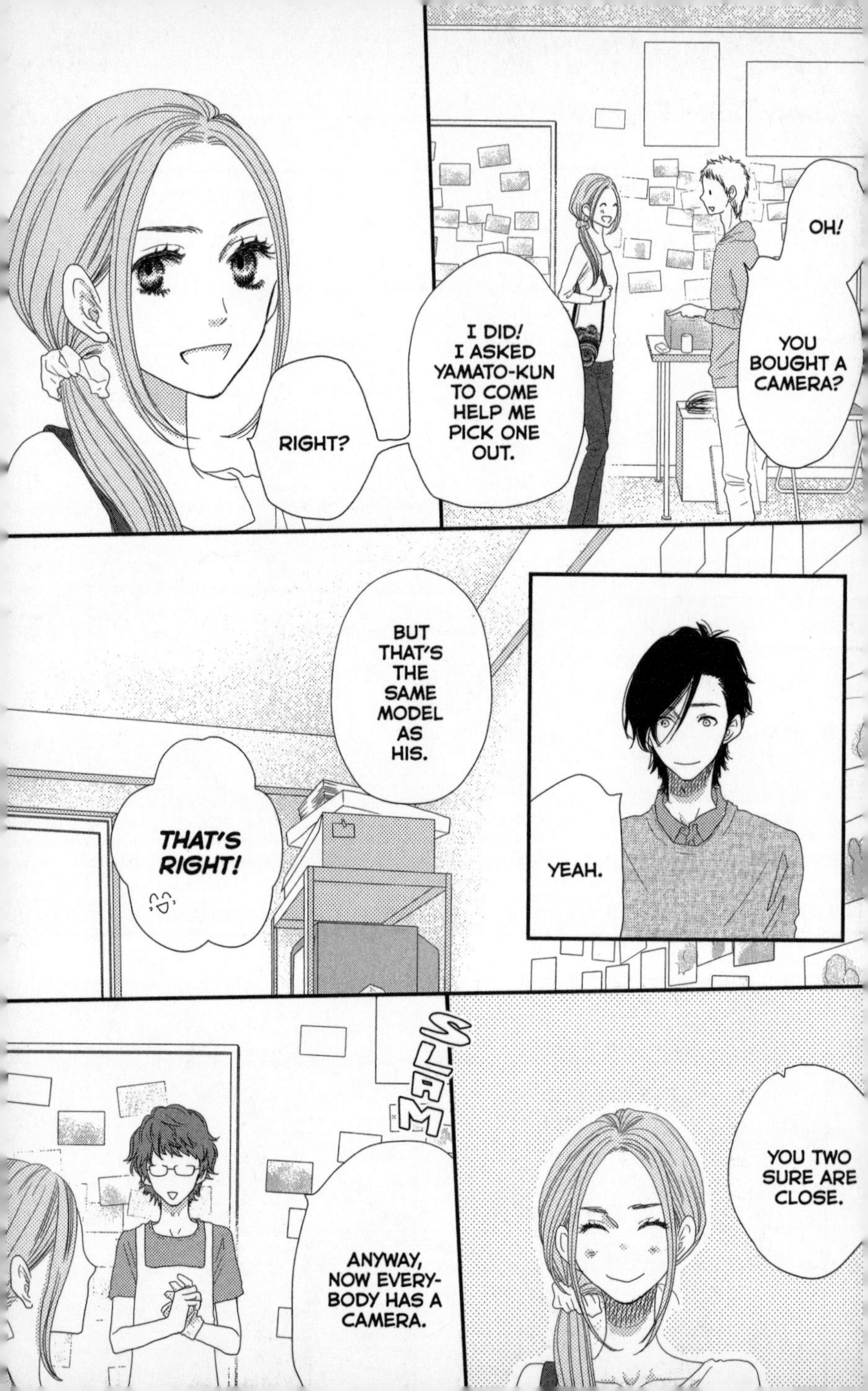
OH!
YOU BOUGHT A CAMERA?
I DID! I ASKED YAMATO-KUN TO COME HELP ME PICK ONE OUT.
RIGHT?
YEAH.
BUT THAT'S THE SAME MODEL AS HIS.
THAT'S RIGHT!
YOU TWO SURE ARE CLOSE.
SLAM
ANYWAY, NOW EVERY-BODY HAS A CAMERA.

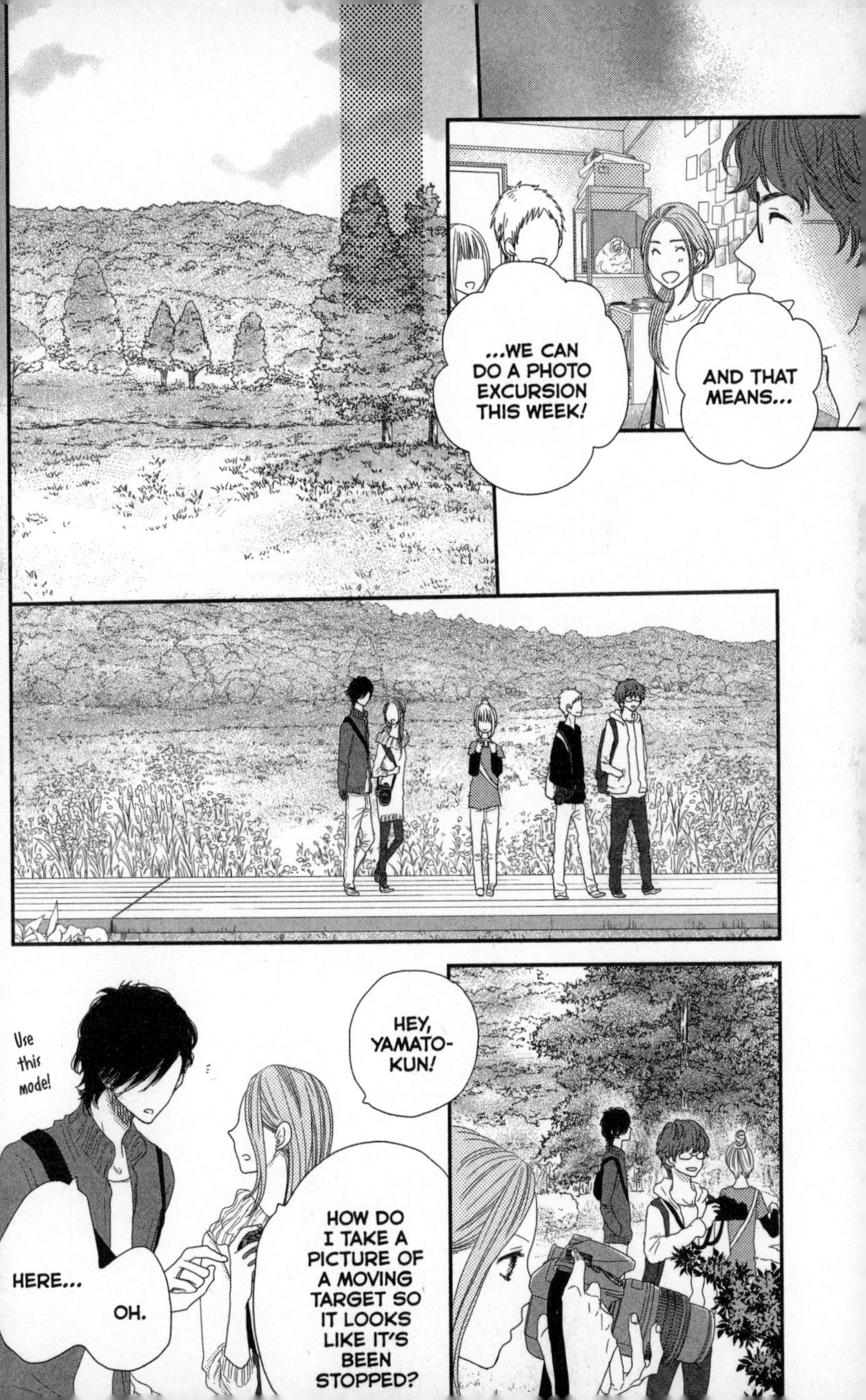
AND THAT MEANS...
...WE CAN DO A PHOTO EXCURSION THIS WEEK!
HEY, YAMATO-KUN!
HOW DO I TAKE A PICTURE OF A MOVING TARGET SO IT LOOKS LIKE IT'S BEEN STOPPED?
Use this mode!
HERE...
OH.

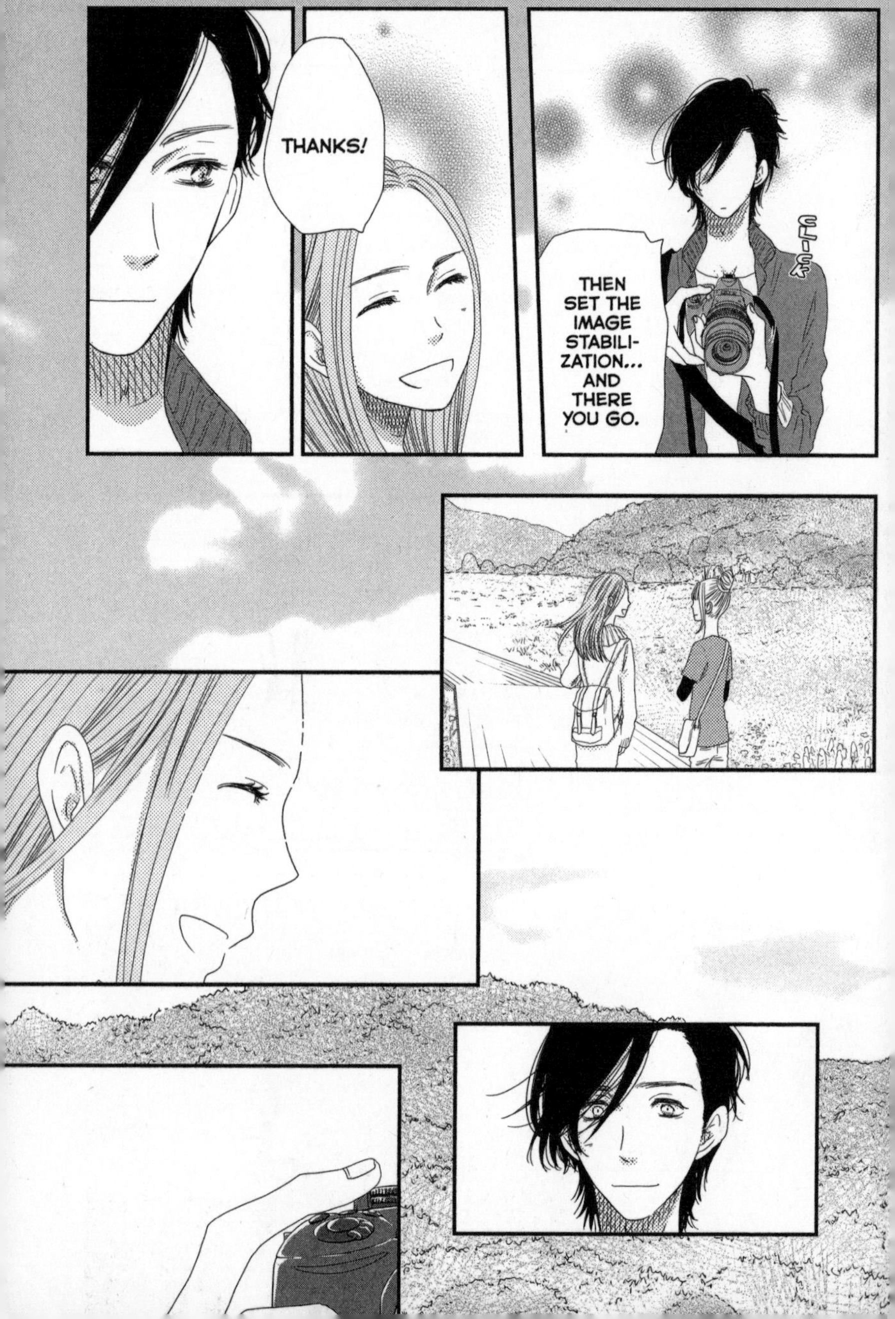
THEN SET THE IMAGE STABILIZATION... AND THERE YOU GO.
CLICK
THANKS!

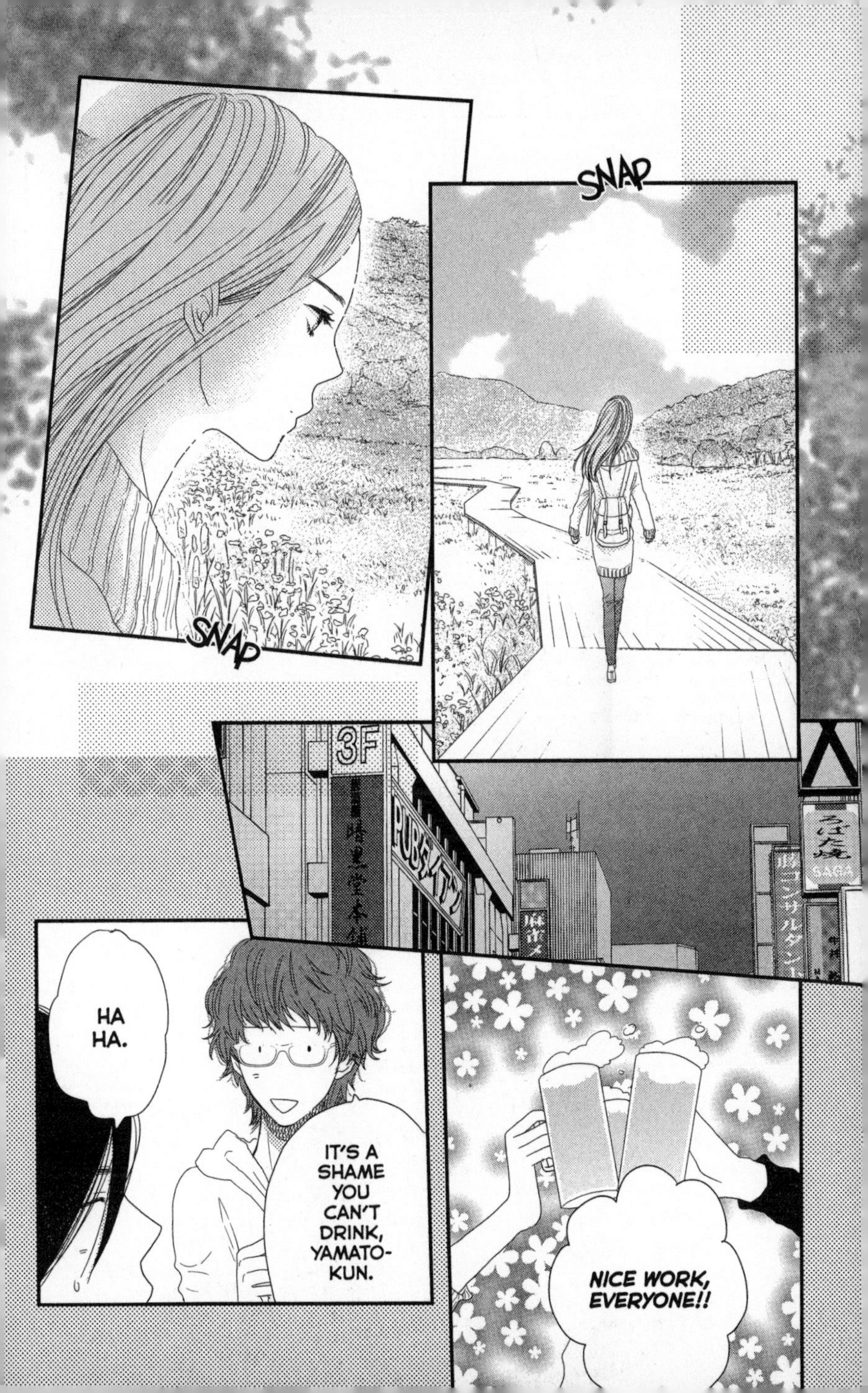
SNAP
SNAP
3F
SAGA
NICE WORK, EVERYONE!!
HA HA.
IT'S A SHAME YOU CAN'T DRINK, YAMATO-KUN.

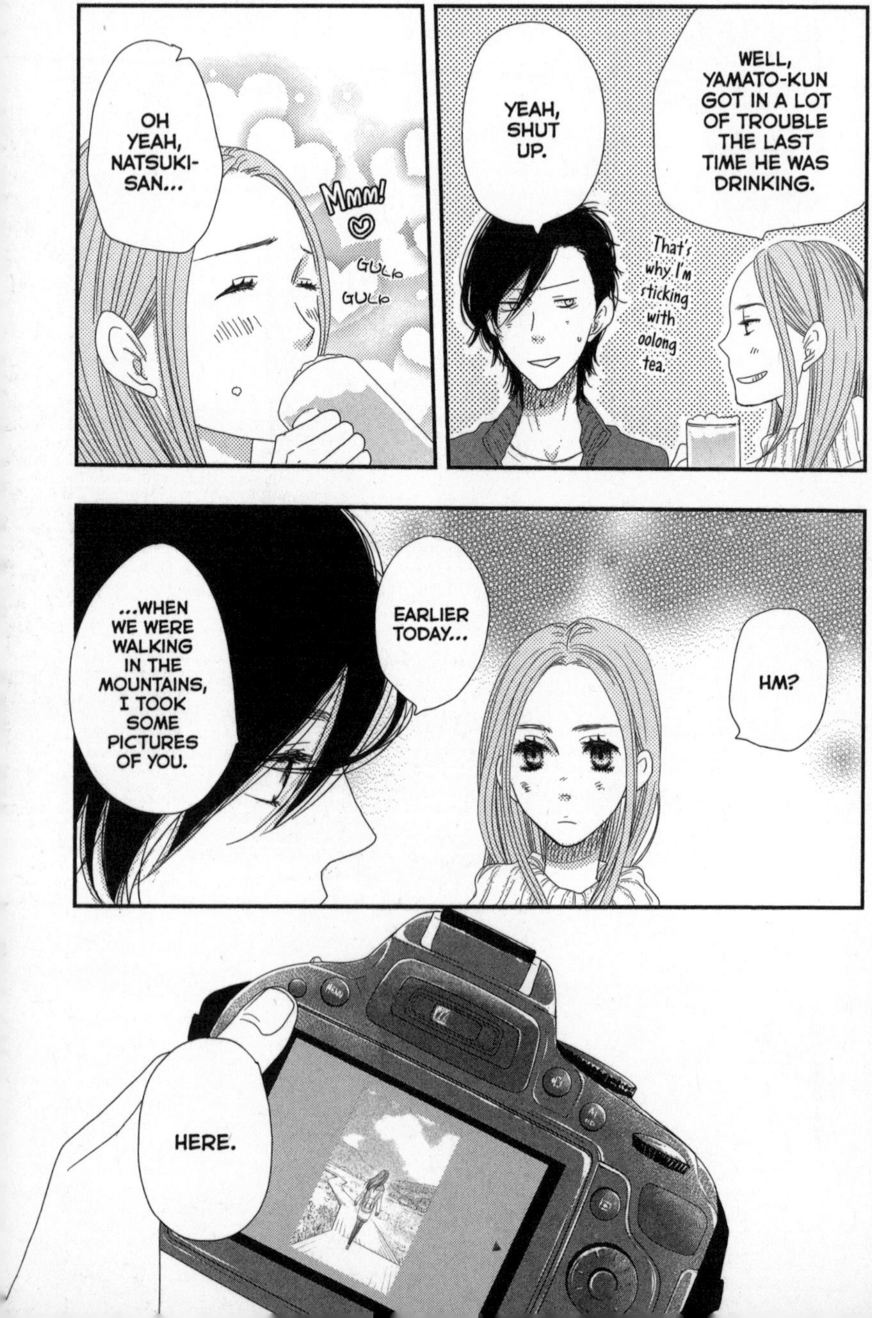
WELL, YAMATO-KUN GOT IN A LOT OF TROUBLE THE LAST TIME HE WAS DRINKING.
That's why I'm sticking with oolong tea.
YEAH, SHUT UP.
Mmm!
GULP
GULP
OH YEAH, NATSUKI-SAN...
HM?
EARLIER TODAY...
...WHEN WE WERE WALKING IN THE MOUNTAINS, I TOOK SOME PICTURES OF YOU.
HERE.

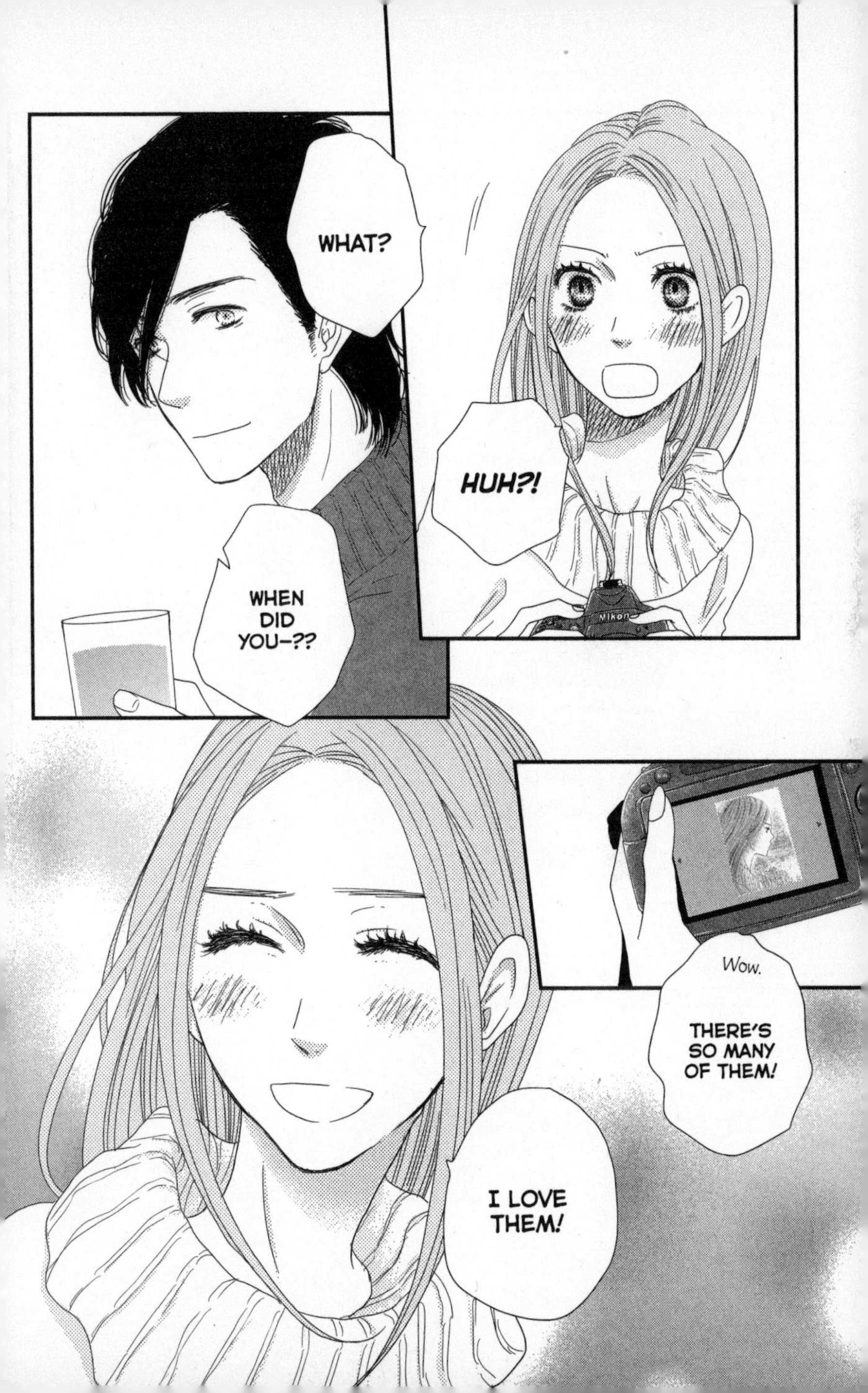
HUH?!
WHAT?
WHEN DID YOU–??
Wow.
THERE'S SO MANY OF THEM!
I LOVE THEM!

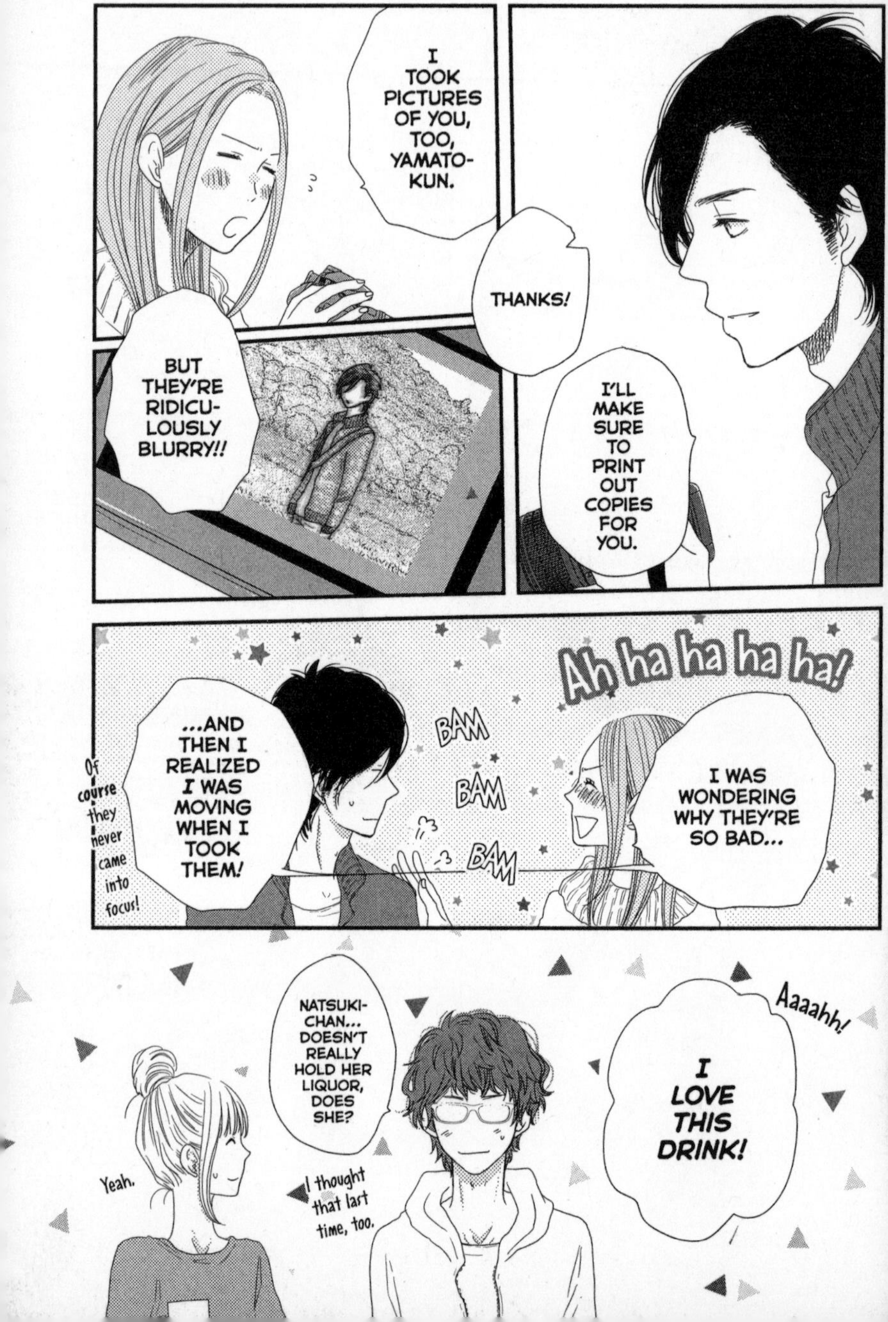
THANKS!
I'LL MAKE SURE TO PRINT OUT COPIES FOR YOU.
I TOOK PICTURES OF YOU, TOO, YAMATO-KUN.
BUT THEY'RE RIDICULOUSLY BLURRY!!
Ah ha ha ha ha!
I WAS WONDERING WHY THEY'RE SO BAD...
BAM
BAM
BAM
...AND THEN I REALIZED *I* WAS MOVING WHEN I TOOK THEM!
Of course they never came into focus!
Aaaahh!
I LOVE THIS DRINK!
NATSUKI-CHAN... DOESN'T REALLY HOLD HER LIQUOR, DOES SHE?
I thought that last time, too.
Yeah.

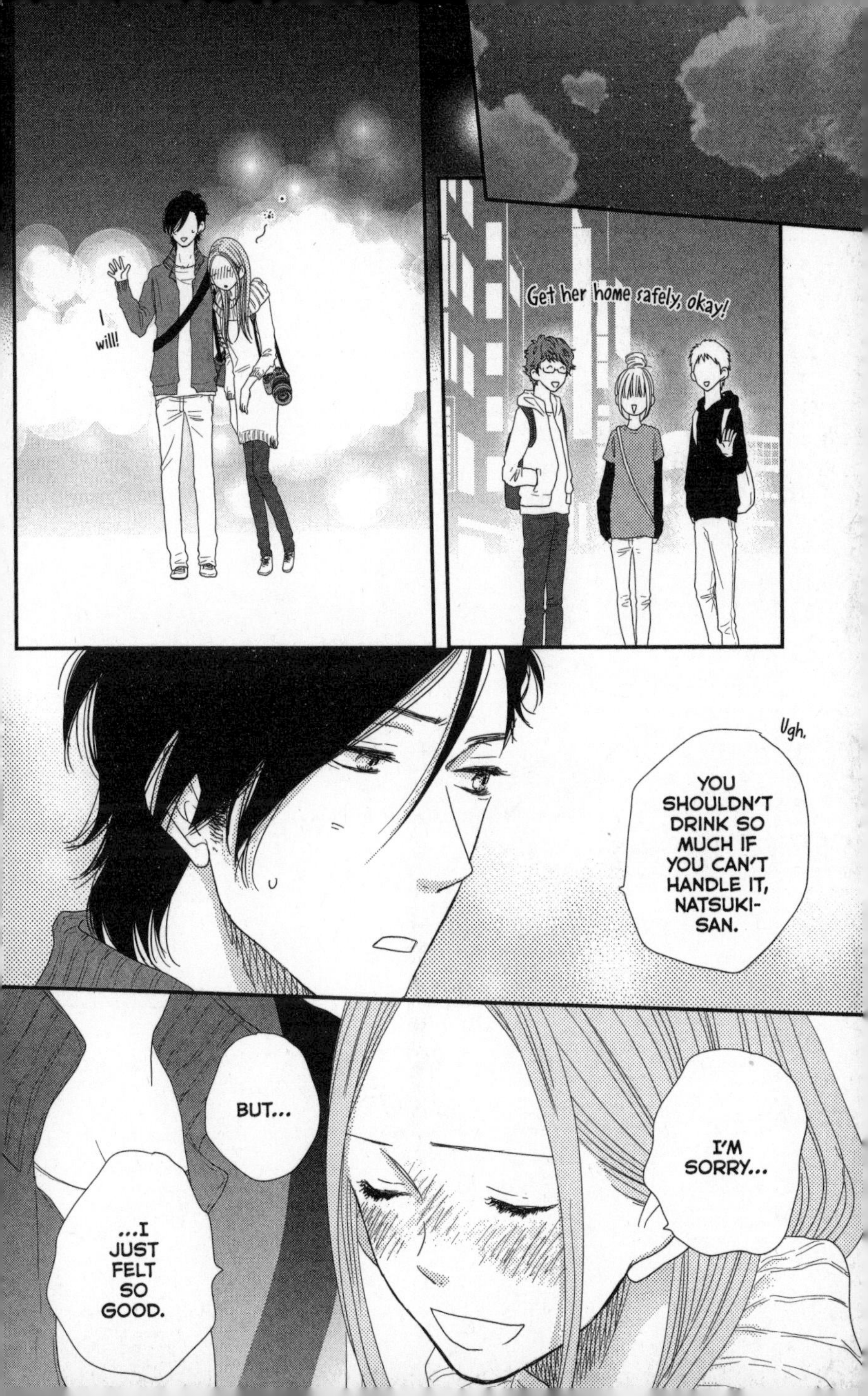
Get her home safely, okay!
I will!
Ugh.
YOU SHOULDN'T DRINK SO MUCH IF YOU CAN'T HANDLE IT, NATSUKI-SAN.
I'M SORRY...
BUT...
...I JUST FELT SO GOOD.

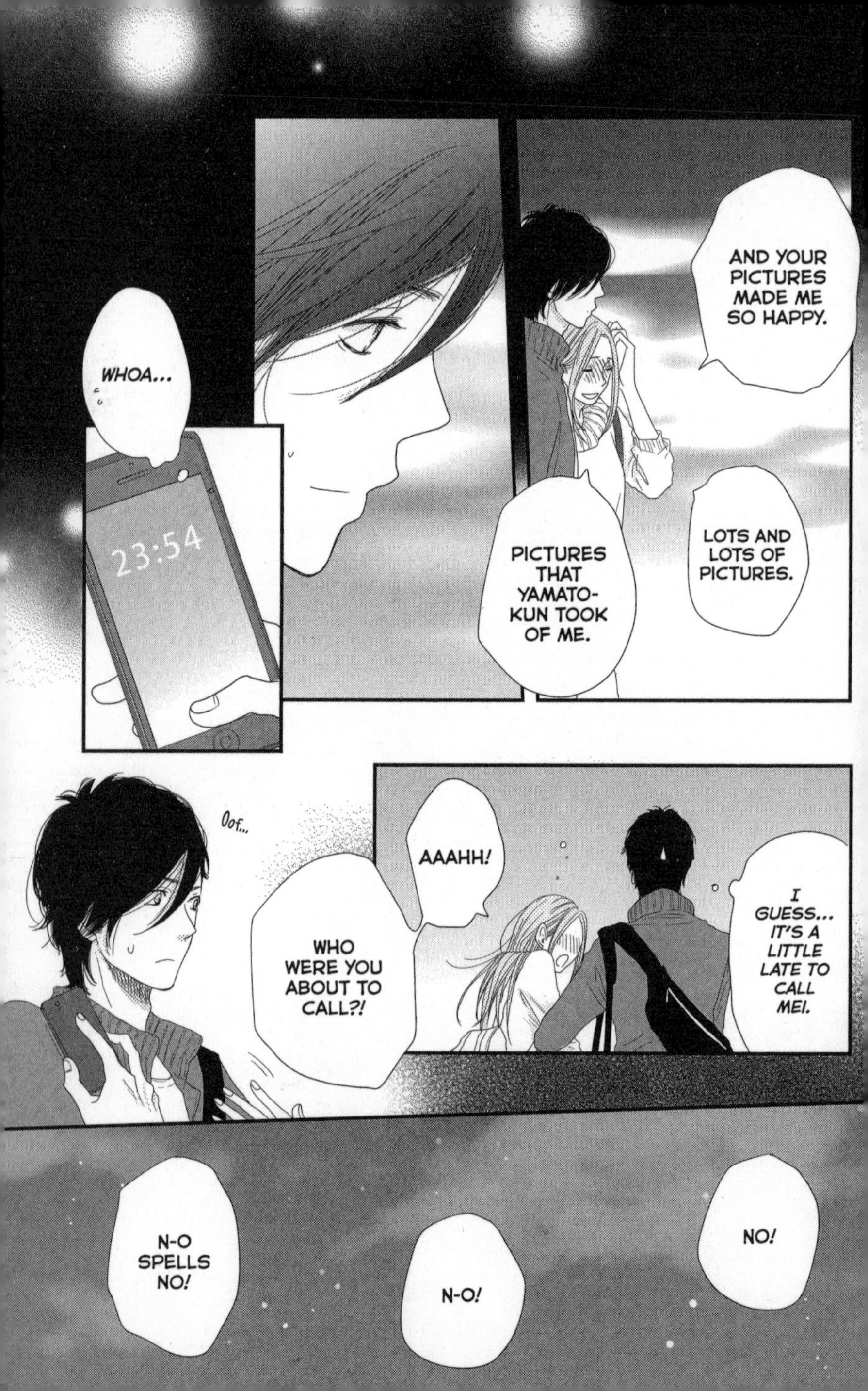
AND YOUR PICTURES MADE ME SO HAPPY.
LOTS AND LOTS OF PICTURES.
PICTURES THAT YAMATO-KUN TOOK OF ME.
WHOA...
23:54
I GUESS... IT'S A LITTLE LATE TO CALL MEI.
AAAHH!
Oof...
WHO WERE YOU ABOUT TO CALL?!
NO!
N-O!
N-O SPELLS NO!

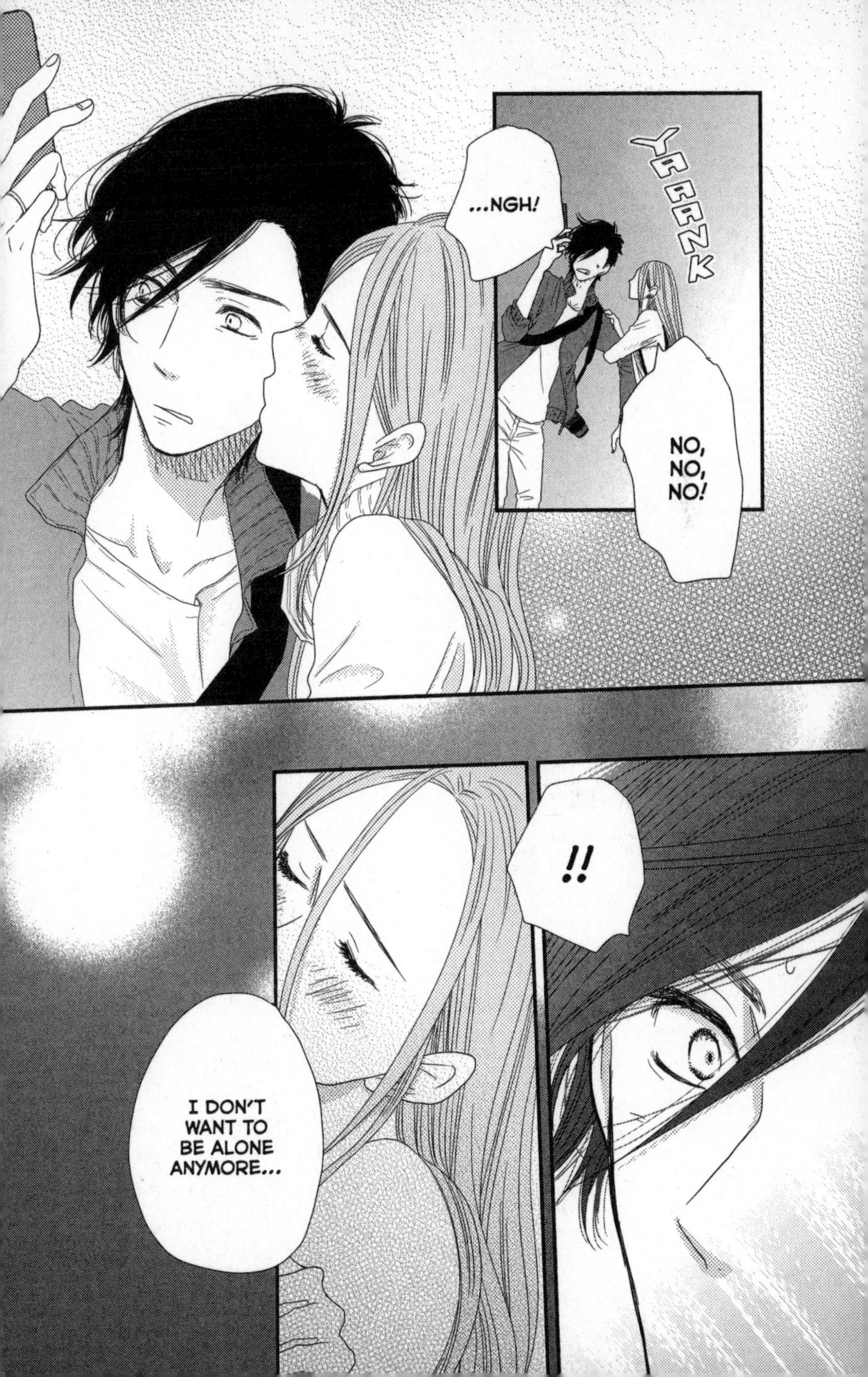
YAAANK
...NGH!
NO, NO, NO!
!!
I DON'T WANT TO BE ALONE ANYMORE...

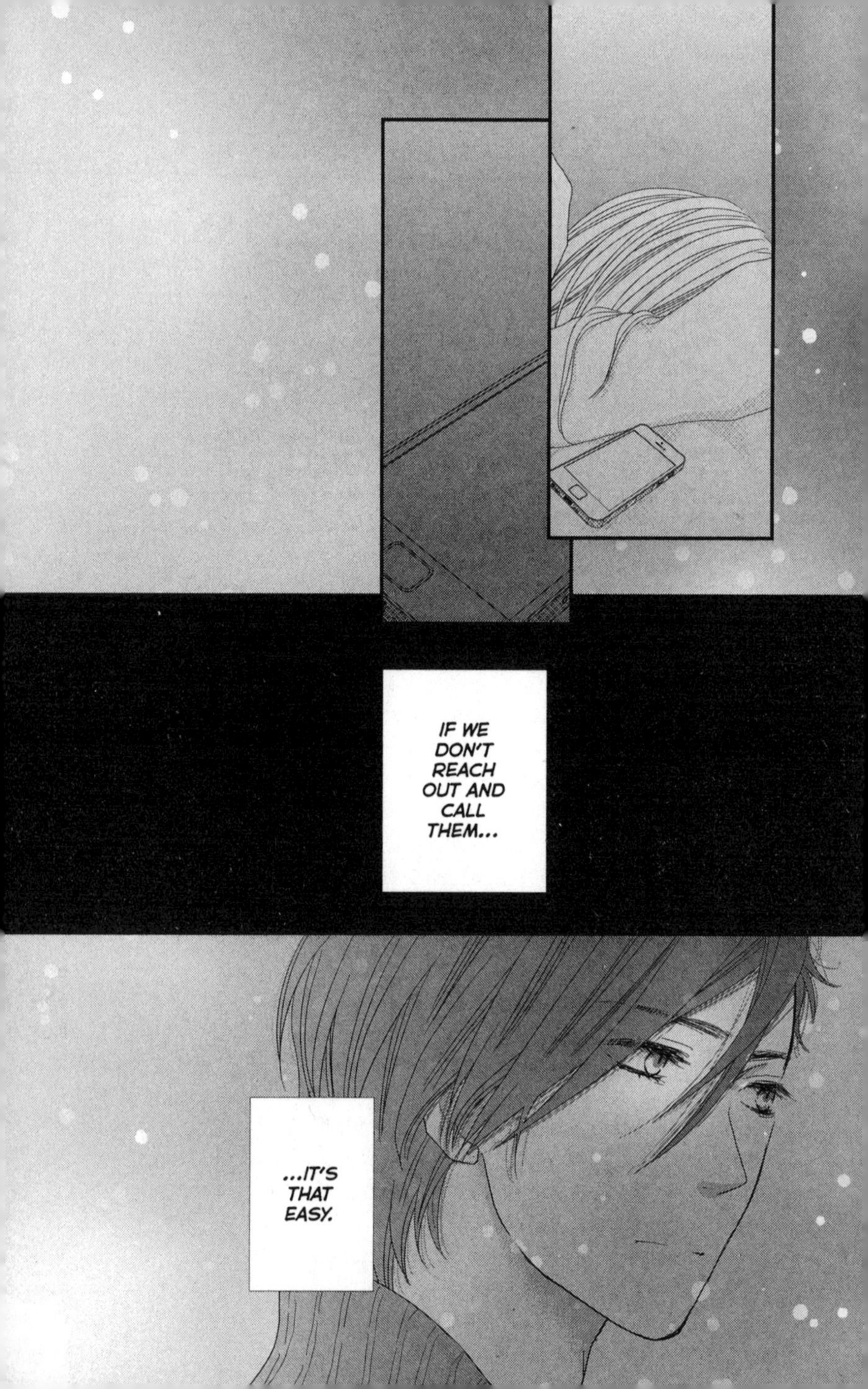
IF WE DON'T REACH OUT AND CALL THEM...
...IT'S THAT EASY.

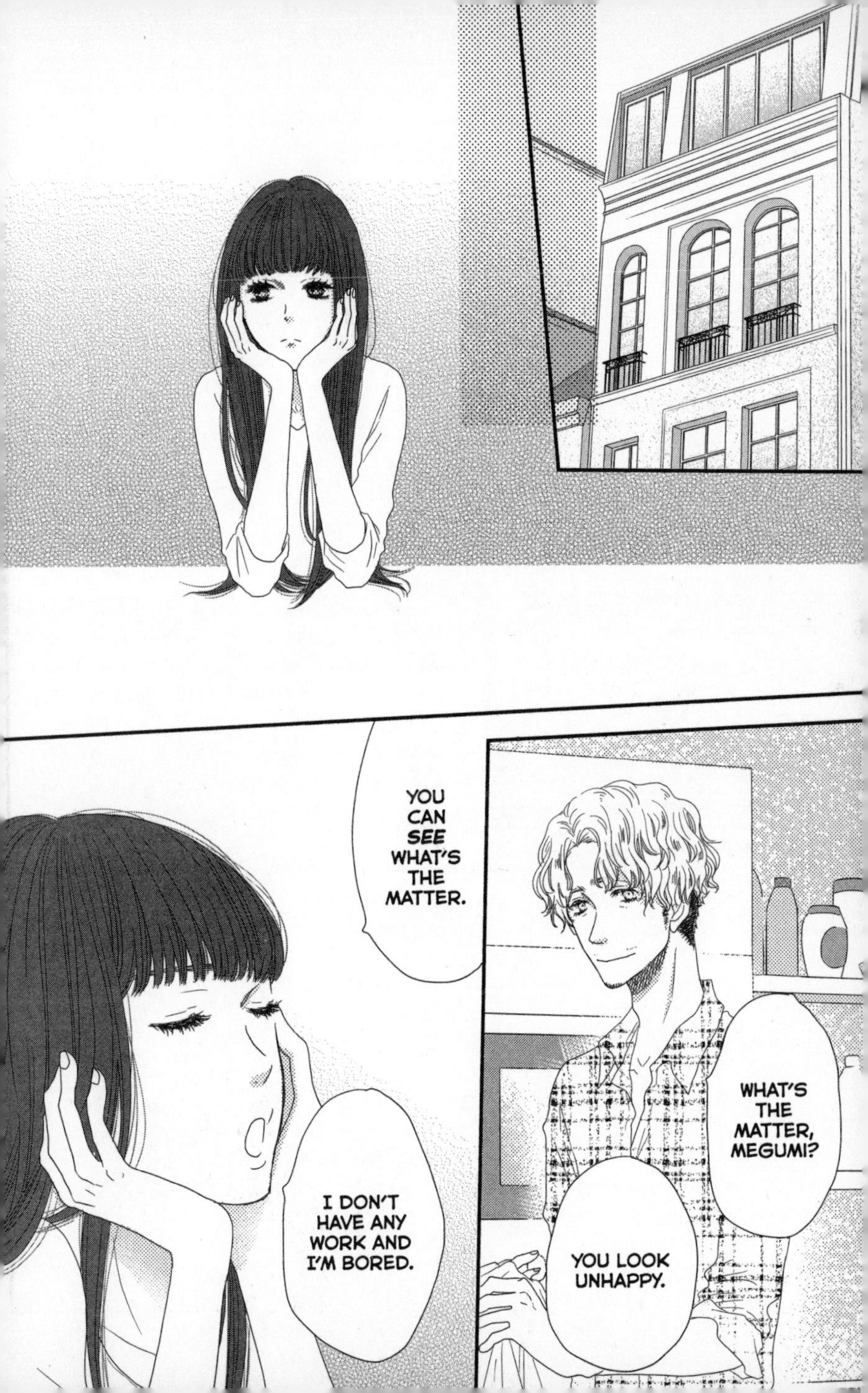
WHAT'S THE MATTER, MEGUMI?
YOU LOOK UNHAPPY.
YOU CAN SEE WHAT'S THE MATTER.
I DON'T HAVE ANY WORK AND I'M BORED.

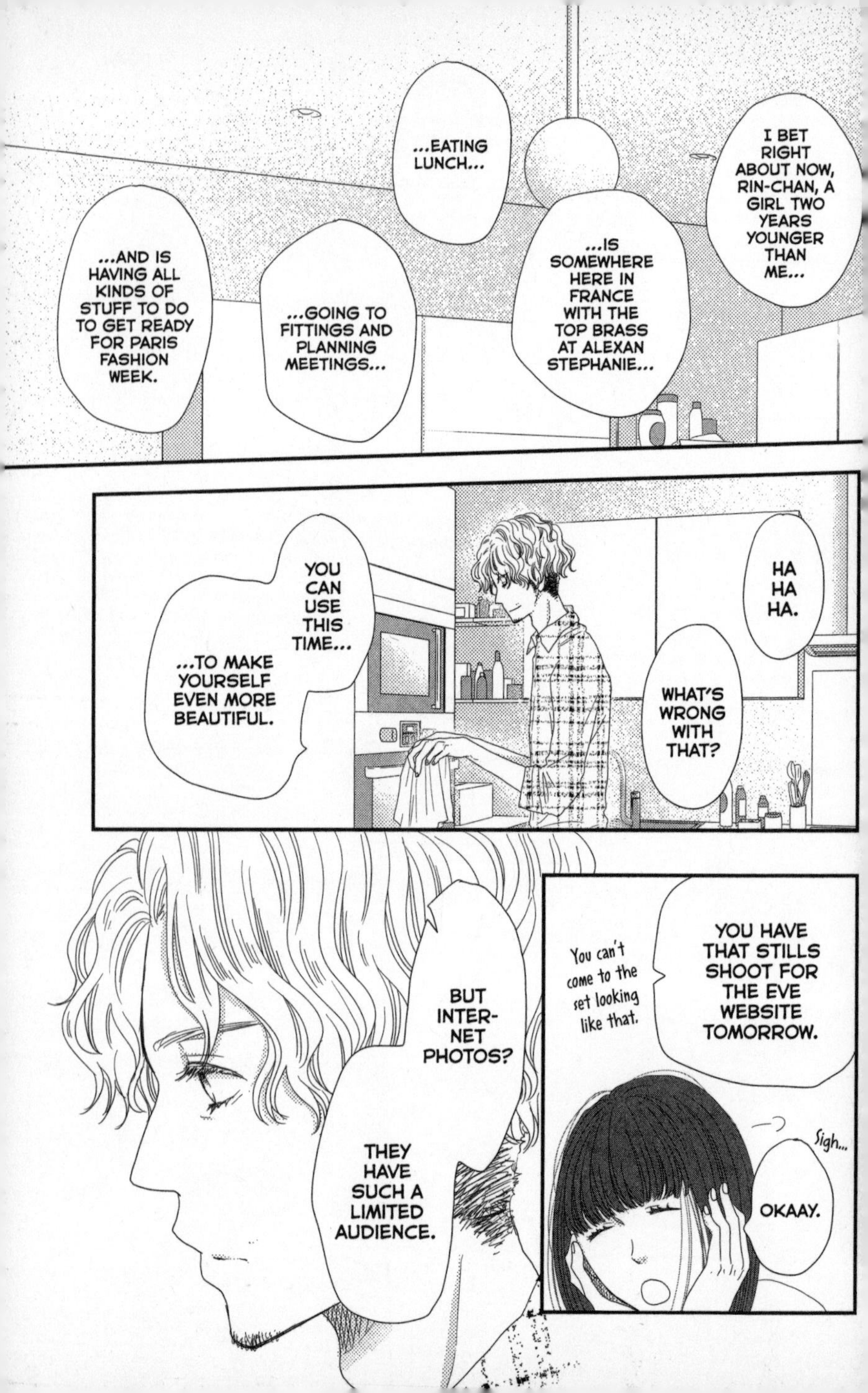
I BET RIGHT ABOUT NOW, RIN-CHAN, A GIRL TWO YEARS YOUNGER THAN ME...
...IS SOMEWHERE HERE IN FRANCE WITH THE TOP BRASS AT ALEXAN STEPHANIE...
...EATING LUNCH...
...GOING TO FITTINGS AND PLANNING MEETINGS...
...AND IS HAVING ALL KINDS OF STUFF TO DO TO GET READY FOR PARIS FASHION WEEK.
HA HA HA.
WHAT'S WRONG WITH THAT?
YOU CAN USE THIS TIME...
...TO MAKE YOURSELF EVEN MORE BEAUTIFUL.
YOU HAVE THAT STILLS SHOOT FOR THE EVE WEBSITE TOMORROW.
You can't come to the set looking like that.
Sigh...
OKAAY.
BUT INTER-NET PHOTOS?
THEY HAVE SUCH A LIMITED AUDIENCE.

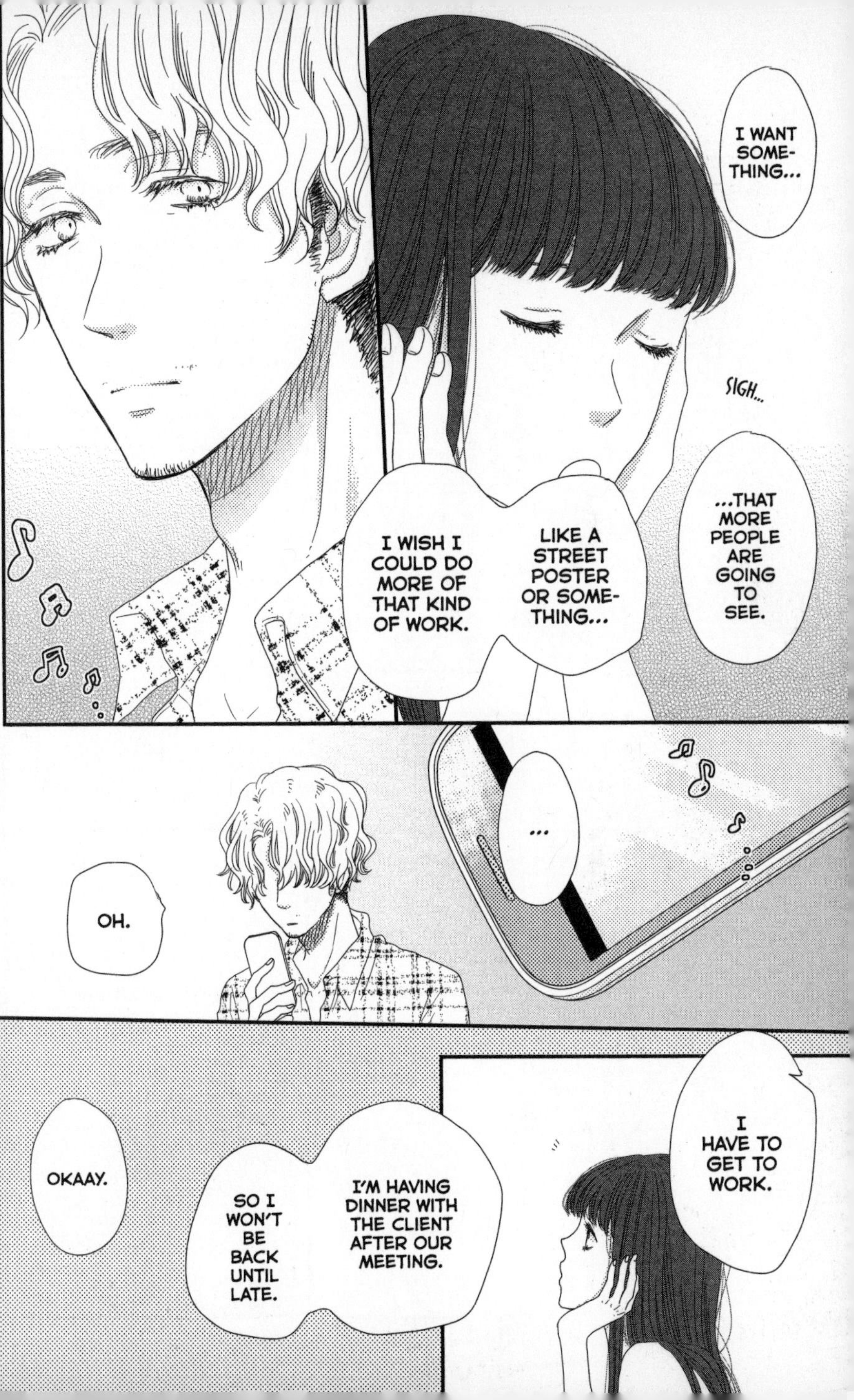
I WANT SOME- THING...
SIGH...
...THAT MORE PEOPLE ARE GOING TO SEE.
LIKE A STREET POSTER OR SOME- THING...
I WISH I COULD DO MORE OF THAT KIND OF WORK.
...
OH.
I HAVE TO GET TO WORK.
I'M HAVING DINNER WITH THE CLIENT AFTER OUR MEETING.
SO I WON'T BE BACK UNTIL LATE.
OKAAY.

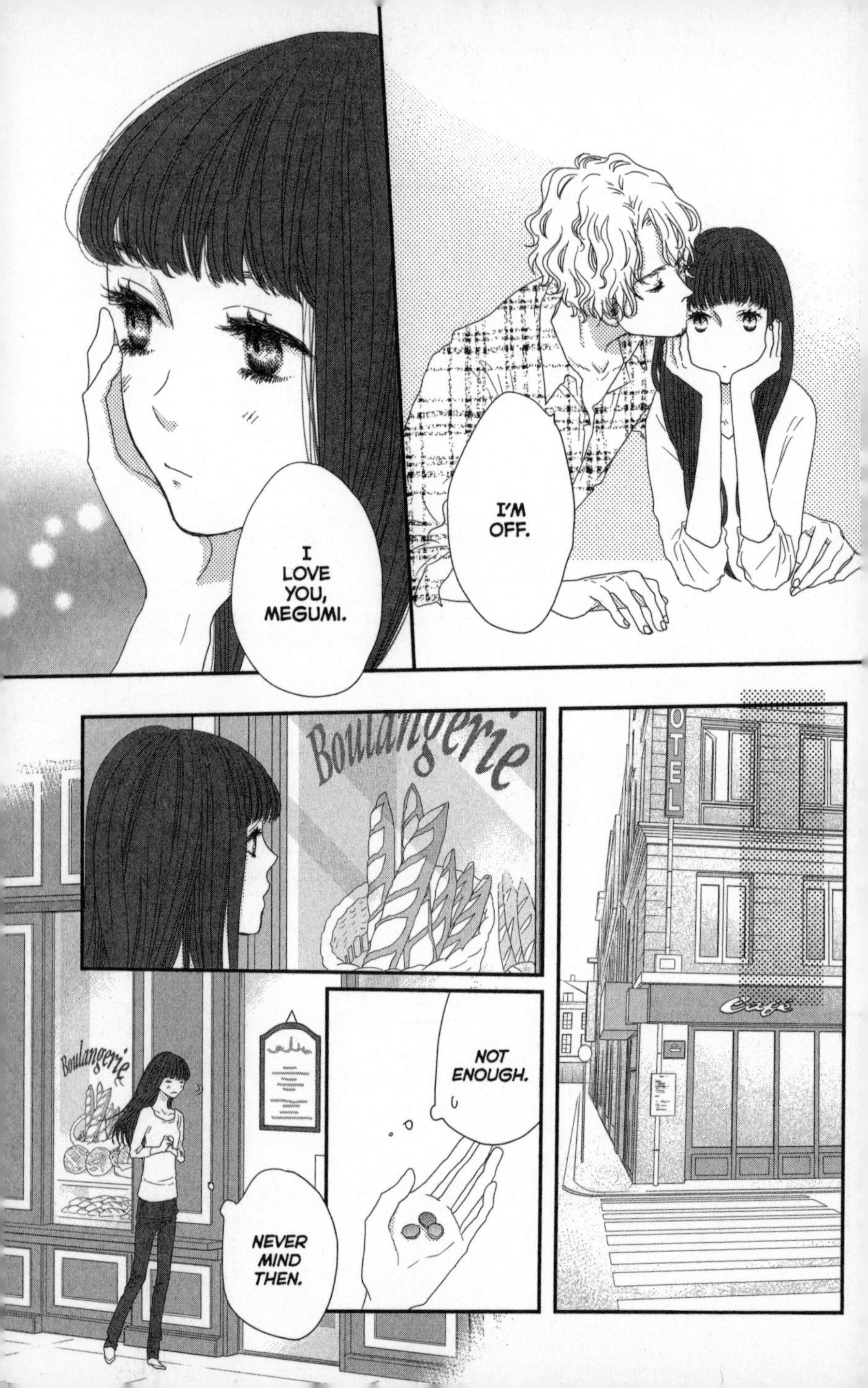
I'M OFF.
I LOVE YOU, MEGUMI.
Café
Boulangerie
NOT ENOUGH.
Boulangerie
NEVER MIND THEN.

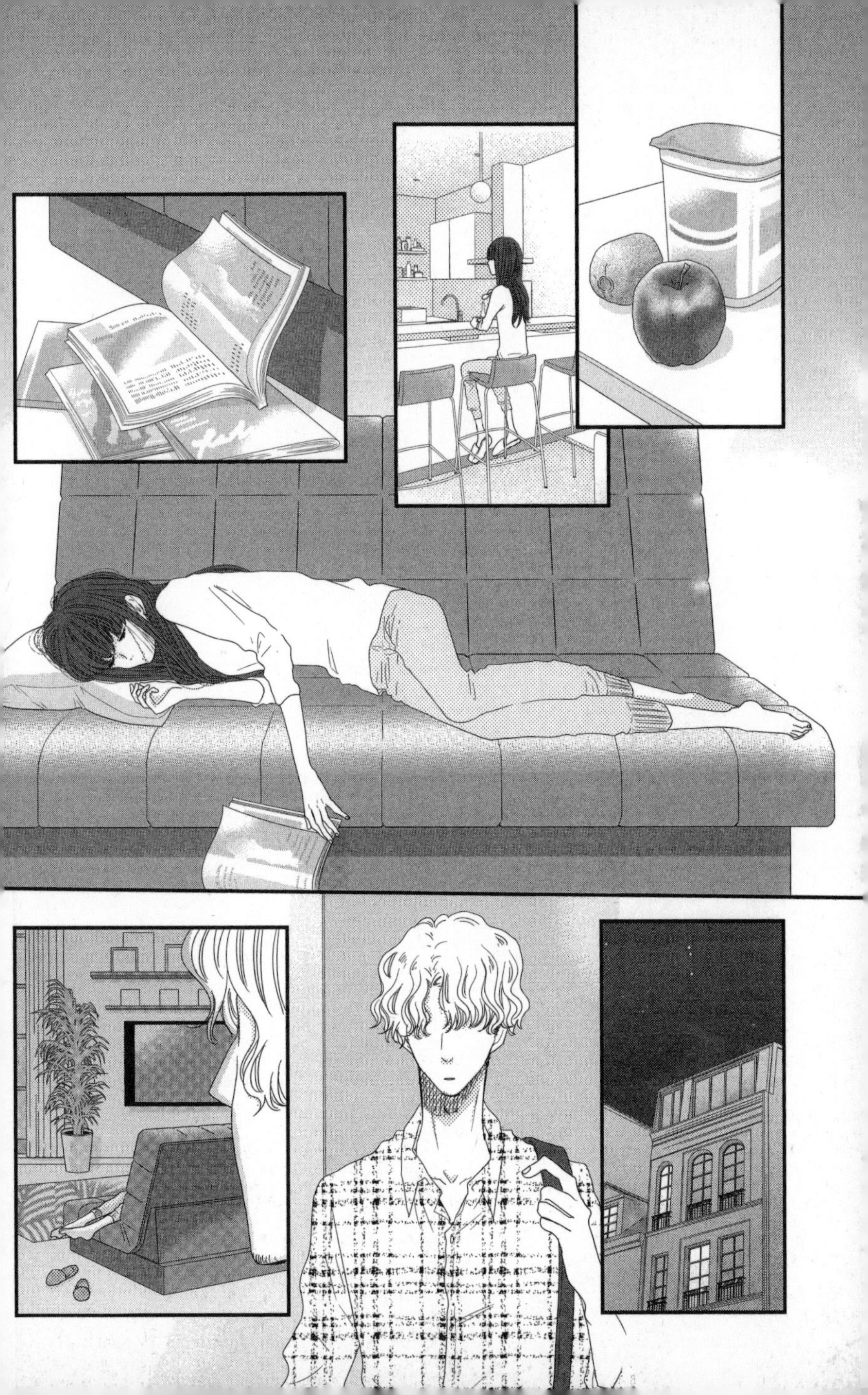

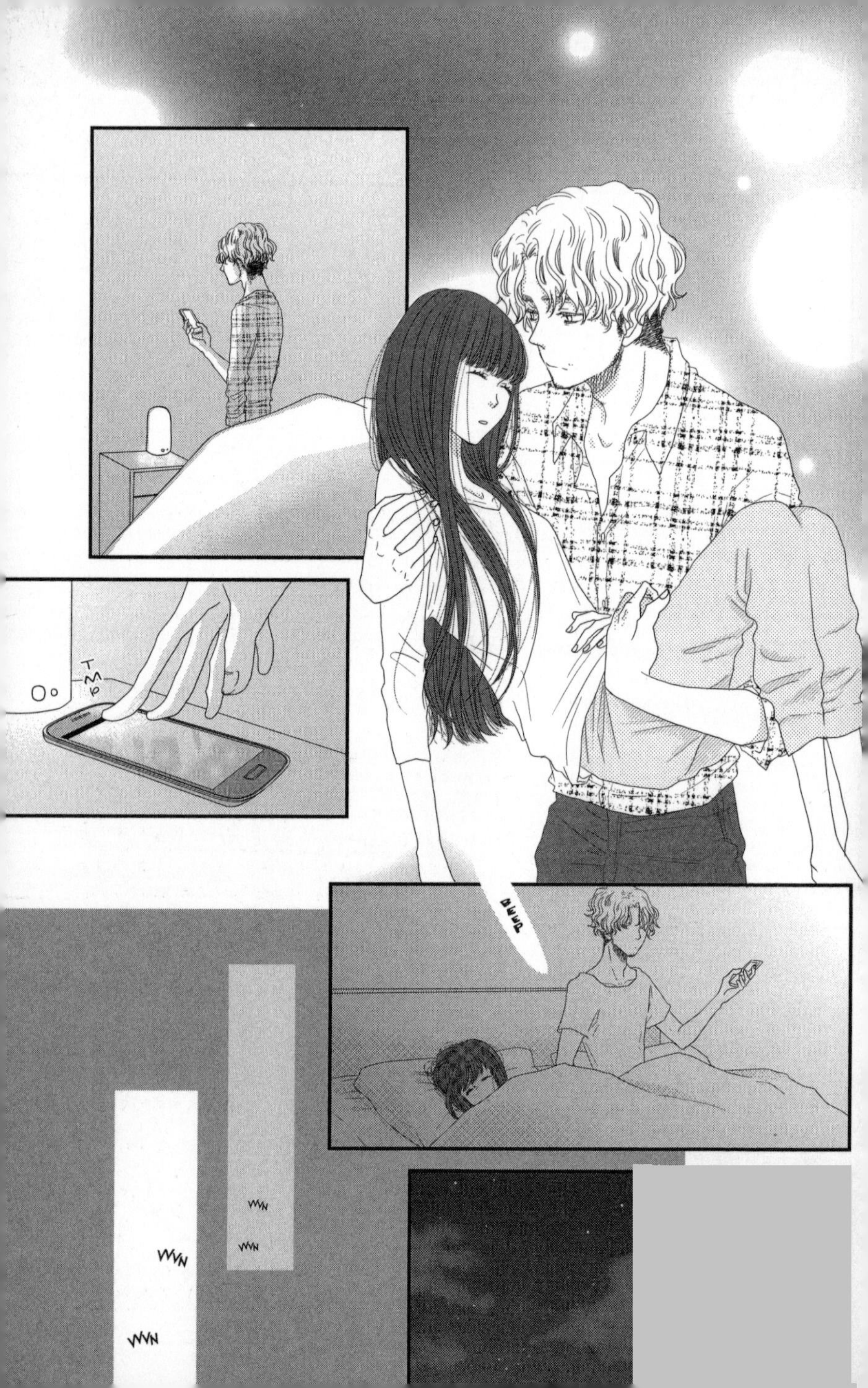
Oo
TMP
BEEP
VVVN
VVVN
VVVN
VVVN

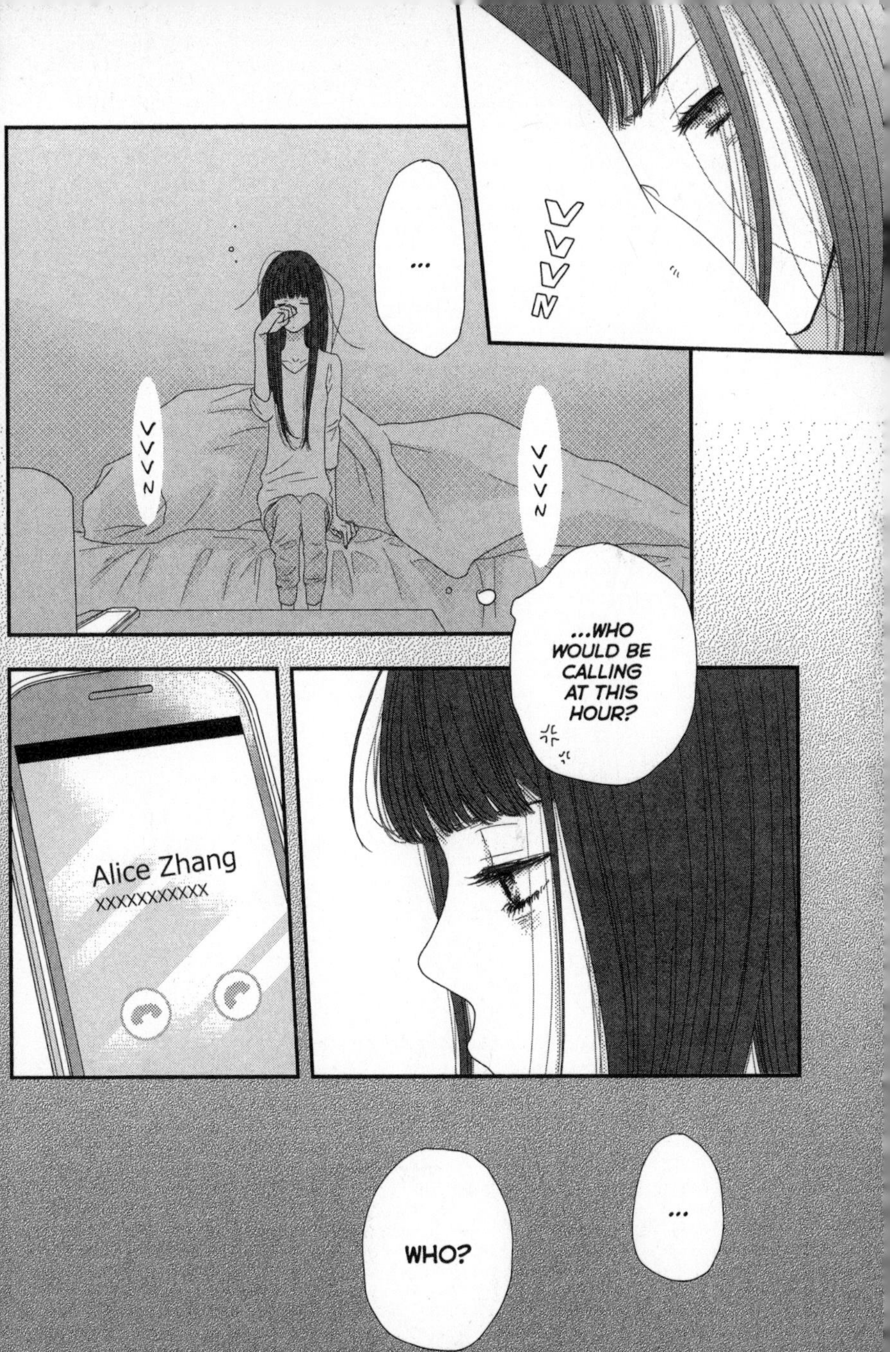
VVVN
...
VVVN
VVVN
...WHO WOULD BE CALLING AT THIS HOUR?
Alice Zhang
XXXXXXXXXX
...
WHO?

Chapter 65 — End

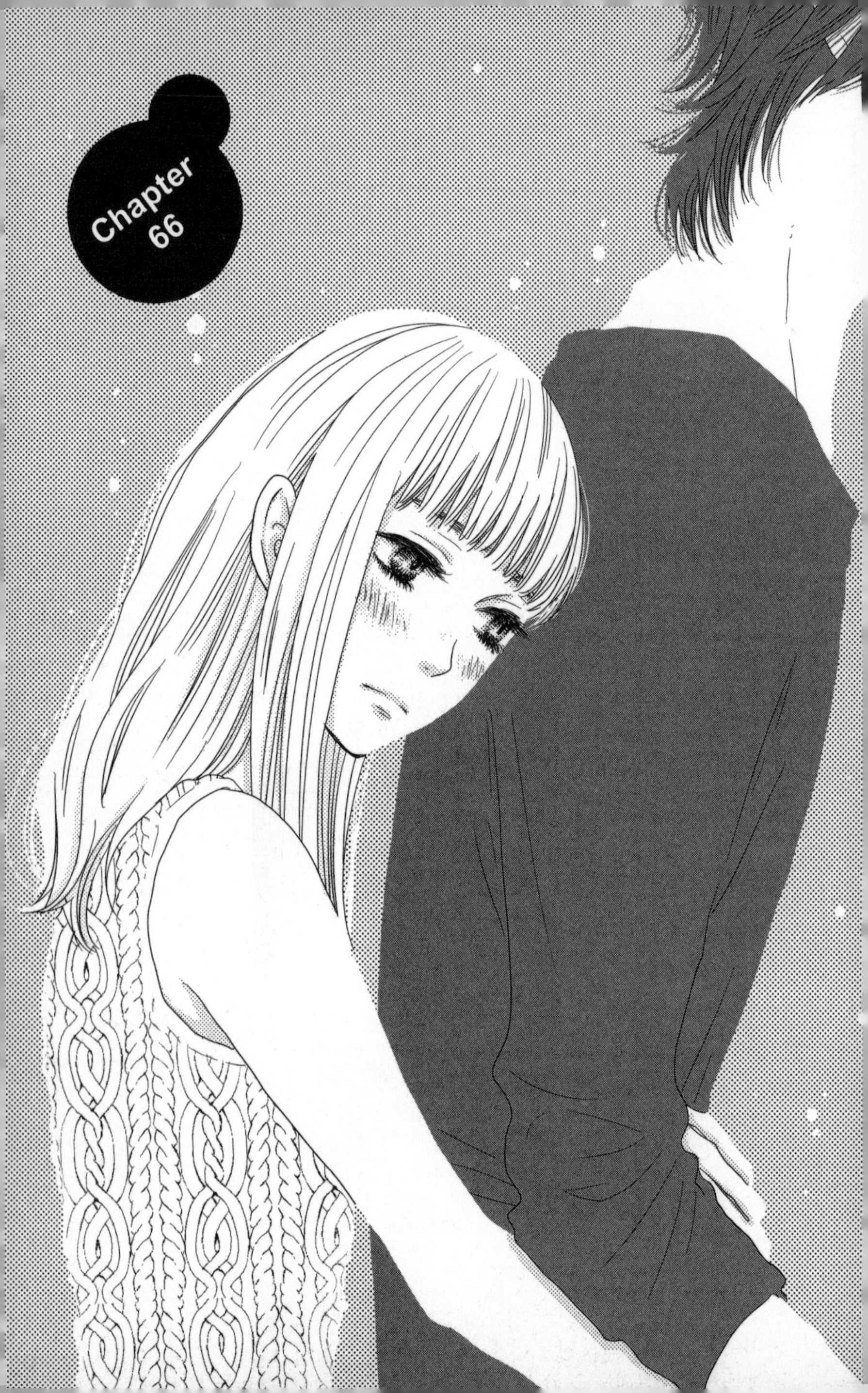
Chapter
66

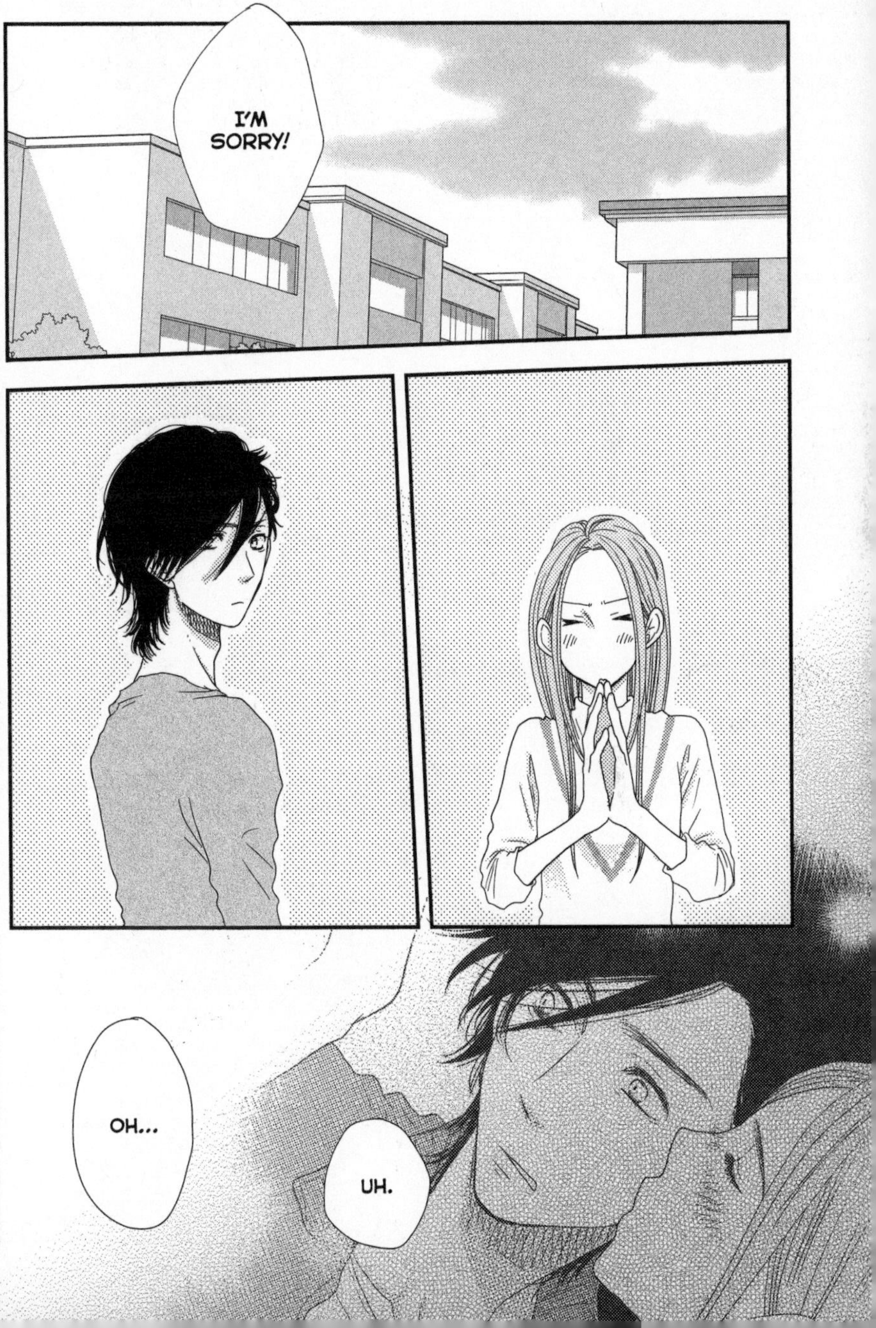
I'M SORRY!
OH...
UH.

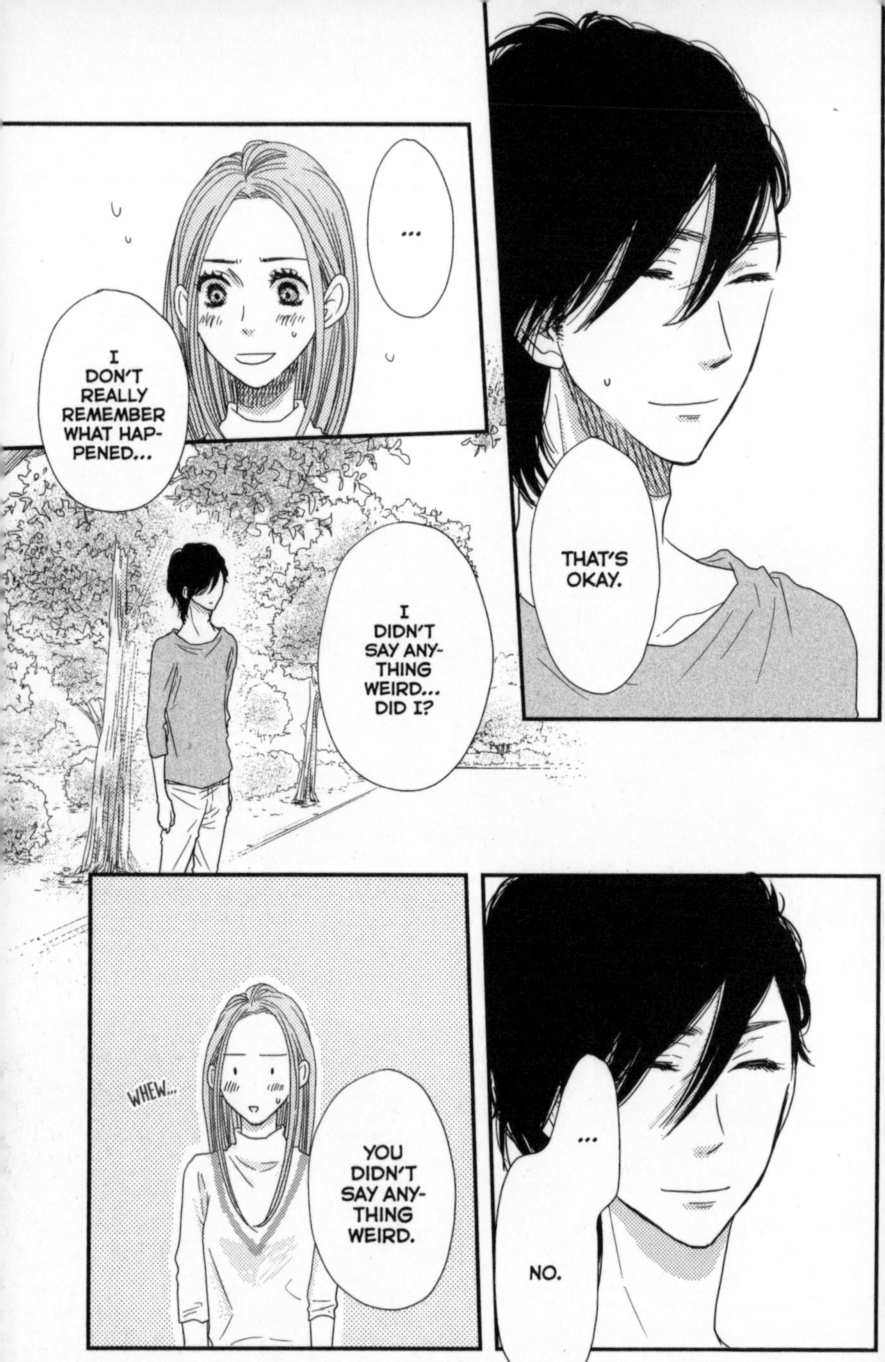
THAT'S OKAY.
...
I DON'T REALLY REMEMBER WHAT HAP-PENED...
I DIDN'T SAY ANY-THING WEIRD... DID I?
...
NO.
YOU DIDN'T SAY ANY-THING WEIRD.
WHEW...

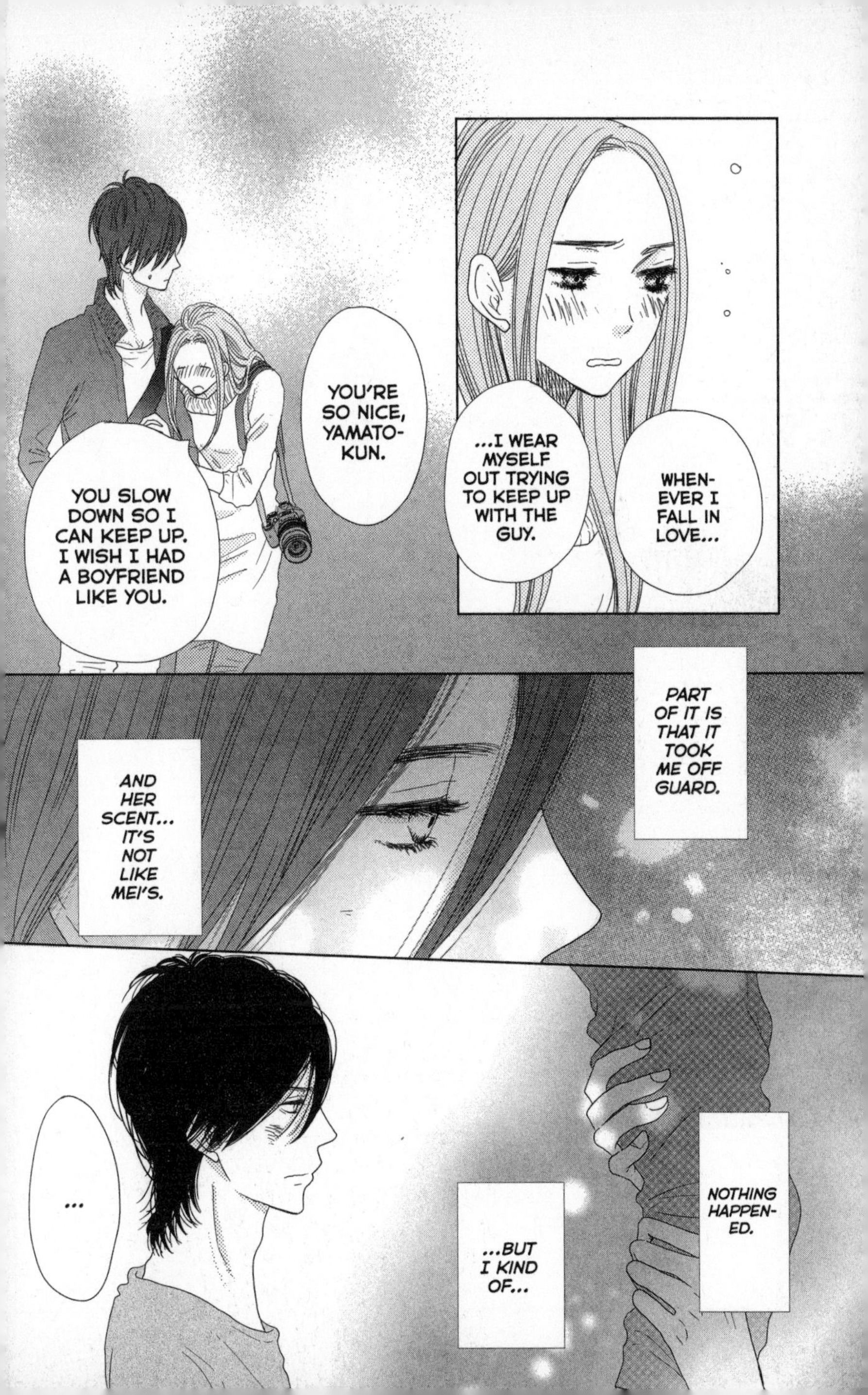
WHEN-EVER I FALL IN LOVE...
...I WEAR MYSELF OUT TRYING TO KEEP UP WITH THE GUY.
YOU'RE SO NICE, YAMATO-KUN.
YOU SLOW DOWN SO I CAN KEEP UP. I WISH I HAD A BOYFRIEND LIKE YOU.
PART OF IT IS THAT IT TOOK ME OFF GUARD.
AND HER SCENT... IT'S NOT LIKE MEI'S.
NOTHING HAPPEN-ED.
...BUT I KIND OF...
...

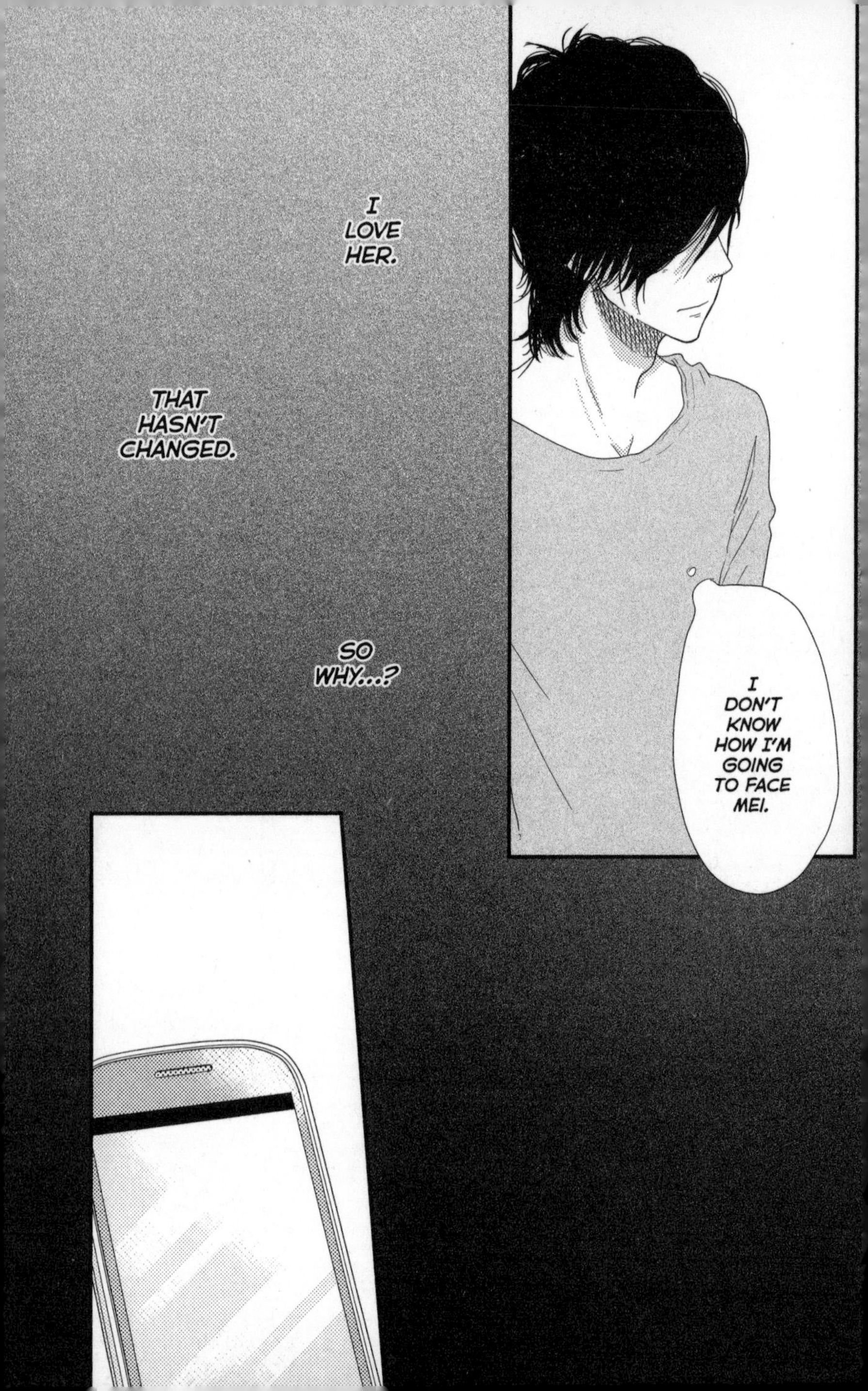
I DON'T KNOW HOW I'M GOING TO FACE MEI.
I LOVE HER.
THAT HASN'T CHANGED.
SO WHY...?

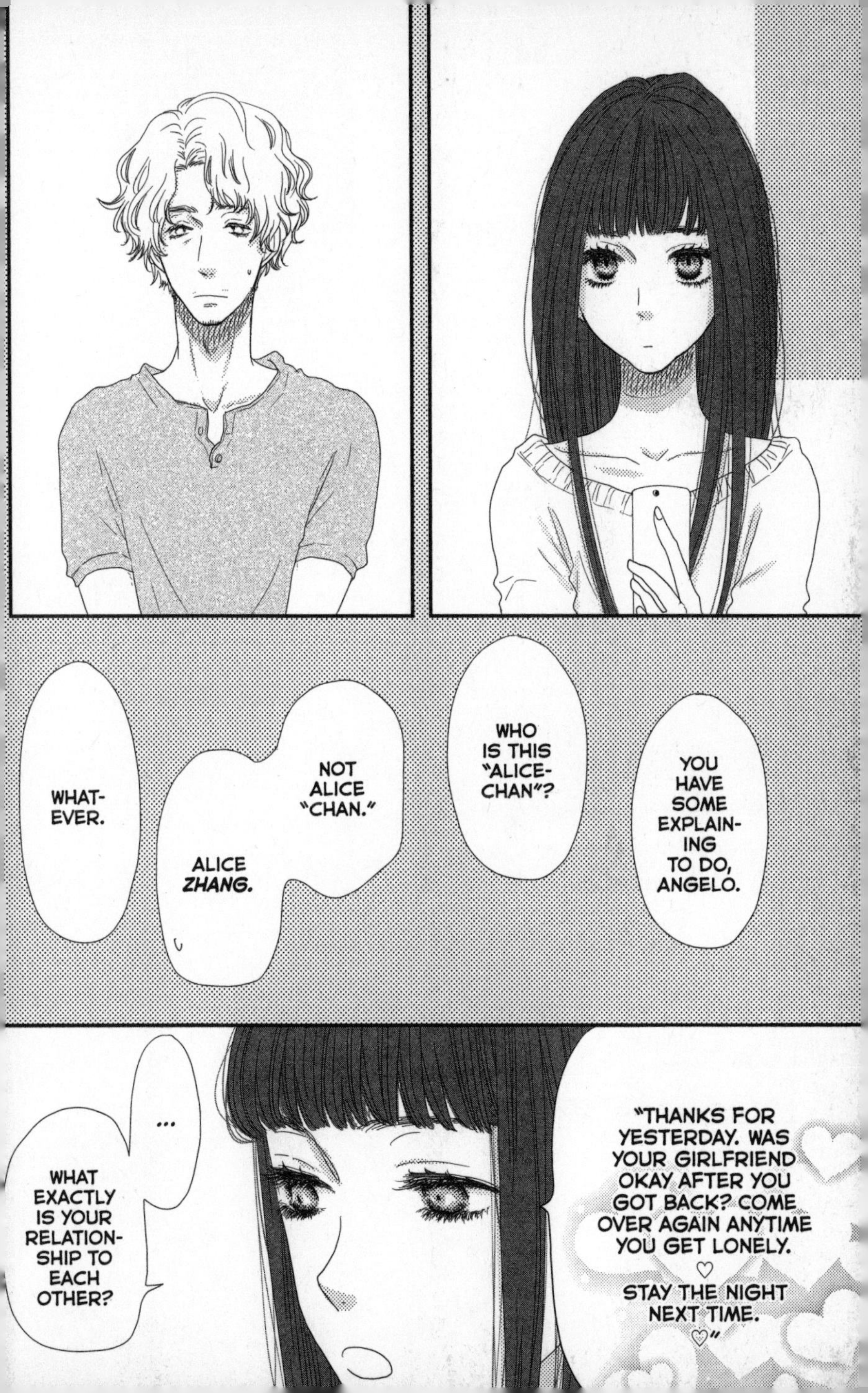
YOU HAVE SOME EXPLAIN-ING TO DO, ANGELO.
WHO IS THIS "ALICE-CHAN"?
NOT ALICE "CHAN."
ALICE *ZHANG.*
WHAT-EVER.
"THANKS FOR YESTERDAY. WAS YOUR GIRLFRIEND OKAY AFTER YOU GOT BACK? COME OVER AGAIN ANYTIME YOU GET LONELY. ♡
STAY THE NIGHT NEXT TIME. ♡"
...
WHAT EXACTLY IS YOUR RELATION-SHIP TO EACH OTHER?

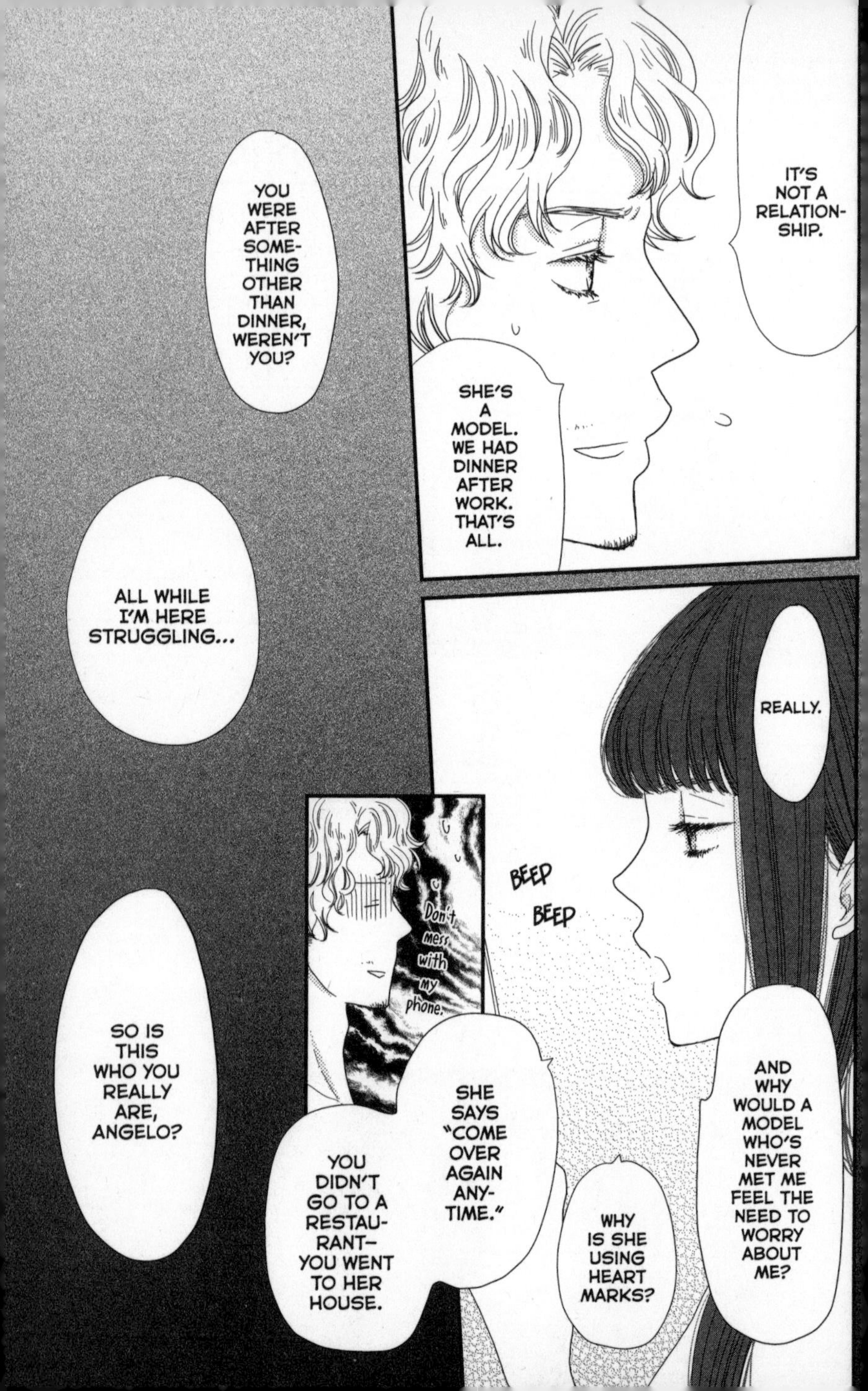
IT'S NOT A RELATIONSHIP.
SHE'S A MODEL. WE HAD DINNER AFTER WORK. THAT'S ALL.
REALLY.
BEEP
BEEP
AND WHY WOULD A MODEL WHO'S NEVER MET ME FEEL THE NEED TO WORRY ABOUT ME?
WHY IS SHE USING HEART MARKS?
SHE SAYS "COME OVER AGAIN ANYTIME."
YOU DIDN'T GO TO A RESTAURANT—YOU WENT TO HER HOUSE.
Don't mess with my phone.
YOU WERE AFTER SOMETHING OTHER THAN DINNER, WEREN'T YOU?
ALL WHILE I'M HERE STRUGGLING...
SO IS THIS WHO YOU REALLY ARE, ANGELO?

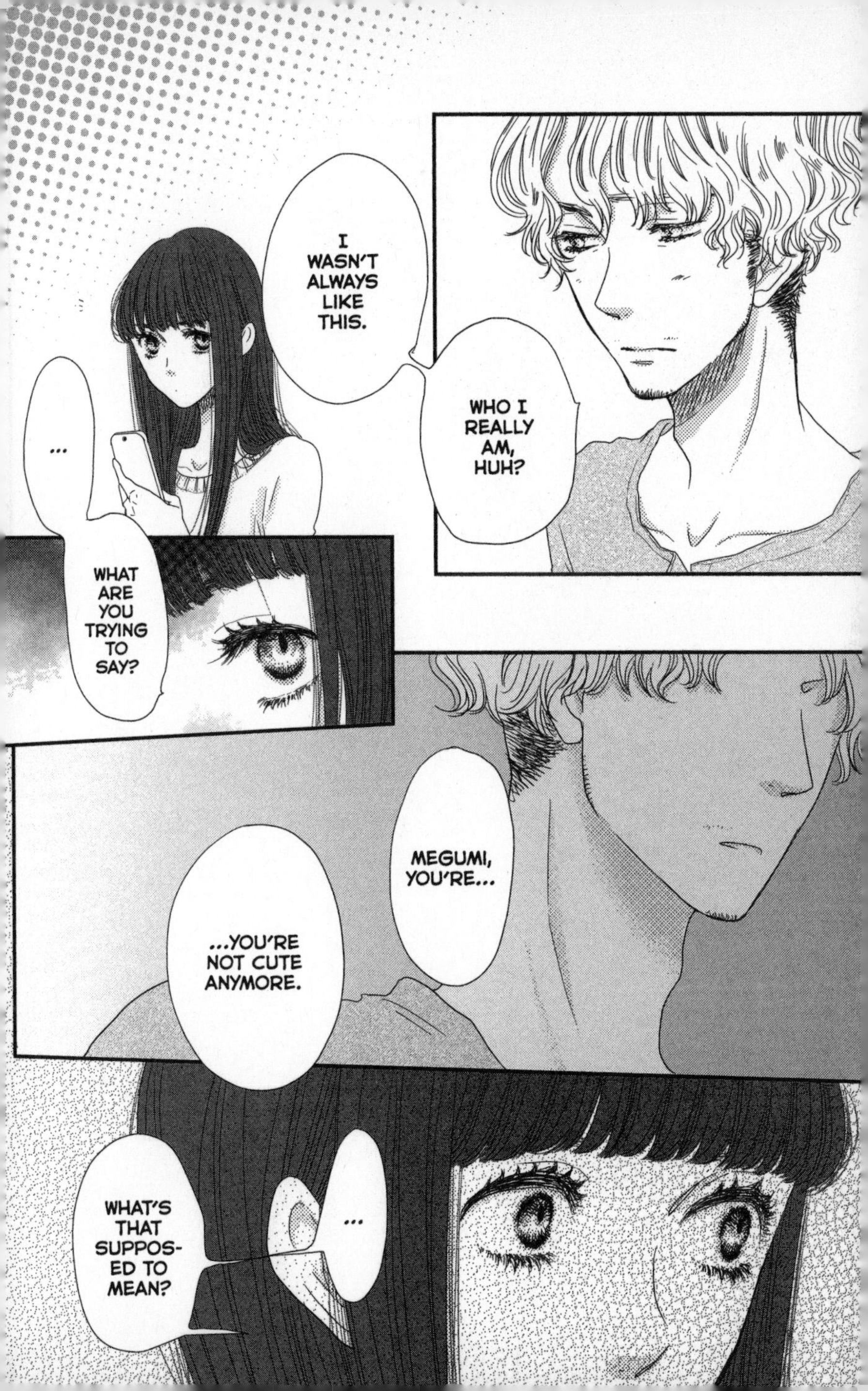
WHO I REALLY AM, HUH?
I WASN'T ALWAYS LIKE THIS.
...
WHAT ARE YOU TRYING TO SAY?
MEGUMI, YOU'RE...
...YOU'RE NOT CUTE ANYMORE.
...
WHAT'S THAT SUPPOS-ED TO MEAN?

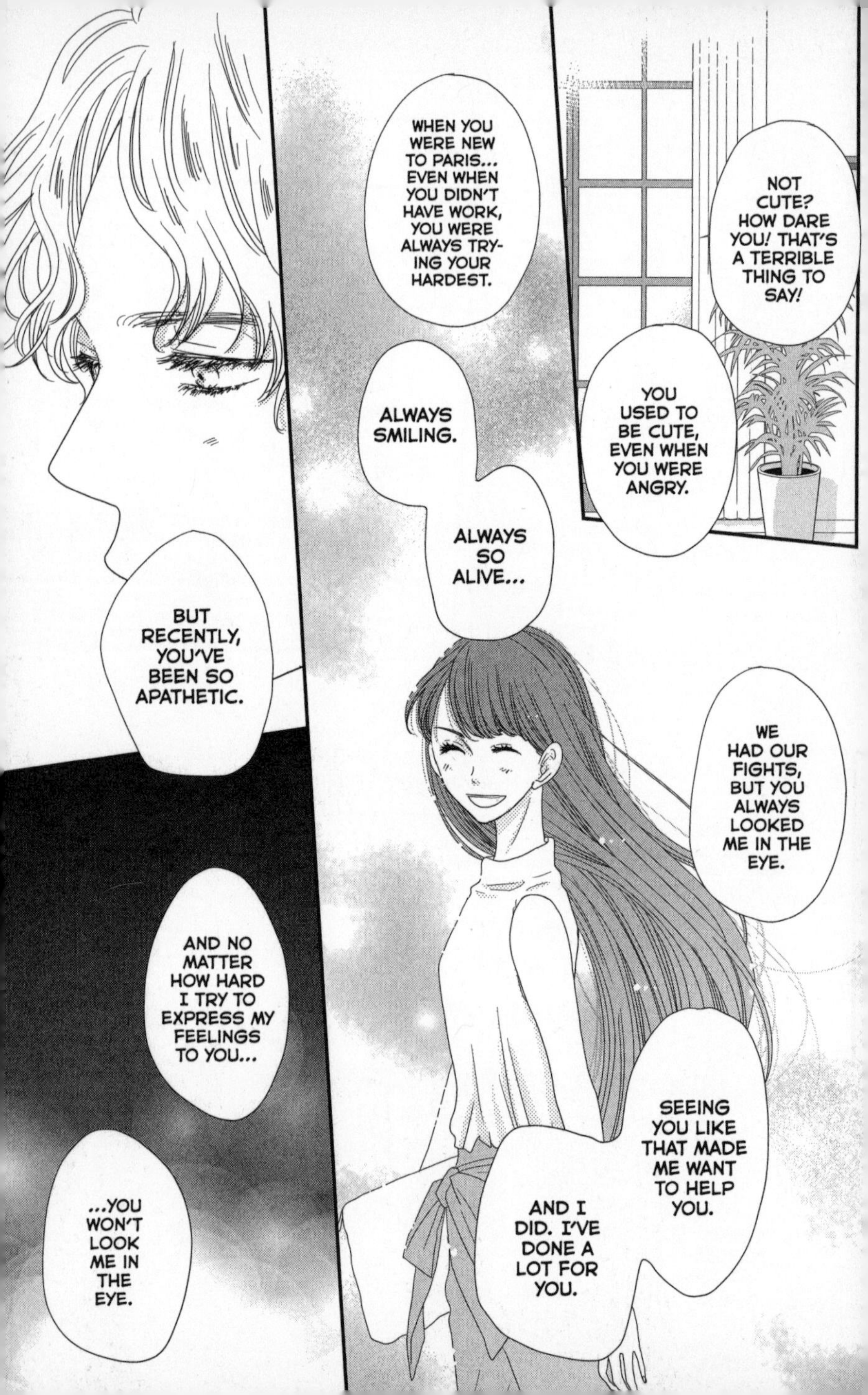
NOT CUTE? HOW DARE YOU! THAT'S A TERRIBLE THING TO SAY!
YOU USED TO BE CUTE, EVEN WHEN YOU WERE ANGRY.
WHEN YOU WERE NEW TO PARIS... EVEN WHEN YOU DIDN'T HAVE WORK, YOU WERE ALWAYS TRY-ING YOUR HARDEST.
ALWAYS SMILING.
ALWAYS SO ALIVE...
WE HAD OUR FIGHTS, BUT YOU ALWAYS LOOKED ME IN THE EYE.
SEEING YOU LIKE THAT MADE ME WANT TO HELP YOU.
AND I DID. I'VE DONE A LOT FOR YOU.
BUT RECENTLY, YOU'VE BEEN SO APATHETIC.
AND NO MATTER HOW HARD I TRY TO EXPRESS MY FEELINGS TO YOU...
...YOU WON'T LOOK ME IN THE EYE.

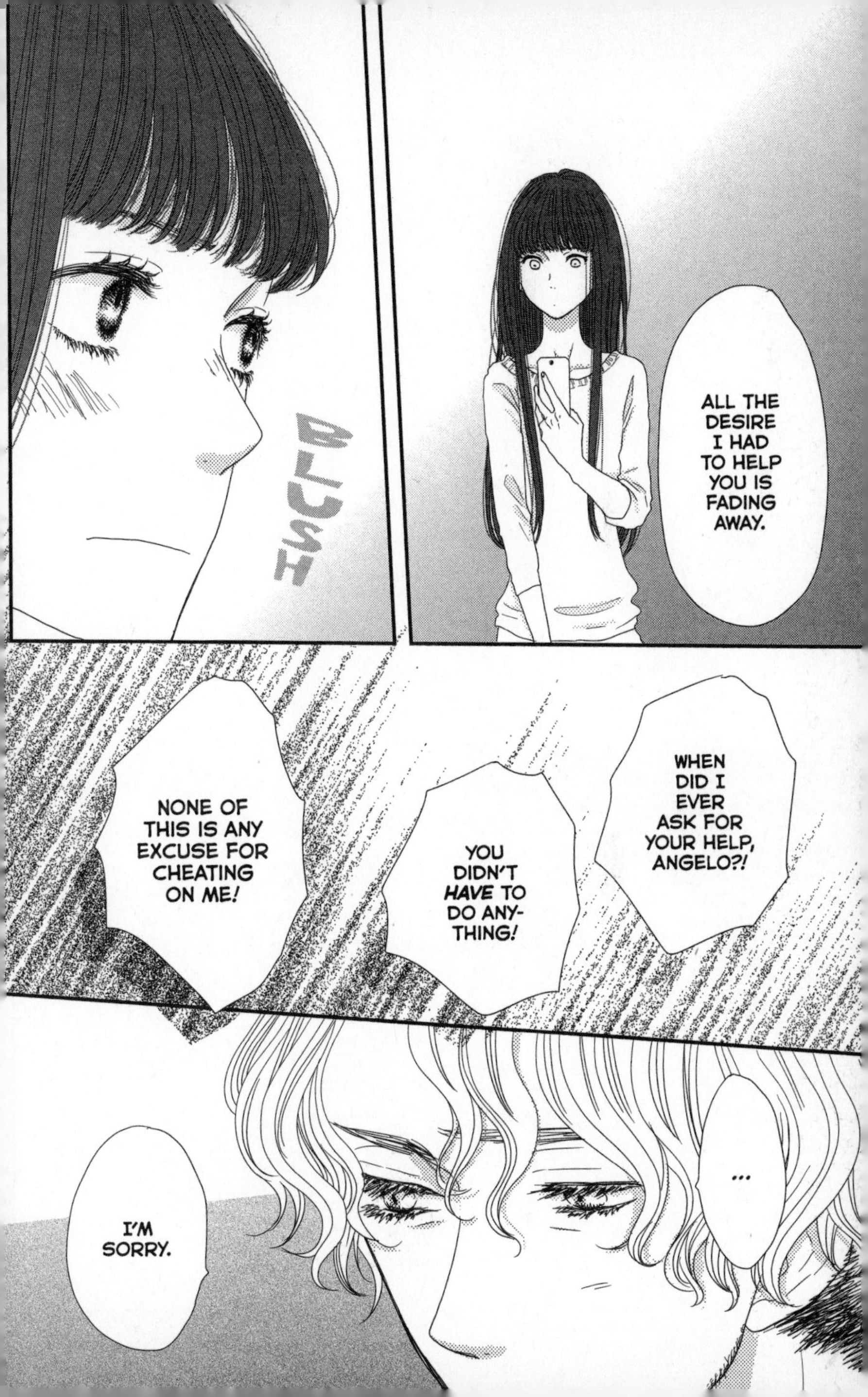
ALL THE DESIRE I HAD TO HELP YOU IS FADING AWAY.
BLUSH
WHEN DID I EVER ASK FOR YOUR HELP, ANGELO?!
YOU DIDN'T *HAVE* TO DO ANY-THING!
NONE OF THIS IS ANY EXCUSE FOR CHEATING ON ME!
...
I'M SORRY.

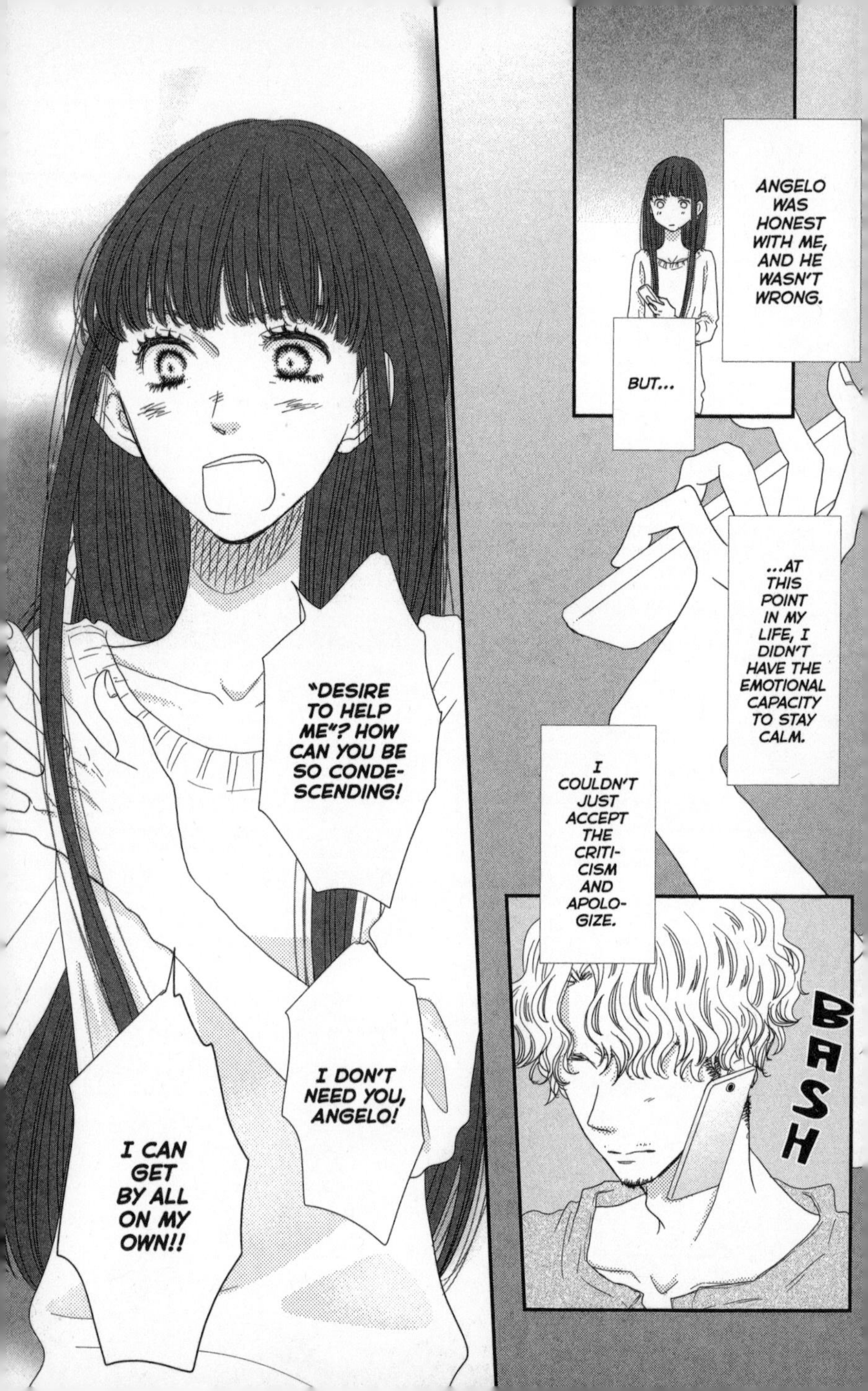
ANGELO WAS HONEST WITH ME, AND HE WASN'T WRONG.
BUT...
...AT THIS POINT IN MY LIFE, I DIDN'T HAVE THE EMOTIONAL CAPACITY TO STAY CALM.
I COULDN'T JUST ACCEPT THE CRITI-CISM AND APOLO-GIZE.
BASH
"DESIRE TO HELP ME"? HOW CAN YOU BE SO CONDE-SCENDING!
I DON'T NEED YOU, ANGELO!
I CAN GET BY ALL ON MY OWN!!

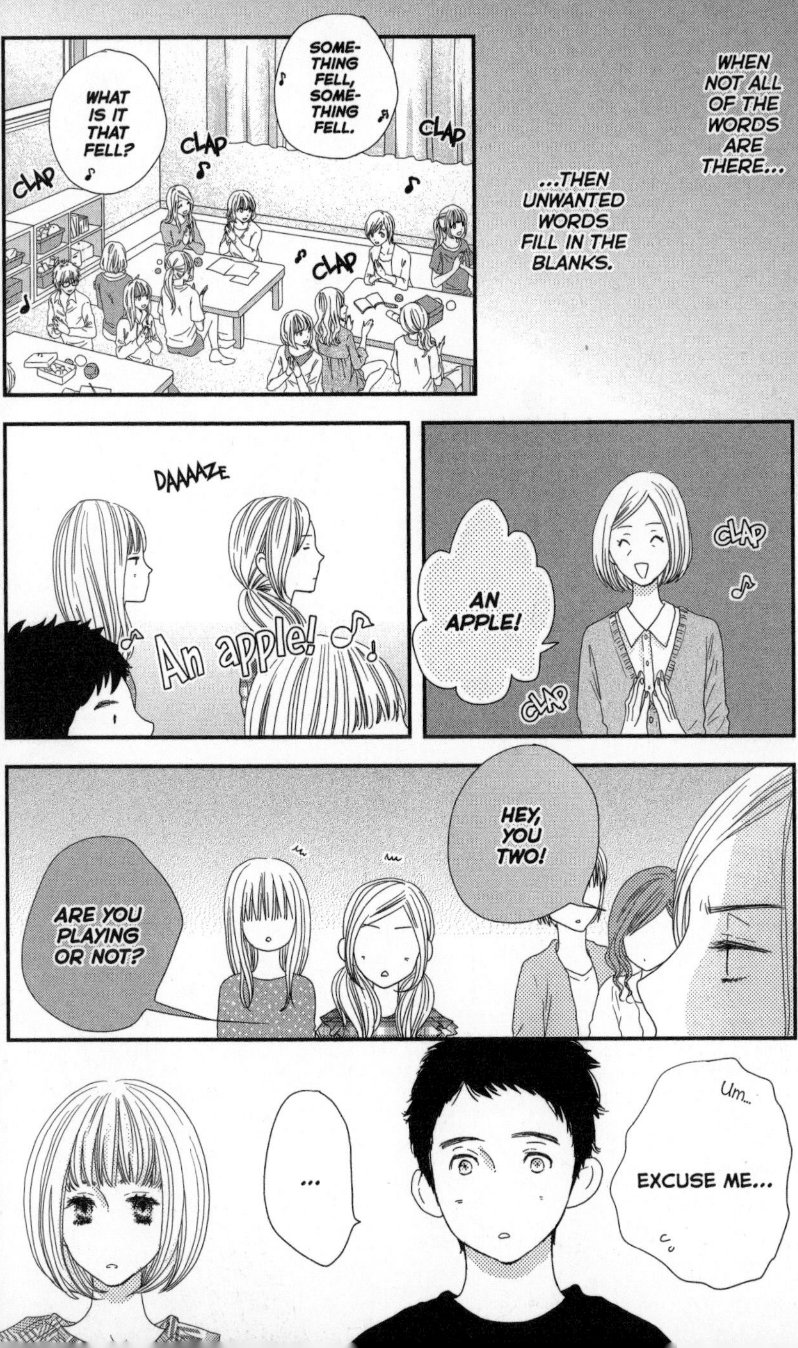
WHEN NOT ALL OF THE WORDS ARE THERE...
...THEN UNWANTED WORDS FILL IN THE BLANKS.
CLAP
SOMETHING FELL, SOMETHING FELL.
CLAP
WHAT IS IT THAT FELL?
CLAP
CLAP
CLAP
AN APPLE!
CLAP
CLAP
DAAAAZE
An apple!
HEY, YOU TWO!
ARE YOU PLAYING OR NOT?
Um...
EXCUSE ME...
...

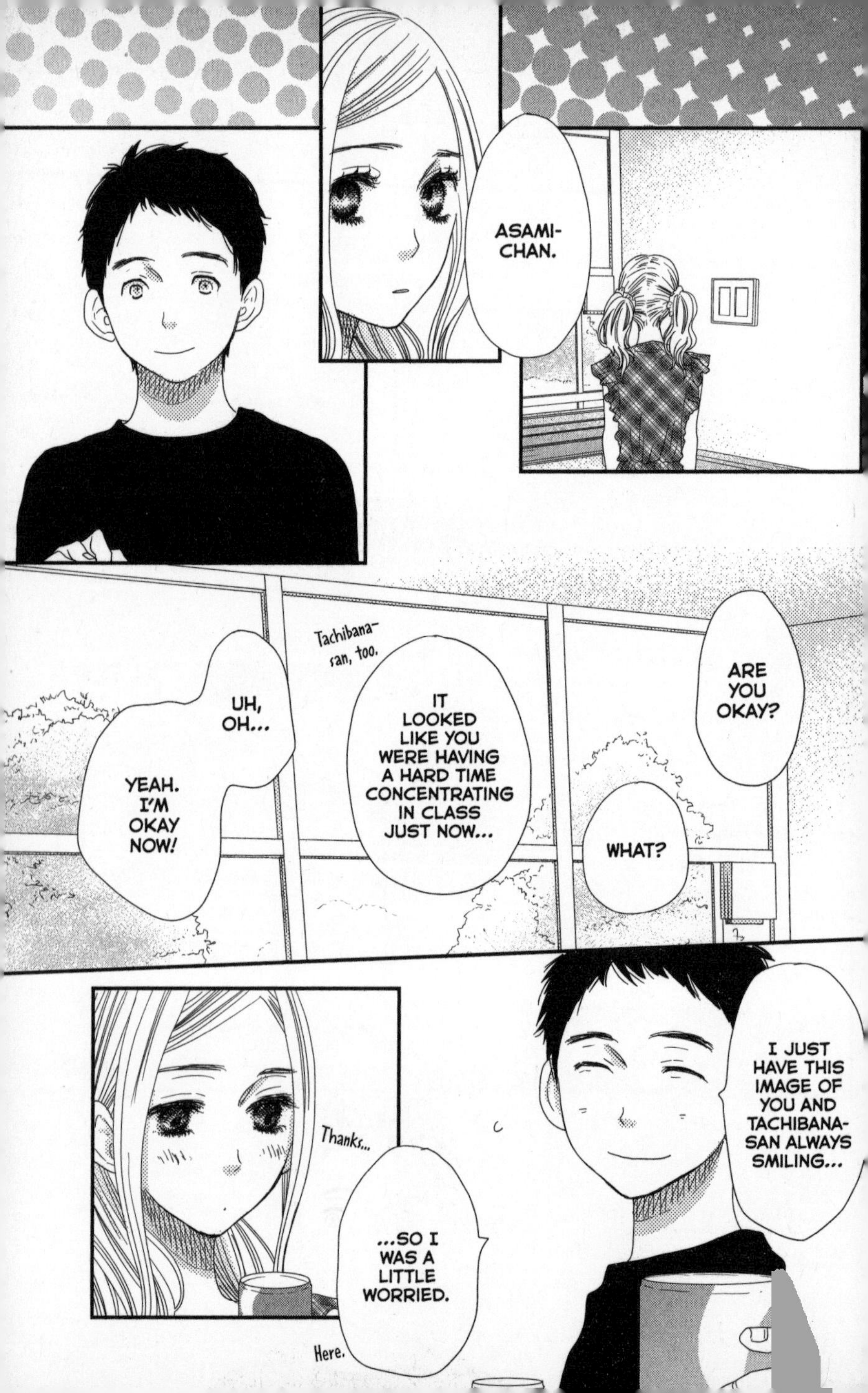
ASAMI-CHAN.
ARE YOU OKAY?
WHAT?
IT LOOKED LIKE YOU WERE HAVING A HARD TIME CONCENTRATING IN CLASS JUST NOW...
Tachibana-san, too.
UH, OH...
YEAH. I'M OKAY NOW!
I JUST HAVE THIS IMAGE OF YOU AND TACHIBANA-SAN ALWAYS SMILING...
...SO I WAS A LITTLE WORRIED.
Here.
Thanks...

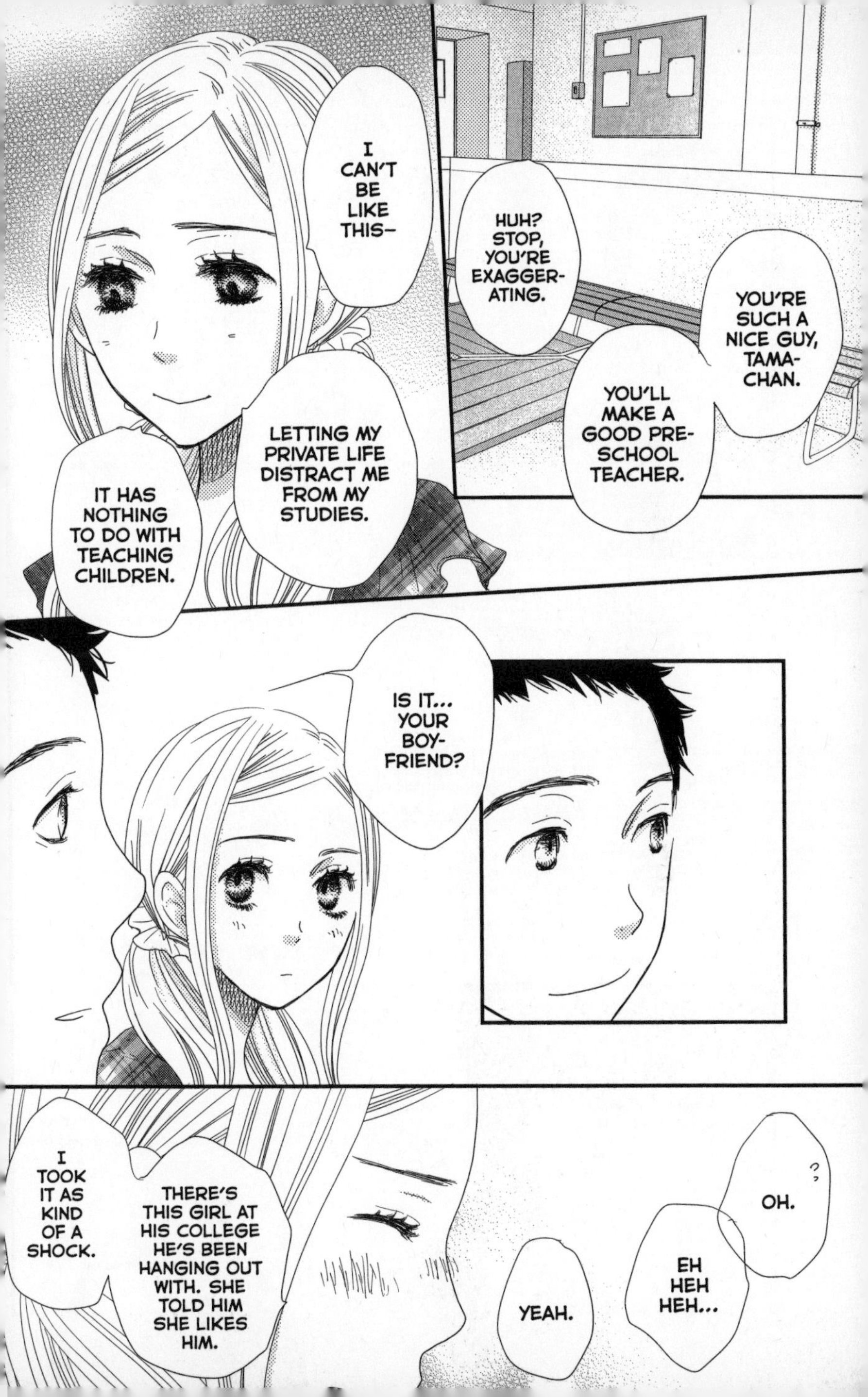
YOU'RE SUCH A NICE GUY, TAMA-CHAN.
YOU'LL MAKE A GOOD PRE-SCHOOL TEACHER.
HUH? STOP, YOU'RE EXAGGER-ATING.
I CAN'T BE LIKE THIS–
LETTING MY PRIVATE LIFE DISTRACT ME FROM MY STUDIES.
IT HAS NOTHING TO DO WITH TEACHING CHILDREN.
IS IT... YOUR BOY-FRIEND?
OH.
EH HEH HEH...
YEAH.
THERE'S THIS GIRL AT HIS COLLEGE HE'S BEEN HANGING OUT WITH. SHE TOLD HIM SHE LIKES HIM.
I TOOK IT AS KIND OF A SHOCK.

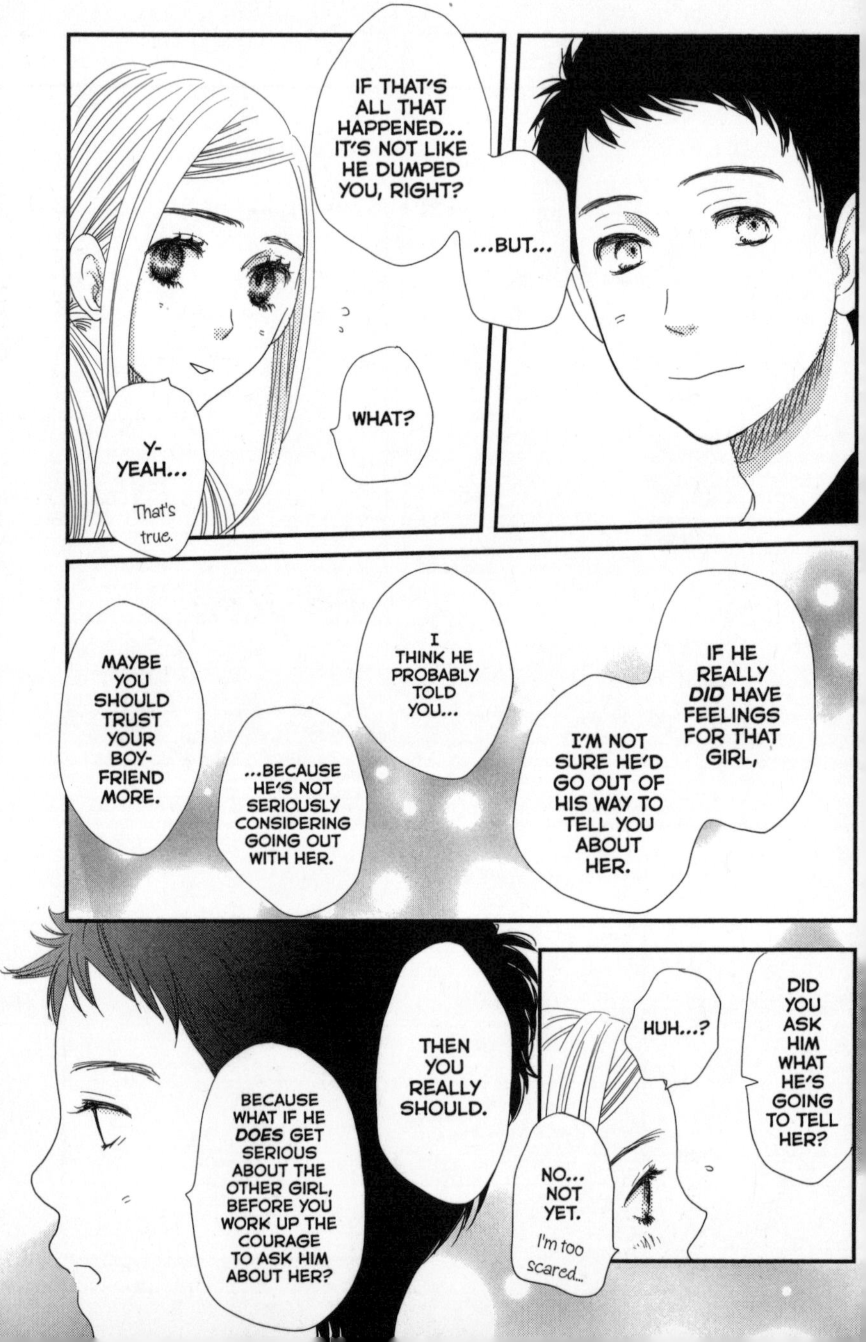
IF THAT'S ALL THAT HAPPENED... IT'S NOT LIKE HE DUMPED YOU, RIGHT?
Y-YEAH... That's true.
...BUT...
WHAT?
IF HE REALLY *DID* HAVE FEELINGS FOR THAT GIRL,
I'M NOT SURE HE'D GO OUT OF HIS WAY TO TELL YOU ABOUT HER.
I THINK HE PROBABLY TOLD YOU...
...BECAUSE HE'S NOT SERIOUSLY CONSIDERING GOING OUT WITH HER.
MAYBE YOU SHOULD TRUST YOUR BOY-FRIEND MORE.
DID YOU ASK HIM WHAT HE'S GOING TO TELL HER?
HUH...?
NO... NOT YET. I'm too scared...
THEN YOU REALLY SHOULD.
BECAUSE WHAT IF HE *DOES* GET SERIOUS ABOUT THE OTHER GIRL, BEFORE YOU WORK UP THE COURAGE TO ASK HIM ABOUT HER?

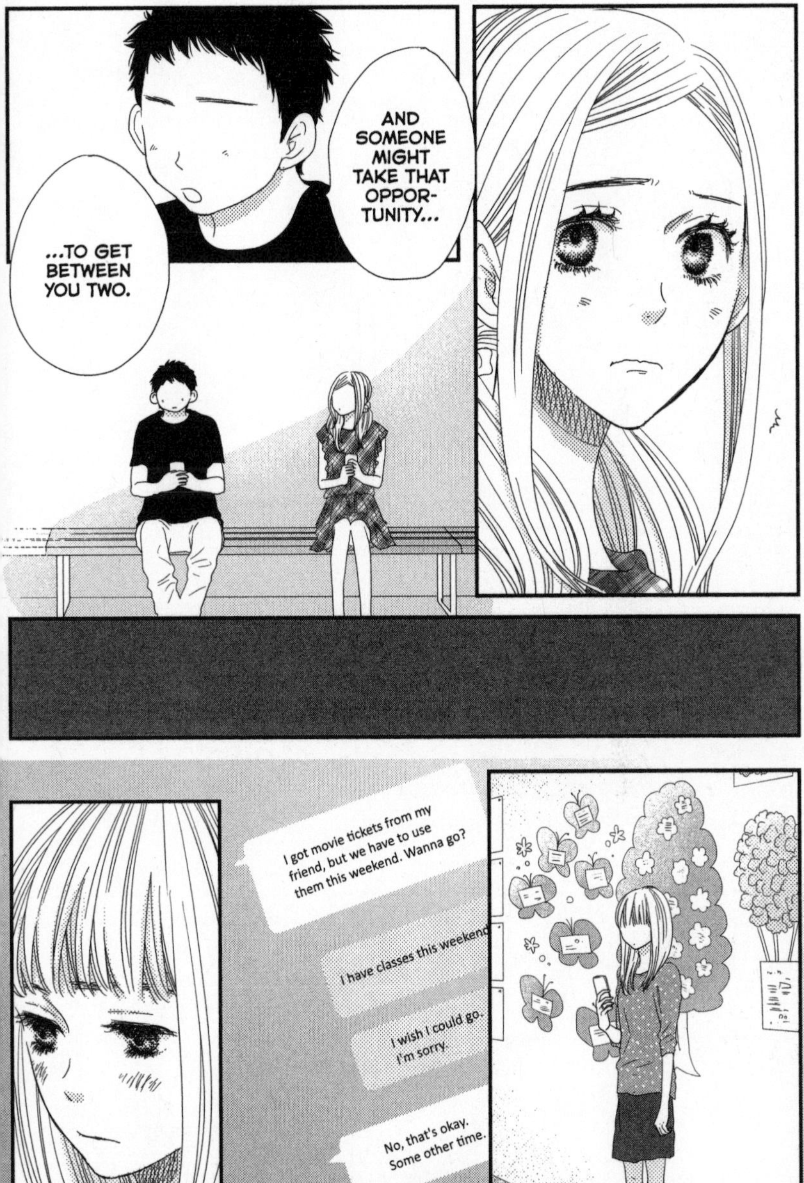
AND SOMEONE MIGHT TAKE THAT OPPOR-TUNITY...
...TO GET BETWEEN YOU TWO.
I got movie tickets from my friend, but we have to use them this weekend. Wanna go?
I have classes this weekend
I wish I could go. I'm sorry.
No, that's okay. Some other time.

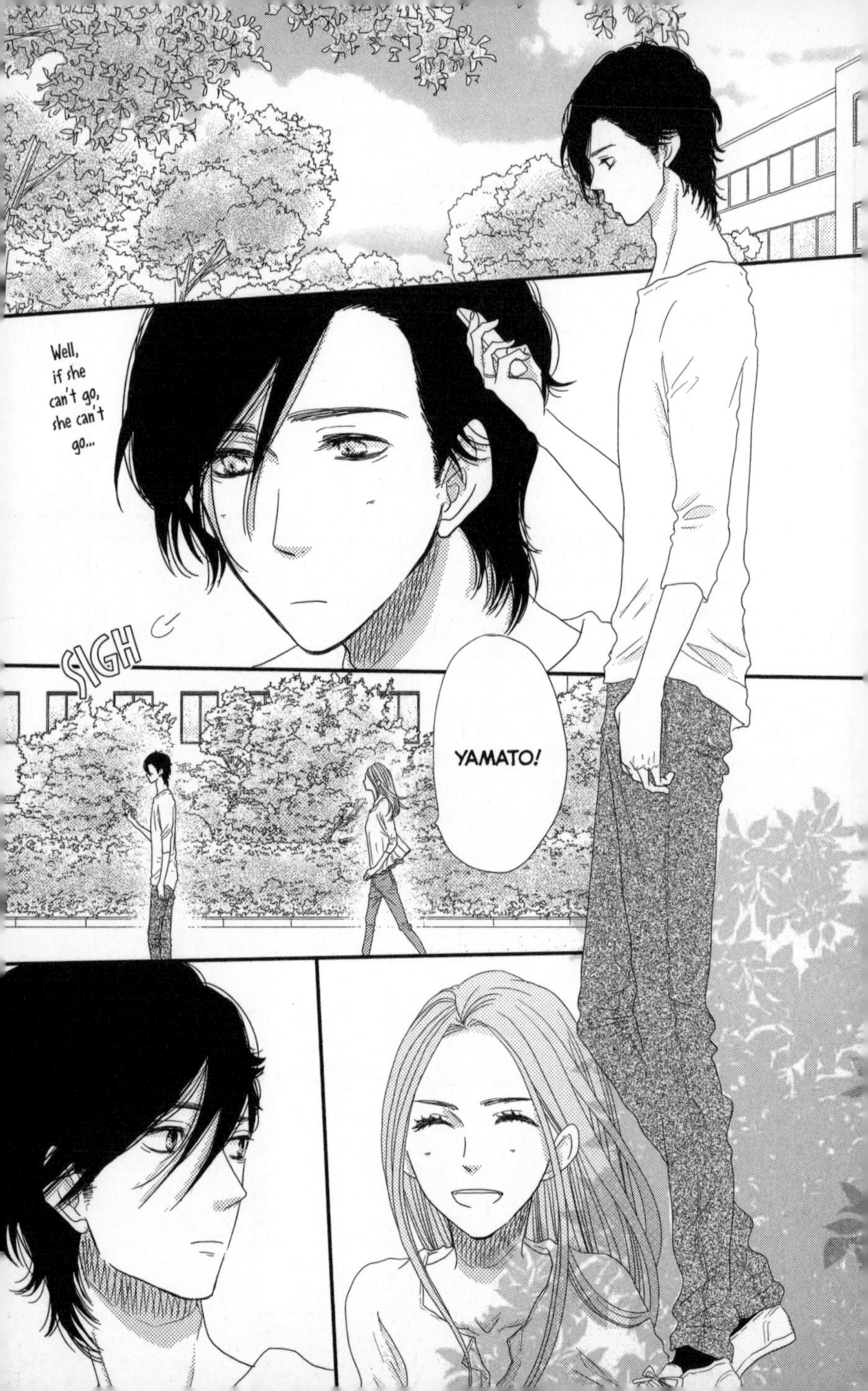
Well, if she can't go, she can't go...
SIGH
YAMATO!

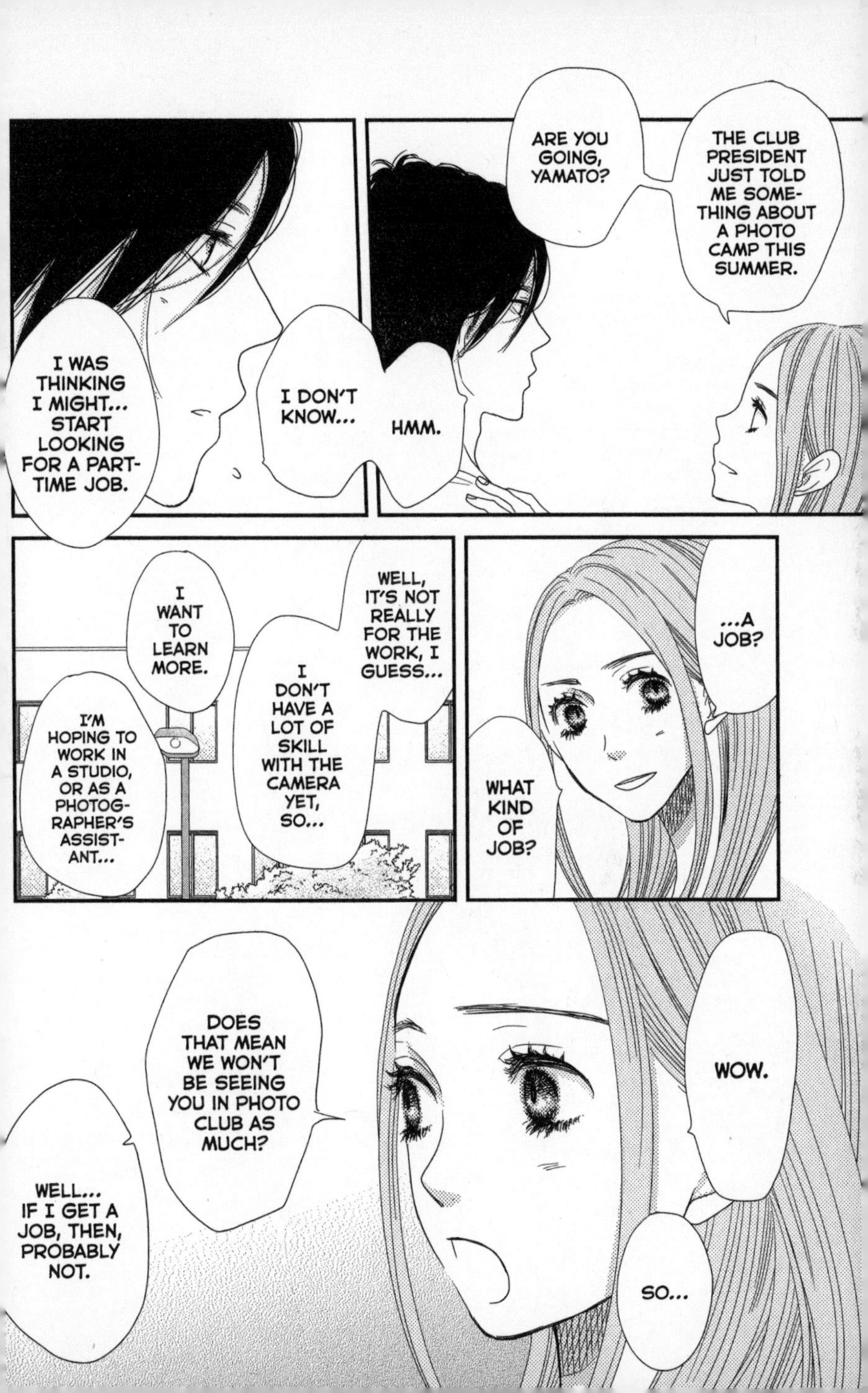
THE CLUB PRESIDENT JUST TOLD ME SOMETHING ABOUT A PHOTO CAMP THIS SUMMER.
ARE YOU GOING, YAMATO?
HMM.
I DON'T KNOW...
I WAS THINKING I MIGHT... START LOOKING FOR A PART-TIME JOB.
...A JOB?
WHAT KIND OF JOB?
WELL, IT'S NOT REALLY FOR THE WORK, I GUESS...
I DON'T HAVE A LOT OF SKILL WITH THE CAMERA YET, SO...
I WANT TO LEARN MORE.
I'M HOPING TO WORK IN A STUDIO, OR AS A PHOTOGRAPHER'S ASSISTANT...
WOW.
SO...
DOES THAT MEAN WE WON'T BE SEEING YOU IN PHOTO CLUB AS MUCH?
WELL... IF I GET A JOB, THEN, PROBABLY NOT.

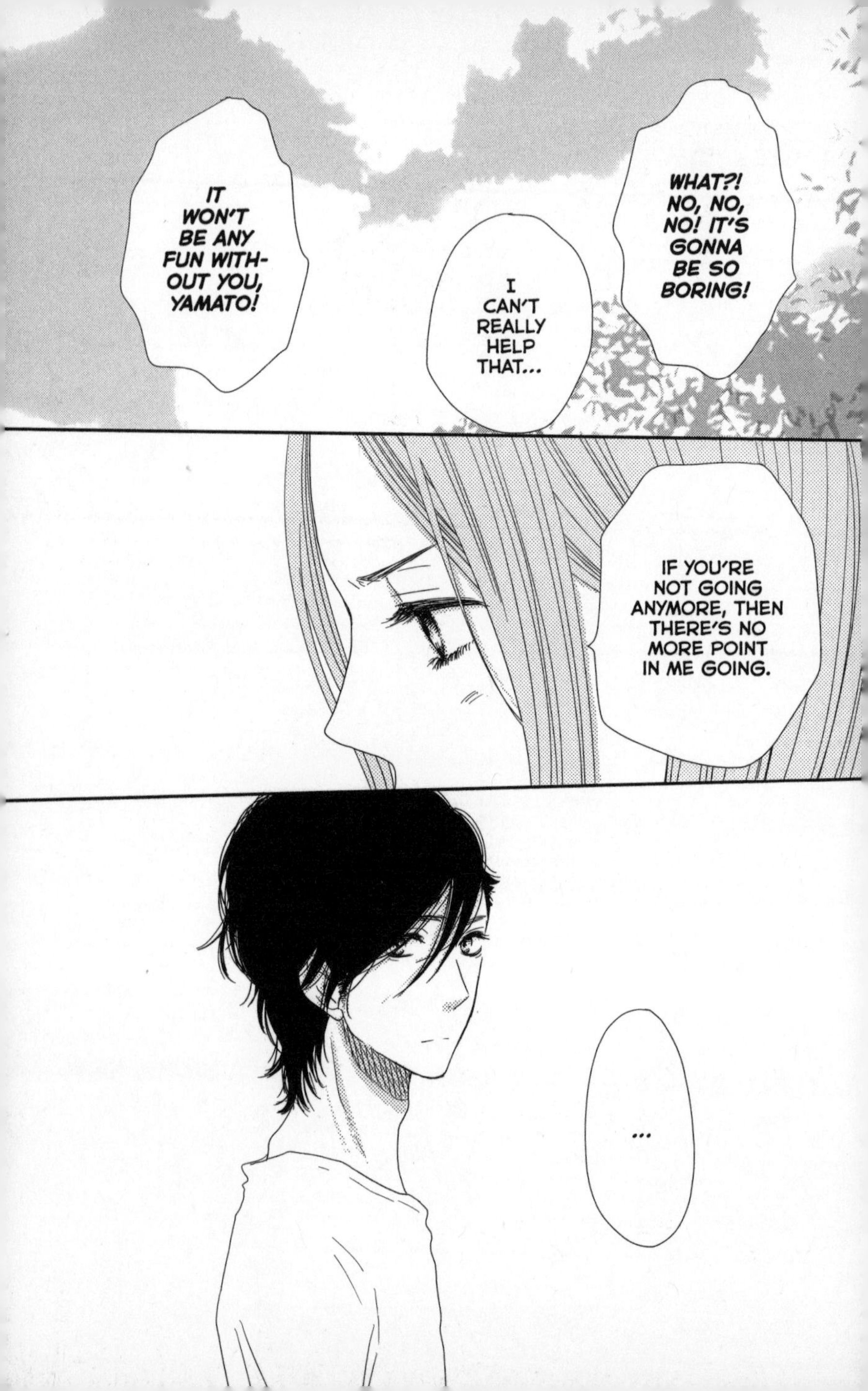
WHAT?! NO, NO, NO! IT'S GONNA BE SO BORING!
I CAN'T REALLY HELP THAT...
IT WON'T BE ANY FUN WITH-OUT YOU, YAMATO!
IF YOU'RE NOT GOING ANYMORE, THEN THERE'S NO MORE POINT IN ME GOING.
...

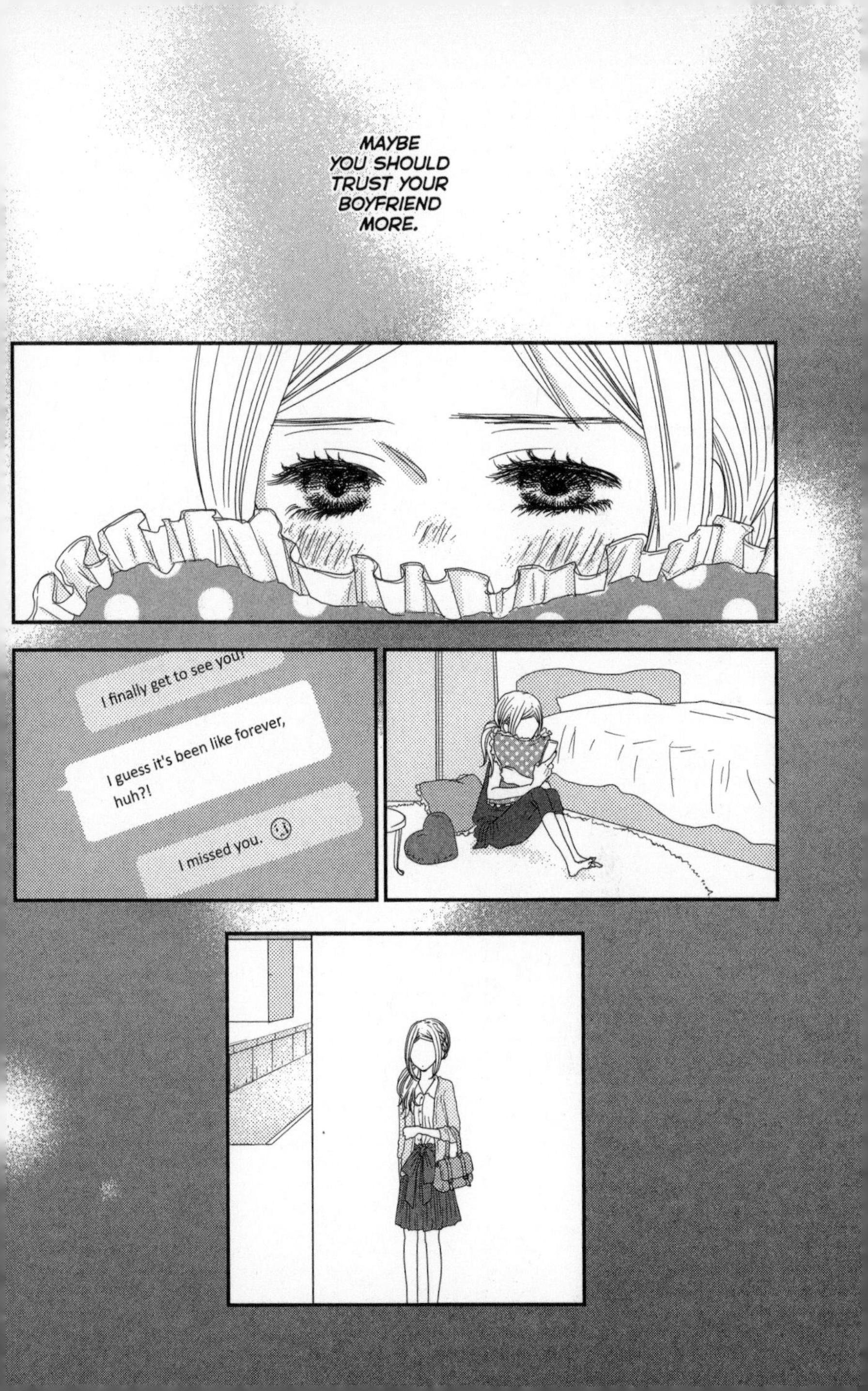
MAYBE YOU SHOULD TRUST YOUR BOYFRIEND MORE.
I finally get to see you!
I guess it's been like forever, huh?!
I missed you.

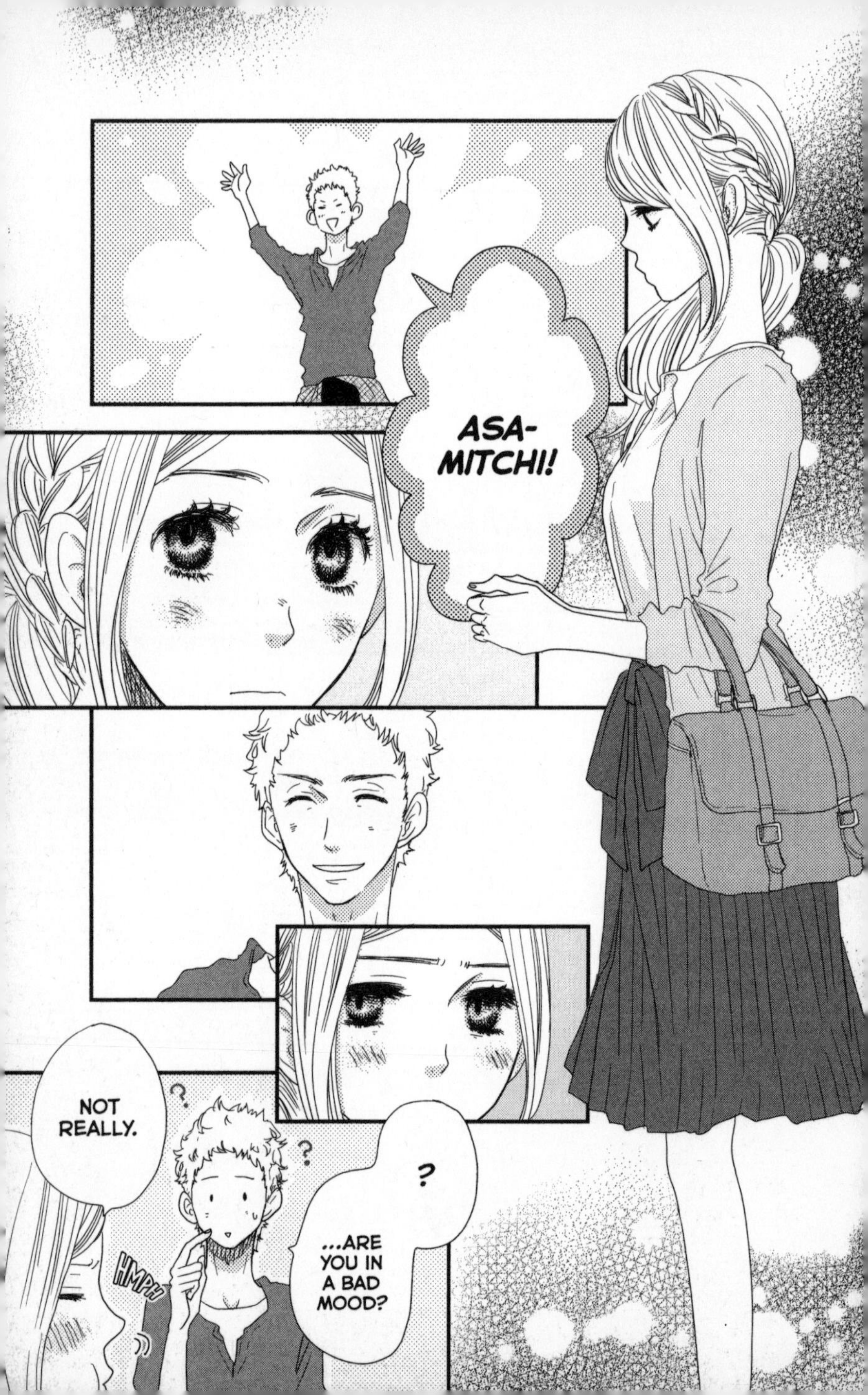
ASA-MITCHI!
?
...ARE YOU IN A BAD MOOD?
NOT REALLY.
HMPH

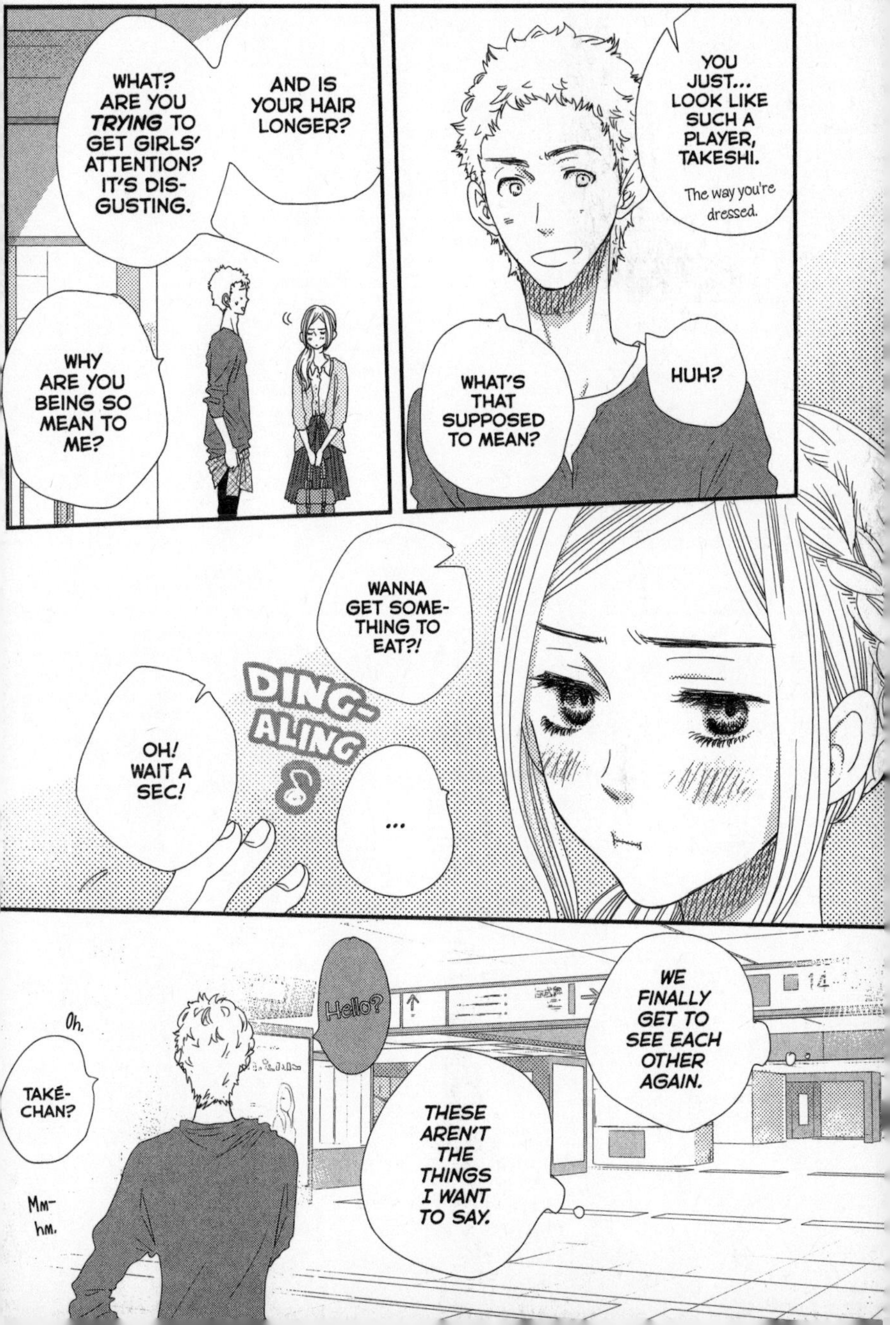
YOU JUST... LOOK LIKE SUCH A PLAYER, TAKESHI.
The way you're dressed.
HUH?
WHAT'S THAT SUPPOSED TO MEAN?
AND IS YOUR HAIR LONGER?
WHAT? ARE YOU *TRYING* TO GET GIRLS' ATTENTION? IT'S DIS-GUSTING.
WHY ARE YOU BEING SO MEAN TO ME?
WANNA GET SOME-THING TO EAT?!
...
DING-ALING
OH! WAIT A SEC!
WE FINALLY GET TO SEE EACH OTHER AGAIN.
THESE AREN'T THE THINGS I WANT TO SAY.
Hello?
Oh.
TAKÉ-CHAN?
Mm-hm.

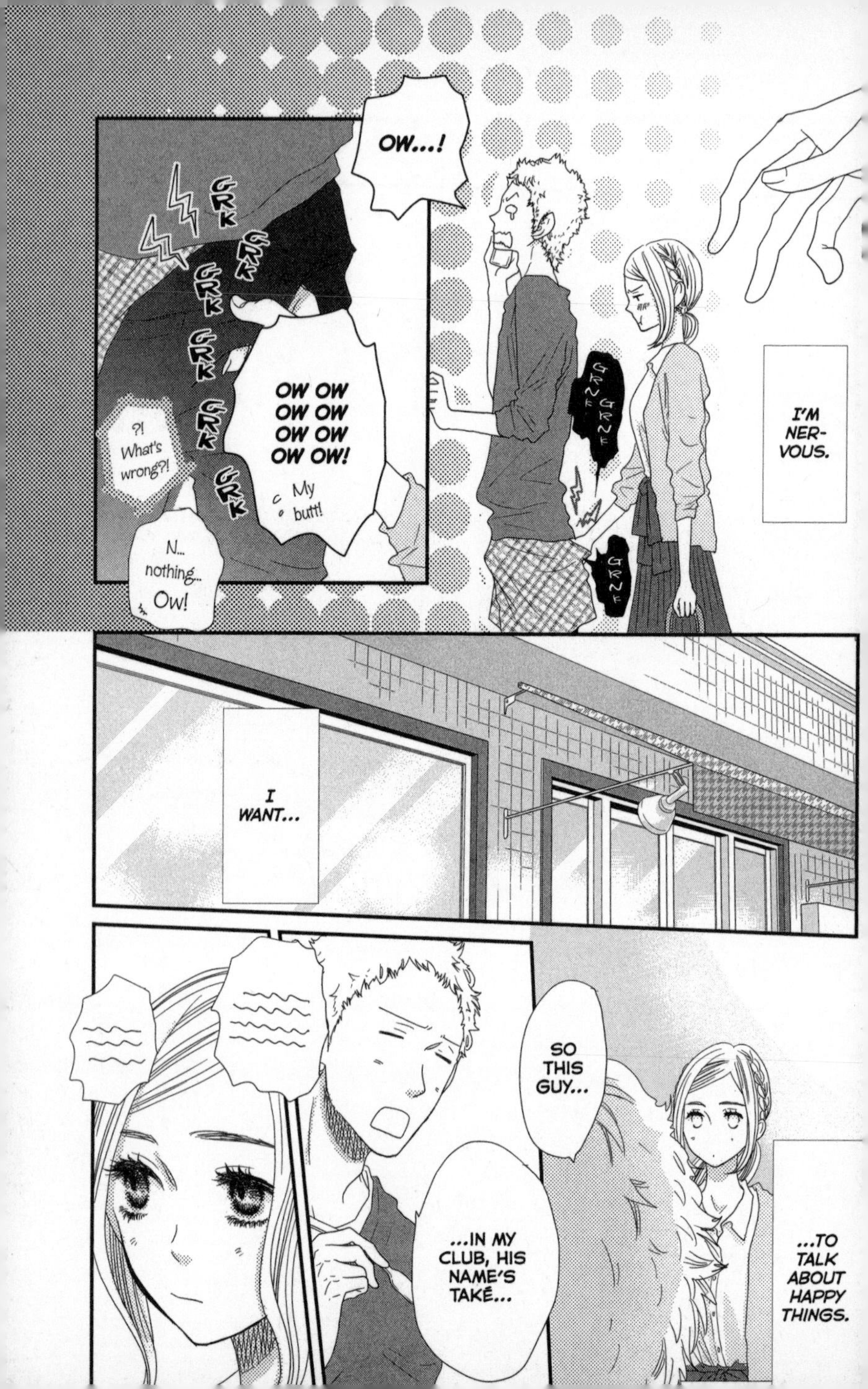
I'M NER-VOUS.
GRNF GRNF
GRNF
OW...!
GRK GRK GRK GRK GRK GRK GRK
OW OW OW OW OW OW OW OW!
My butt!
?! What's wrong?!
N... nothing... Ow!
I WANT...
...TO TALK ABOUT HAPPY THINGS.
SO THIS GUY...
...IN MY CLUB, HIS NAME'S TAKÉ...

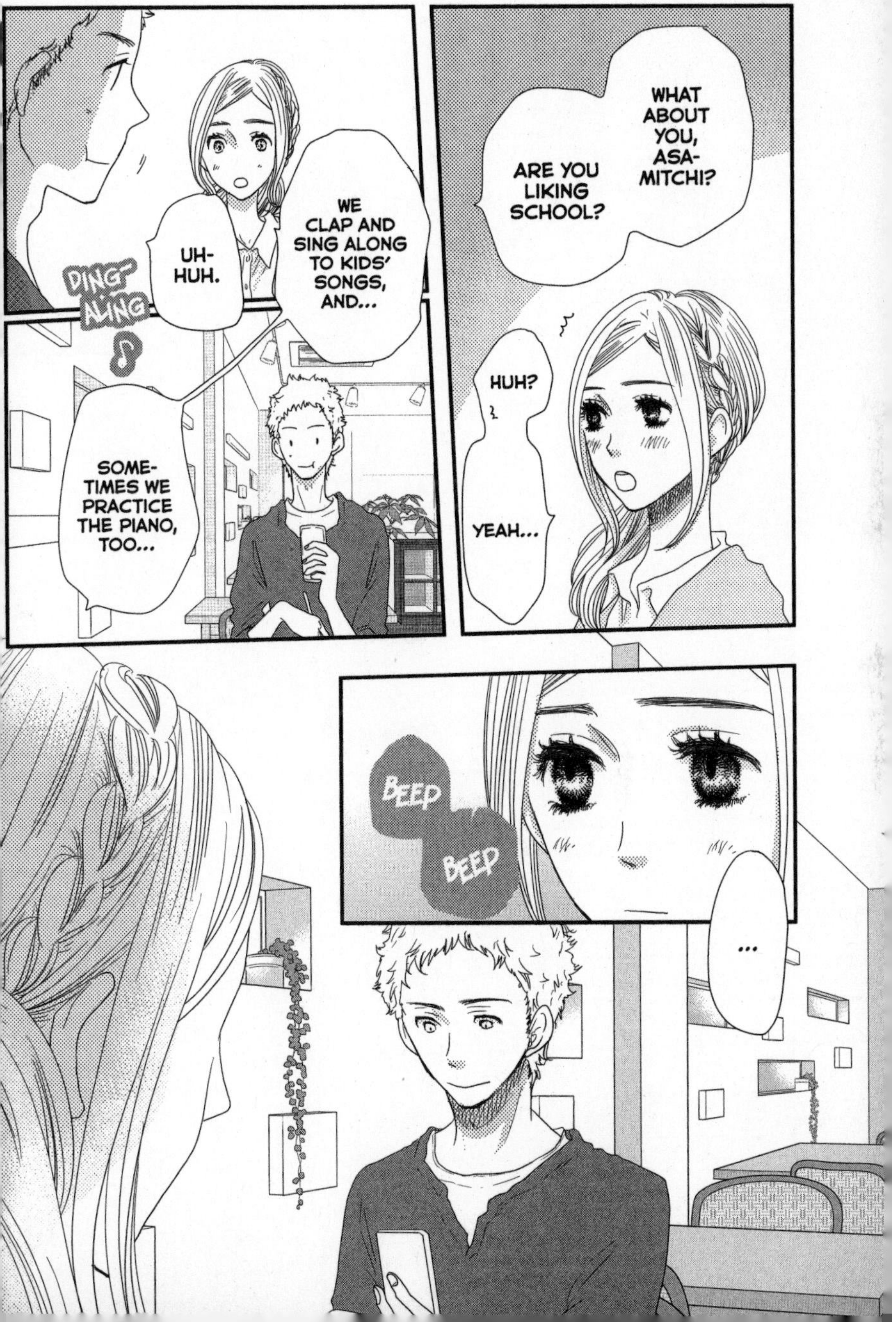
WE CLAP AND SING ALONG TO KIDS' SONGS, AND...
UH-HUH.
DING-ALING
SOMETIMES WE PRACTICE THE PIANO, TOO...
WHAT ABOUT YOU, ASA-MITCHI?
ARE YOU LIKING SCHOOL?
HUH?
YEAH...
BEEP
BEEP
...

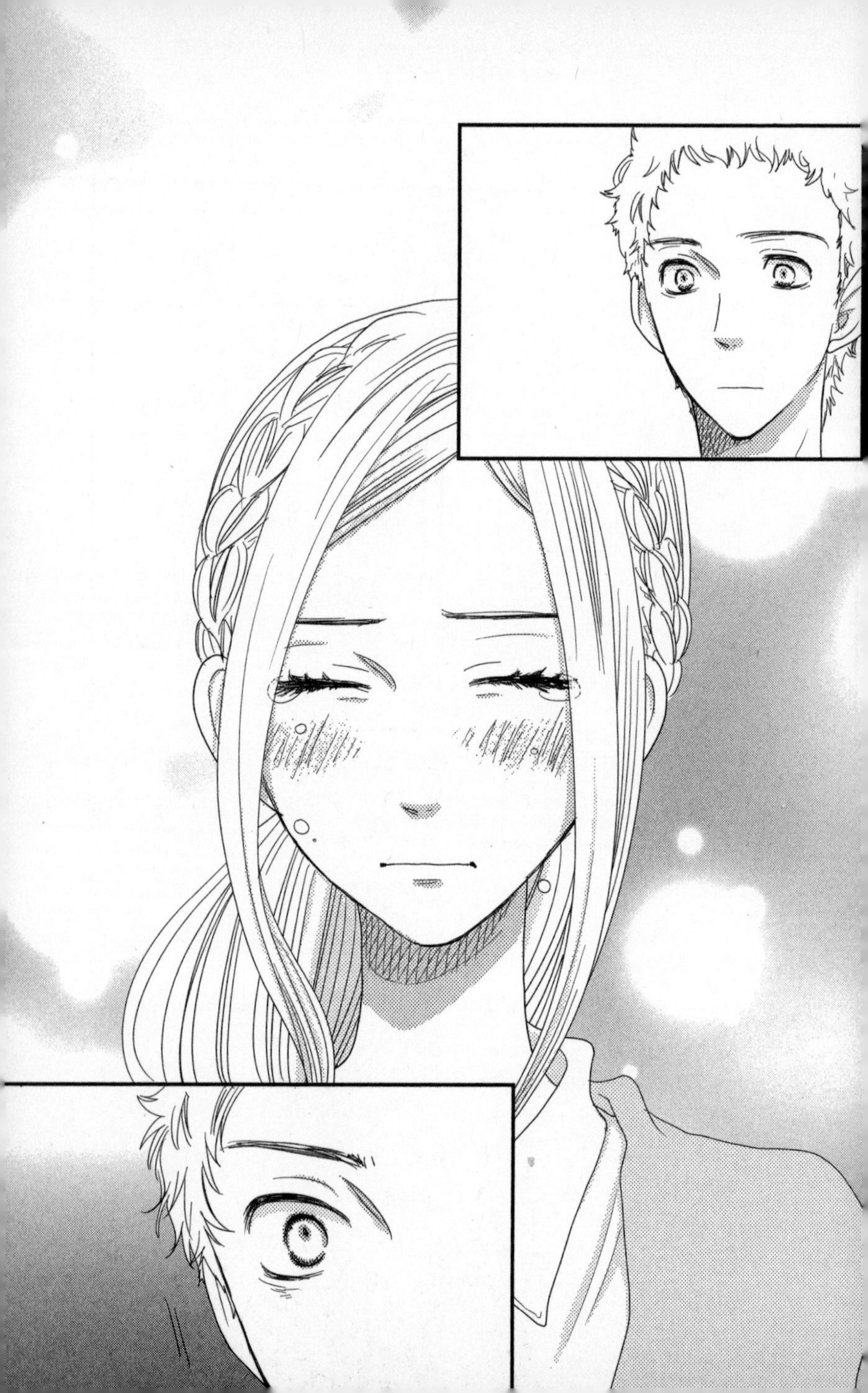

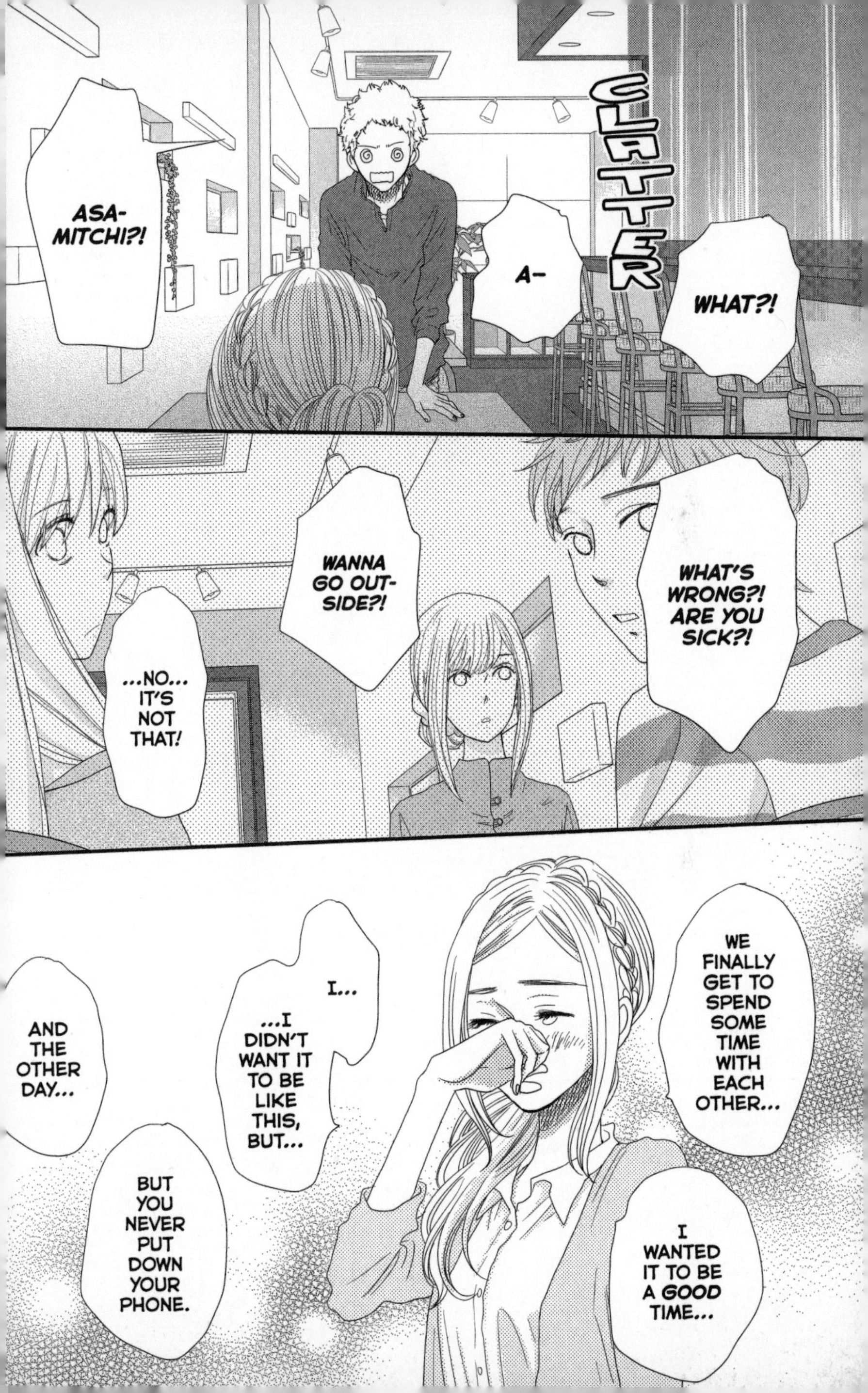
CLATTER
WHAT?!
A-
ASA-MITCHI?!
WHAT'S WRONG?! ARE YOU SICK?!
WANNA GO OUT-SIDE?!
...NO... IT'S NOT THAT!
WE FINALLY GET TO SPEND SOME TIME WITH EACH OTHER...
I WANTED IT TO BE A GOOD TIME...
I...
...I DIDN'T WANT IT TO BE LIKE THIS, BUT...
AND THE OTHER DAY...
BUT YOU NEVER PUT DOWN YOUR PHONE.

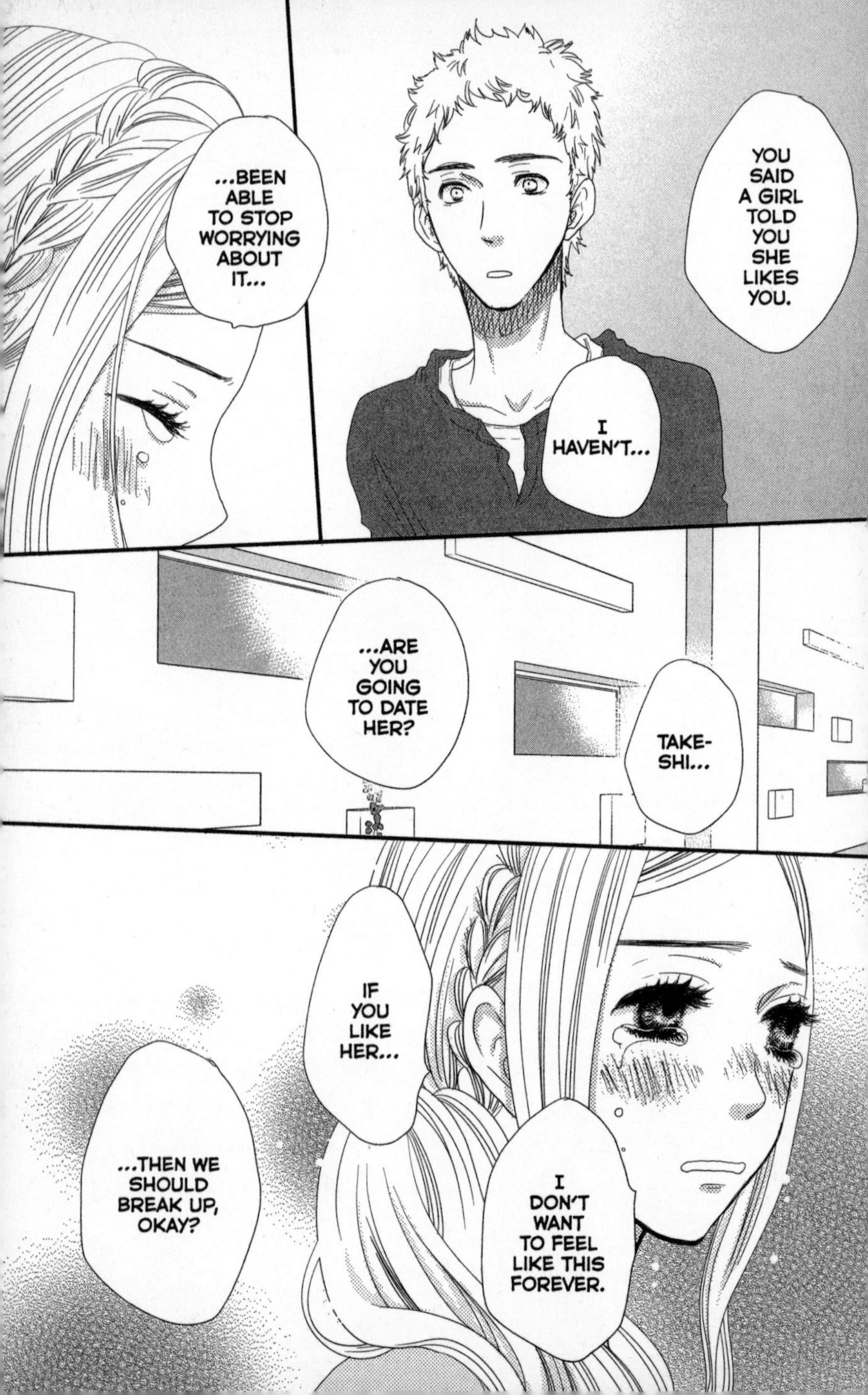
YOU SAID A GIRL TOLD YOU SHE LIKES YOU.
I HAVEN'T...
...BEEN ABLE TO STOP WORRYING ABOUT IT...
TAKE-SHI...
...ARE YOU GOING TO DATE HER?
I DON'T WANT TO FEEL LIKE THIS FOREVER.
IF YOU LIKE HER...
...THEN WE SHOULD BREAK UP, OKAY?

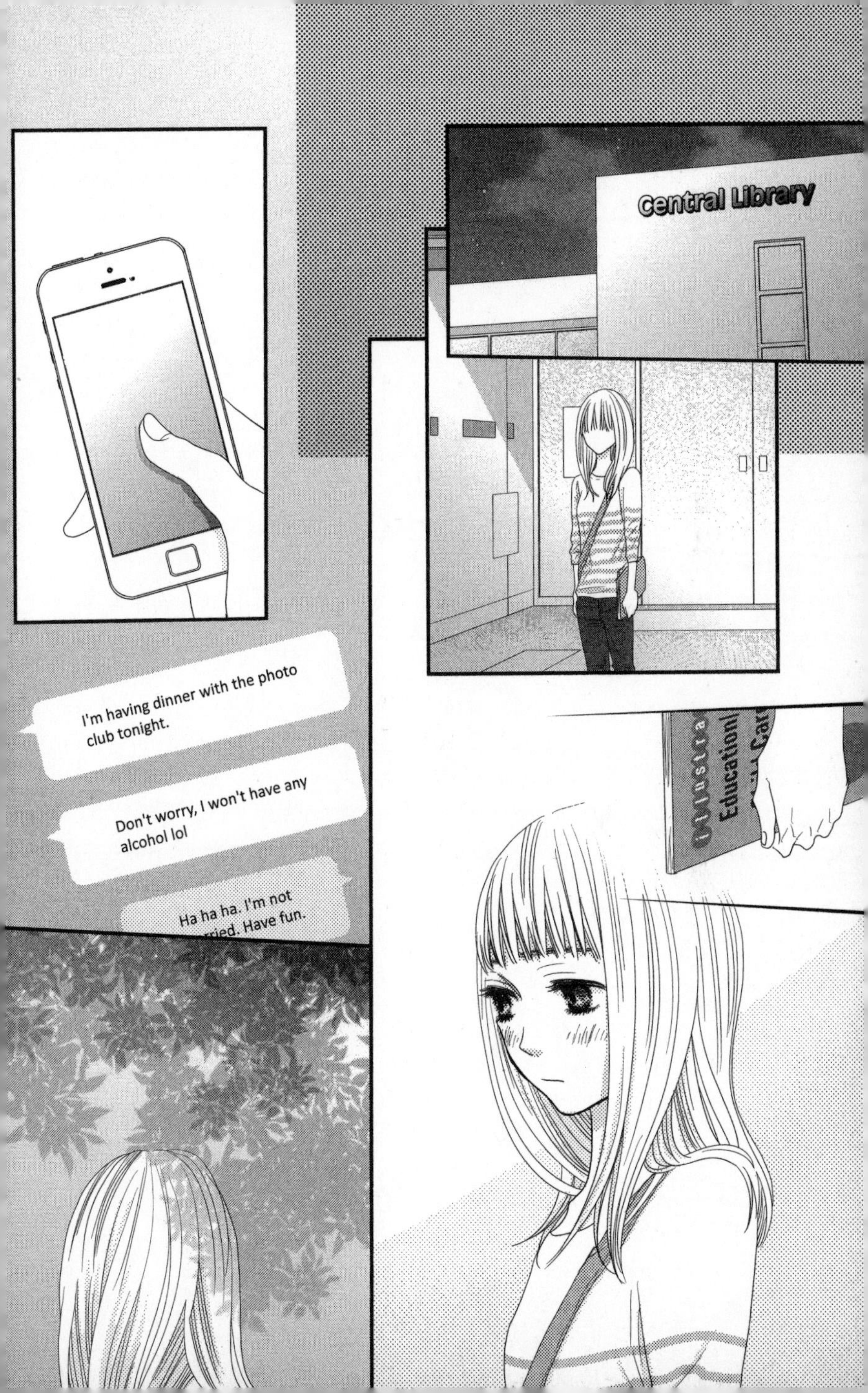
Central Library
I'm having dinner with the photo club tonight.
Don't worry, I won't have any alcohol lol
Ha ha ha. I'm not
rried. Have fun.
Education

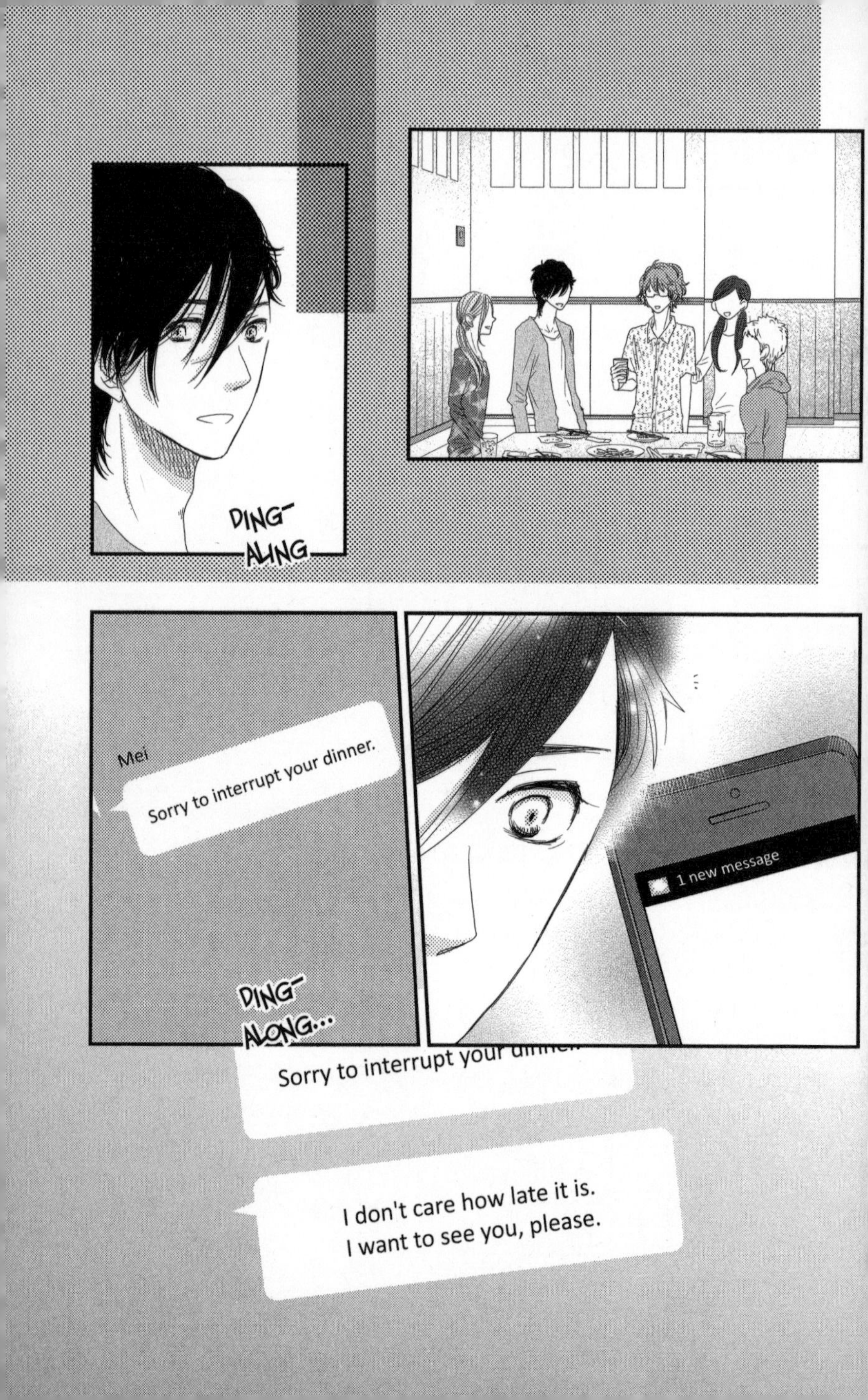
DING-ALING
1 new message
Mei
Sorry to interrupt your dinner.
DING-ALONG...
Sorry to interrupt your dinner.
I don't care how late it is.
I want to see you, please.

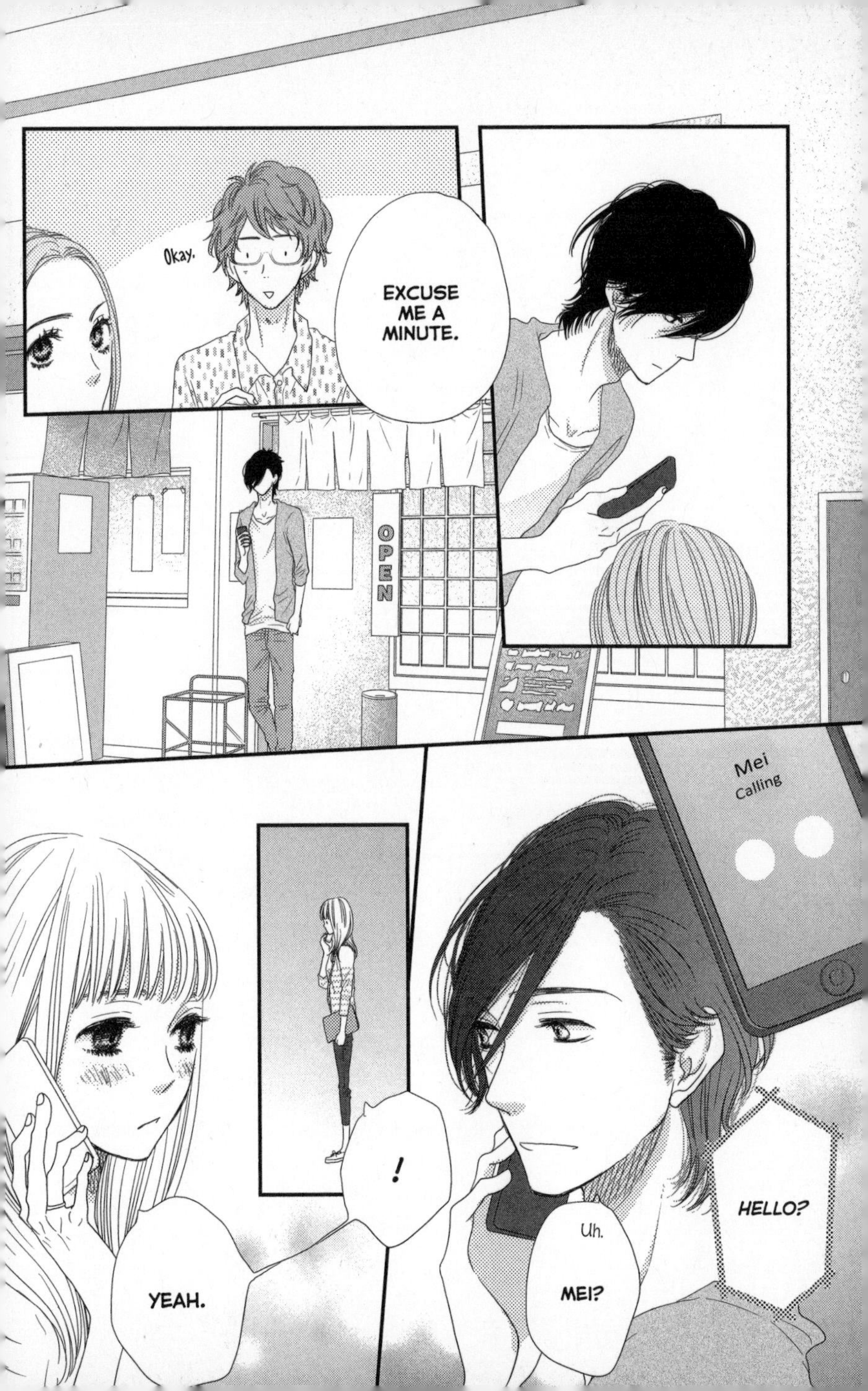
EXCUSE ME A MINUTE.
Okay.
OPEN
Mei
Calling
HELLO?
Uh.
MEI?
!
YEAH.

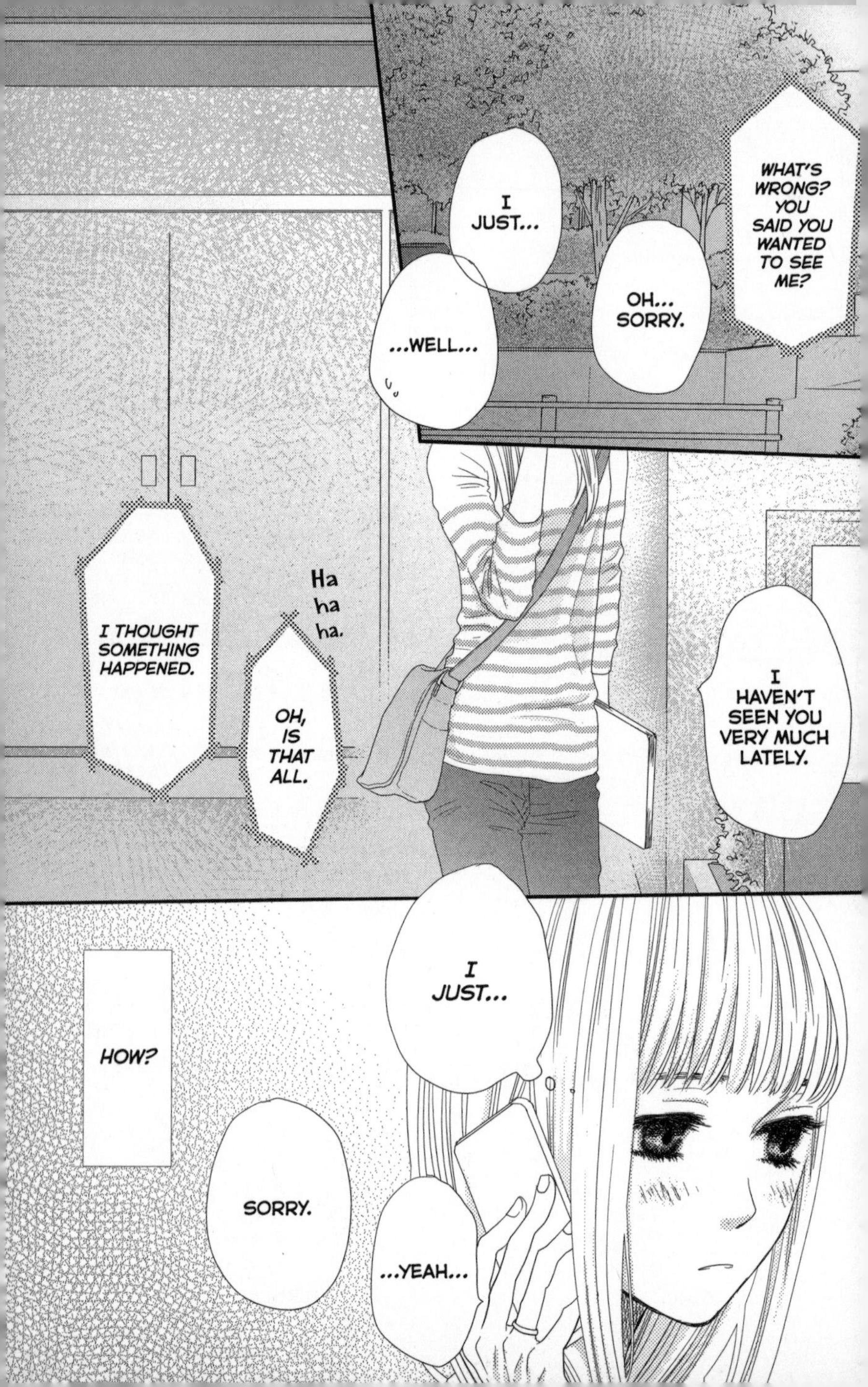
WHAT'S WRONG? YOU SAID YOU WANTED TO SEE ME?
OH... SORRY.
I JUST...
...WELL...
I HAVEN'T SEEN YOU VERY MUCH LATELY.
I THOUGHT SOMETHING HAPPENED.
Ha ha ha.
OH, IS THAT ALL.
I JUST...
...YEAH...
SORRY.
HOW?

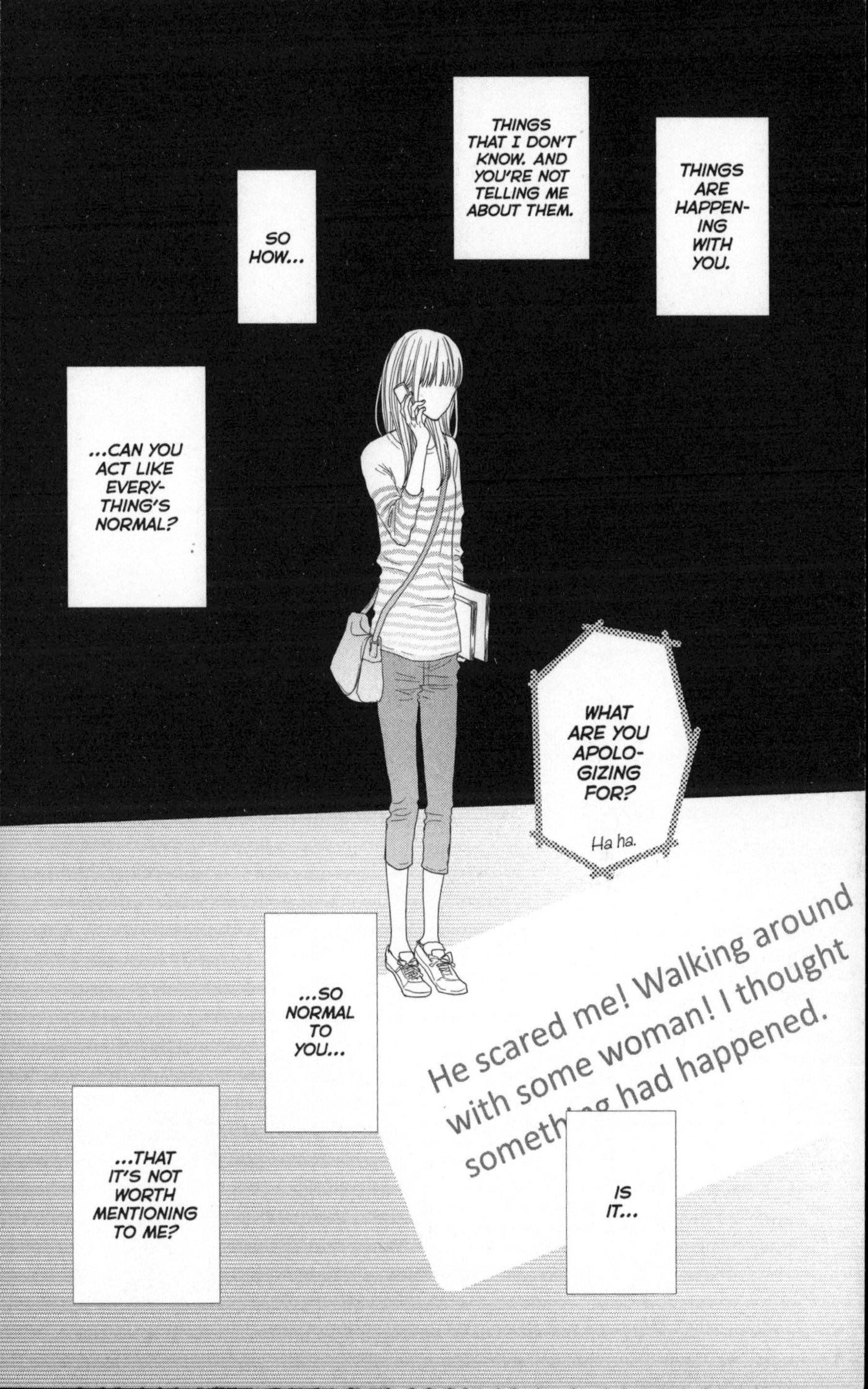
THINGS ARE HAPPEN-ING WITH YOU.
THINGS THAT I DON'T KNOW. AND YOU'RE NOT TELLING ME ABOUT THEM.
SO HOW...
...CAN YOU ACT LIKE EVERY-THING'S NORMAL?
WHAT ARE YOU APOLO-GIZING FOR?
Ha ha.
He scared me! Walking around with some woman! I thought someth had happened.
IS IT...
...SO NORMAL TO YOU...
...THAT IT'S NOT WORTH MENTIONING TO ME?

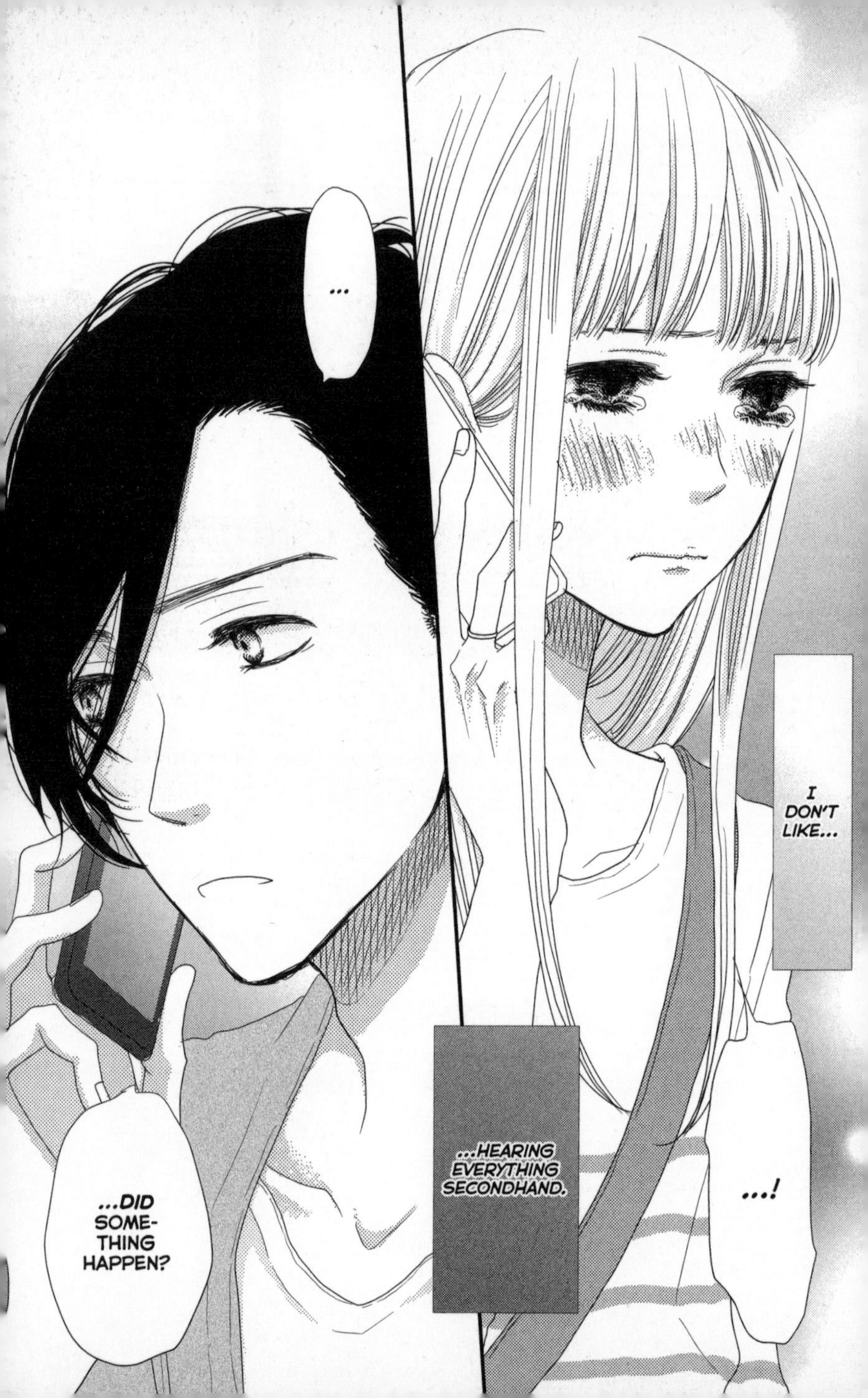
I DON'T LIKE...
...!
...HEARING EVERYTHING SECONDHAND.
...
...DID SOME-THING HAPPEN?

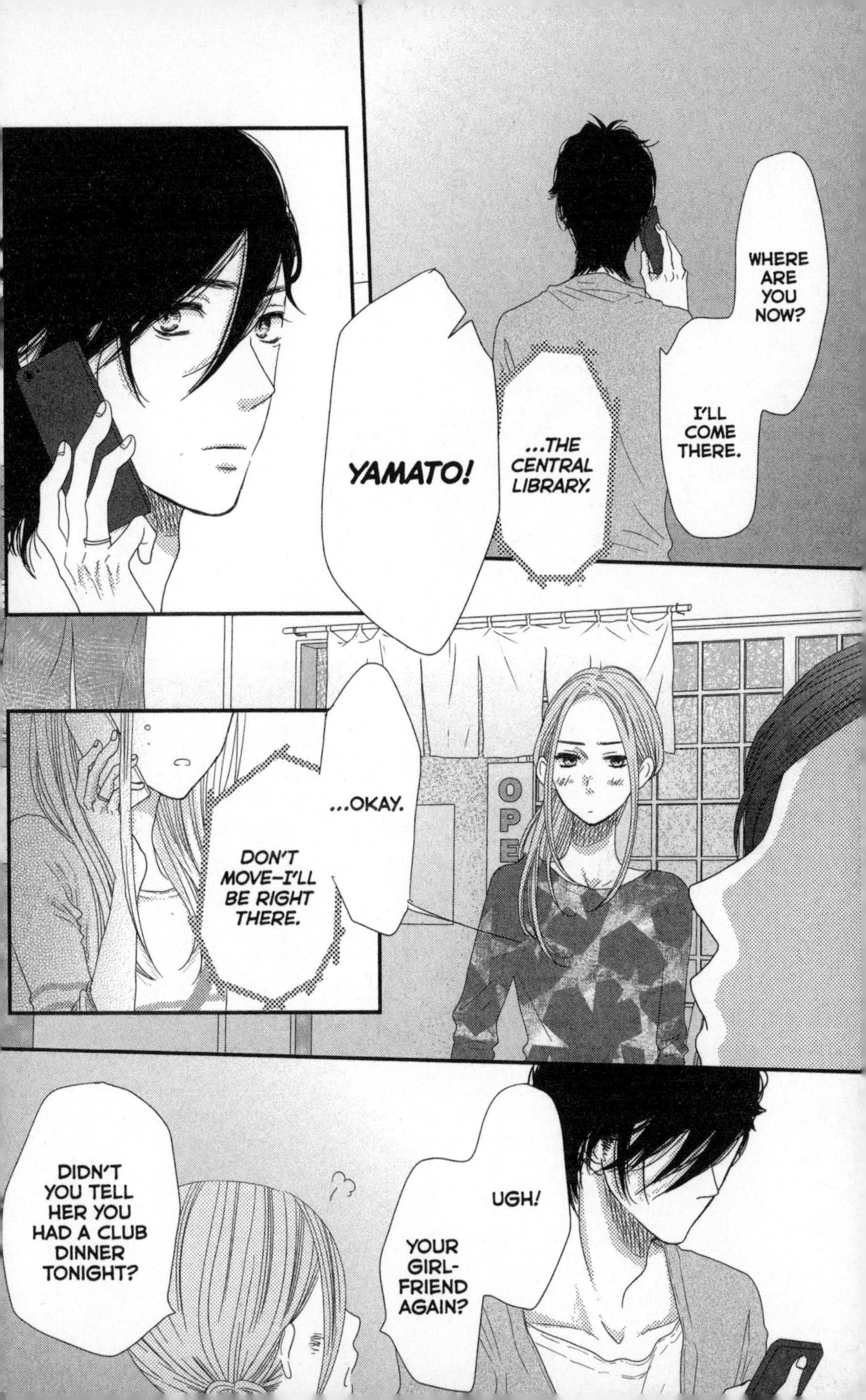
WHERE ARE YOU NOW?
I'LL COME THERE.
...THE CENTRAL LIBRARY.
YAMATO!
...OKAY.
DON'T MOVE—I'LL BE RIGHT THERE.
UGH!
YOUR GIRL-FRIEND AGAIN?
DIDN'T YOU TELL HER YOU HAD A CLUB DINNER TONIGHT?

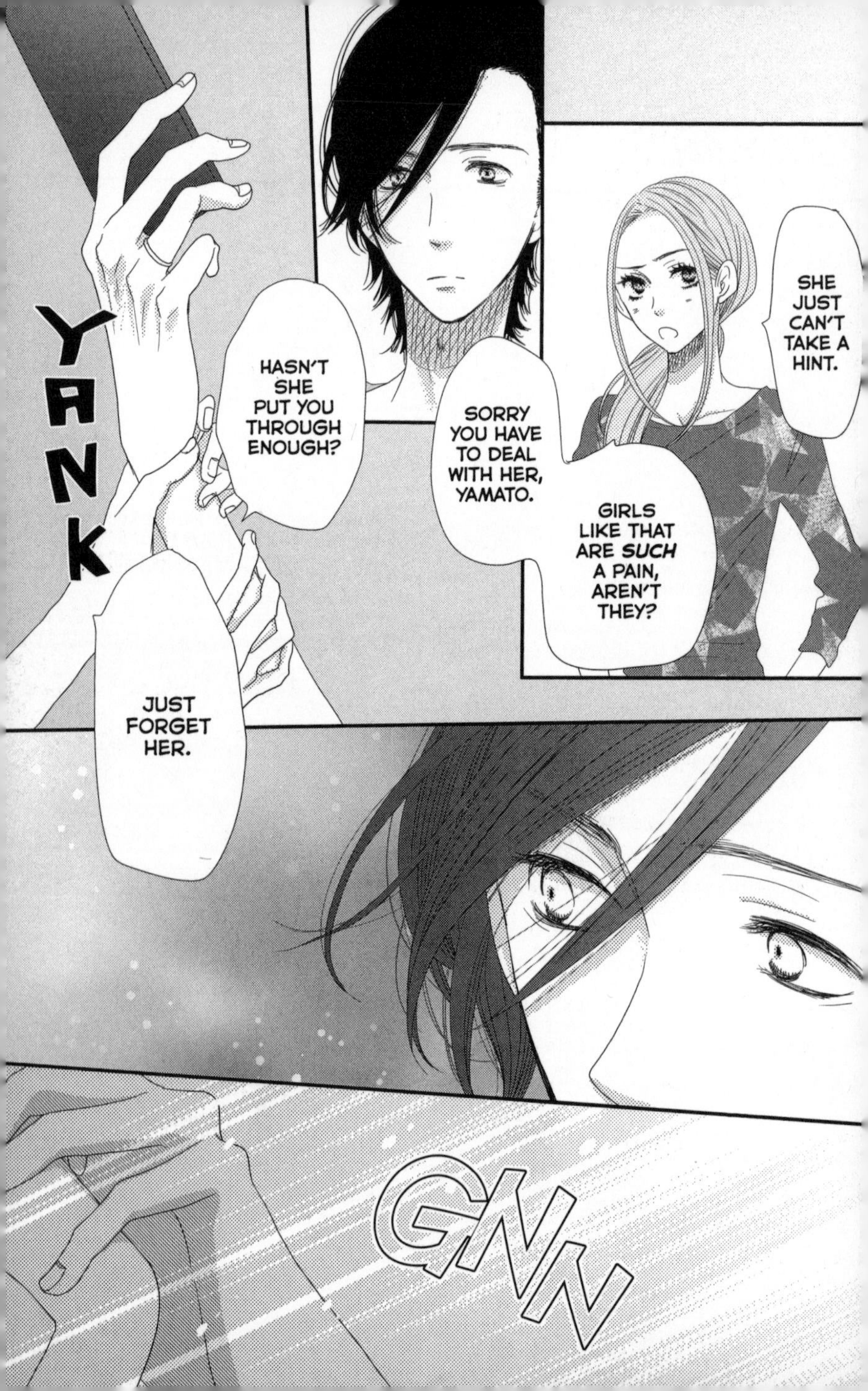
SHE JUST CAN'T TAKE A HINT.
SORRY YOU HAVE TO DEAL WITH HER, YAMATO.
GIRLS LIKE THAT ARE *SUCH* A PAIN, AREN'T THEY?
HASN'T SHE PUT YOU THROUGH ENOUGH?
YANK
JUST FORGET HER.
GNN

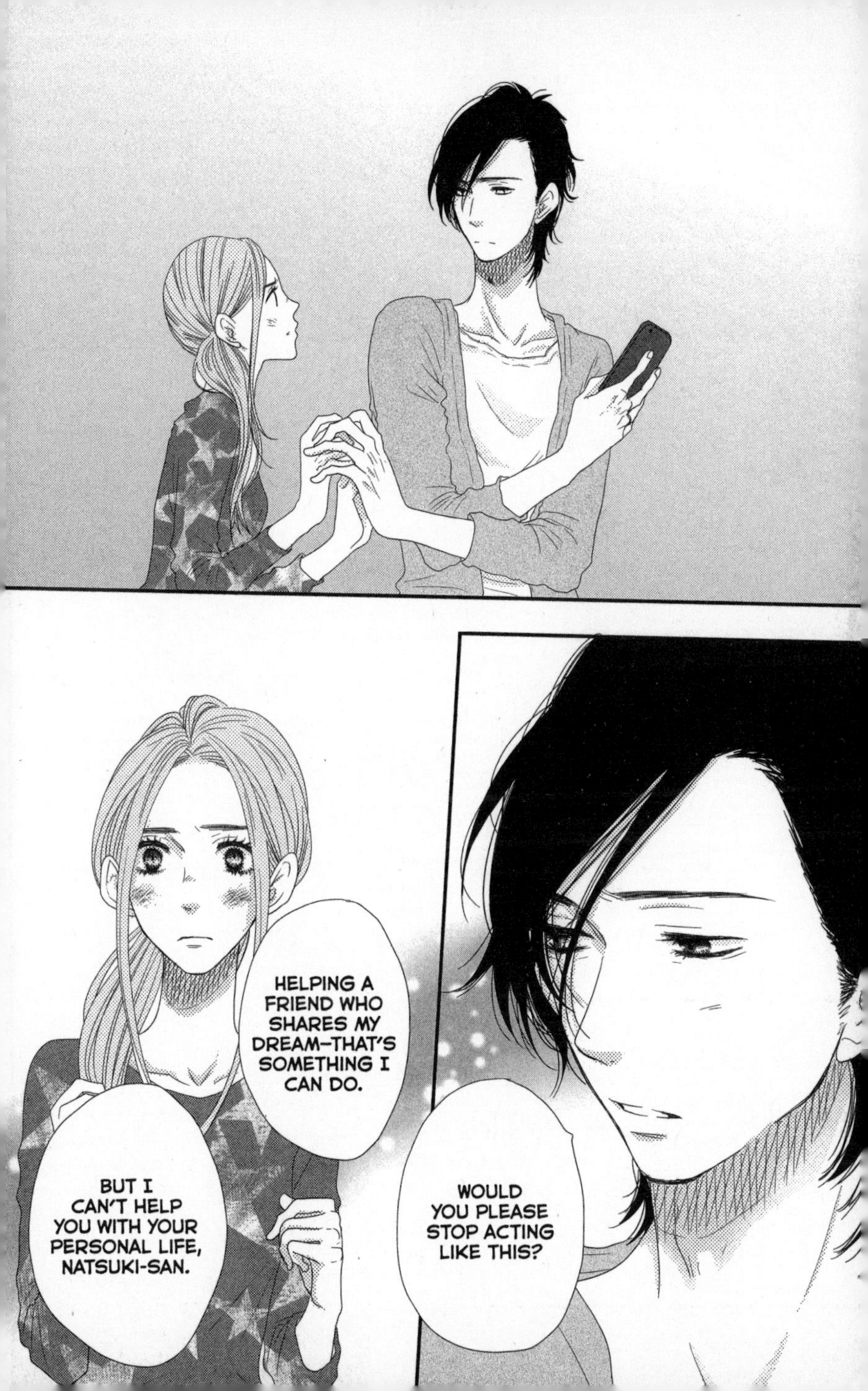
WOULD YOU PLEASE STOP ACTING LIKE THIS?
HELPING A FRIEND WHO SHARES MY DREAM—THAT'S SOMETHING I CAN DO.
BUT I CAN'T HELP YOU WITH YOUR PERSONAL LIFE, NATSUKI-SAN.

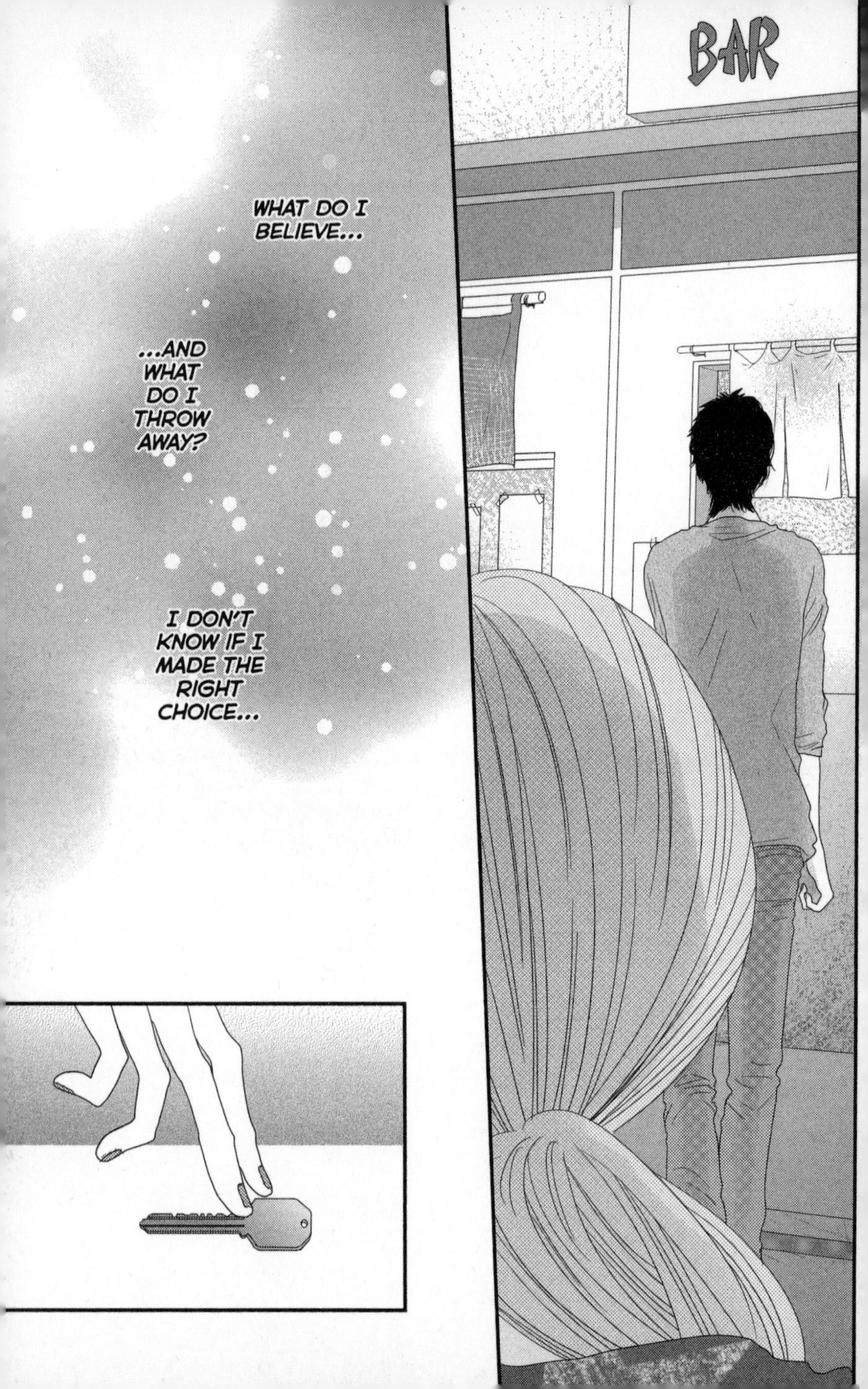
BAR
WHAT DO I BELIEVE...
...AND WHAT DO I THROW AWAY?
I DON'T KNOW IF I MADE THE RIGHT CHOICE...

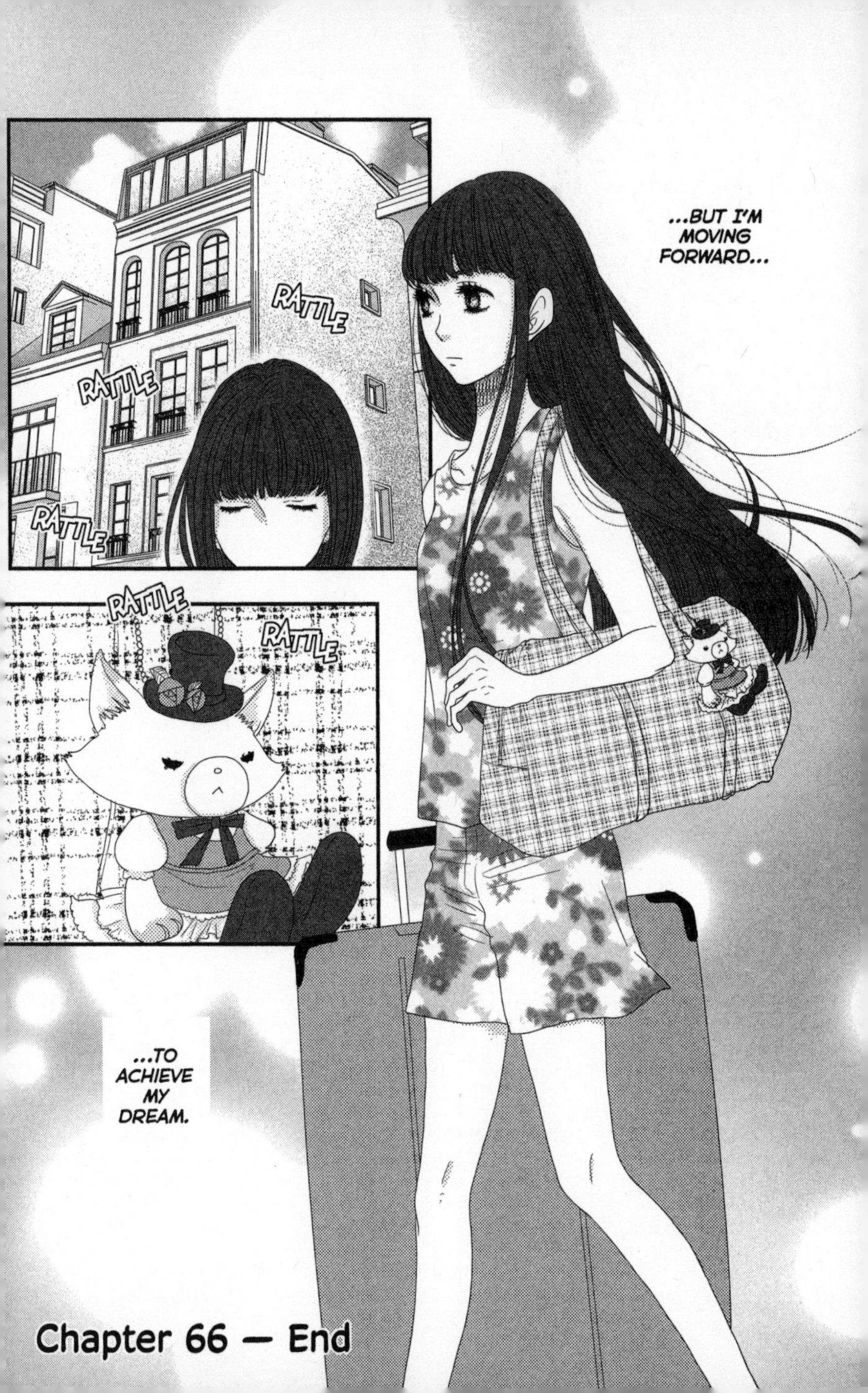
...BUT I'M MOVING FORWARD...
RATTLE
RATTLE
RATTLE
RATTLE
RATTLE
...TO ACHIEVE MY DREAM.
Chapter 66 — End

Say "I love you".

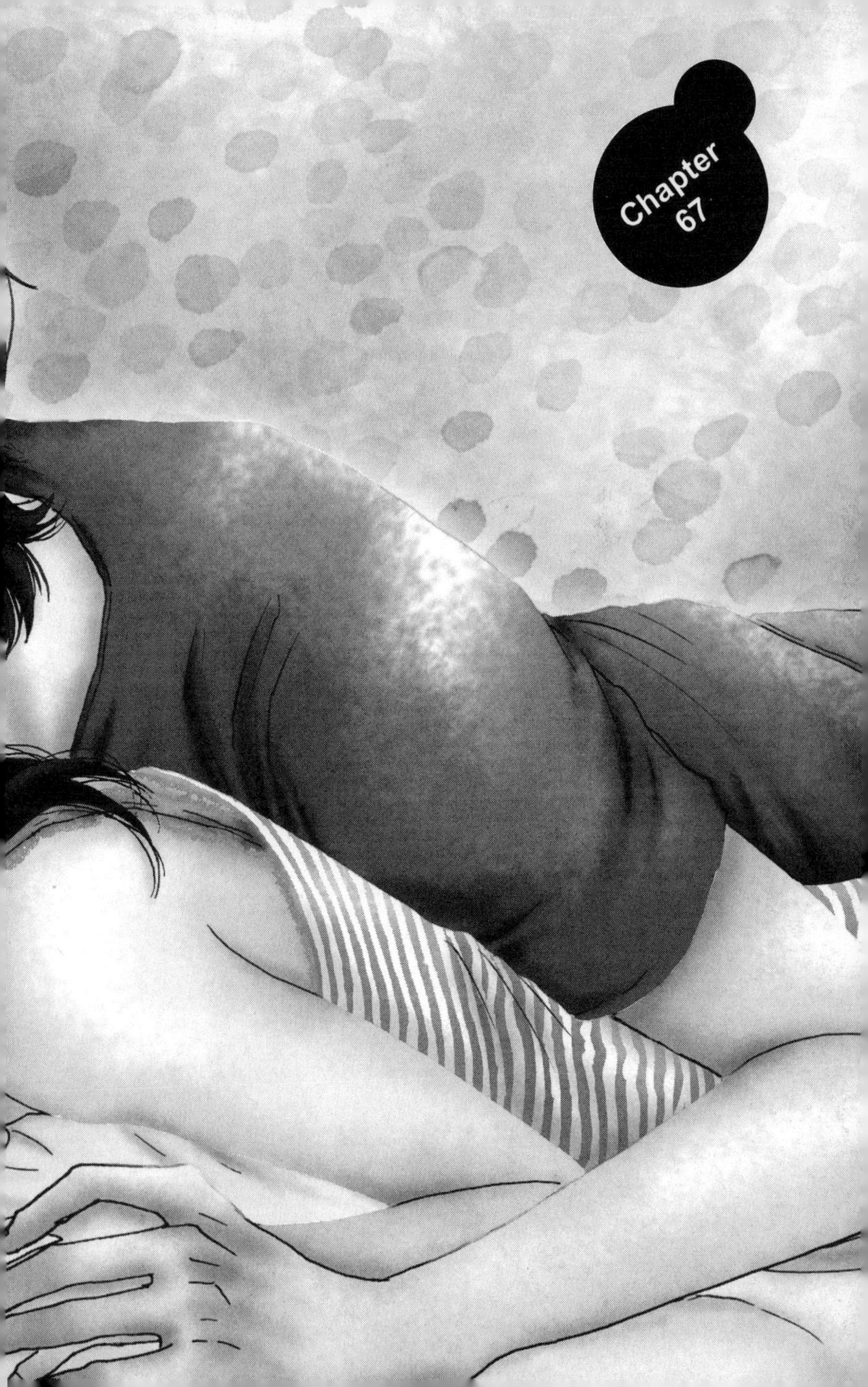
Chapter 67

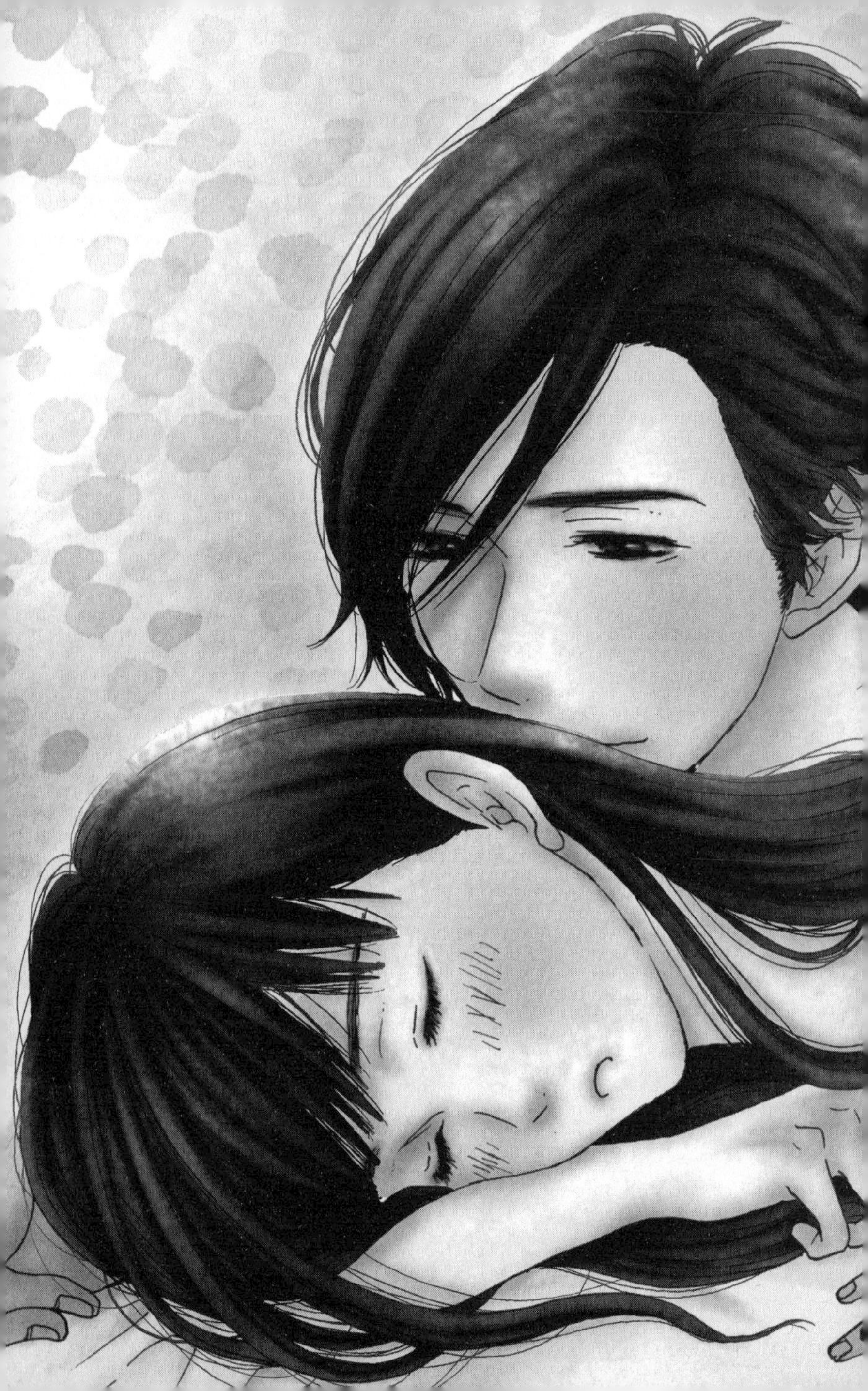

Say "I love you".

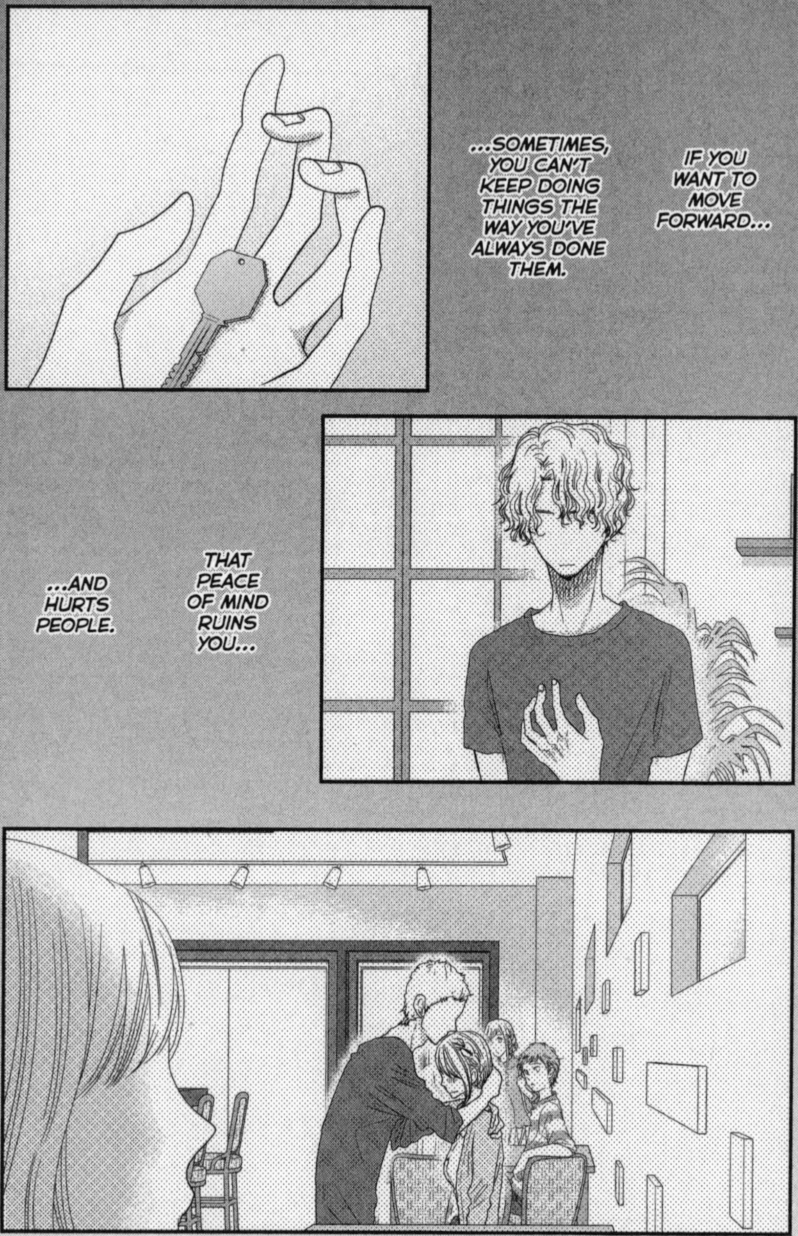
IF YOU WANT TO MOVE FORWARD...
...SOMETIMES, YOU CAN'T KEEP DOING THINGS THE WAY YOU'VE ALWAYS DONE THEM.
THAT PEACE OF MIND RUINS YOU...
...AND HURTS PEOPLE.

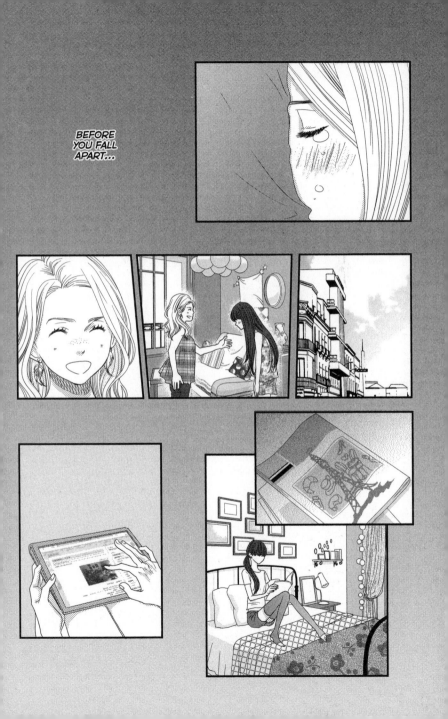

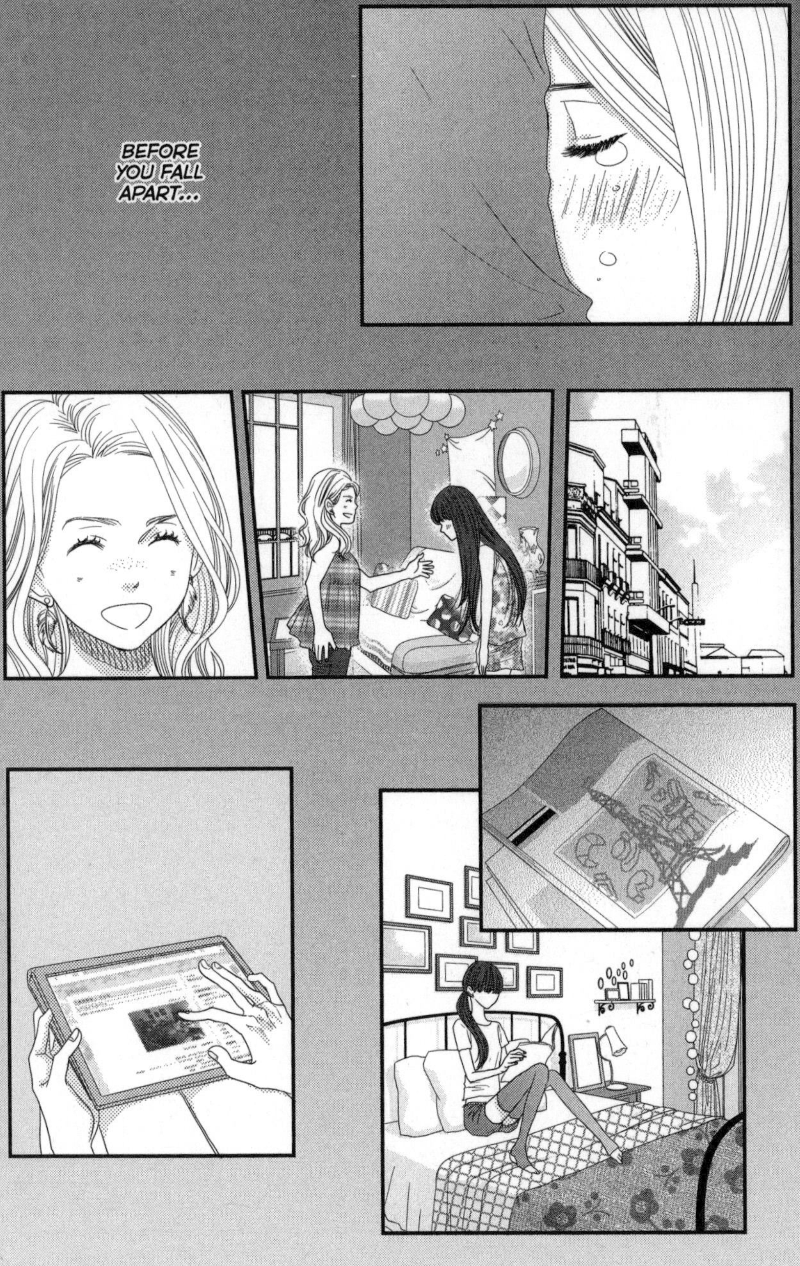
BEFORE
YOU FALL
APART...

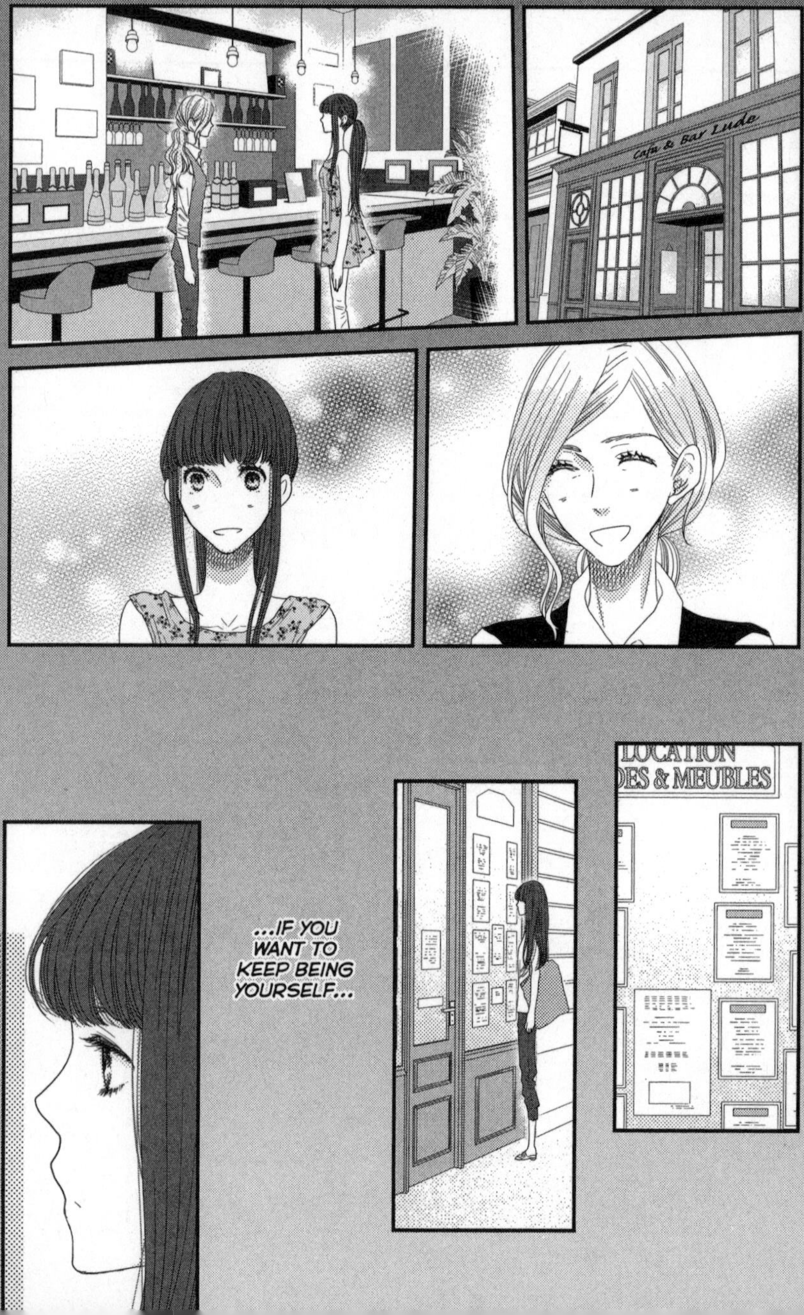
Cafe & Bar Lude
LOCATION
DES & MEUBLES
...IF YOU WANT TO KEEP BEING YOURSELF...

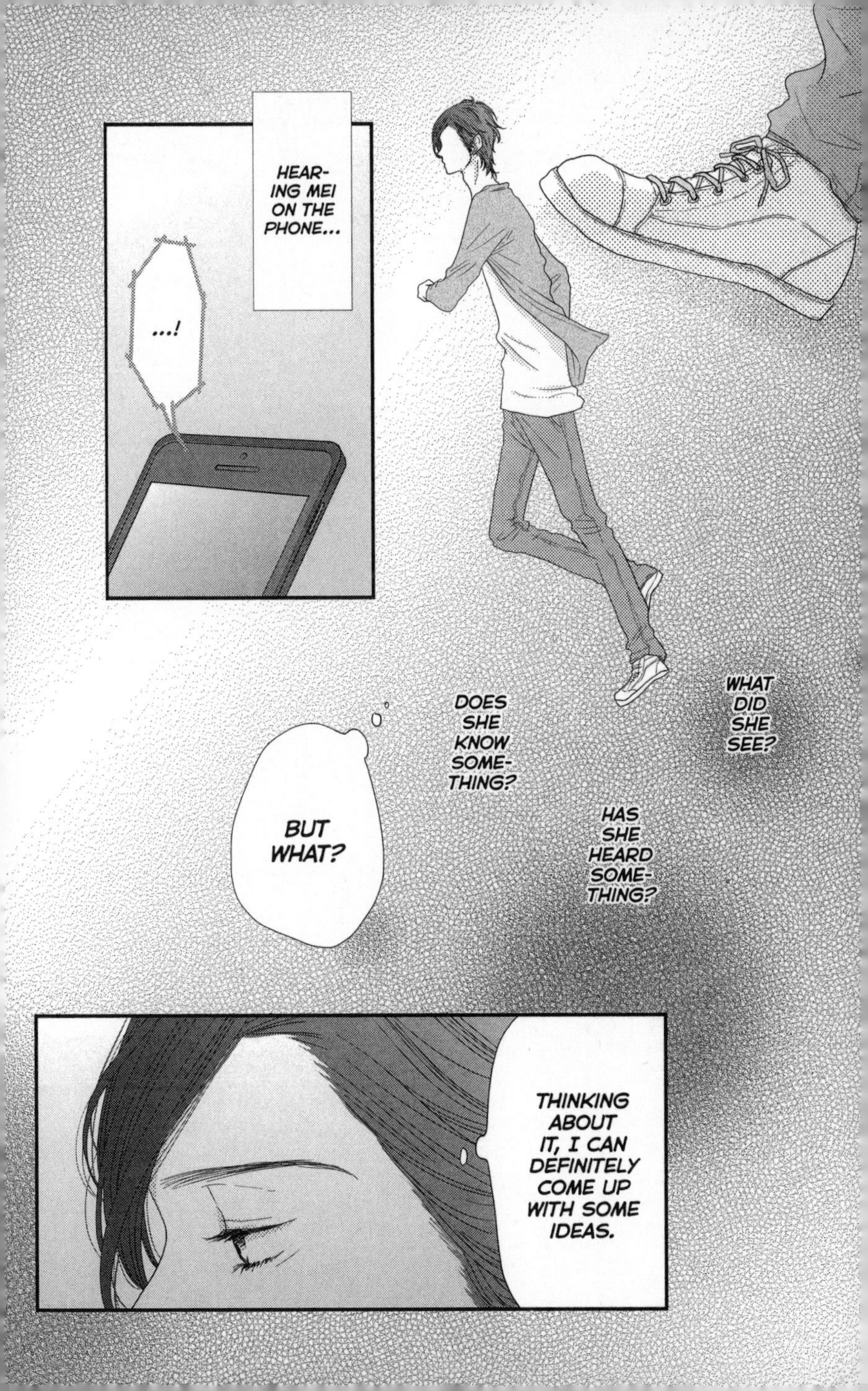
HEARING MEI ON THE PHONE...
...!
WHAT DID SHE SEE?
DOES SHE KNOW SOMETHING?
HAS SHE HEARD SOMETHING?
BUT WHAT?
THINKING ABOUT IT, I CAN DEFINITELY COME UP WITH SOME IDEAS.

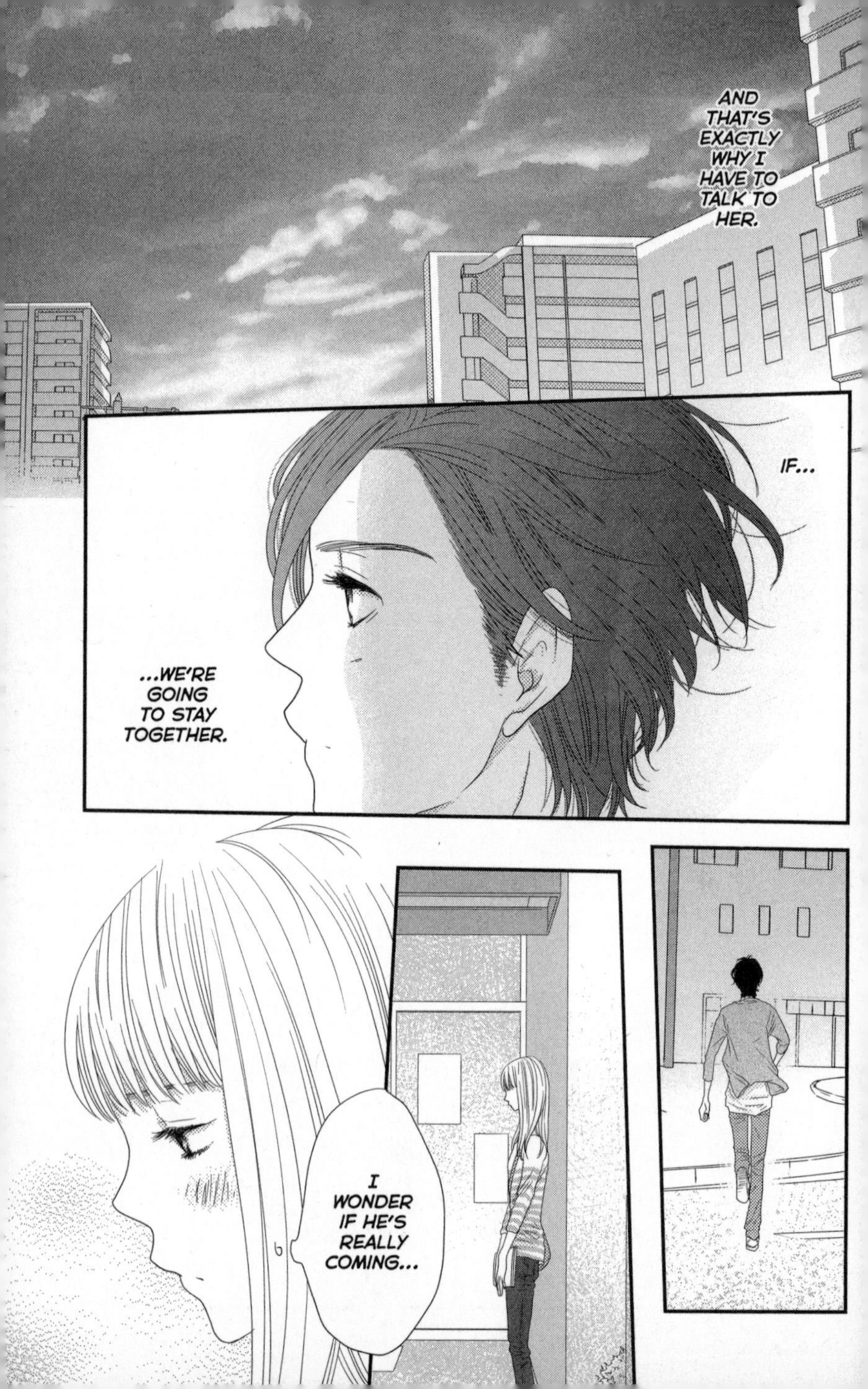
AND THAT'S EXACTLY WHY I HAVE TO TALK TO HER.
IF...
...WE'RE GOING TO STAY TOGETHER.
I WONDER IF HE'S REALLY COMING...

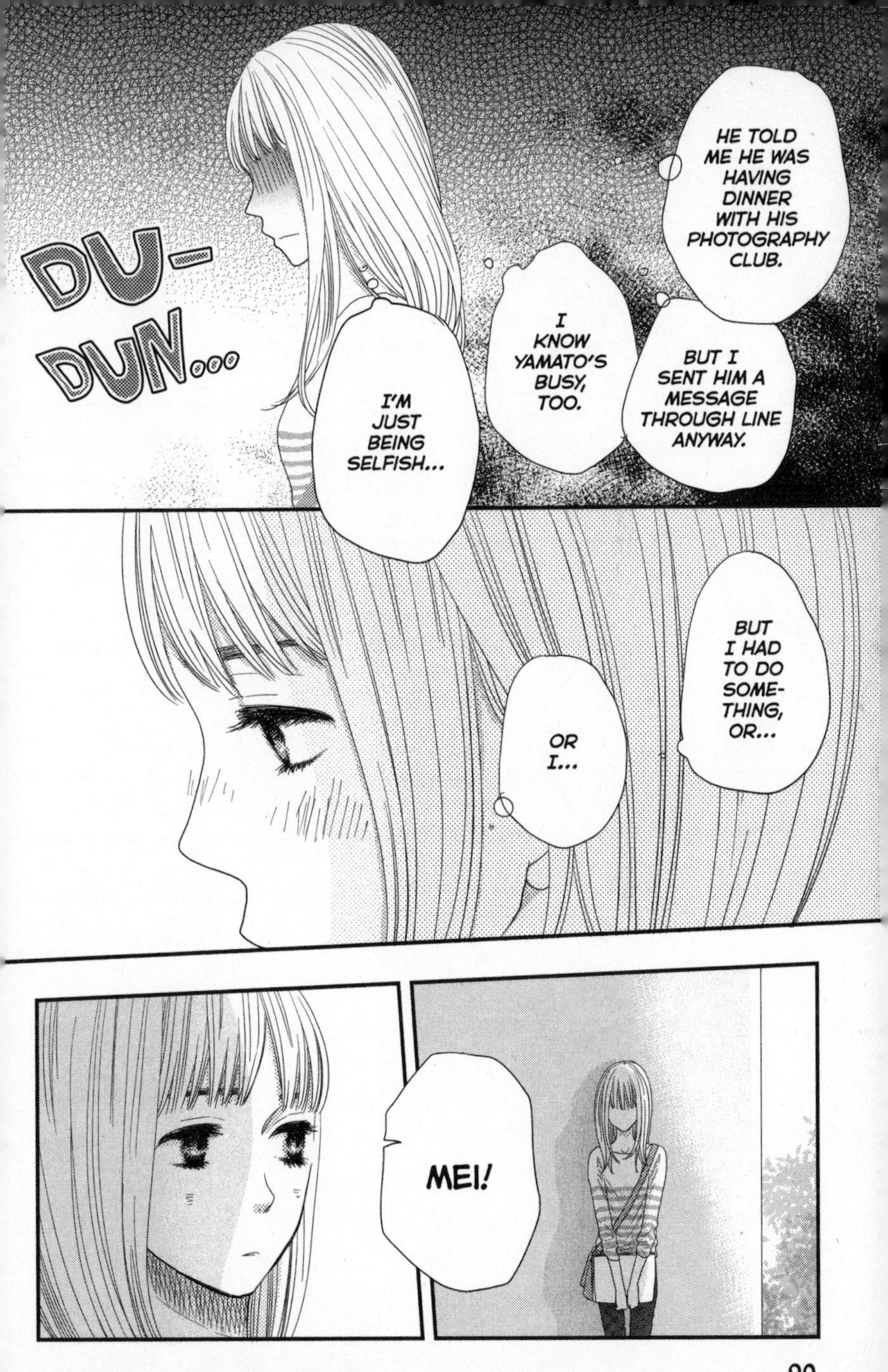
HE TOLD ME HE WAS HAVING DINNER WITH HIS PHOTOGRAPHY CLUB.
BUT I SENT HIM A MESSAGE THROUGH LINE ANYWAY.
I KNOW YAMATO'S BUSY, TOO.
I'M JUST BEING SELFISH...
DU-DUN...
BUT I HAD TO DO SOME-THING, OR...
OR I...
MEI!

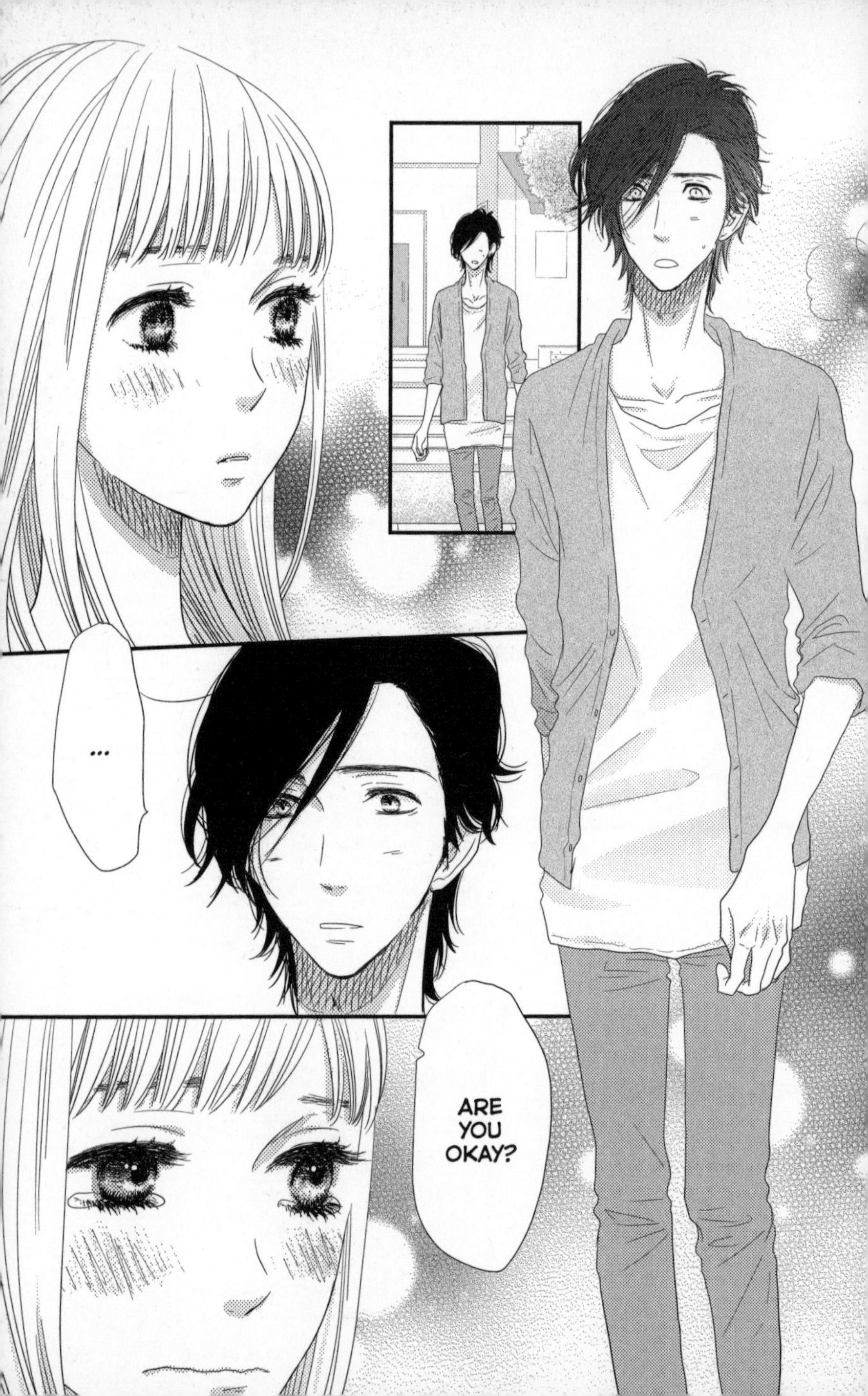
...
ARE YOU OKAY?

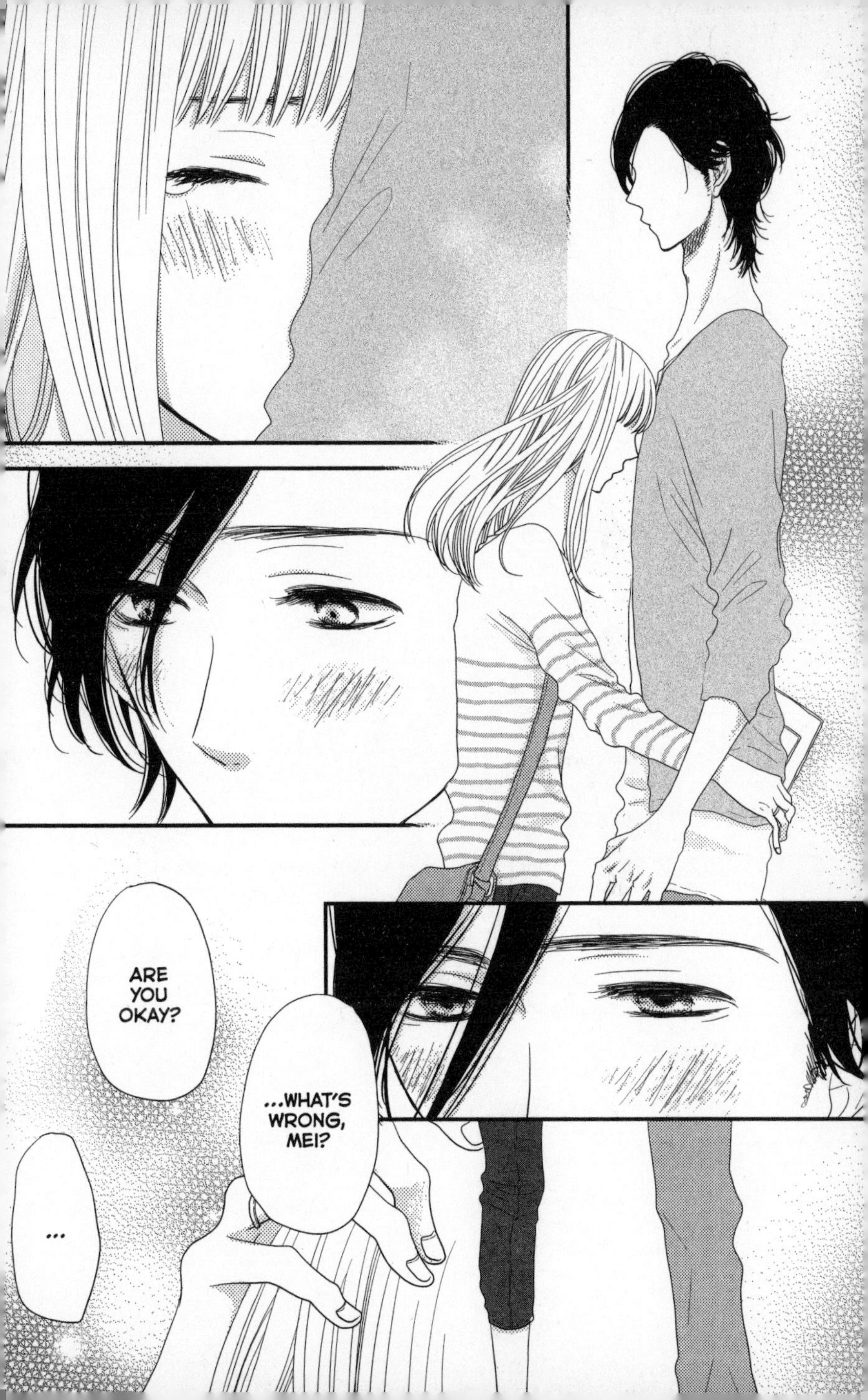
...WHAT'S WRONG, MEI?
ARE YOU OKAY?
...

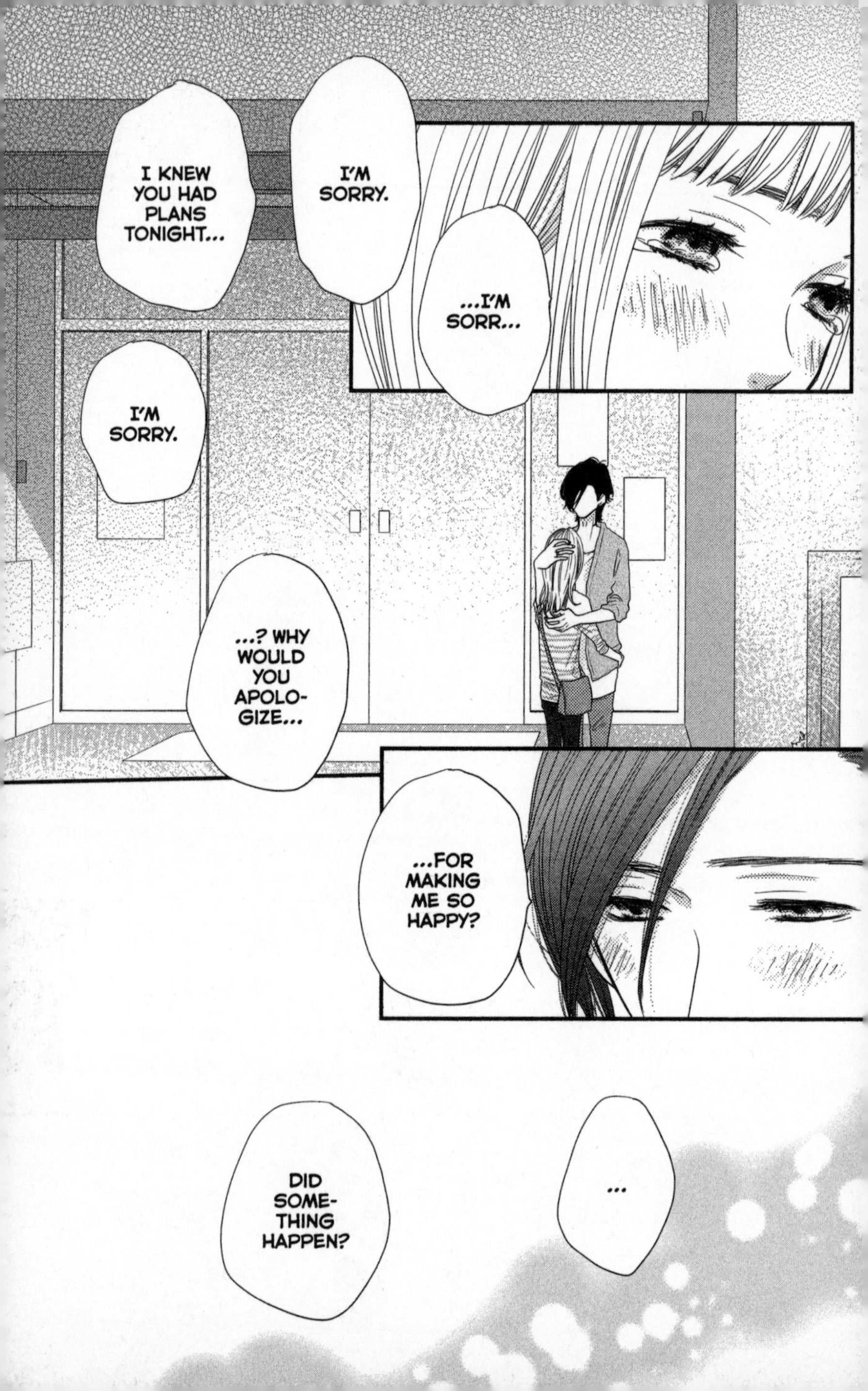
I'M SORRY.
...I'M SORR...
I KNEW YOU HAD PLANS TONIGHT...
I'M SORRY.
...? WHY WOULD YOU APOLOGIZE...
...FOR MAKING ME SO HAPPY?
...
DID SOMETHING HAPPEN?

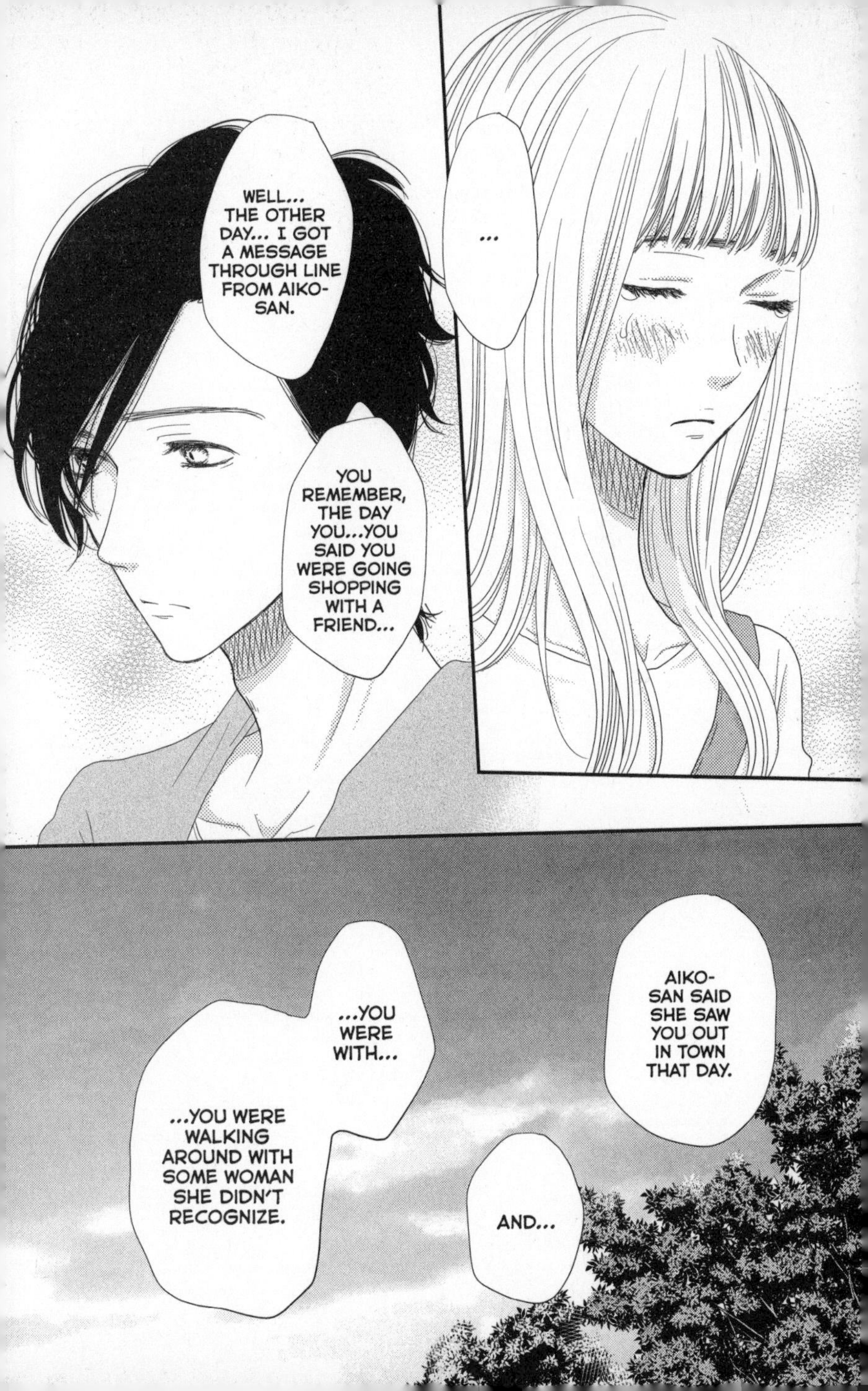
...
WELL... THE OTHER DAY... I GOT A MESSAGE THROUGH LINE FROM AIKO-SAN.
YOU REMEMBER, THE DAY YOU...YOU SAID YOU WERE GOING SHOPPING WITH A FRIEND...
AIKO-SAN SAID SHE SAW YOU OUT IN TOWN THAT DAY.
AND...
...YOU WERE WITH...
...YOU WERE WALKING AROUND WITH SOME WOMAN SHE DIDN'T RECOGNIZE.

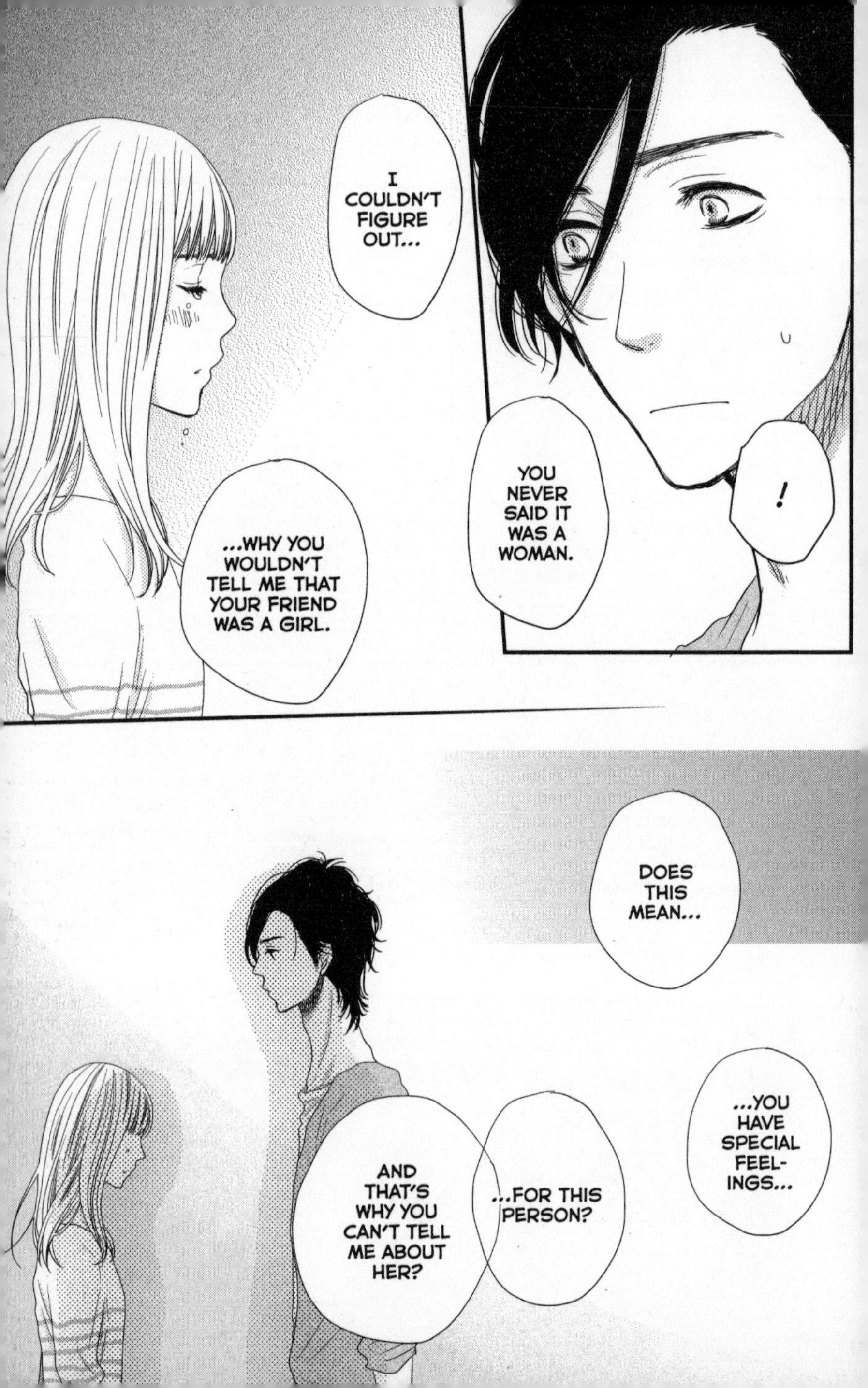
!
YOU NEVER SAID IT WAS A WOMAN.
I COULDN'T FIGURE OUT...
...WHY YOU WOULDN'T TELL ME THAT YOUR FRIEND WAS A GIRL.
DOES THIS MEAN...
...YOU HAVE SPECIAL FEEL- INGS...
...FOR THIS PERSON?
AND THAT'S WHY YOU CAN'T TELL ME ABOUT HER?

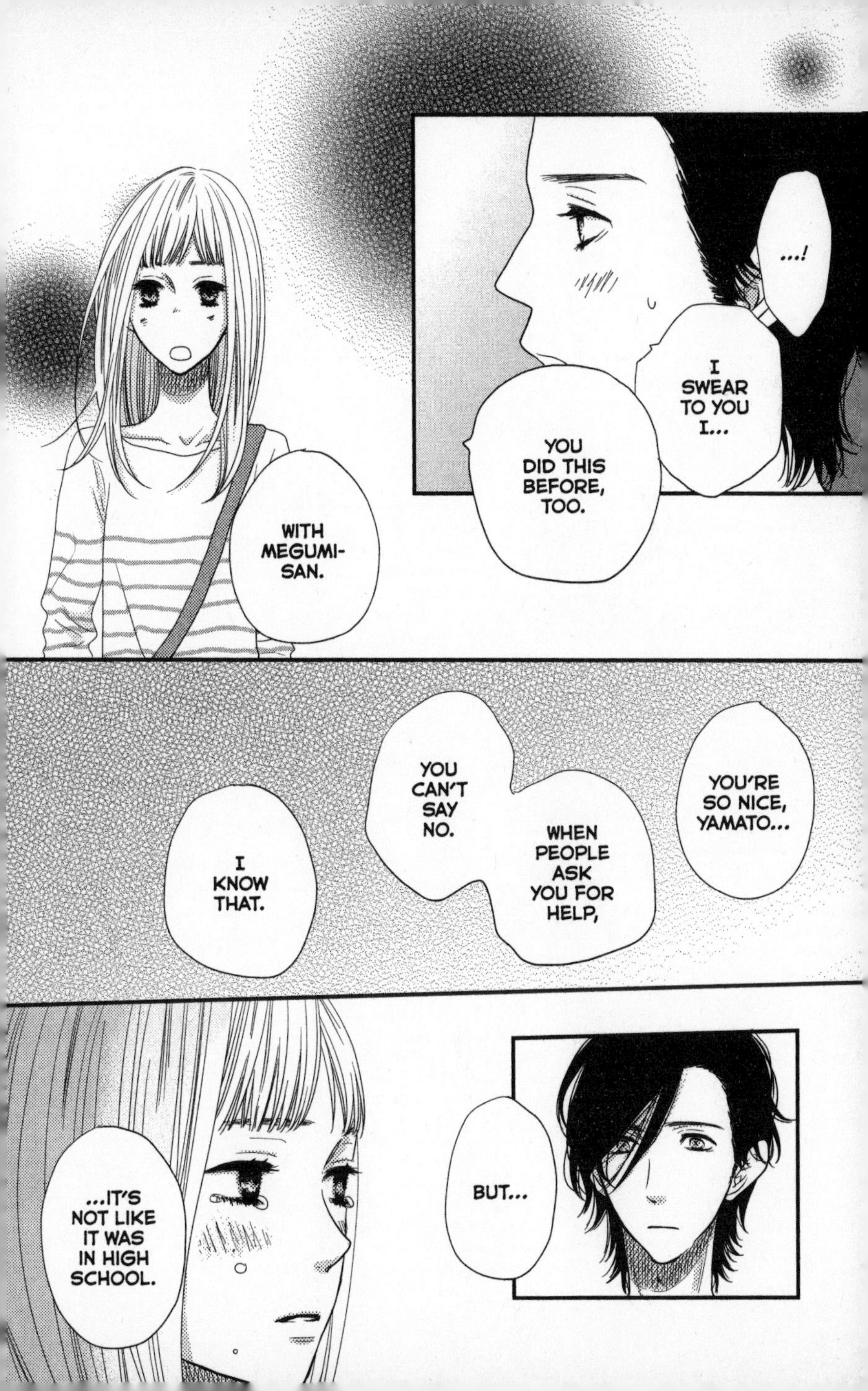
...!
I SWEAR TO YOU I...
YOU DID THIS BEFORE, TOO.
WITH MEGUMI-SAN.
YOU'RE SO NICE, YAMATO...
WHEN PEOPLE ASK YOU FOR HELP,
YOU CAN'T SAY NO.
I KNOW THAT.
BUT...
...IT'S NOT LIKE IT WAS IN HIGH SCHOOL.

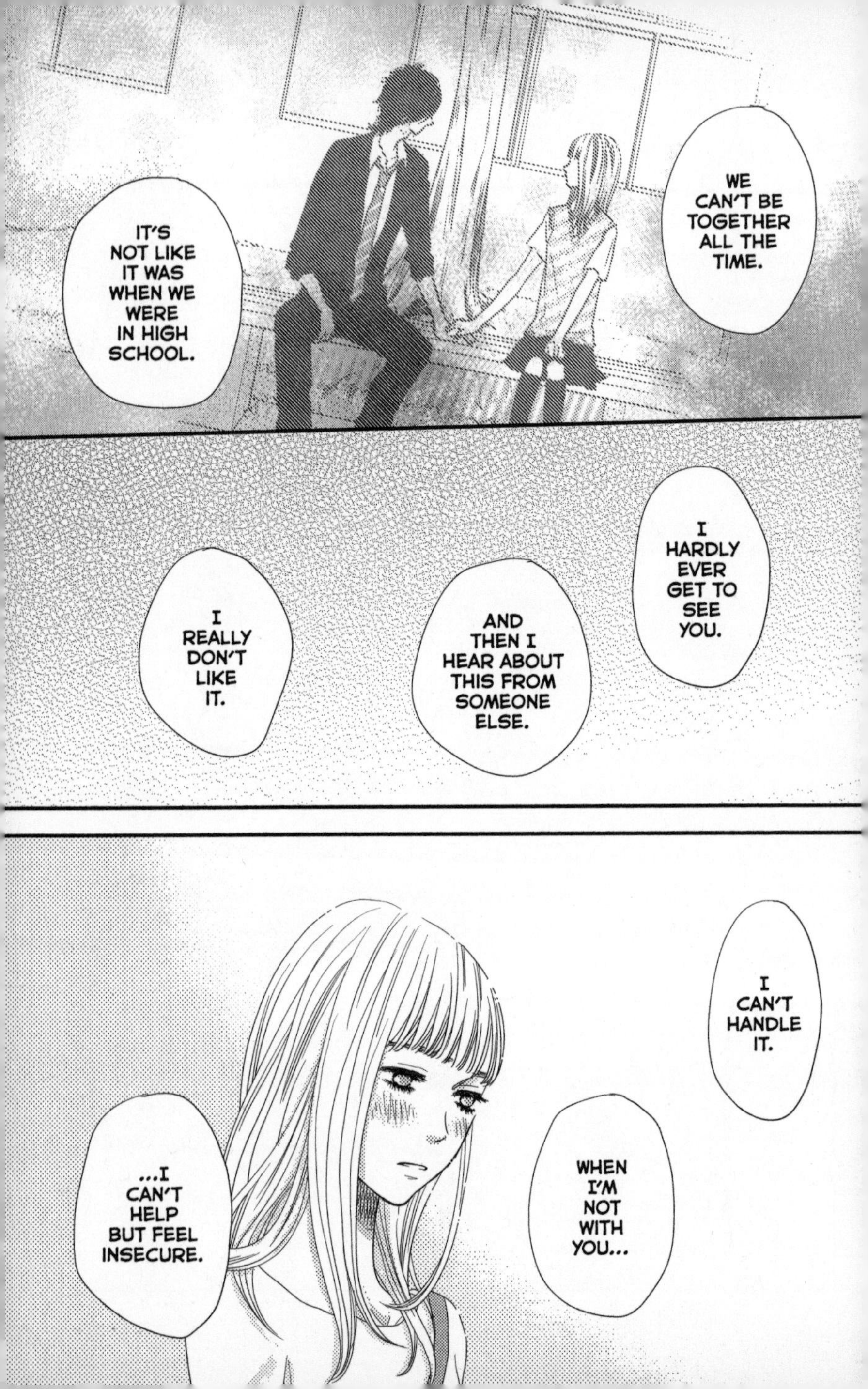
WE CAN'T BE TOGETHER ALL THE TIME.
IT'S NOT LIKE IT WAS WHEN WE WERE IN HIGH SCHOOL.
I HARDLY EVER GET TO SEE YOU.
AND THEN I HEAR ABOUT THIS FROM SOMEONE ELSE.
I REALLY DON'T LIKE IT.
I CAN'T HANDLE IT.
WHEN I'M NOT WITH YOU...
...I CAN'T HELP BUT FEEL INSECURE.

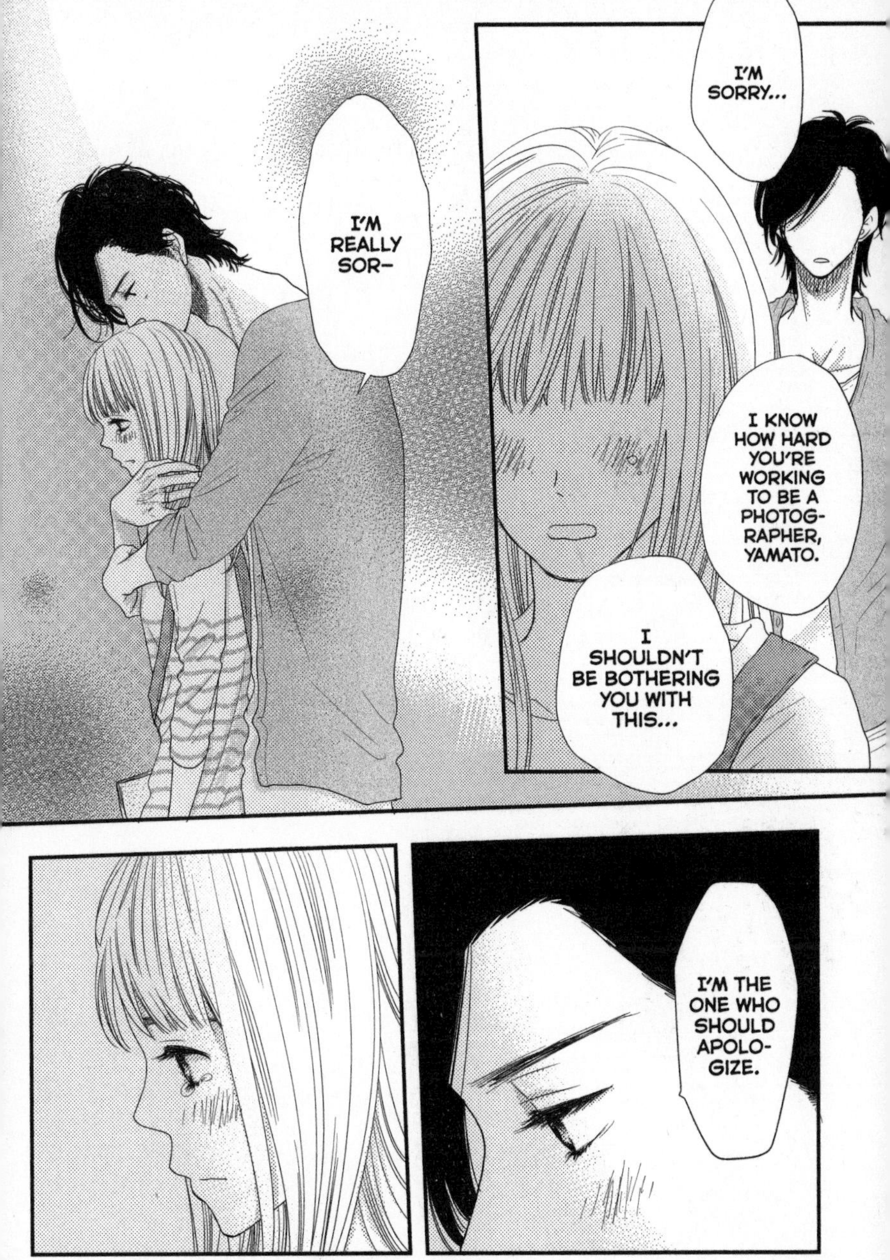
I'M SORRY...
I KNOW HOW HARD YOU'RE WORKING TO BE A PHOTOG-RAPHER, YAMATO.
I SHOULDN'T BE BOTHERING YOU WITH THIS...
I'M REALLY SOR-
I'M THE ONE WHO SHOULD APOLO-GIZE.

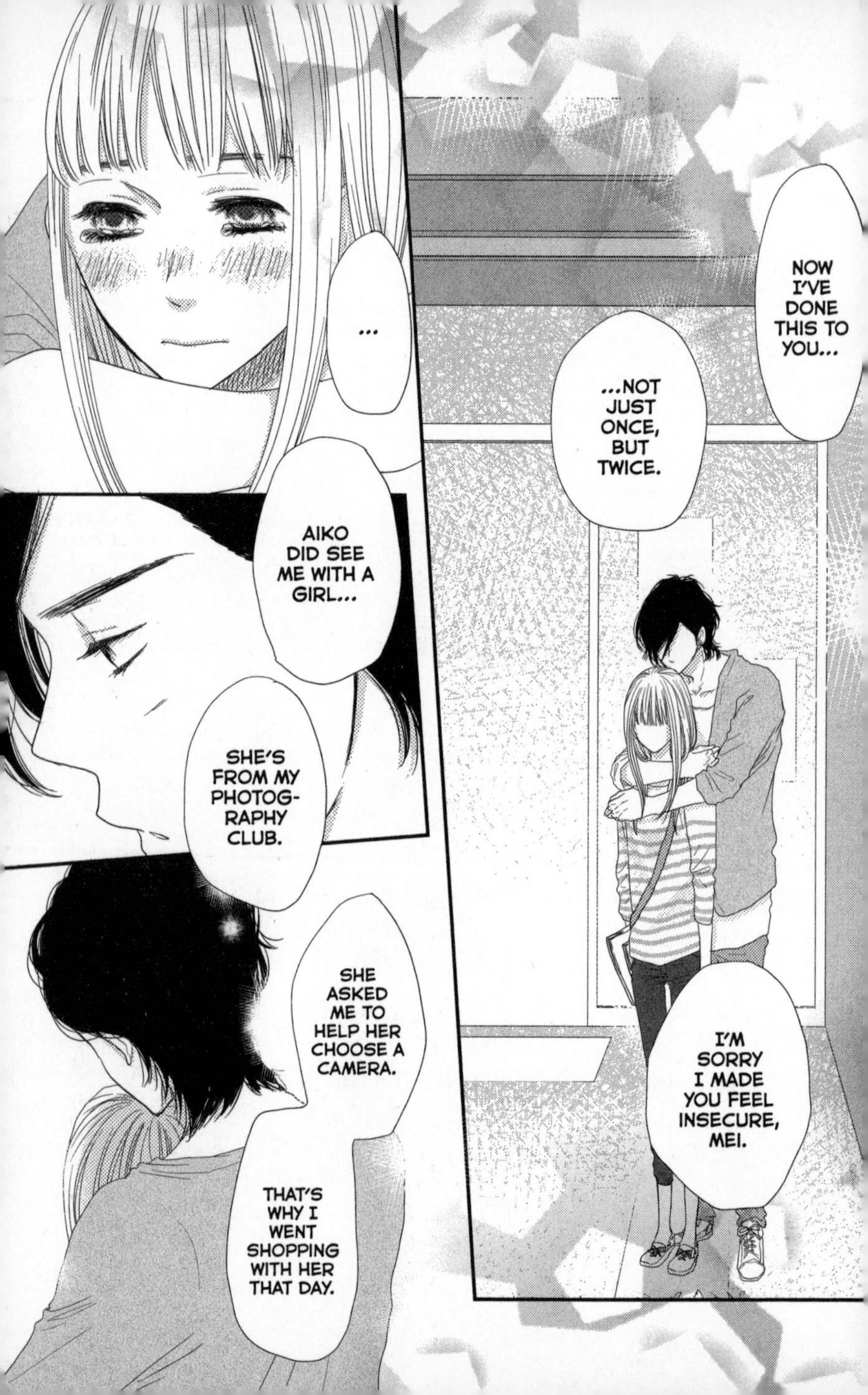
NOW I'VE DONE THIS TO YOU...
...NOT JUST ONCE, BUT TWICE.
I'M SORRY I MADE YOU FEEL INSECURE, MEI.
...
AIKO DID SEE ME WITH A GIRL...
SHE'S FROM MY PHOTOG-RAPHY CLUB.
SHE ASKED ME TO HELP HER CHOOSE A CAMERA.
THAT'S WHY I WENT SHOPPING WITH HER THAT DAY.

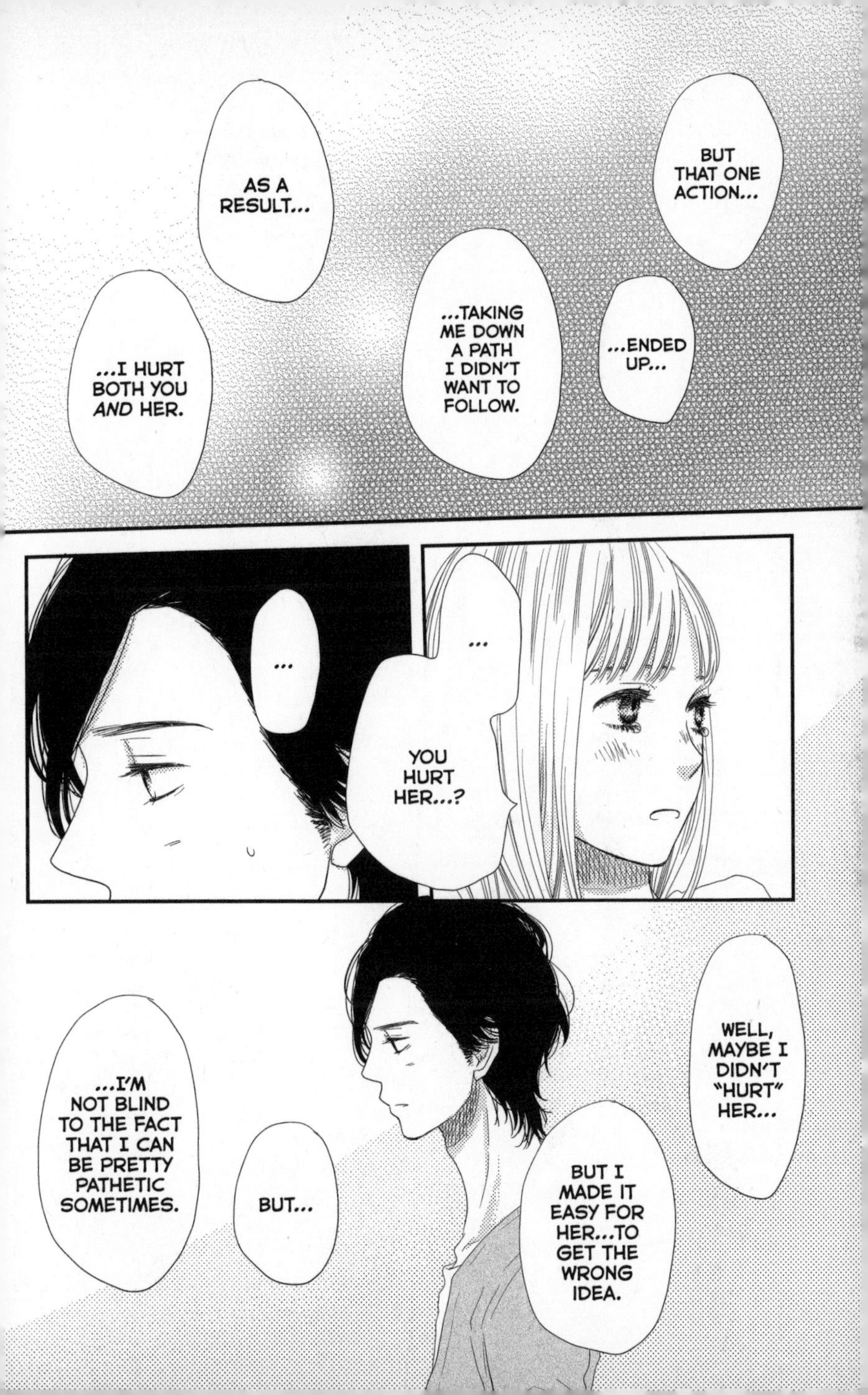
BUT THAT ONE ACTION...
...ENDED UP...
...TAKING ME DOWN A PATH I DIDN'T WANT TO FOLLOW.
AS A RESULT...
...I HURT BOTH YOU *AND* HER.
...
YOU HURT HER...?
...
WELL, MAYBE I DIDN'T "HURT" HER...
BUT I MADE IT EASY FOR HER...TO GET THE WRONG IDEA.
BUT...
...I'M NOT BLIND TO THE FACT THAT I CAN BE PRETTY PATHETIC SOMETIMES.

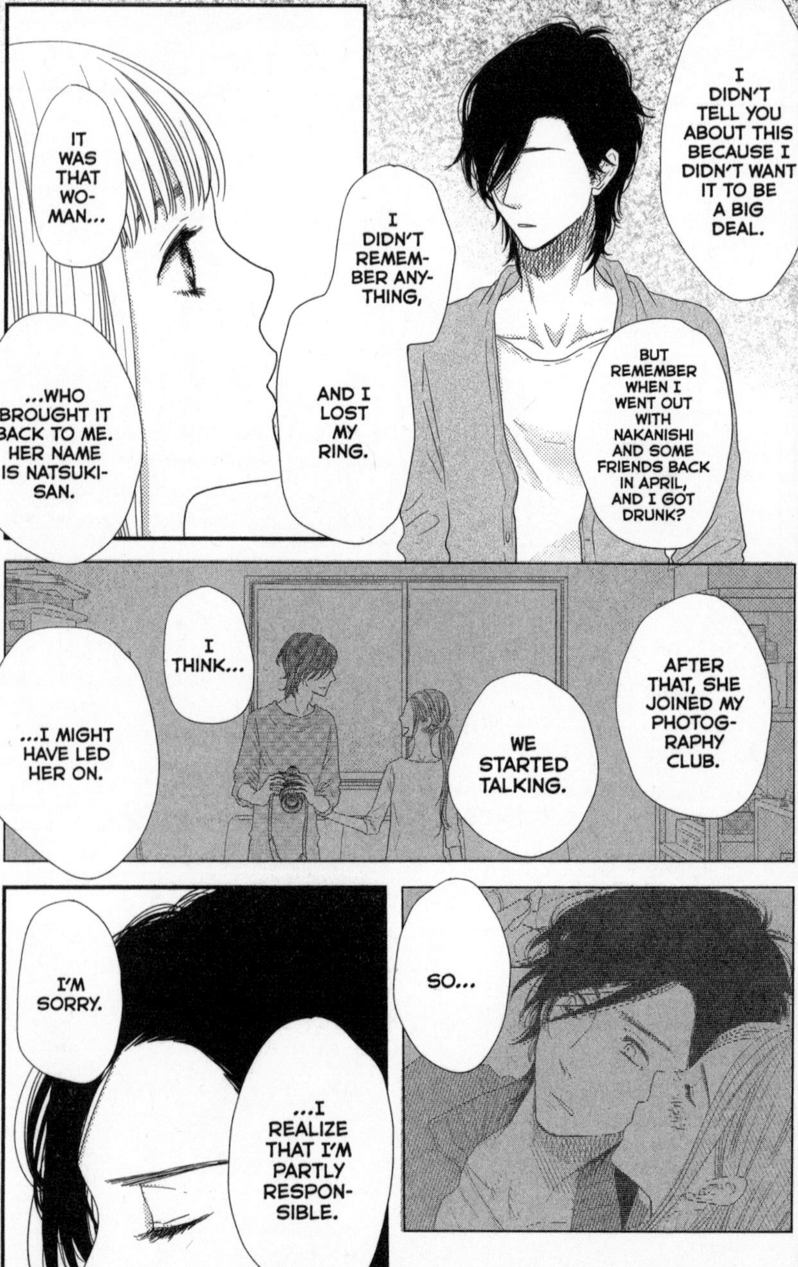
I DIDN'T TELL YOU ABOUT THIS BECAUSE I DIDN'T WANT IT TO BE A BIG DEAL.
BUT REMEMBER WHEN I WENT OUT WITH NAKANISHI AND SOME FRIENDS BACK IN APRIL, AND I GOT DRUNK?
I DIDN'T REMEMBER ANYTHING,
AND I LOST MY RING.
IT WAS THAT WOMAN...
...WHO BROUGHT IT BACK TO ME. HER NAME IS NATSUKI-SAN.
AFTER THAT, SHE JOINED MY PHOTOGRAPHY CLUB.
WE STARTED TALKING.
I THINK...
...I MIGHT HAVE LED HER ON.
SO...
...I REALIZE THAT I'M PARTLY RESPONSIBLE.
I'M SORRY.

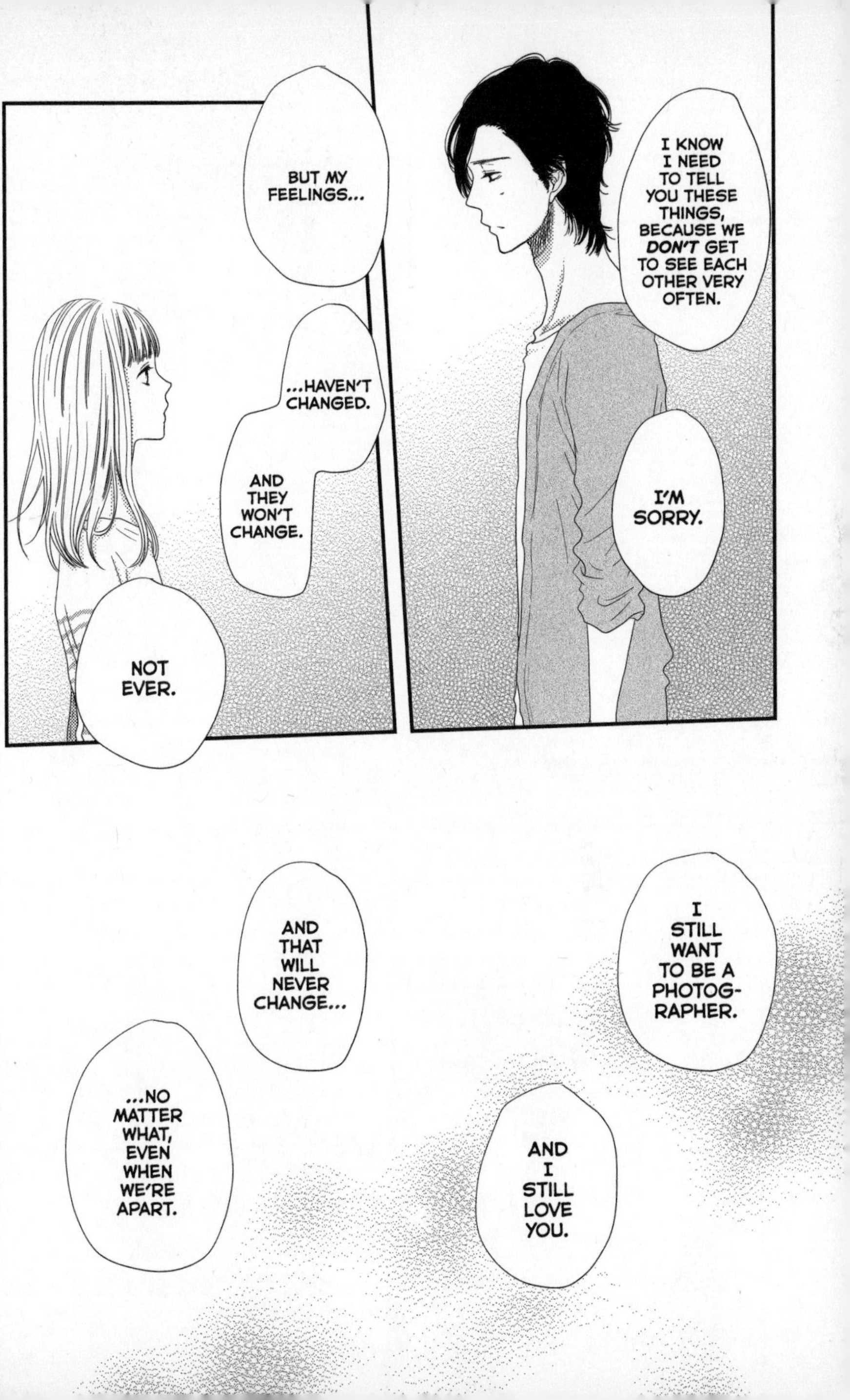
I KNOW I NEED TO TELL YOU THESE THINGS, BECAUSE WE *DON'T* GET TO SEE EACH OTHER VERY OFTEN.
I'M SORRY.
BUT MY FEELINGS...
...HAVEN'T CHANGED.
AND THEY WON'T CHANGE.
NOT EVER.
I STILL WANT TO BE A PHOTOG-RAPHER.
AND THAT WILL NEVER CHANGE...
AND I STILL LOVE YOU.
...NO MATTER WHAT, EVEN WHEN WE'RE APART.

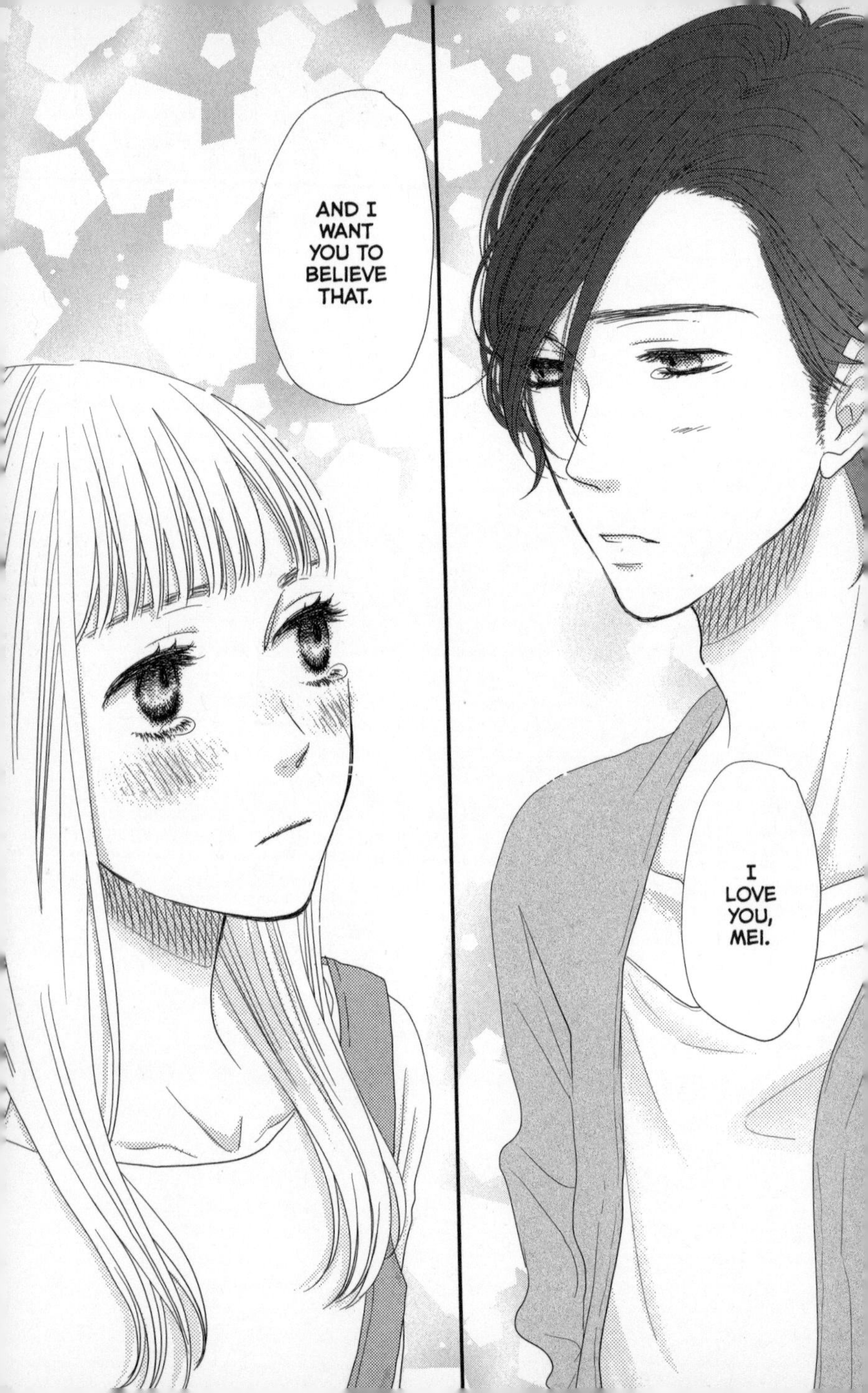
I LOVE YOU, MEI.
AND I WANT YOU TO BELIEVE THAT.

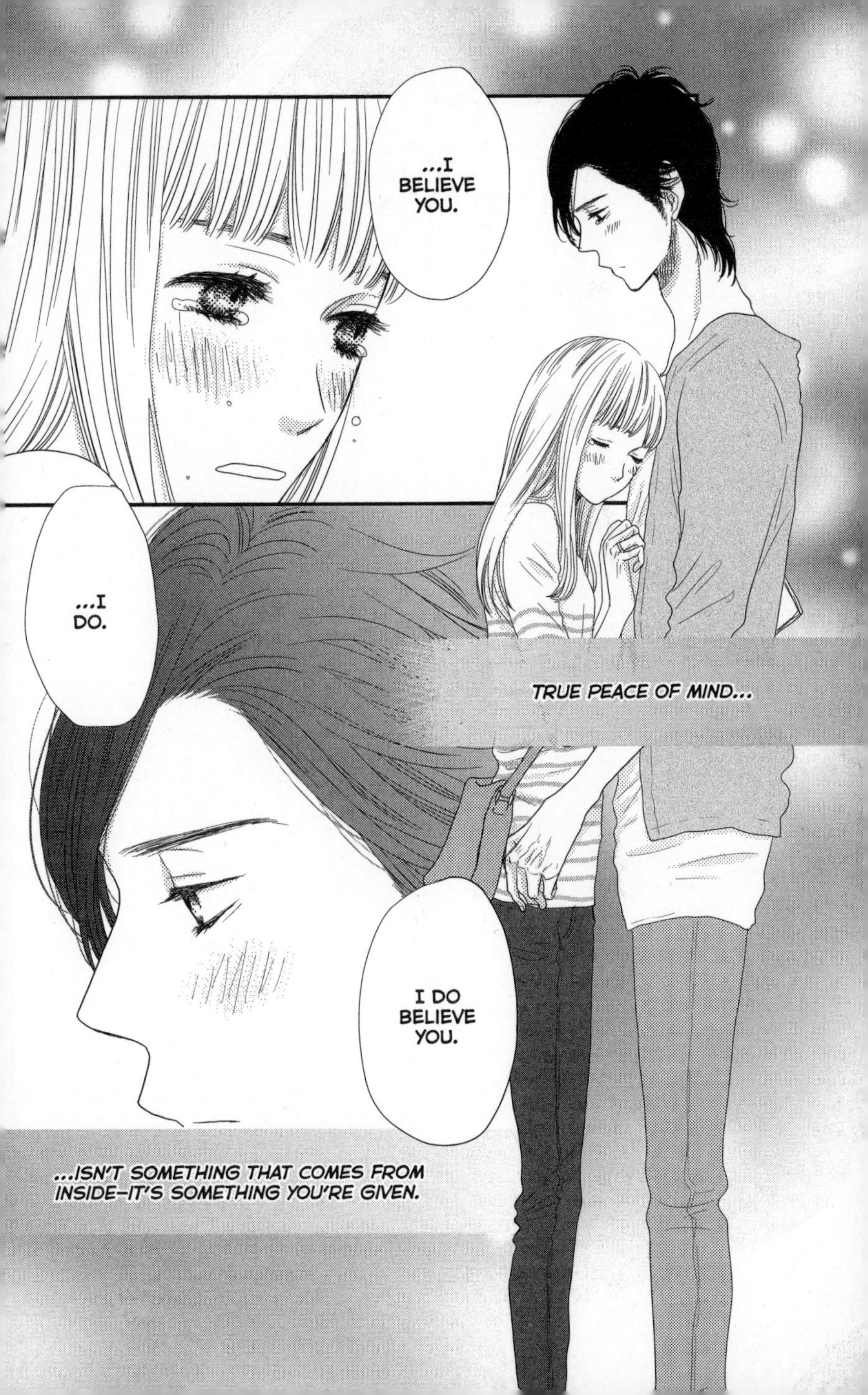
...I BELIEVE YOU.
...I DO.
I DO BELIEVE YOU.
TRUE PEACE OF MIND...
...ISN'T SOMETHING THAT COMES FROM INSIDE—IT'S SOMETHING YOU'RE GIVEN.

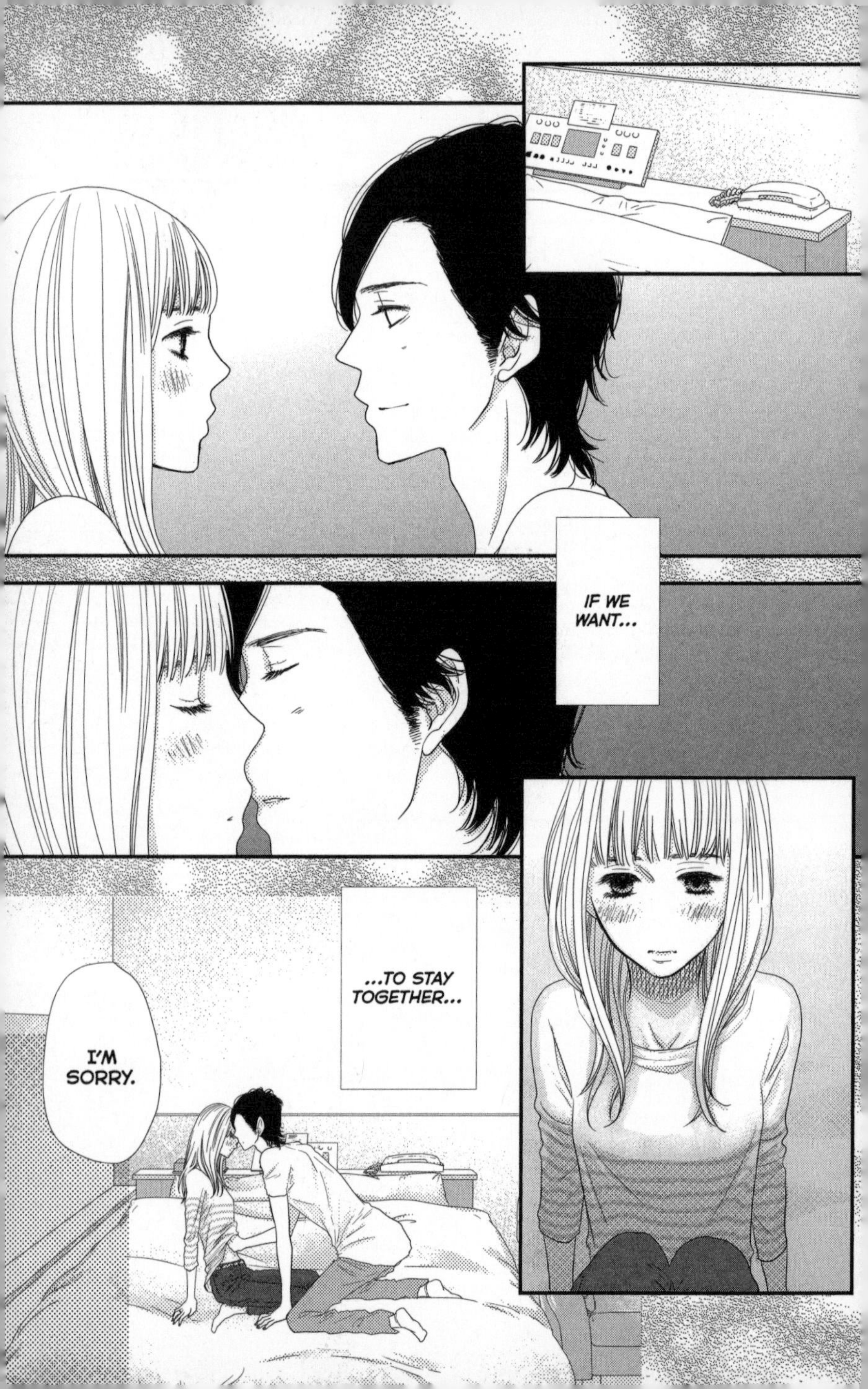
IF WE WANT...
...TO STAY TOGETHER...
I'M SORRY.

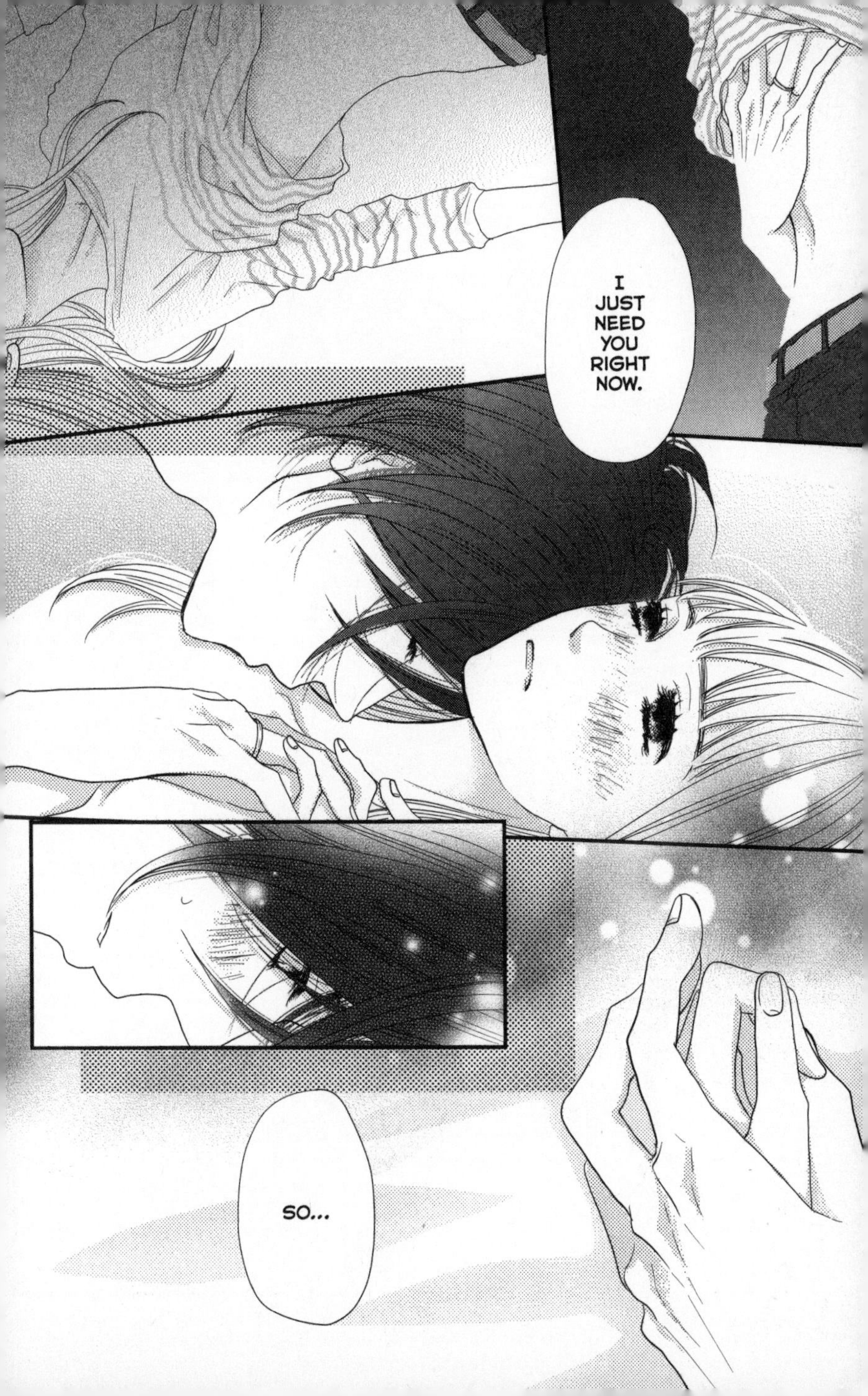
I JUST NEED YOU RIGHT NOW.
SO...

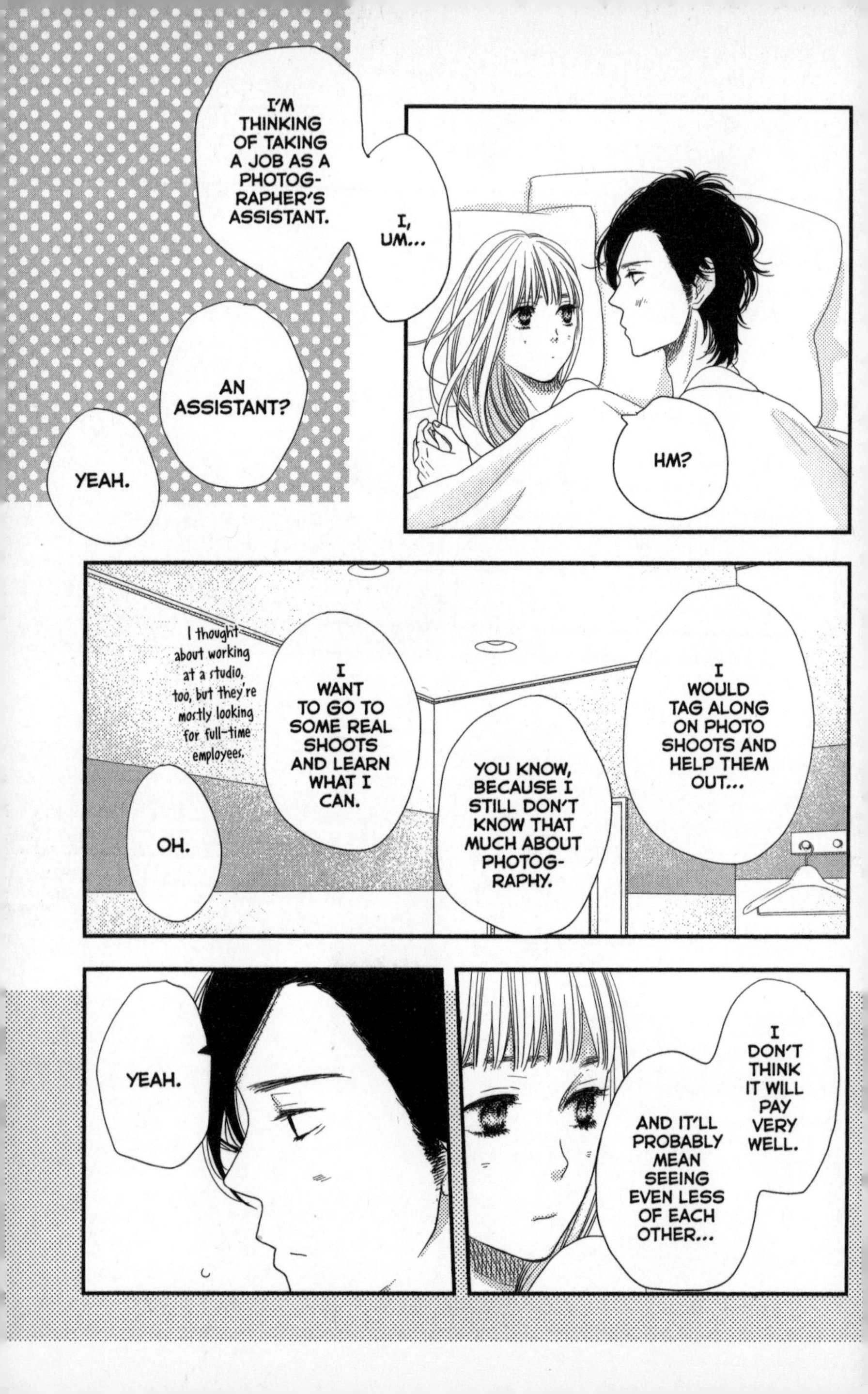
I, UM...
HM?
I'M THINKING OF TAKING A JOB AS A PHOTOG-RAPHER'S ASSISTANT.
AN ASSISTANT?
YEAH.
I WOULD TAG ALONG ON PHOTO SHOOTS AND HELP THEM OUT...
YOU KNOW, BECAUSE I STILL DON'T KNOW THAT MUCH ABOUT PHOTOG-RAPHY.
I WANT TO GO TO SOME REAL SHOOTS AND LEARN WHAT I CAN.
I thought about working at a studio, too, but they're mostly looking for full-time employees.
OH.
I DON'T THINK IT WILL PAY VERY WELL.
AND IT'LL PROBABLY MEAN SEEING EVEN LESS OF EACH OTHER...
YEAH.

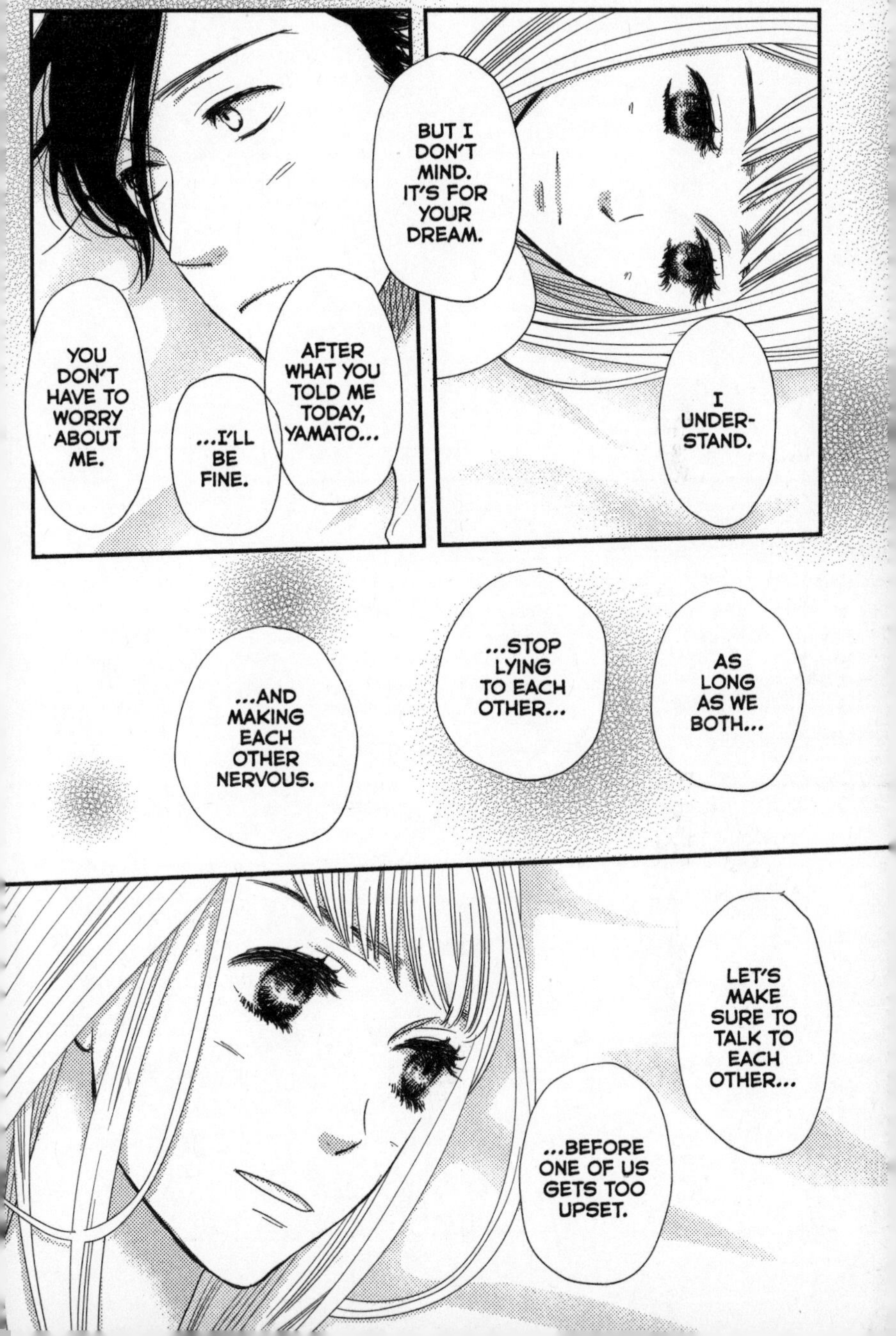
BUT I DON'T MIND. IT'S FOR YOUR DREAM.
I UNDER-STAND.
AFTER WHAT YOU TOLD ME TODAY, YAMATO...
...I'LL BE FINE.
YOU DON'T HAVE TO WORRY ABOUT ME.
AS LONG AS WE BOTH...
...STOP LYING TO EACH OTHER...
...AND MAKING EACH OTHER NERVOUS.
LET'S MAKE SURE TO TALK TO EACH OTHER...
...BEFORE ONE OF US GETS TOO UPSET.

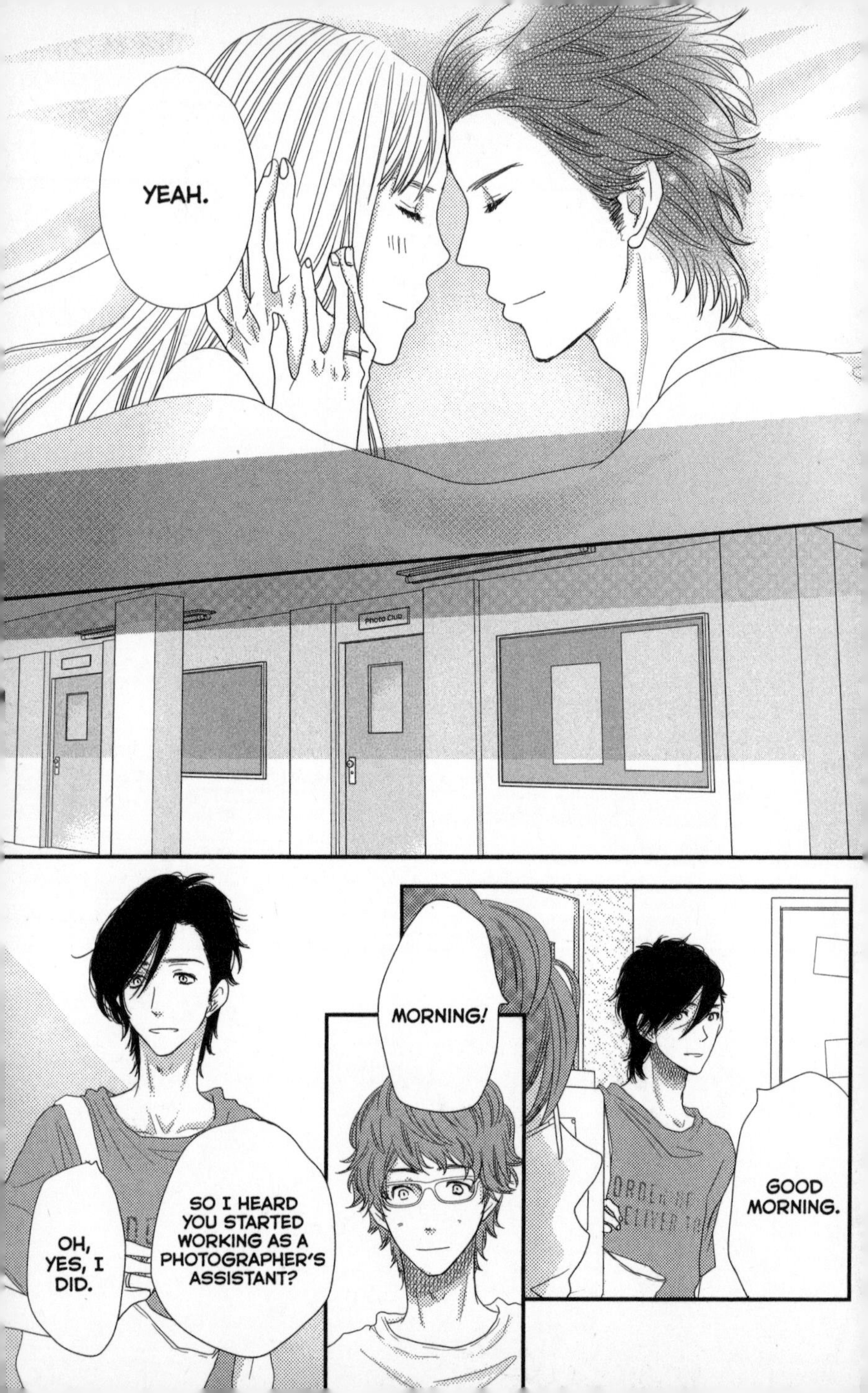
YEAH.
MORNING!
GOOD MORNING.
SO I HEARD YOU STARTED WORKING AS A PHOTOGRAPHER'S ASSISTANT?
OH, YES, I DID.

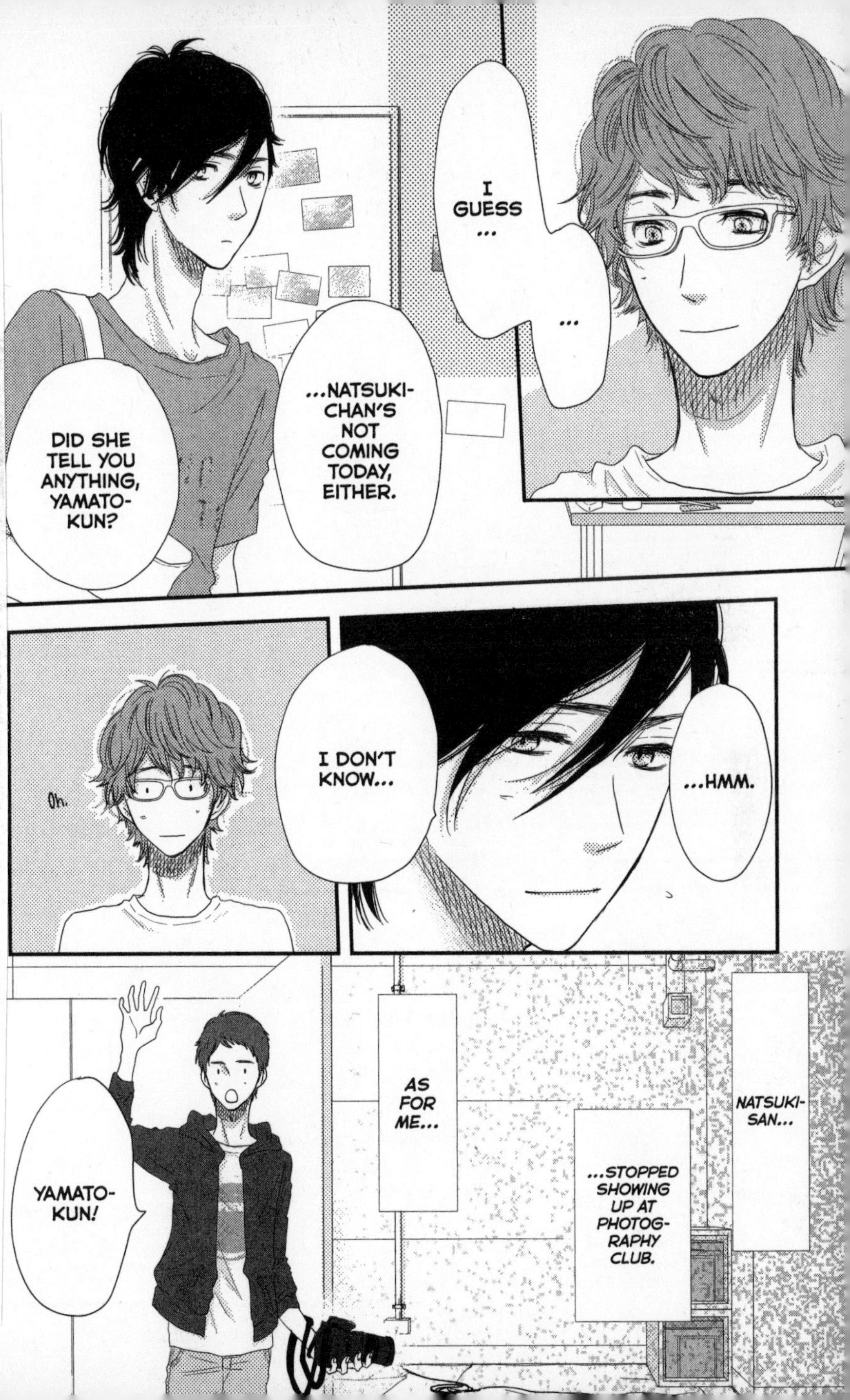
I GUESS ...
...
...NATSUKI-CHAN'S NOT COMING TODAY, EITHER.
DID SHE TELL YOU ANYTHING, YAMATO-KUN?
...HMM.
I DON'T KNOW...
Oh.
NATSUKI-SAN...
...STOPPED SHOWING UP AT PHOTOGRAPHY CLUB.
AS FOR ME...
YAMATO-KUN!

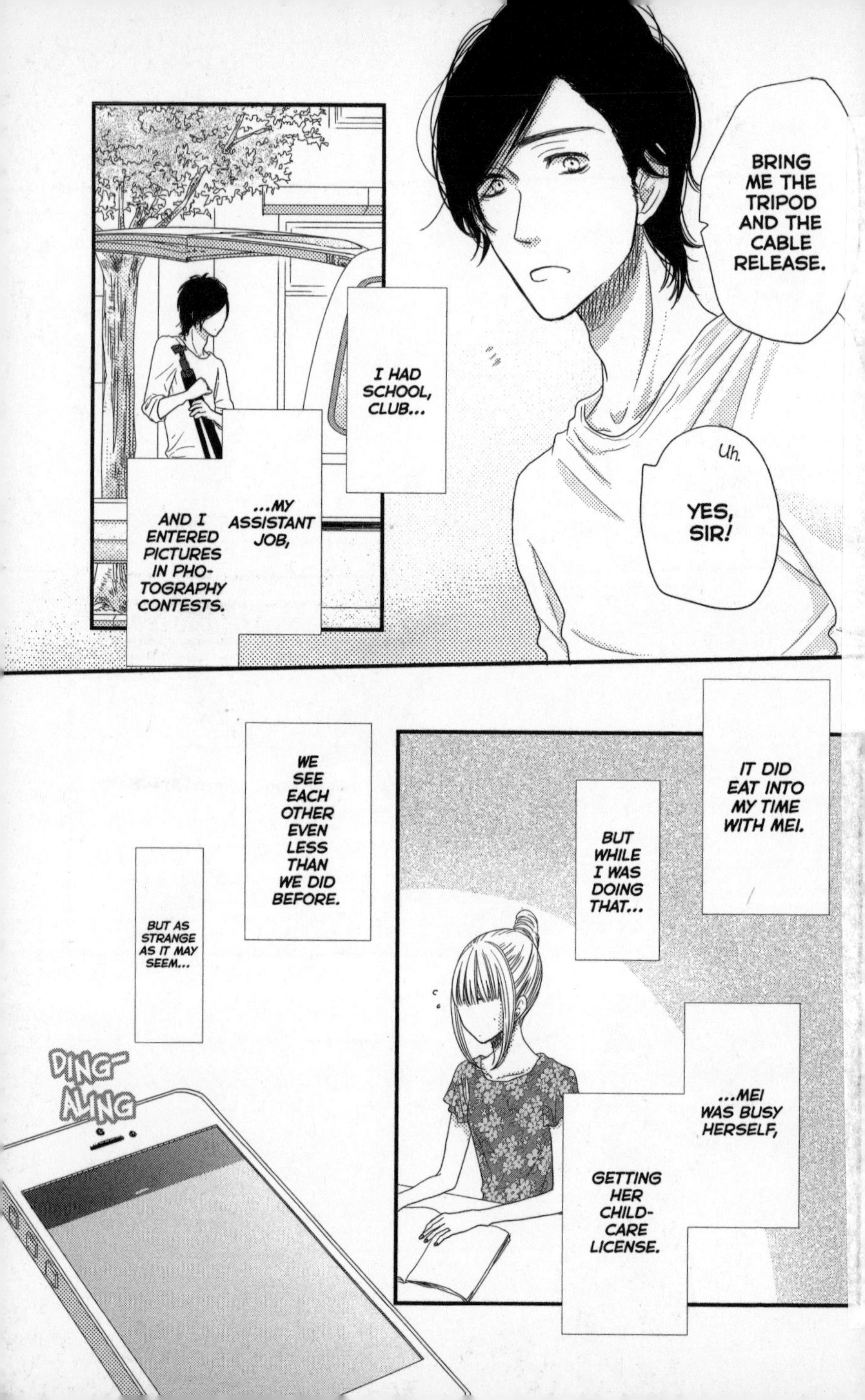
BRING ME THE TRIPOD AND THE CABLE RELEASE.
Uh.
YES, SIR!
I HAD SCHOOL, CLUB...
...MY ASSISTANT JOB,
AND I ENTERED PICTURES IN PHOTOGRAPHY CONTESTS.
IT DID EAT INTO MY TIME WITH MEI.
BUT WHILE I WAS DOING THAT...
...MEI WAS BUSY HERSELF,
GETTING HER CHILD-CARE LICENSE.
WE SEE EACH OTHER EVEN LESS THAN WE DID BEFORE.
BUT AS STRANGE AS IT MAY SEEM...
DING-ALING

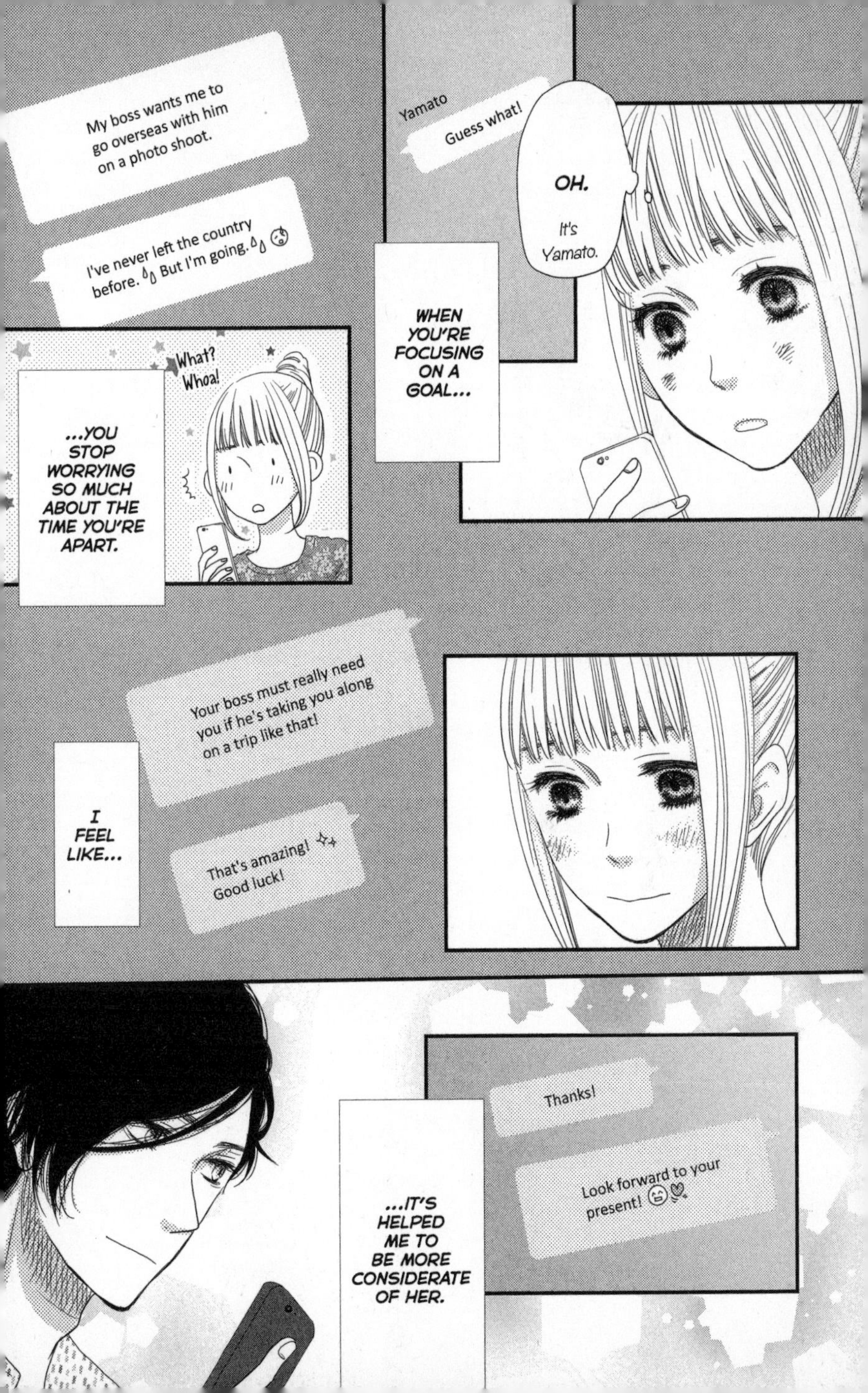
Yamato
Guess what!
OH.
It's Yamato.
WHEN YOU'RE FOCUSING ON A GOAL...
My boss wants me to go overseas with him on a photo shoot.
I've never left the country before. But I'm going.
What? Whoa!
...YOU STOP WORRYING SO MUCH ABOUT THE TIME YOU'RE APART.
Your boss must really need you if he's taking you along on a trip like that!
That's amazing! Good luck!
I FEEL LIKE...
Thanks!
Look forward to your present!
...IT'S HELPED ME TO BE MORE CONSIDERATE OF HER.

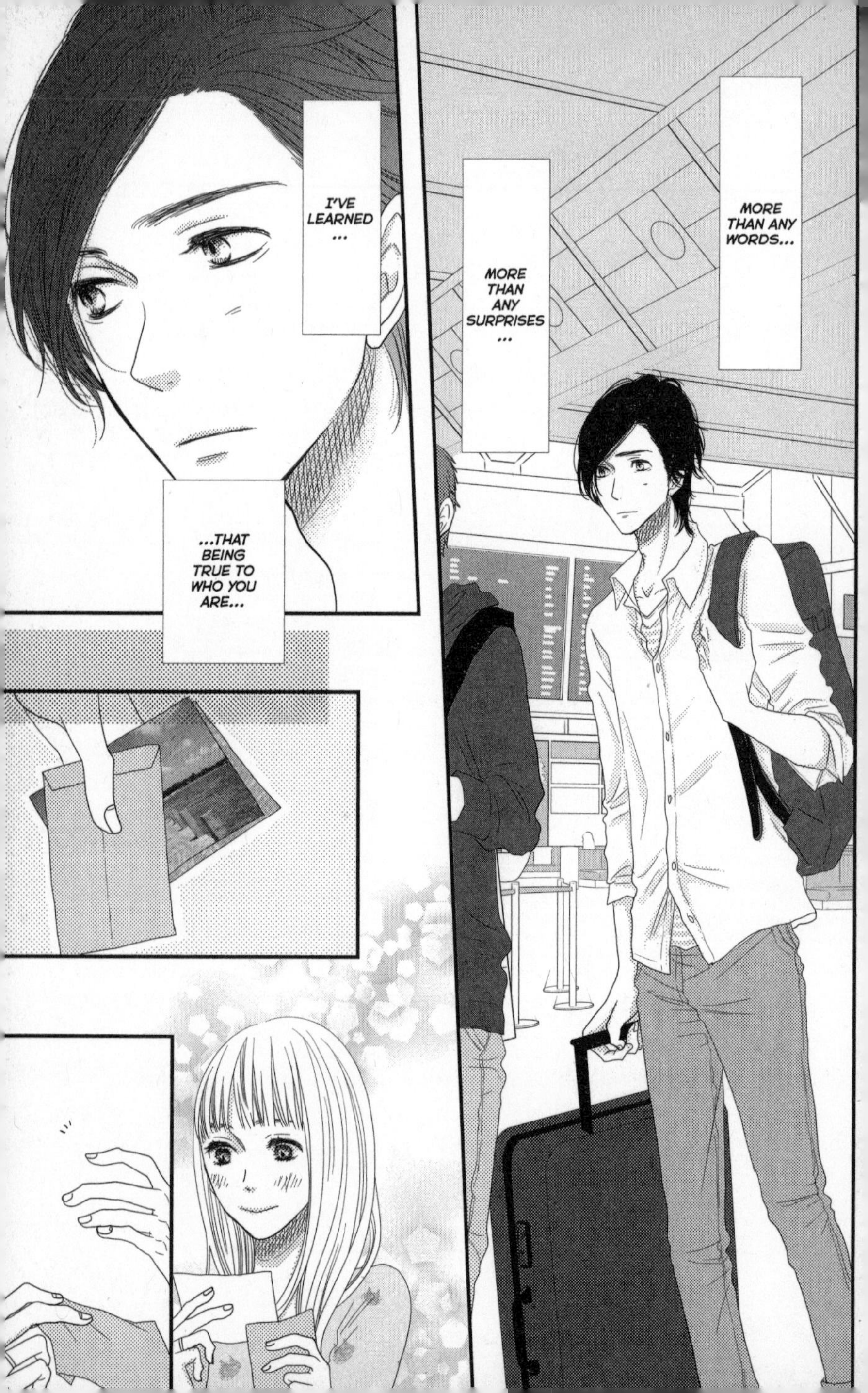
MORE THAN ANY WORDS...
MORE THAN ANY SURPRISES...
I'VE LEARNED...
...THAT BEING TRUE TO WHO YOU ARE...

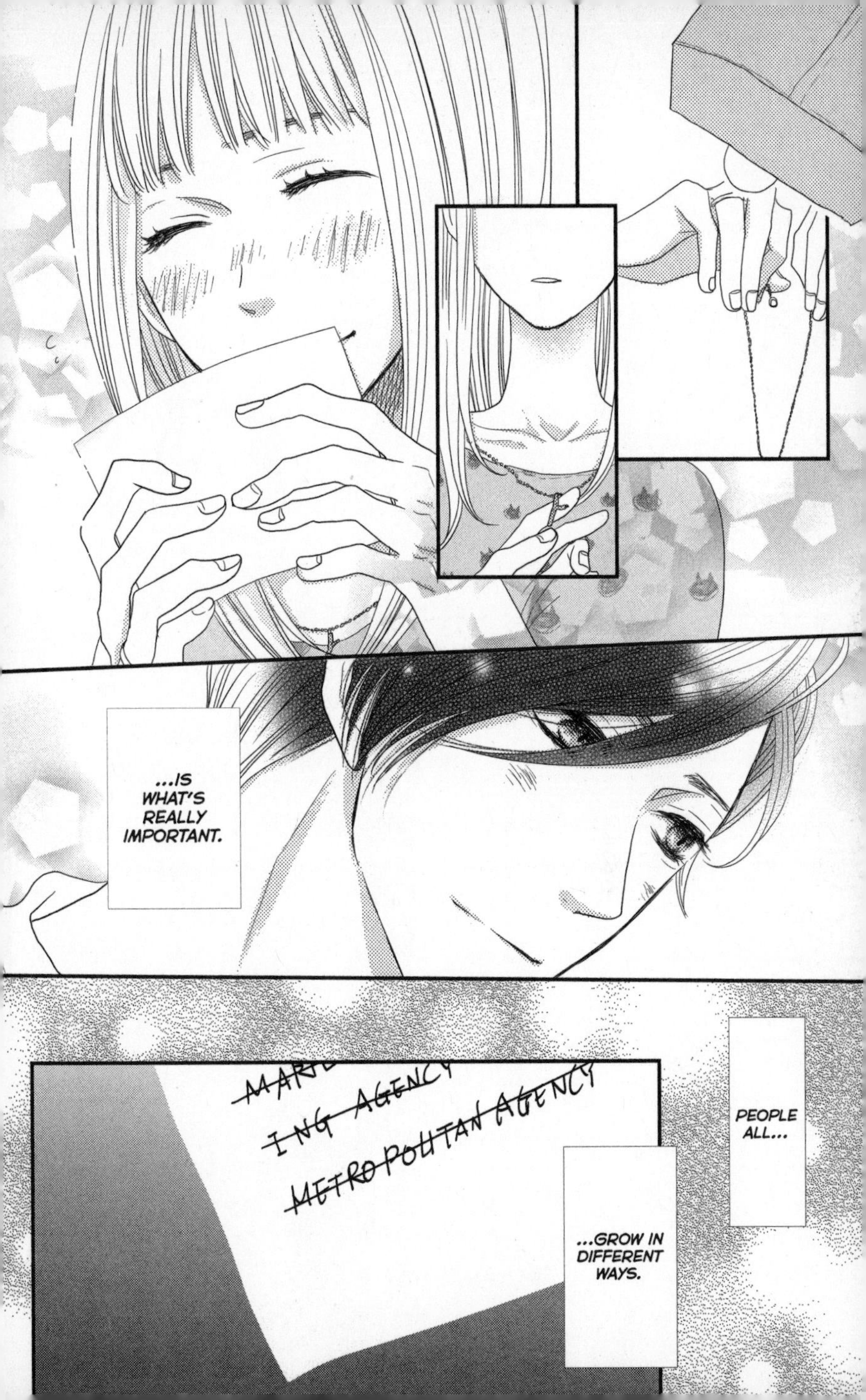
...IS WHAT'S REALLY IMPORTANT.
PEOPLE ALL...
...GROW IN DIFFERENT WAYS.
ING AGENCY
METROPOLITAN AGENCY

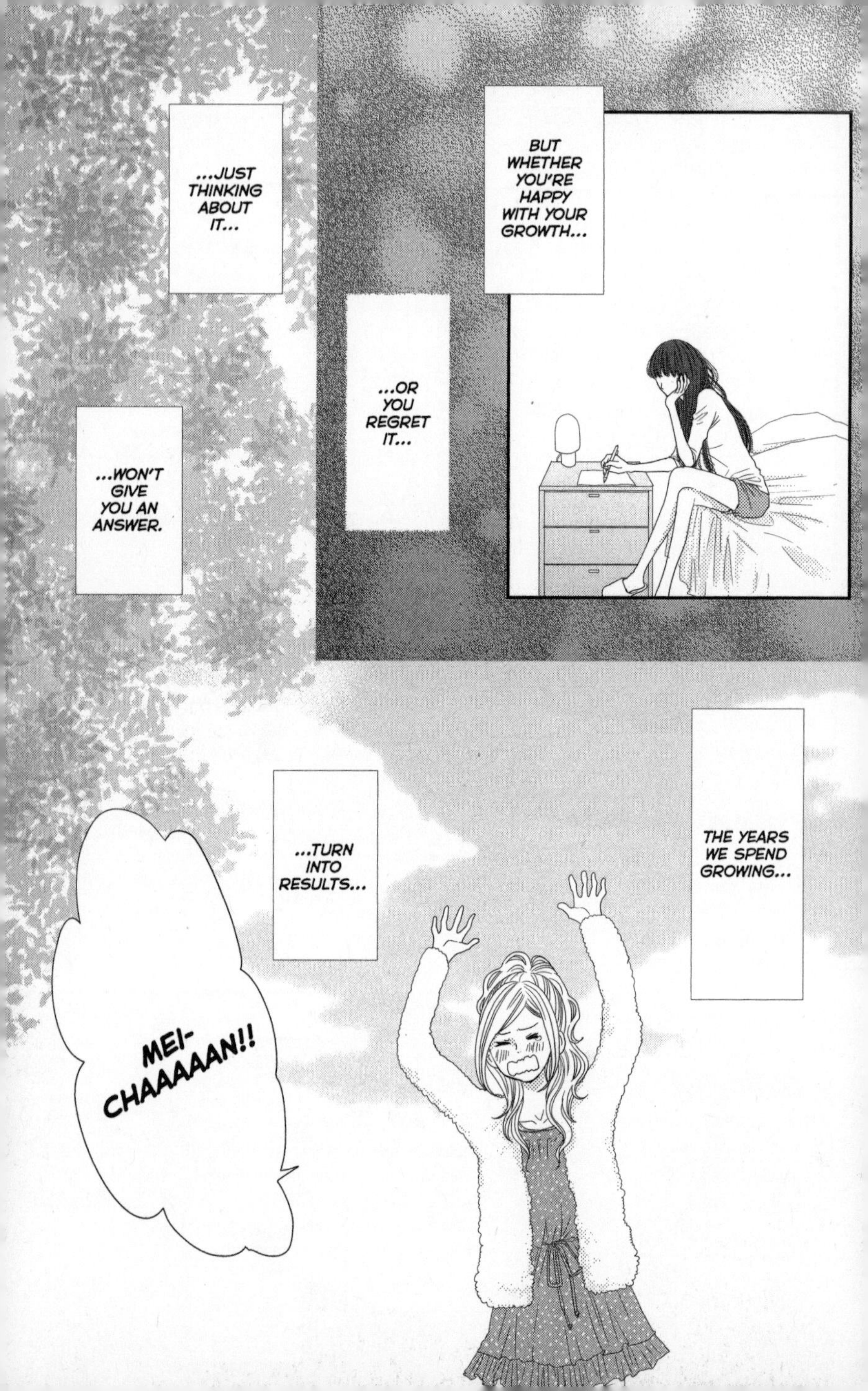
BUT WHETHER YOU'RE HAPPY WITH YOUR GROWTH...
...OR YOU REGRET IT...
...JUST THINKING ABOUT IT...
...WON'T GIVE YOU AN ANSWER.
THE YEARS WE SPEND GROWING...
...TURN INTO RESULTS...
MEI-CHAAAAAN!!

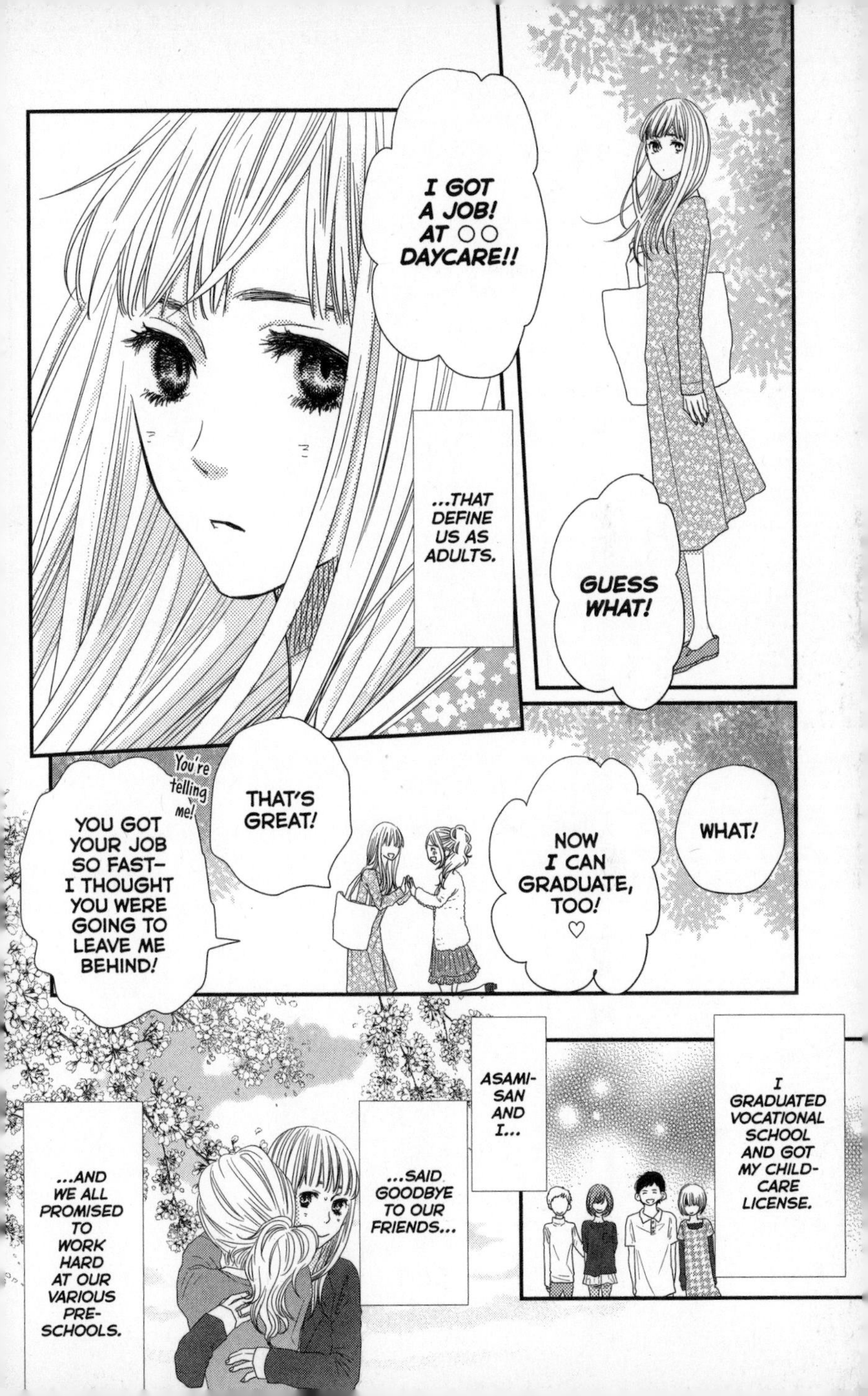
GUESS WHAT!
I GOT A JOB! AT ○○ DAYCARE!!
...THAT DEFINE US AS ADULTS.
WHAT!
NOW I CAN GRADUATE, TOO! ♡
THAT'S GREAT!
You're telling me!
YOU GOT YOUR JOB SO FAST— I THOUGHT YOU WERE GOING TO LEAVE ME BEHIND!
I GRADUATED VOCATIONAL SCHOOL AND GOT MY CHILD-CARE LICENSE.
ASAMI-SAN AND I...
...SAID GOODBYE TO OUR FRIENDS...
...AND WE ALL PROMISED TO WORK HARD AT OUR VARIOUS PRE-SCHOOLS.

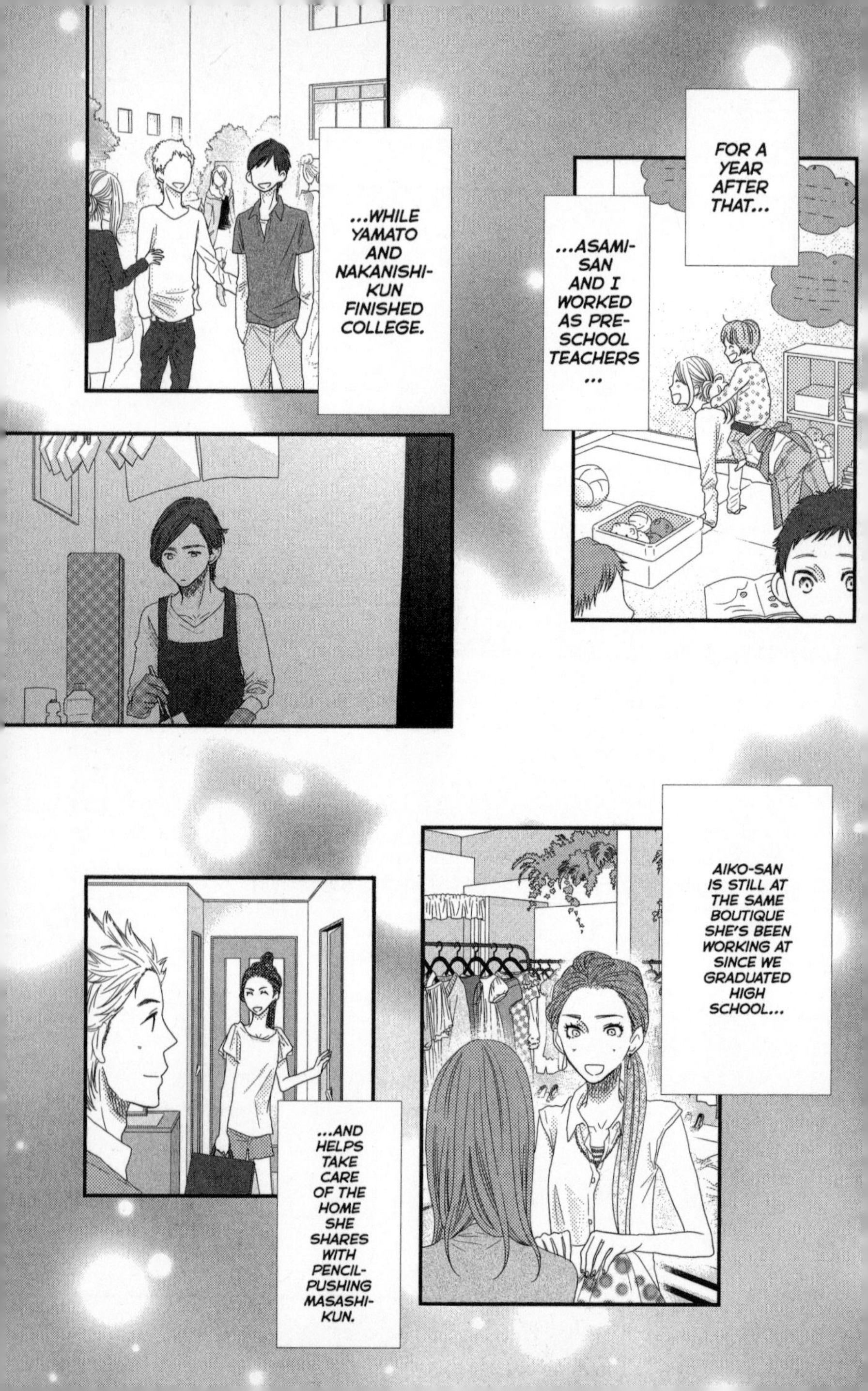
FOR A YEAR AFTER THAT...
...ASAMI-SAN AND I WORKED AS PRE-SCHOOL TEACHERS...
...WHILE YAMATO AND NAKANISHI-KUN FINISHED COLLEGE.
AIKO-SAN IS STILL AT THE SAME BOUTIQUE SHE'S BEEN WORKING AT SINCE WE GRADUATED HIGH SCHOOL...
...AND HELPS TAKE CARE OF THE HOME SHE SHARES WITH PENCIL-PUSHING MASASHI-KUN.

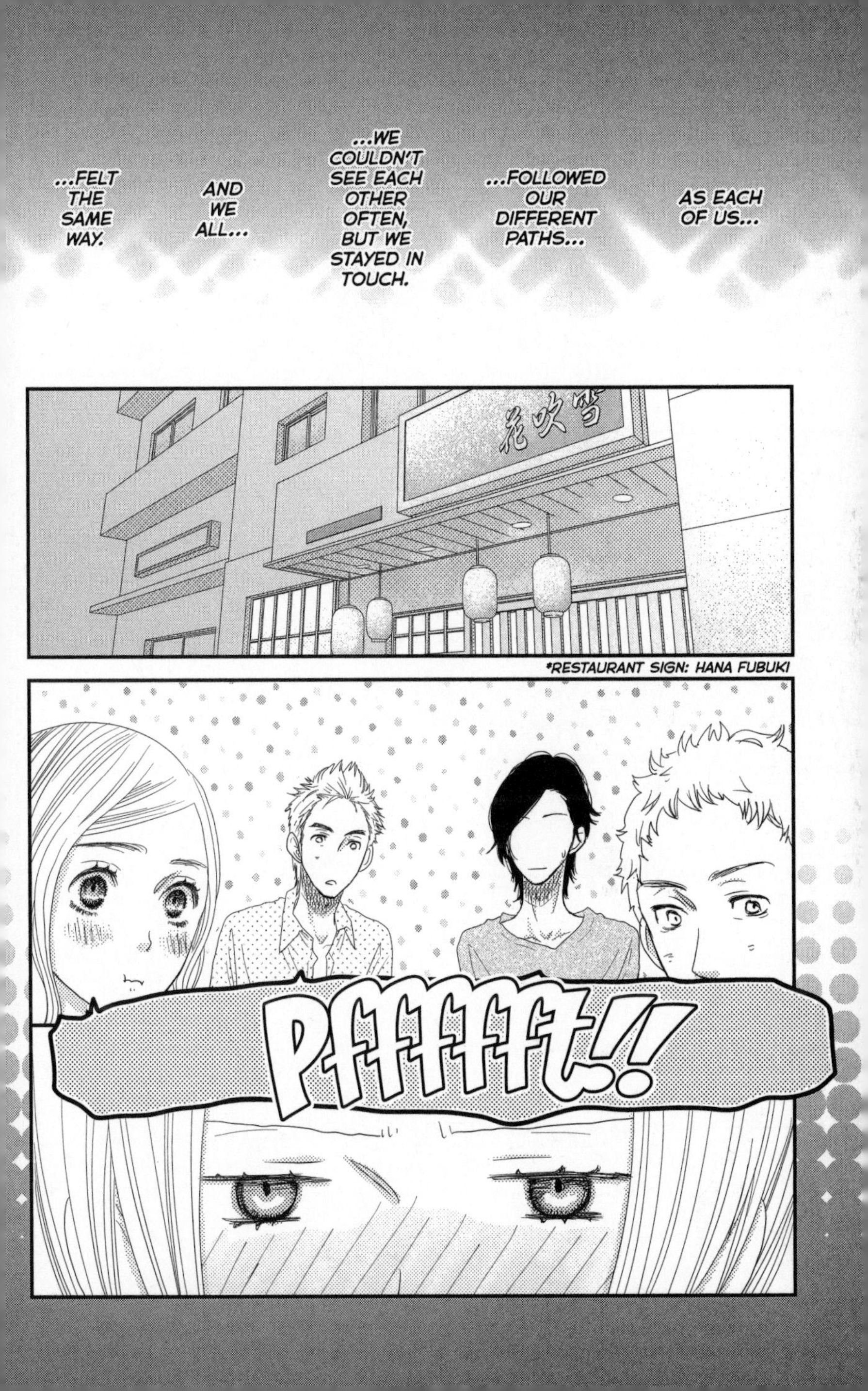
AS EACH OF US...
...FOLLOWED OUR DIFFERENT PATHS...
...WE COULDN'T SEE EACH OTHER OFTEN, BUT WE STAYED IN TOUCH.
AND WE ALL...
...FELT THE SAME WAY.
花吹雪
*RESTAURANT SIGN: HANA FUBUKI
Pffffft!!

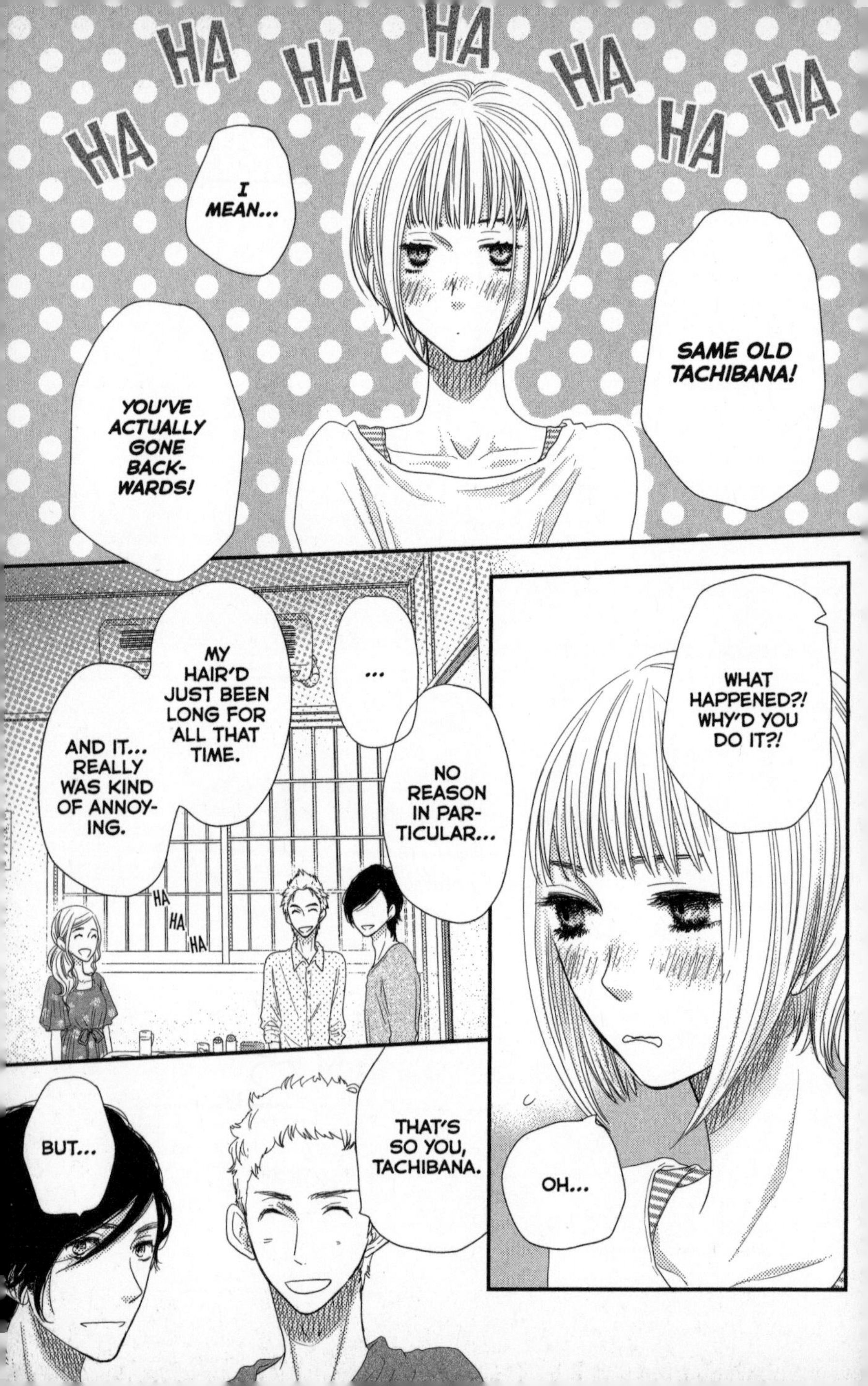
HA HA HA HA HA HA HA HA
SAME OLD TACHIBANA!
I MEAN...
YOU'VE ACTUALLY GONE BACKWARDS!
WHAT HAPPENED?! WHY'D YOU DO IT?!
OH...
...
NO REASON IN PARTICULAR...
MY HAIR'D JUST BEEN LONG FOR ALL THAT TIME.
AND IT... REALLY WAS KIND OF ANNOYING.
HA HA HA
THAT'S SO YOU, TACHIBANA.
BUT...

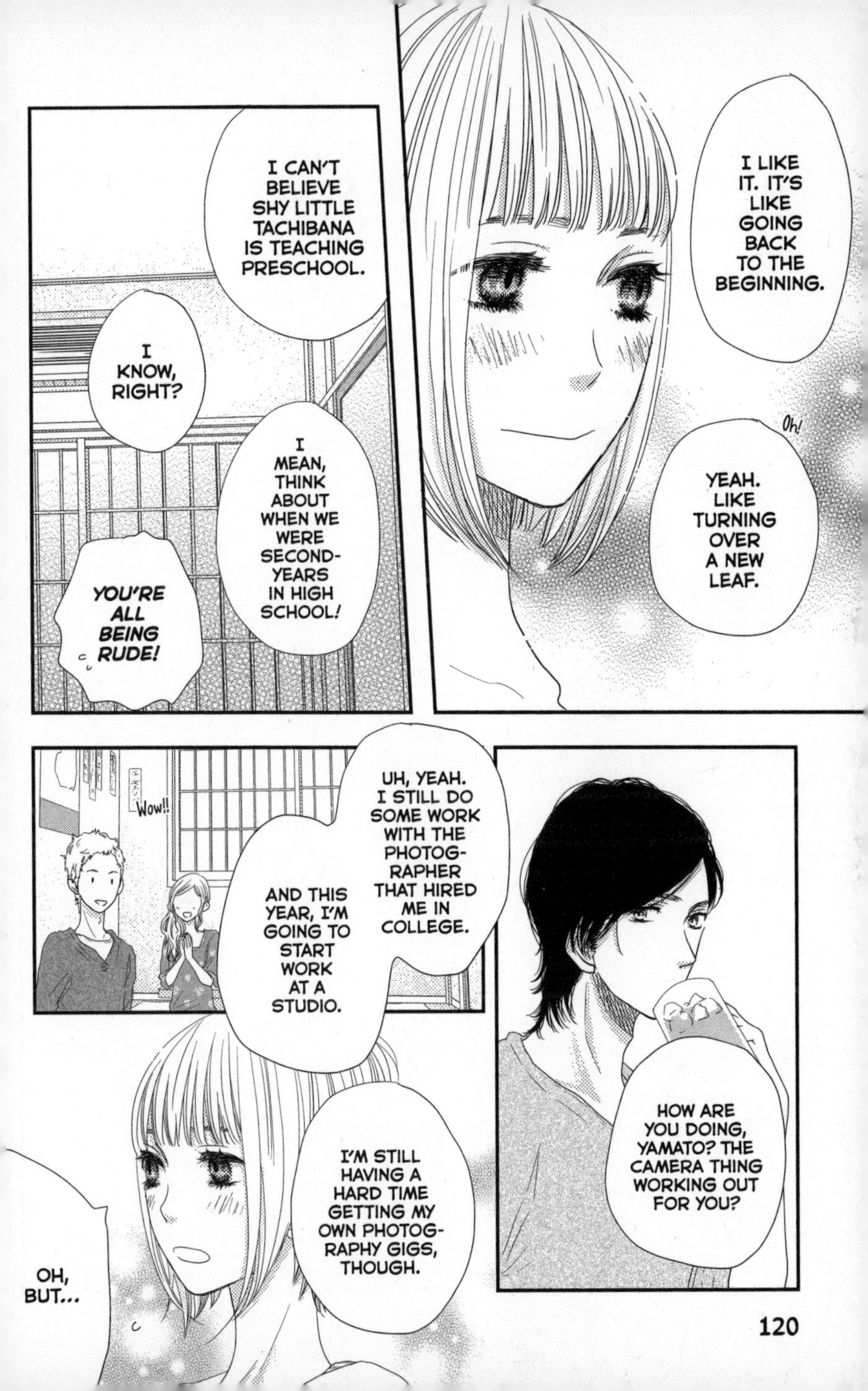
I LIKE IT. IT'S LIKE GOING BACK TO THE BEGINNING.
Oh!
YEAH. LIKE TURNING OVER A NEW LEAF.
I CAN'T BELIEVE SHY LITTLE TACHIBANA IS TEACHING PRESCHOOL.
I KNOW, RIGHT?
I MEAN, THINK ABOUT WHEN WE WERE SECOND-YEARS IN HIGH SCHOOL!
YOU'RE ALL BEING RUDE!
HOW ARE YOU DOING, YAMATO? THE CAMERA THING WORKING OUT FOR YOU?
UH, YEAH. I STILL DO SOME WORK WITH THE PHOTOGRAPHER THAT HIRED ME IN COLLEGE.
AND THIS YEAR, I'M GOING TO START WORK AT A STUDIO.
Wow!!
I'M STILL HAVING A HARD TIME GETTING MY OWN PHOTOGRAPHY GIGS, THOUGH.
OH, BUT...

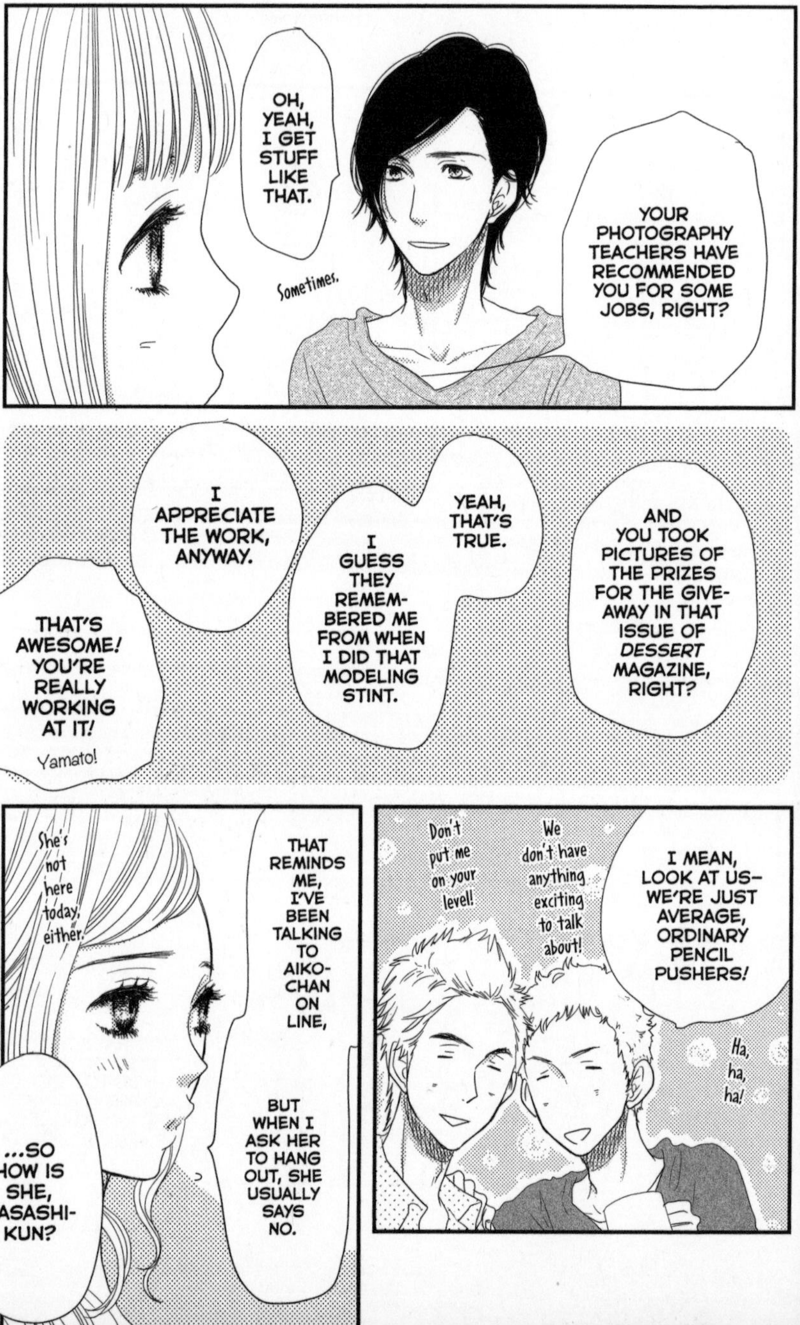
YOUR PHOTOGRAPHY TEACHERS HAVE RECOMMENDED YOU FOR SOME JOBS, RIGHT?
OH, YEAH, I GET STUFF LIKE THAT.
Sometimes.
AND YOU TOOK PICTURES OF THE PRIZES FOR THE GIVE-AWAY IN THAT ISSUE OF *DESSERT* MAGAZINE, RIGHT?
YEAH, THAT'S TRUE.
I GUESS THEY REMEM-BERED ME FROM WHEN I DID THAT MODELING STINT.
I APPRECIATE THE WORK, ANYWAY.
THAT'S AWESOME! YOU'RE REALLY WORKING AT IT!
Yamato!
I MEAN, LOOK AT US— WE'RE JUST AVERAGE, ORDINARY PENCIL PUSHERS!
Ha, ha, ha!
We don't have anything exciting to talk about!
Don't put me on your level!
THAT REMINDS ME, I'VE BEEN TALKING TO AIKO-CHAN ON LINE,
BUT WHEN I ASK HER TO HANG OUT, SHE USUALLY SAYS NO.
She's not here today, either.
...SO HOW IS SHE, MASASHI-KUN?

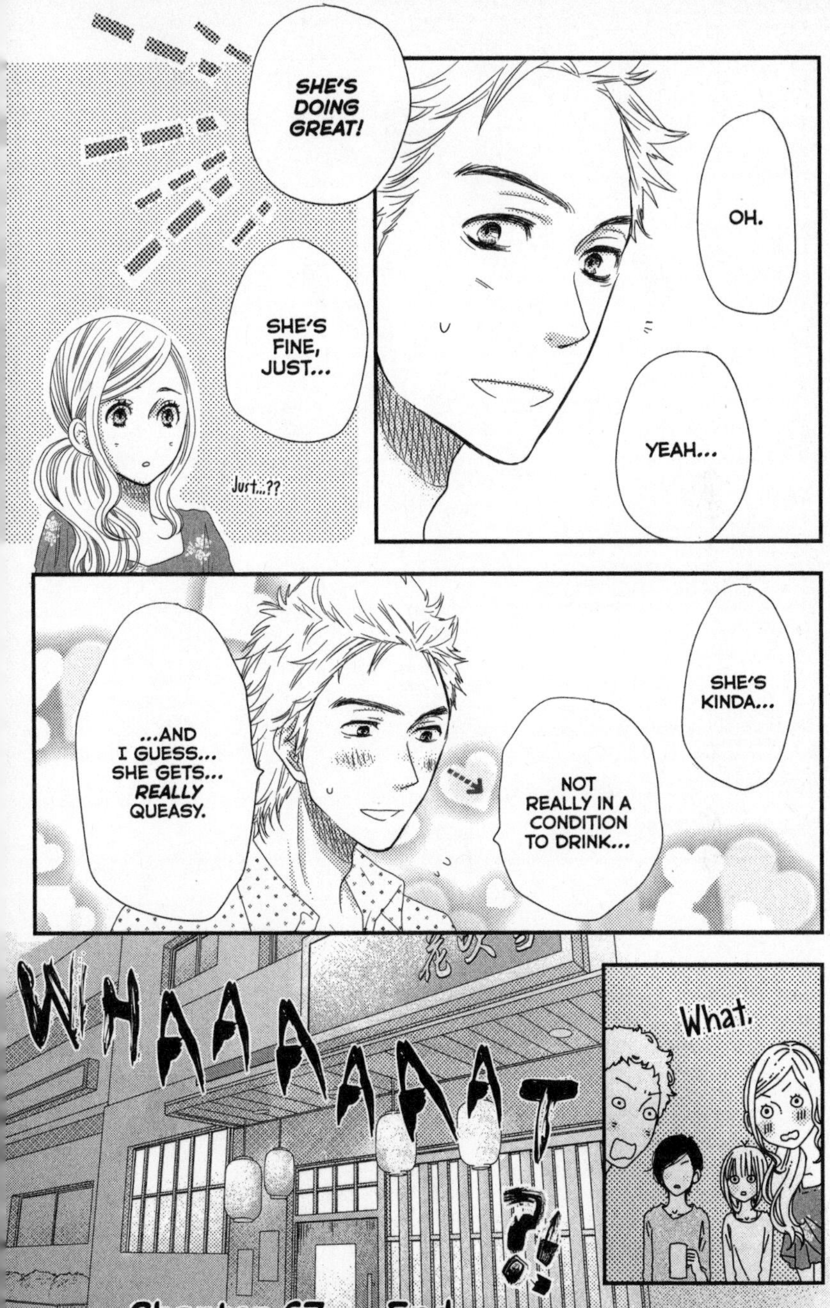
OH.
YEAH...
SHE'S DOING GREAT!
SHE'S FINE, JUST...
Just...??
SHE'S KINDA...
NOT REALLY IN A CONDITION TO DRINK...
...AND I GUESS... SHE GETS... *REALLY* QUEASY.
What.
WHAAAAAAT?!

Chapter 67 — End

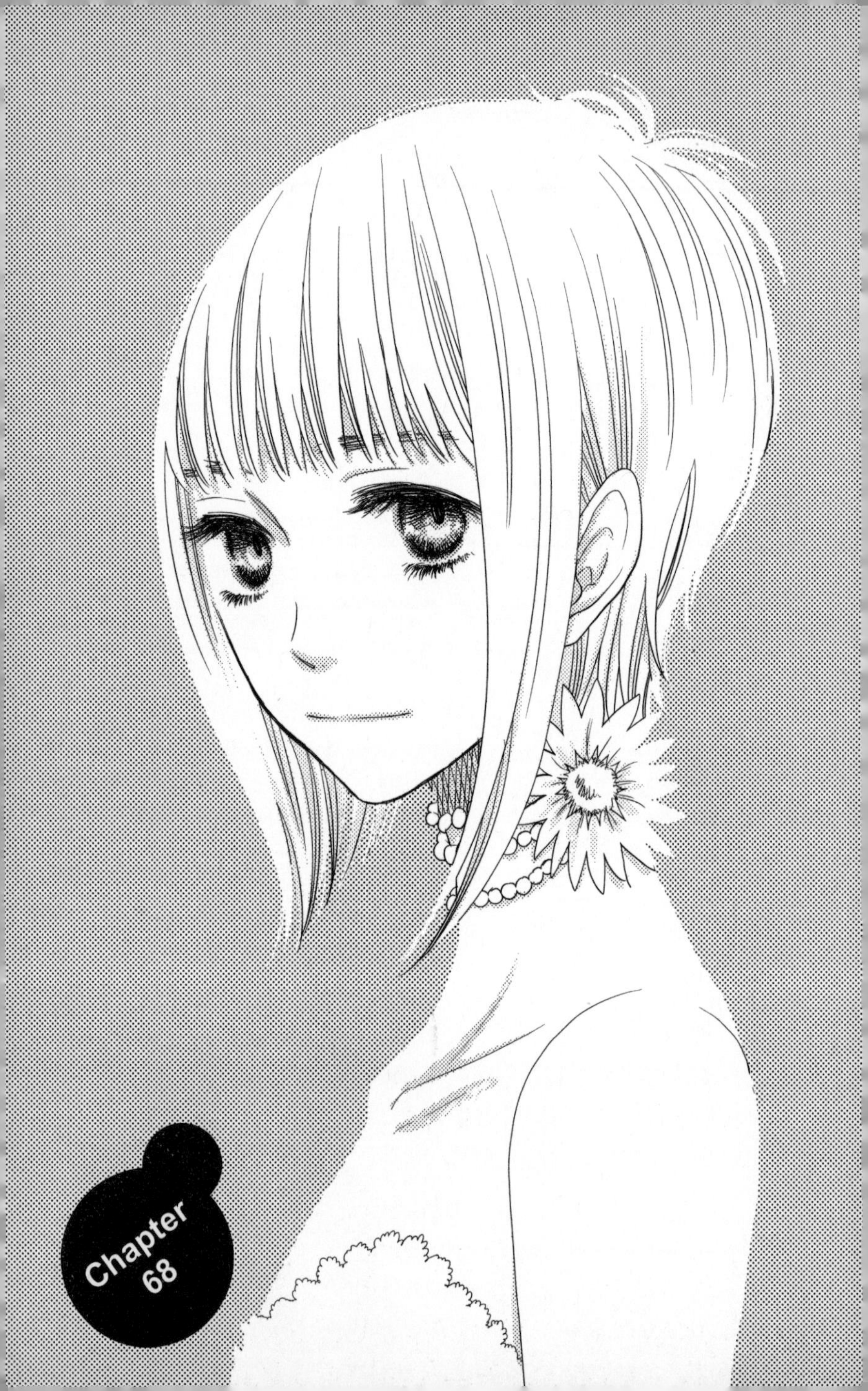
Chapter
68

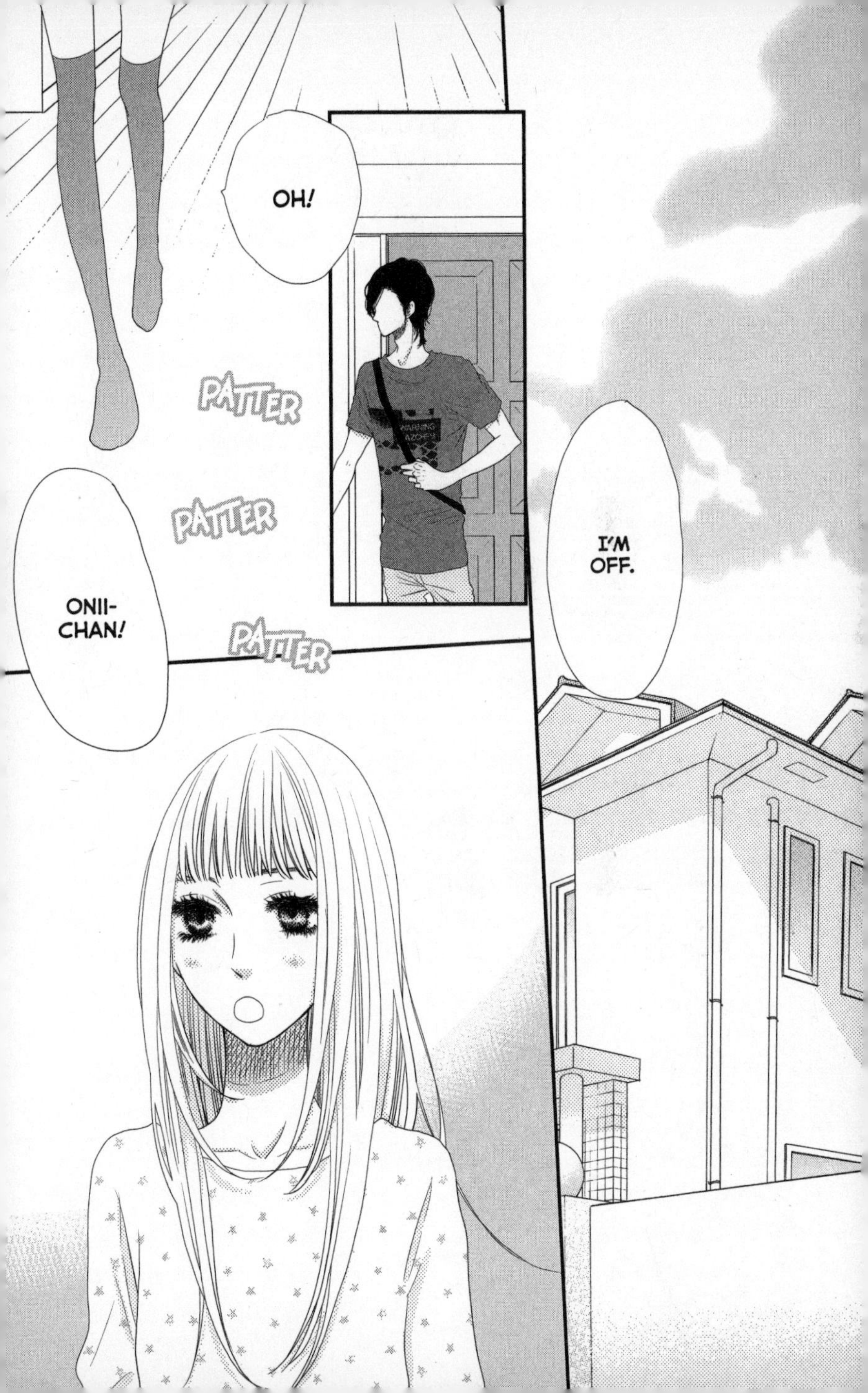
I'M OFF.
OH!
PATTER
PATTER
PATTER
ONII-CHAN!

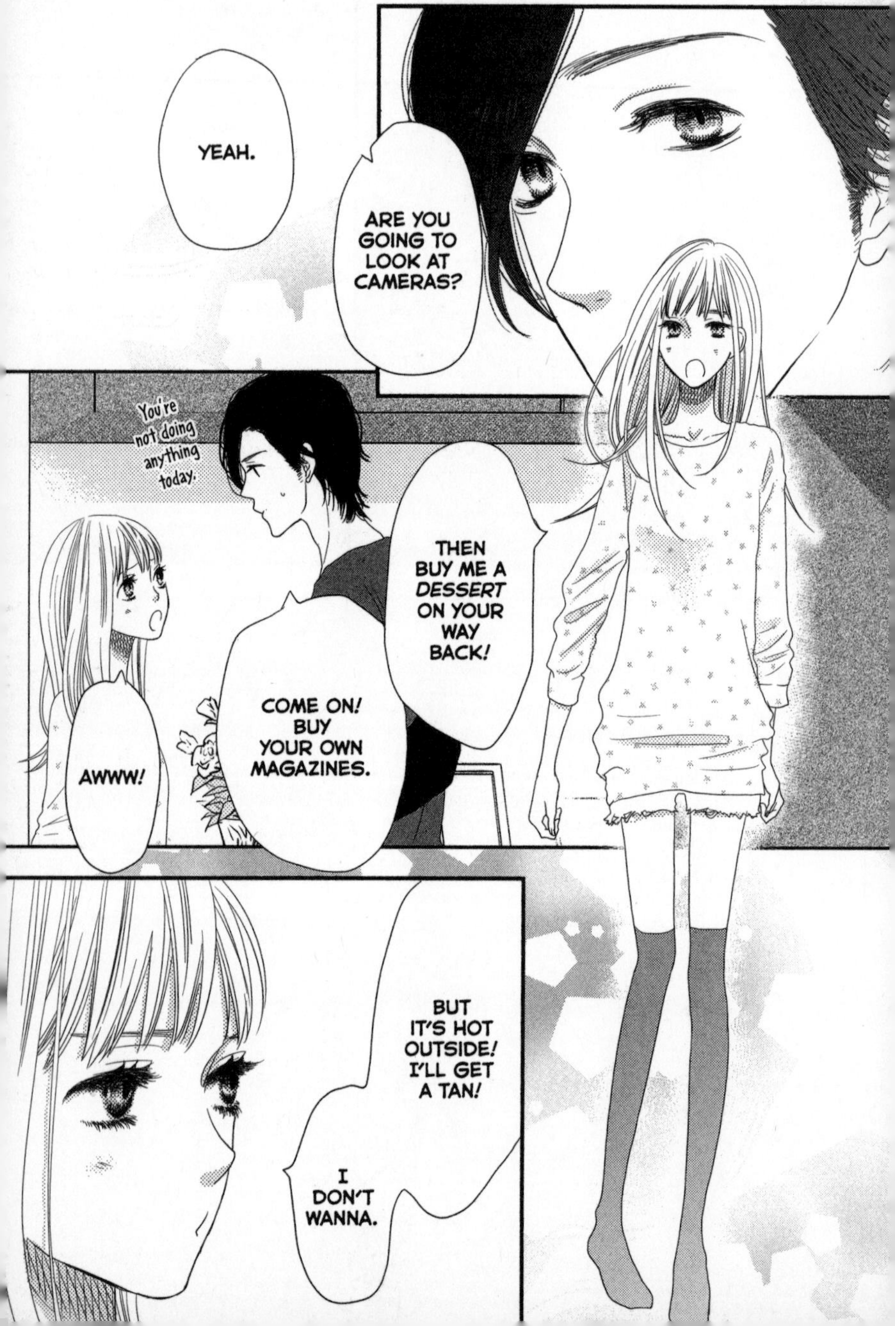
ARE YOU GOING TO LOOK AT CAMERAS?
YEAH.
THEN BUY ME A *DESSERT* ON YOUR WAY BACK!
You're not doing anything today.
COME ON! BUY YOUR OWN MAGAZINES.
AWWW!
BUT IT'S HOT OUTSIDE! I'LL GET A TAN!
I DON'T WANNA.

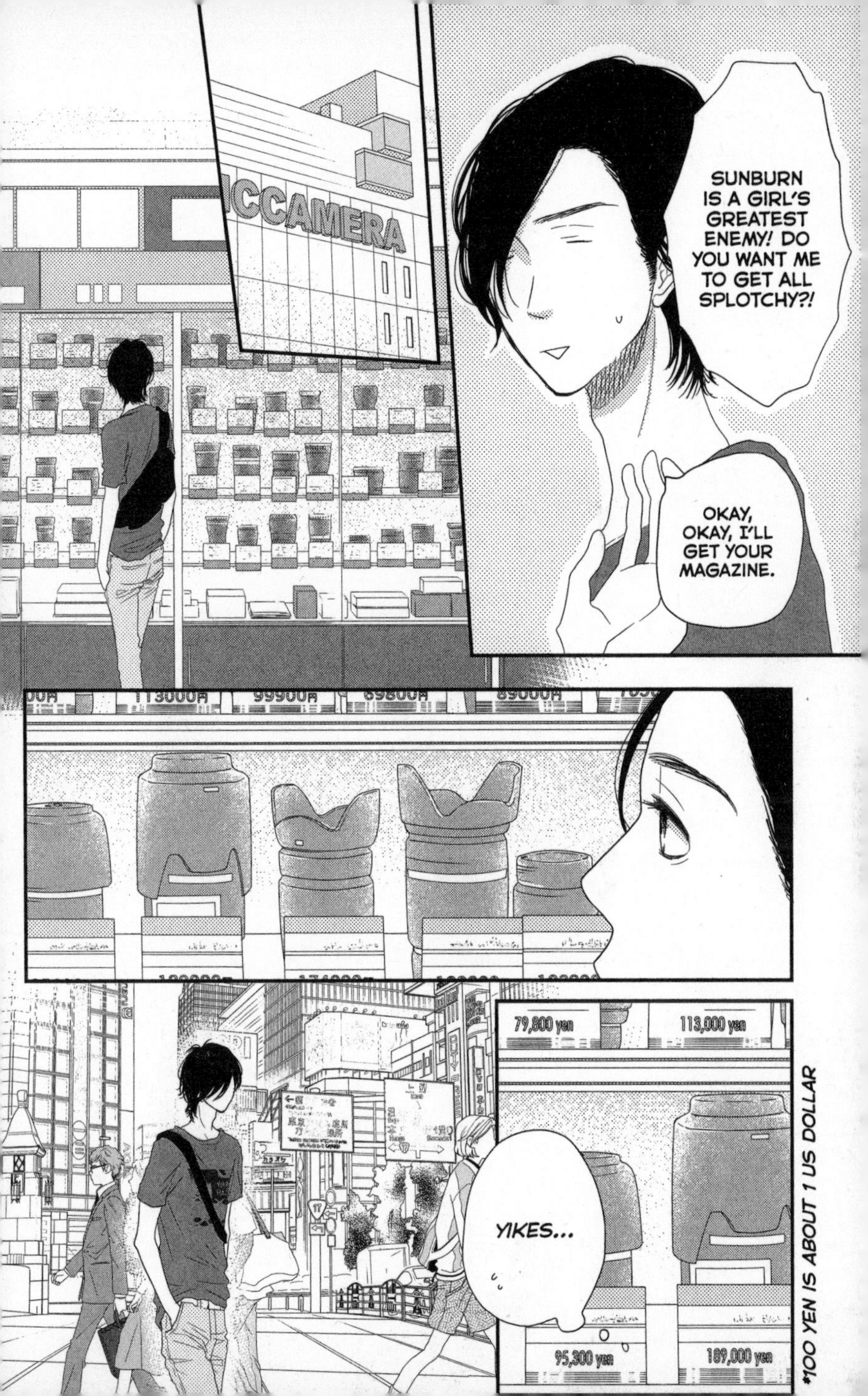
SUNBURN IS A GIRL'S GREATEST ENEMY! DO YOU WANT ME TO GET ALL SPLOTCHY?!
OKAY, OKAY, I'LL GET YOUR MAGAZINE.
CCAMERA
113000円
99900円
69800円
89000円
79,800 yen
113,000 yen
YIKES...
95,300 yen
189,000 yen

*100 YEN IS ABOUT 1 US DOLLAR

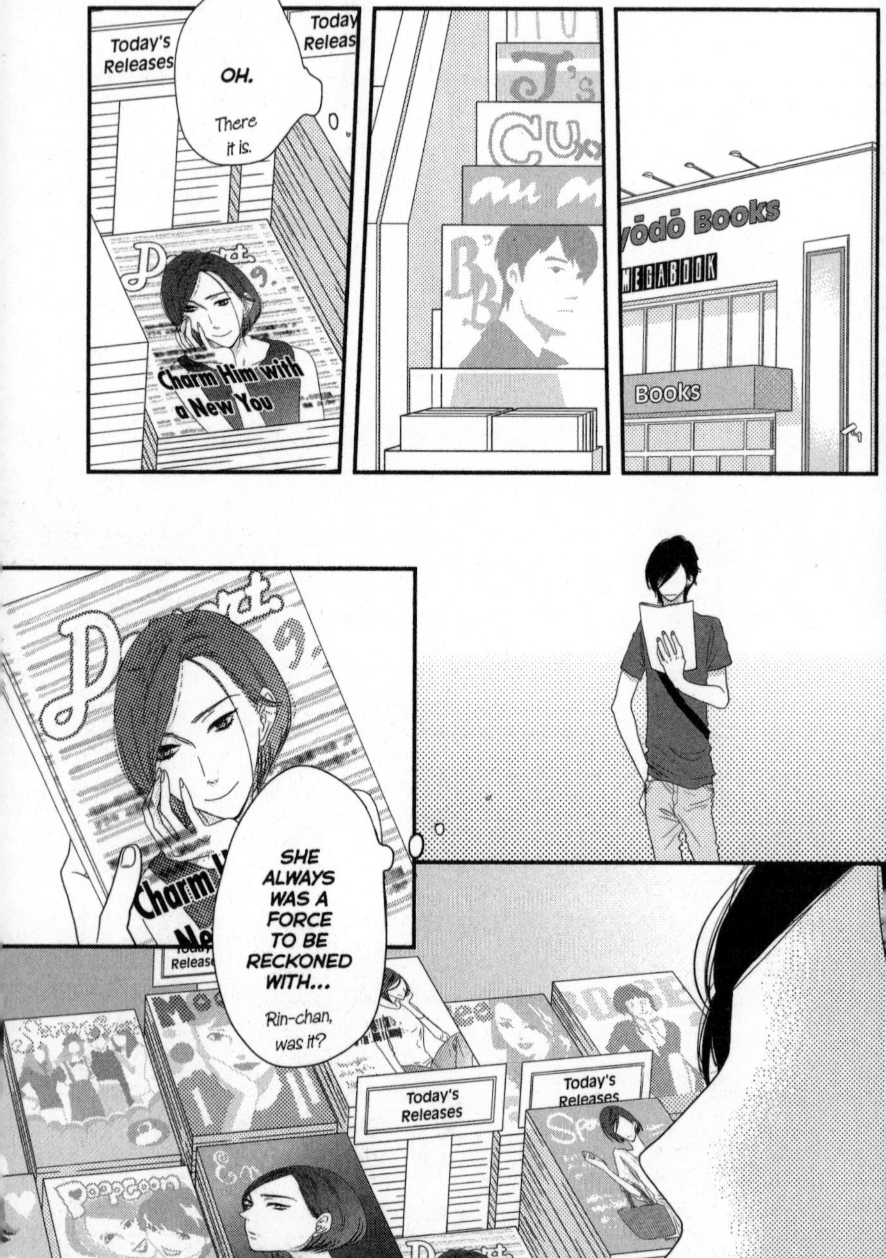

Books
MEGABOOK
Books
Today's Releases
OH.
There it is.
Charm Him with a New You
SHE ALWAYS WAS A FORCE TO BE RECKONED WITH...
Rin-chan, was it?
Today's Releases
Today's Releases

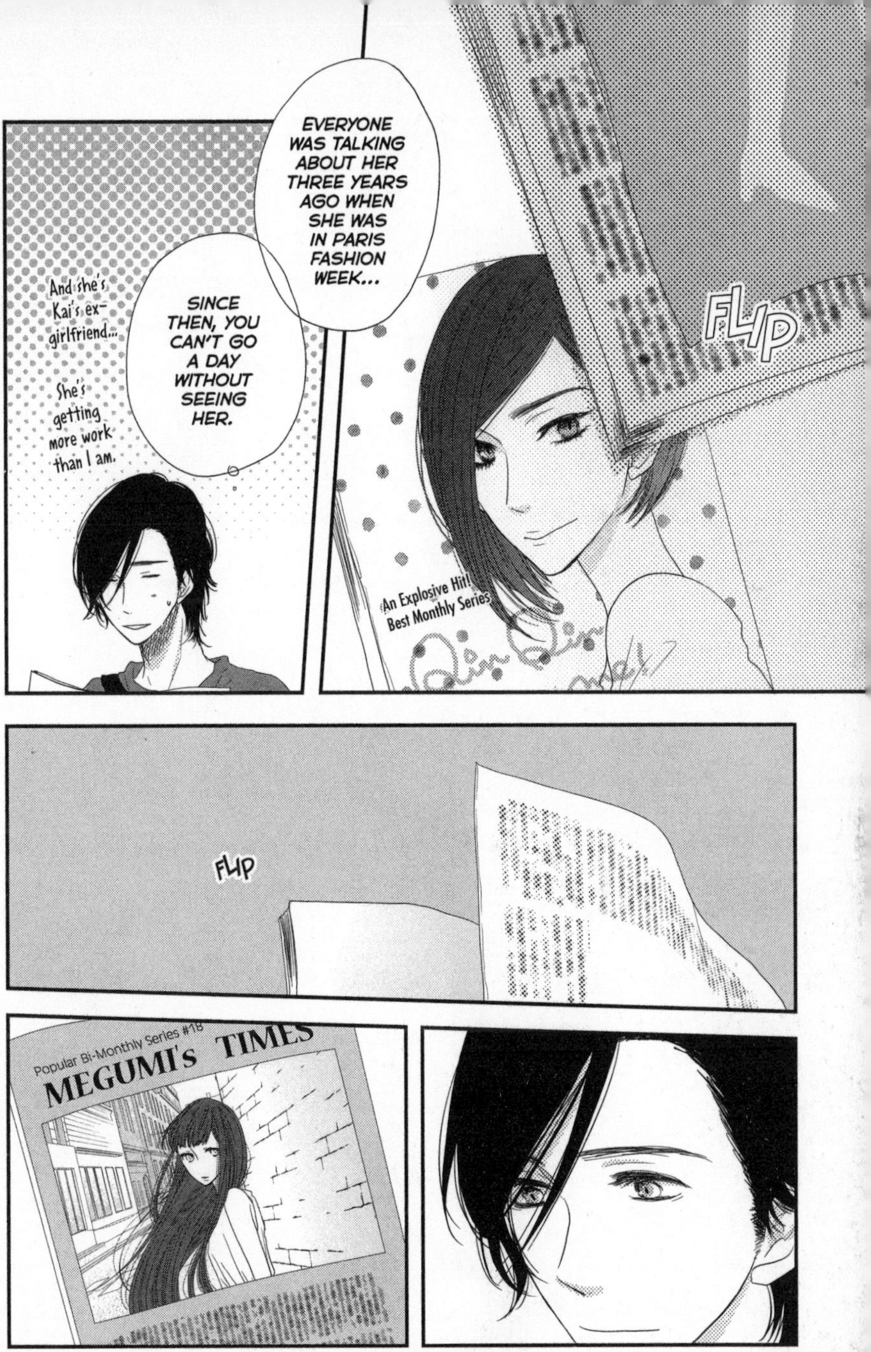
FLIP
An Explosive Hit! Best Monthly Series
EVERYONE WAS TALKING ABOUT HER THREE YEARS AGO WHEN SHE WAS IN PARIS FASHION WEEK...
SINCE THEN, YOU CAN'T GO A DAY WITHOUT SEEING HER.
And she's Kai's ex-girlfriend...
She's getting more work than I am.
FLIP
Popular Bi-Monthly Series #18
MEGUMI's TIMES

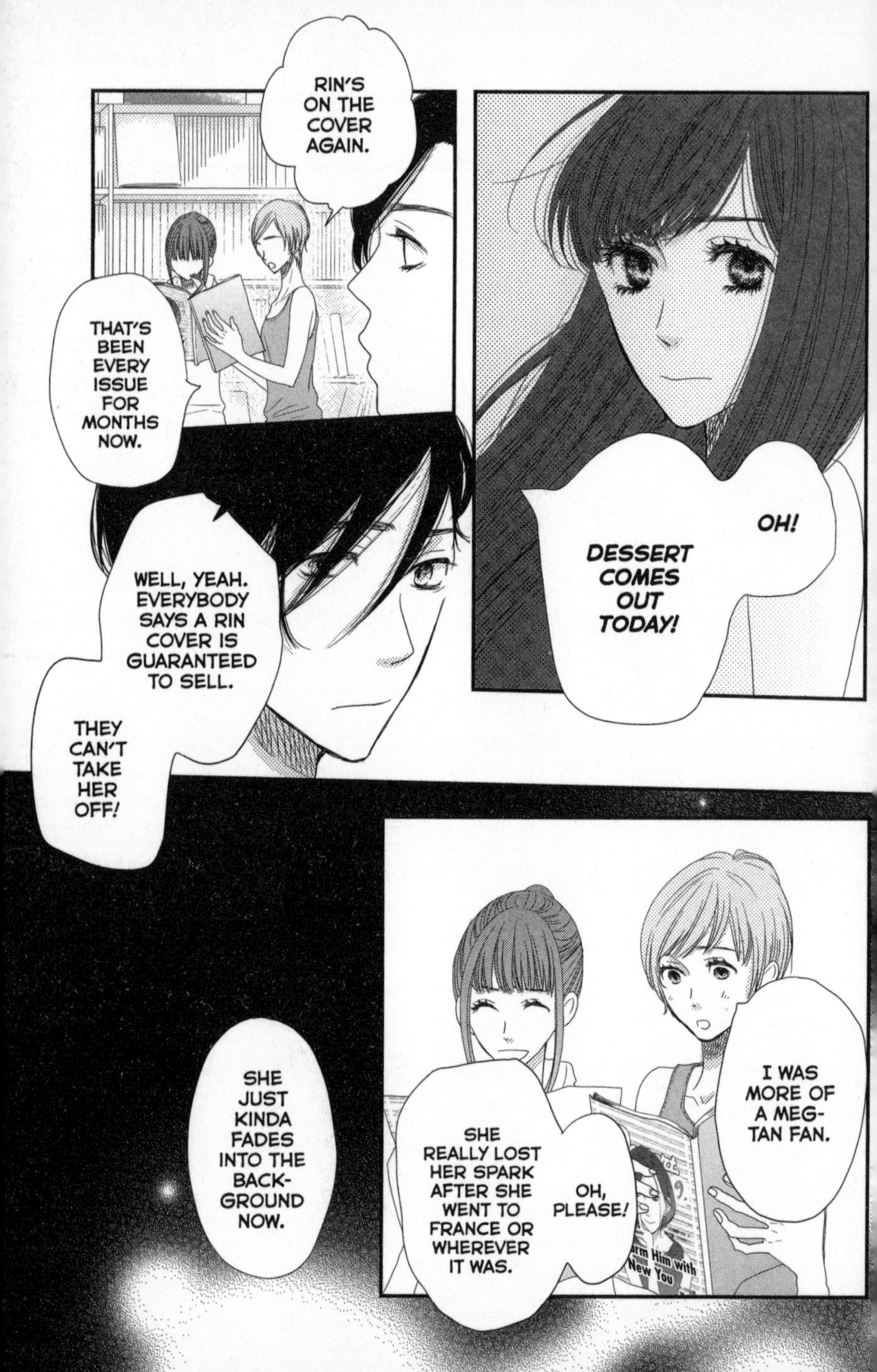
OH!
DESSERT COMES OUT TODAY!
RIN'S ON THE COVER AGAIN.
THAT'S BEEN EVERY ISSUE FOR MONTHS NOW.
WELL, YEAH. EVERYBODY SAYS A RIN COVER IS GUARANTEED TO SELL.
THEY CAN'T TAKE HER OFF!
I WAS MORE OF A MEG-TAN FAN.
OH, PLEASE!
SHE REALLY LOST HER SPARK AFTER SHE WENT TO FRANCE OR WHEREVER IT WAS.
SHE JUST KINDA FADES INTO THE BACK-GROUND NOW.

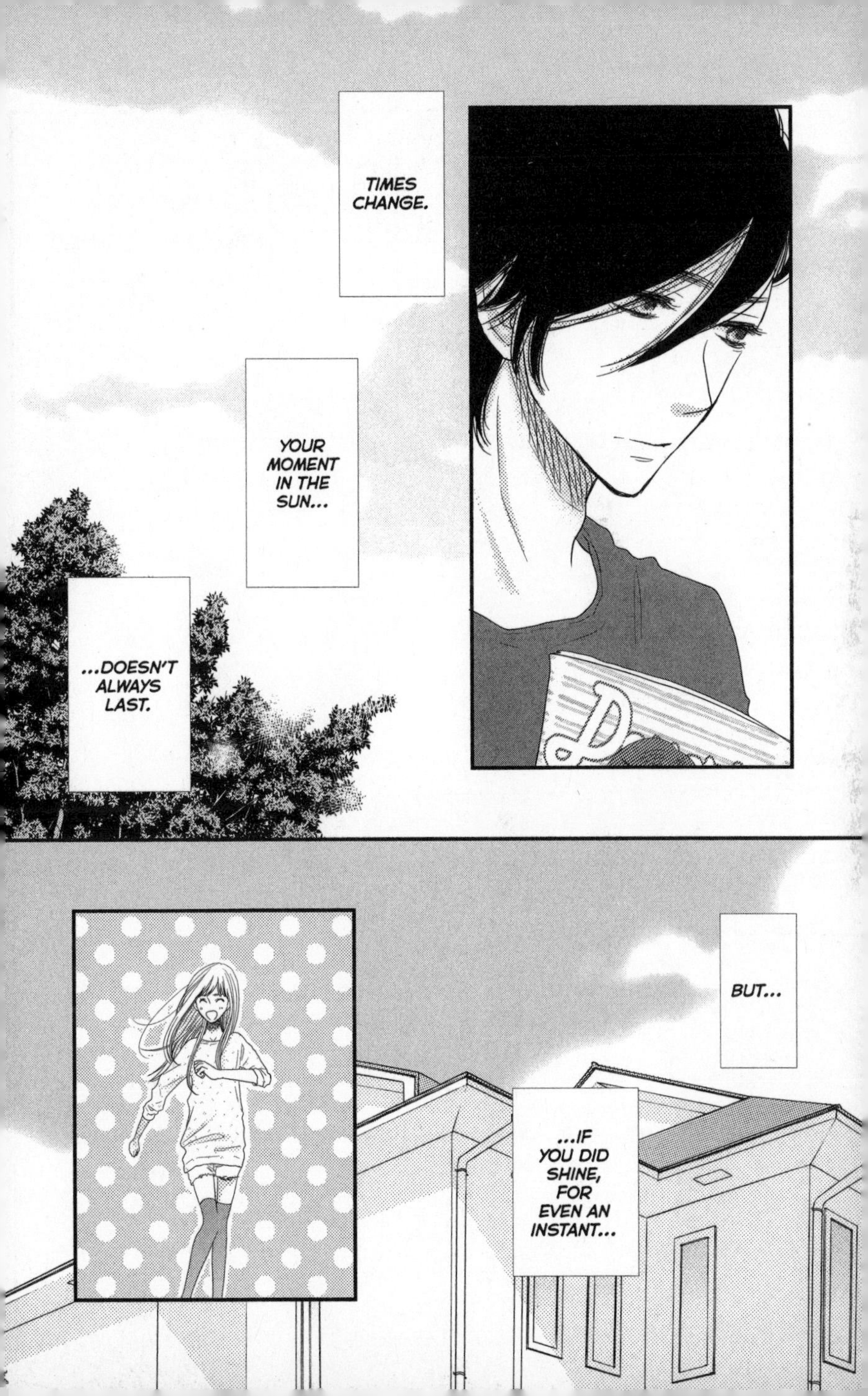
TIMES CHANGE.
YOUR MOMENT IN THE SUN...
...DOESN'T ALWAYS LAST.
BUT...
...IF YOU DID SHINE, FOR EVEN AN INSTANT...

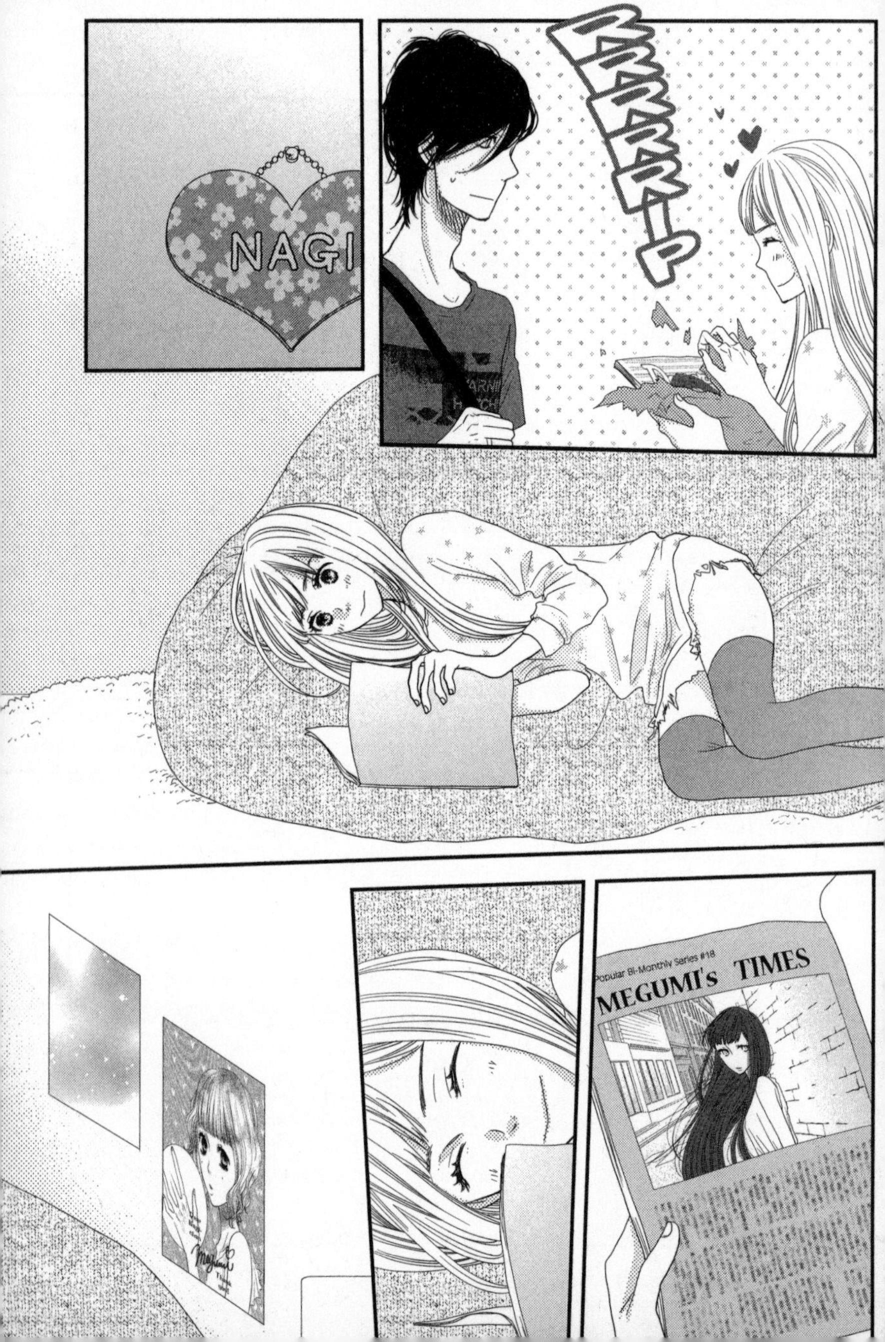
RRRRRIP
NAGI
Popular Bi-Monthly Series #18
MEGUMI's TIMES

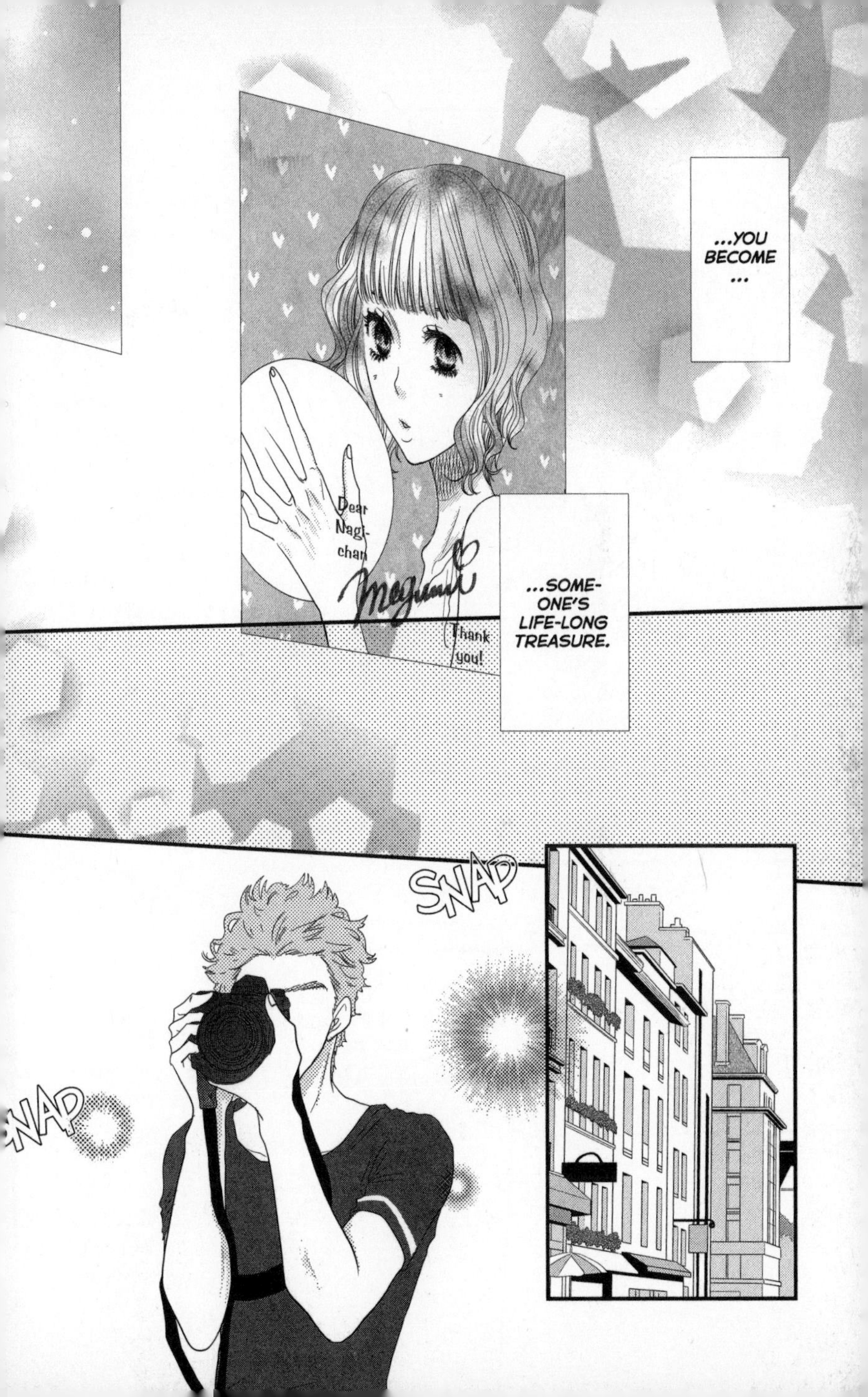
...YOU BECOME ...
Dear Nagi-chan
Megumi
Thank you!
...SOME-ONE'S LIFE-LONG TREASURE.
SNAP
SNAP

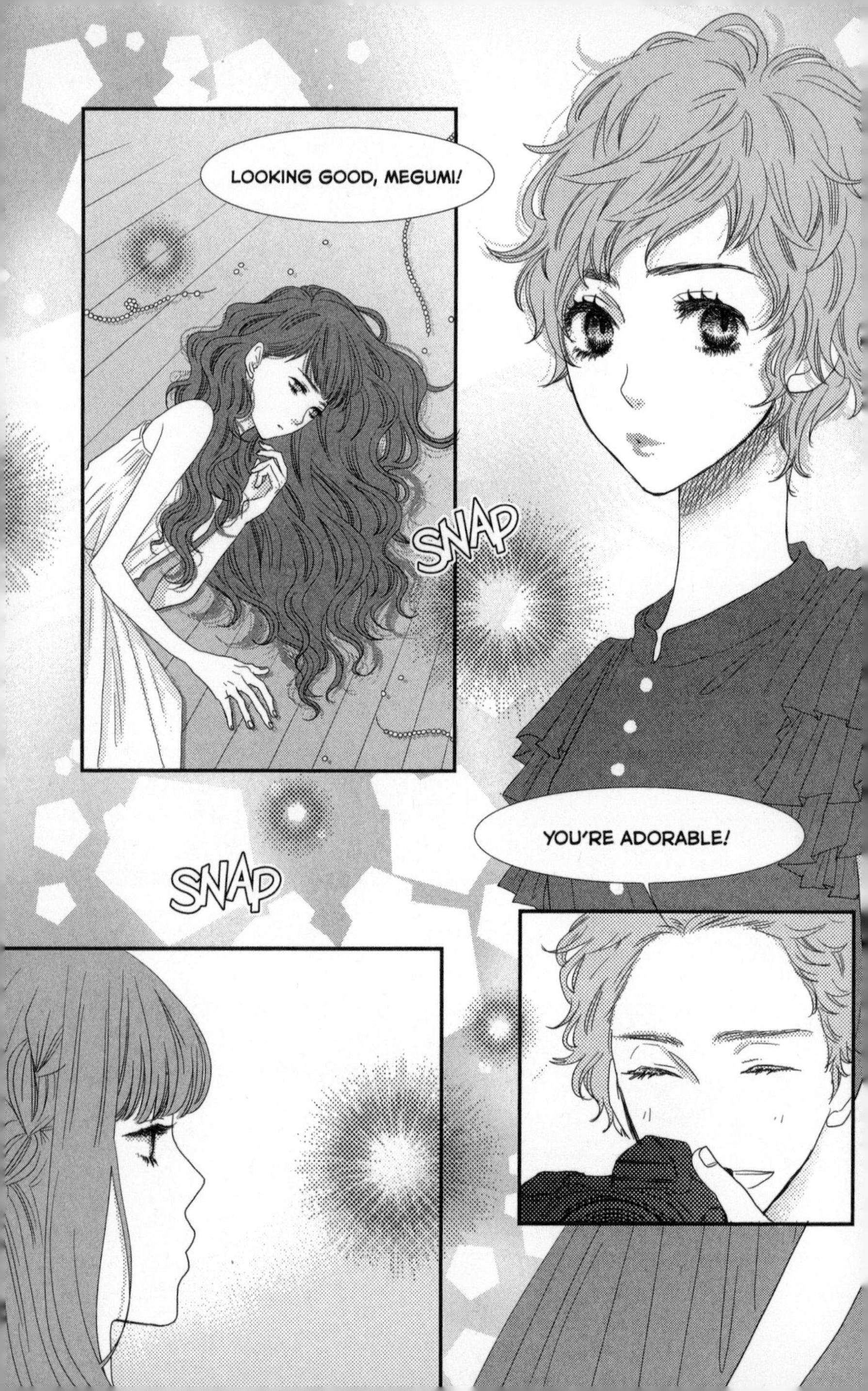
LOOKING GOOD, MEGUMI!
SNAP
SNAP
YOU'RE ADORABLE!

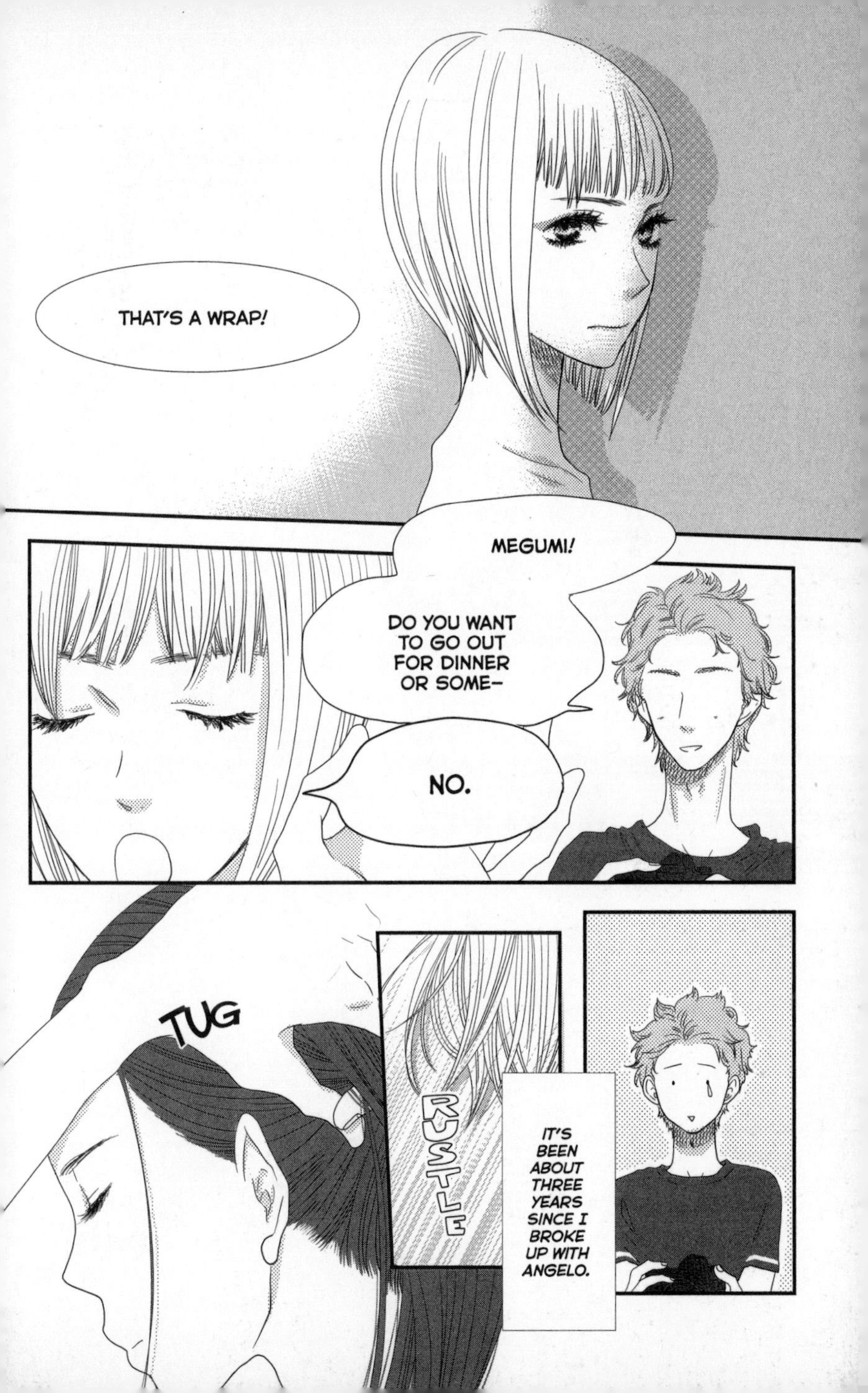
THAT'S A WRAP!
MEGUMI!
DO YOU WANT TO GO OUT FOR DINNER OR SOME-
NO.
IT'S BEEN ABOUT THREE YEARS SINCE I BROKE UP WITH ANGELO.
RUSTLE
TUG

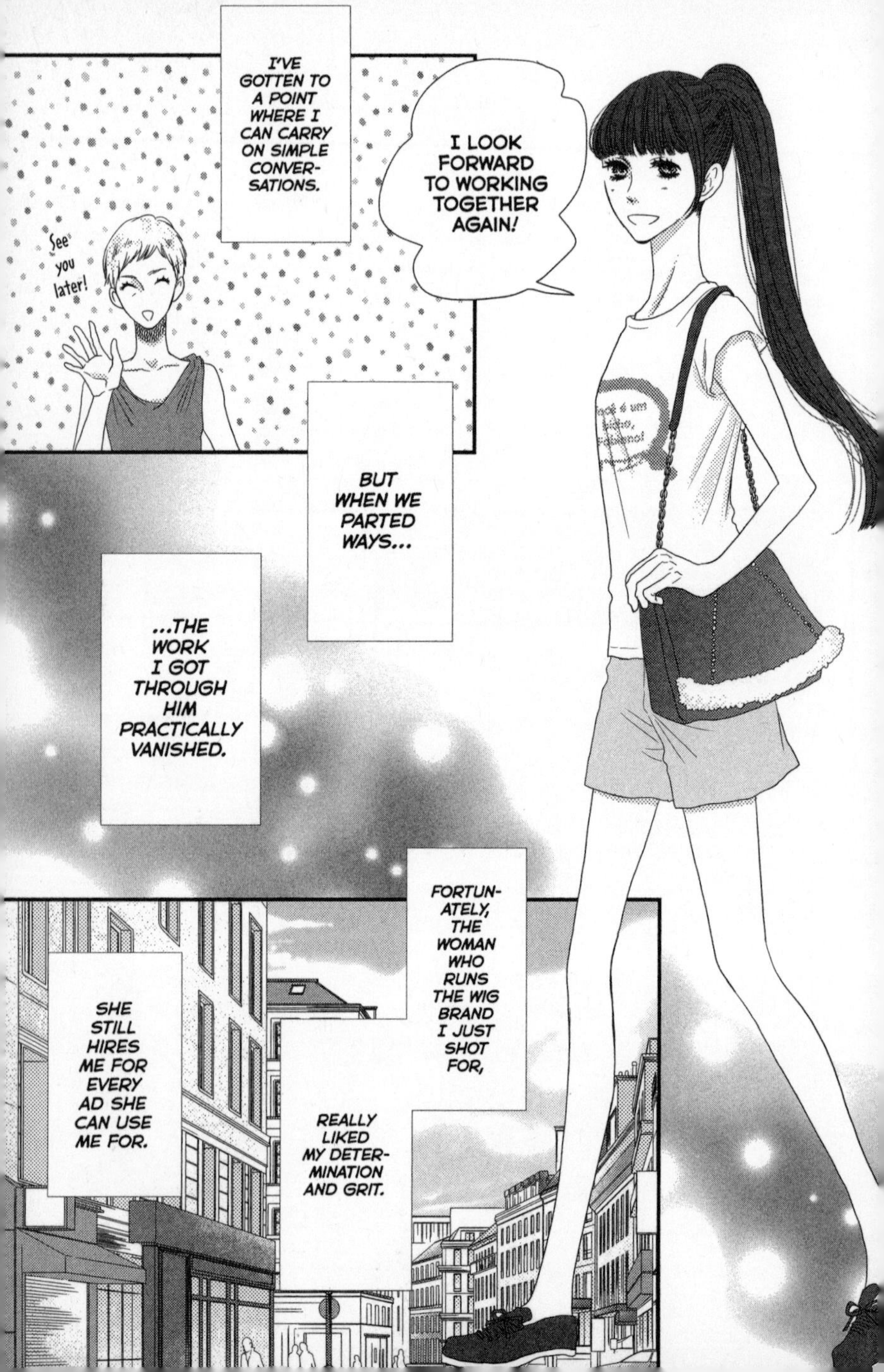
I'VE GOTTEN TO A POINT WHERE I CAN CARRY ON SIMPLE CONVERSATIONS.
I LOOK FORWARD TO WORKING TOGETHER AGAIN!
See you later!
BUT WHEN WE PARTED WAYS...
...THE WORK I GOT THROUGH HIM PRACTICALLY VANISHED.
FORTUNATELY, THE WOMAN WHO RUNS THE WIG BRAND I JUST SHOT FOR,
REALLY LIKED MY DETERMINATION AND GRIT.
SHE STILL HIRES ME FOR EVERY AD SHE CAN USE ME FOR.

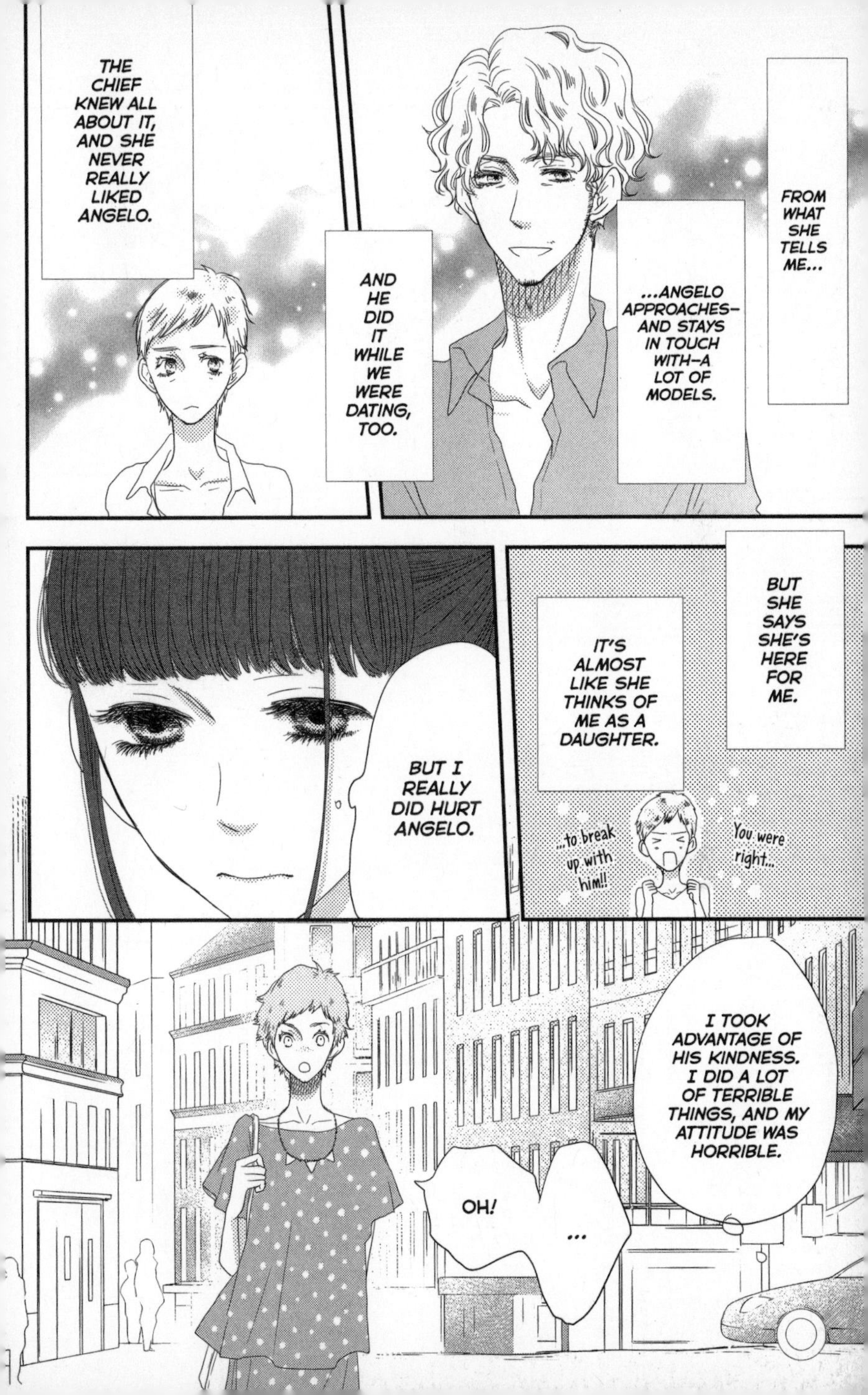
FROM WHAT SHE TELLS ME...
...ANGELO APPROACHES—AND STAYS IN TOUCH WITH—A LOT OF MODELS.
AND HE DID IT WHILE WE WERE DATING, TOO.
THE CHIEF KNEW ALL ABOUT IT, AND SHE NEVER REALLY LIKED ANGELO.
BUT SHE SAYS SHE'S HERE FOR ME.
IT'S ALMOST LIKE SHE THINKS OF ME AS A DAUGHTER.
You were right...
...to break up with him!!
BUT I REALLY DID HURT ANGELO.
I TOOK ADVANTAGE OF HIS KINDNESS. I DID A LOT OF TERRIBLE THINGS, AND MY ATTITUDE WAS HORRIBLE.
OH!
...

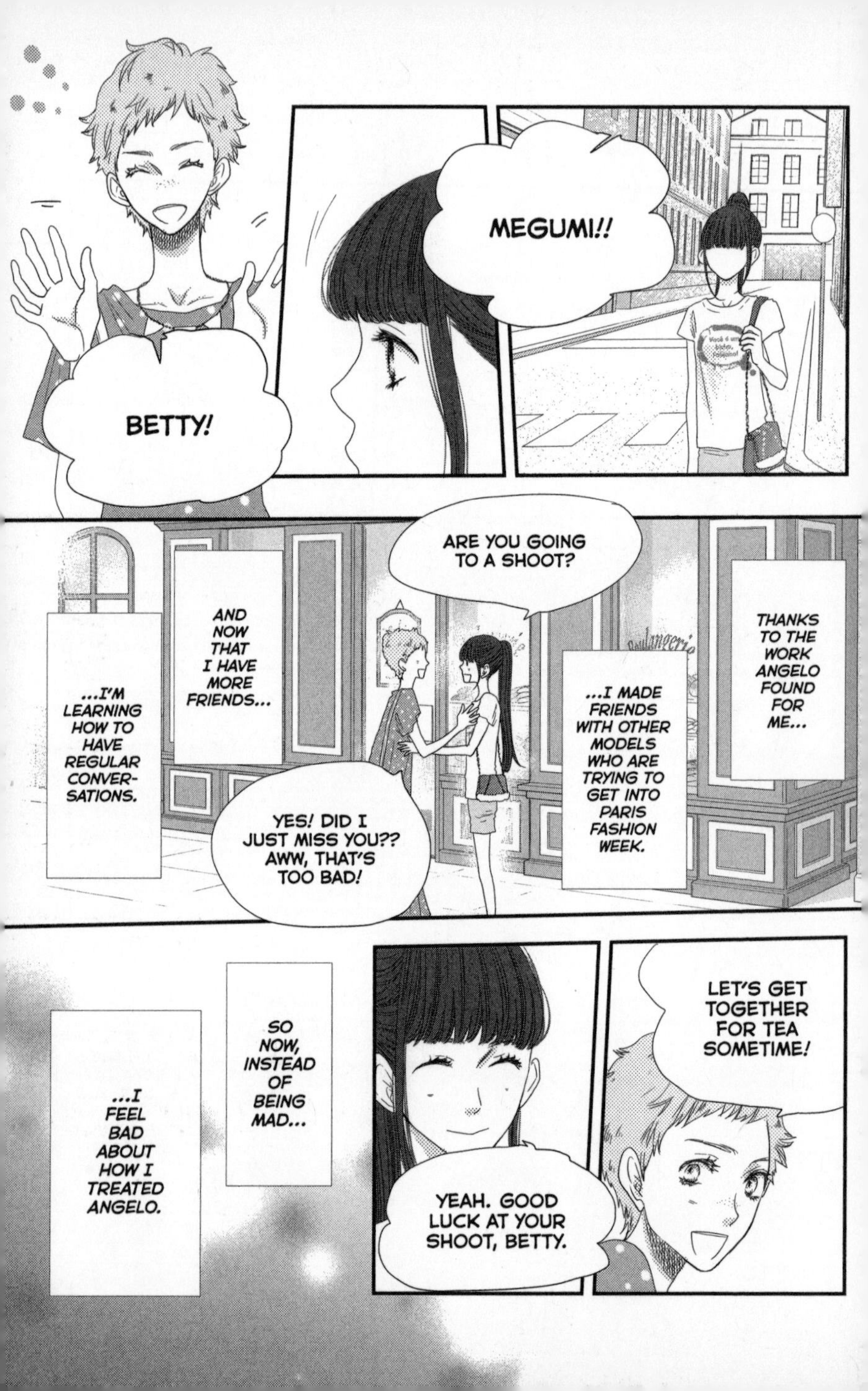
MEGUMI!!
BETTY!
THANKS TO THE WORK ANGELO FOUND FOR ME...
ARE YOU GOING TO A SHOOT?
...I MADE FRIENDS WITH OTHER MODELS WHO ARE TRYING TO GET INTO PARIS FASHION WEEK.
AND NOW THAT I HAVE MORE FRIENDS...
YES! DID I JUST MISS YOU?? AWW, THAT'S TOO BAD!
...I'M LEARNING HOW TO HAVE REGULAR CONVER-SATIONS.
LET'S GET TOGETHER FOR TEA SOMETIME!
YEAH. GOOD LUCK AT YOUR SHOOT, BETTY.
SO NOW, INSTEAD OF BEING MAD...
...I FEEL BAD ABOUT HOW I TREATED ANGELO.

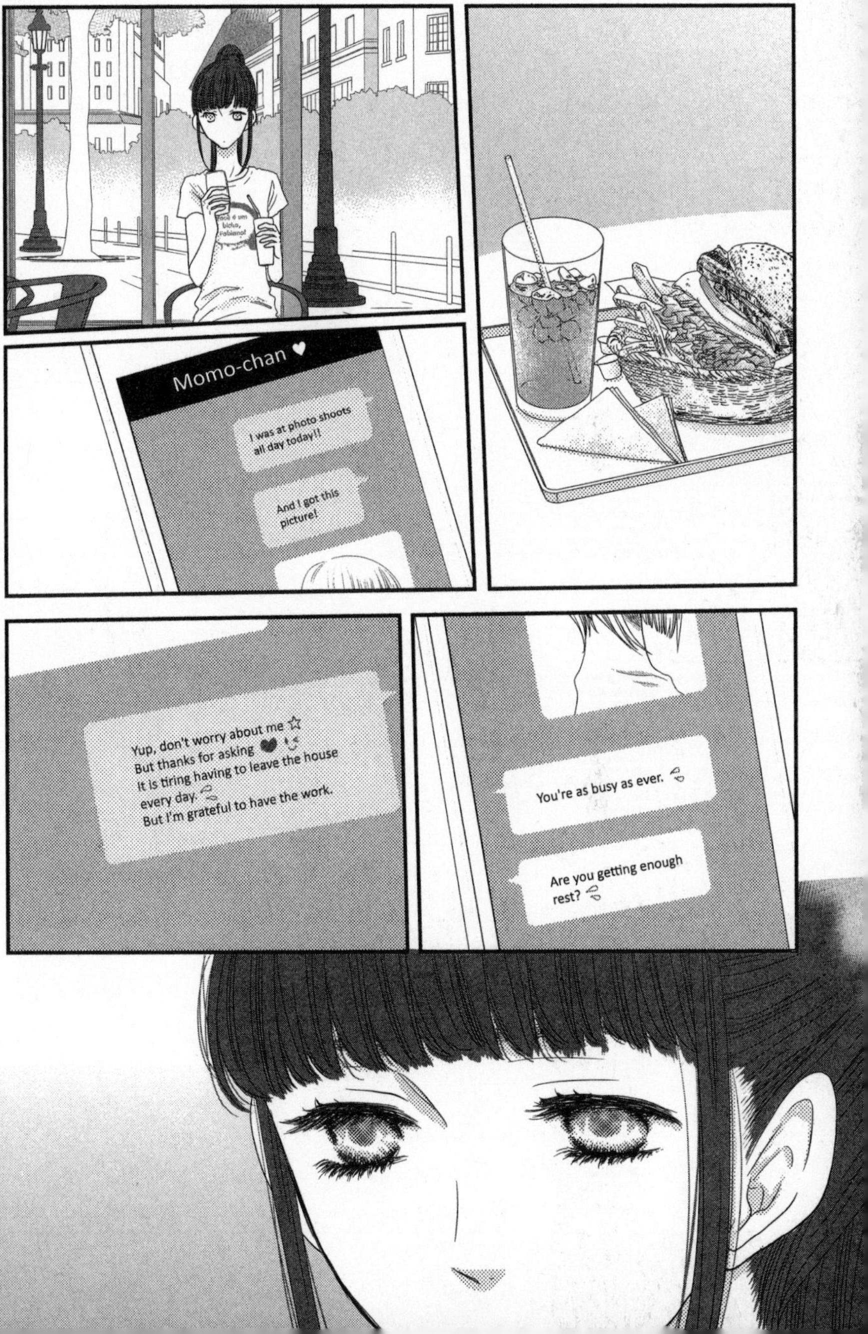
Momo-chan ♥
I was at photo shoots all day today!!
And I got this picture!
You're as busy as ever.
Are you getting enough rest?
Yup, don't worry about me ☆
But thanks for asking
It is tiring having to leave the house every day.
But I'm grateful to have the work.

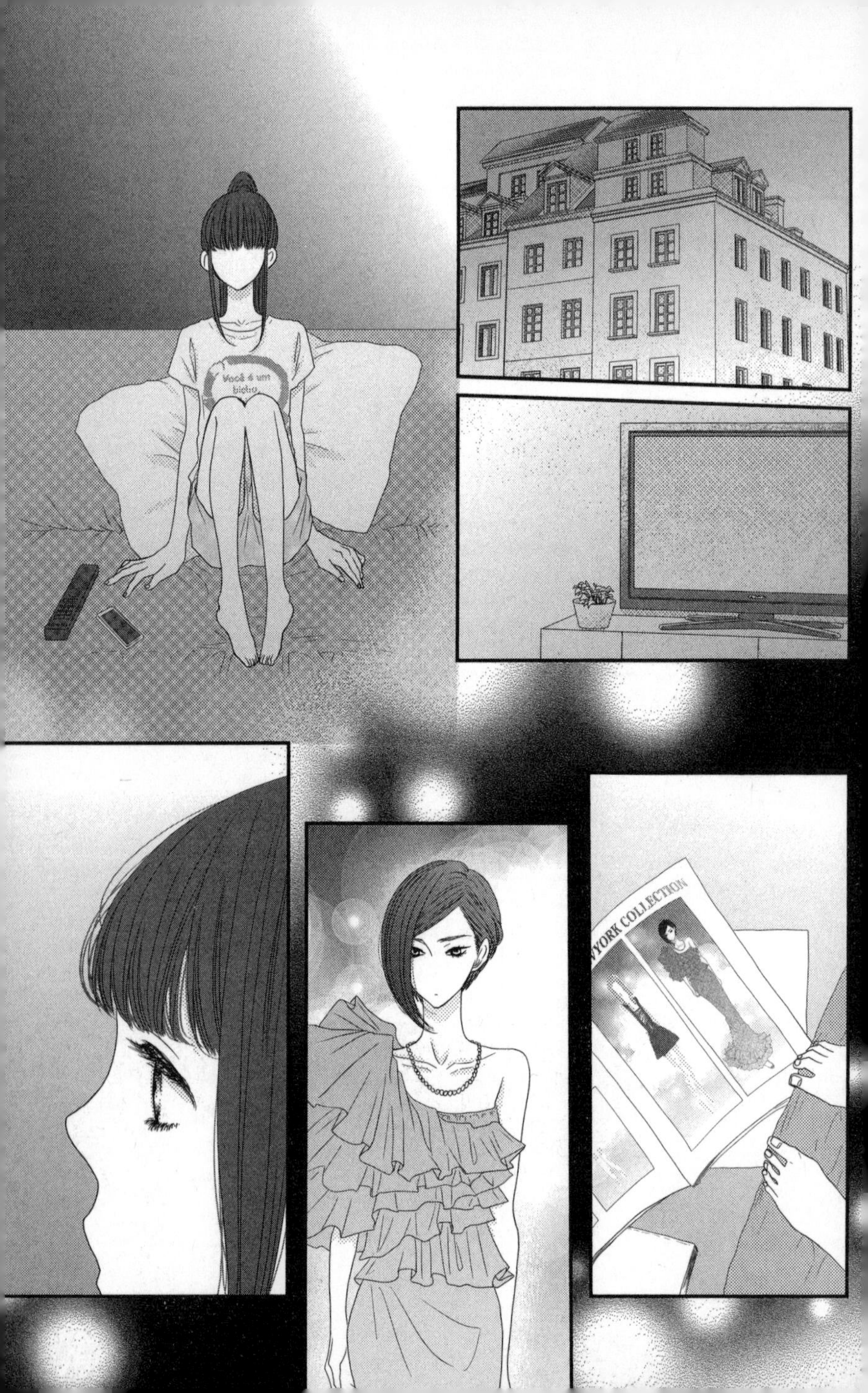
Você é um
bicho
WYORK COLLECTION

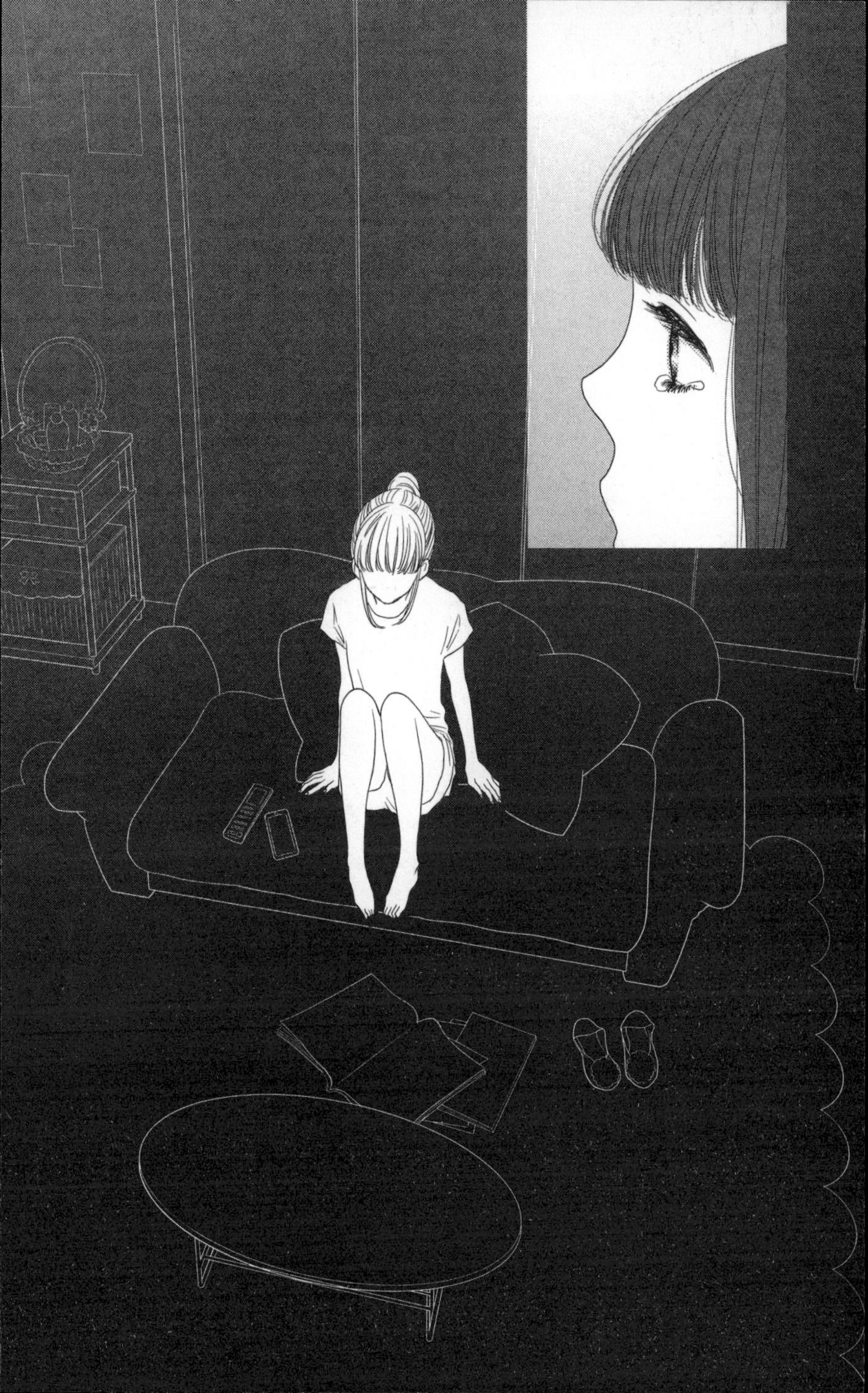

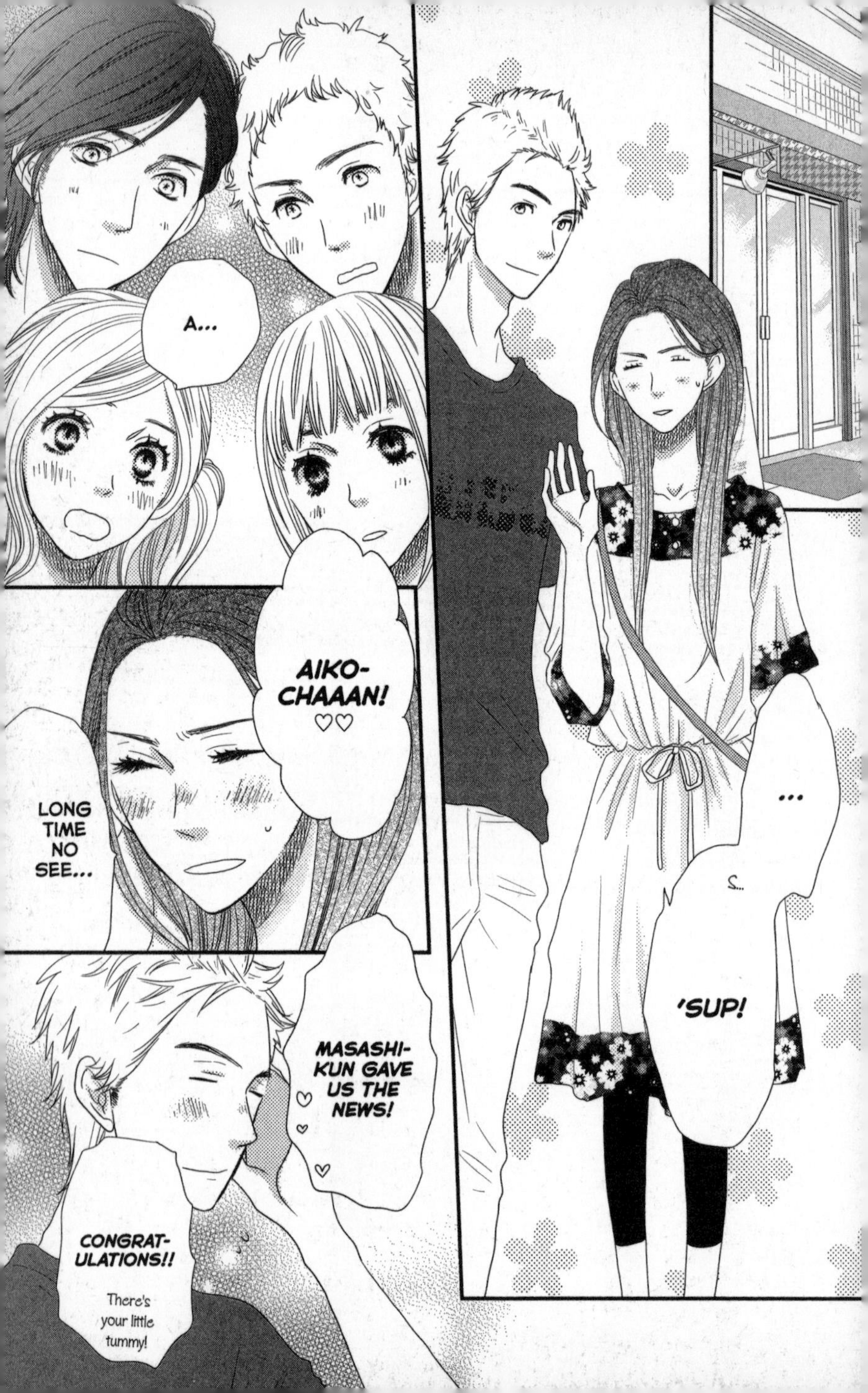
...
S...
'SUP!
A...
AIKO-CHAAAN! ♡♡
LONG TIME NO SEE...
MASASHI-KUN GAVE US THE NEWS!
CONGRATULATIONS!!
There's your little tummy!

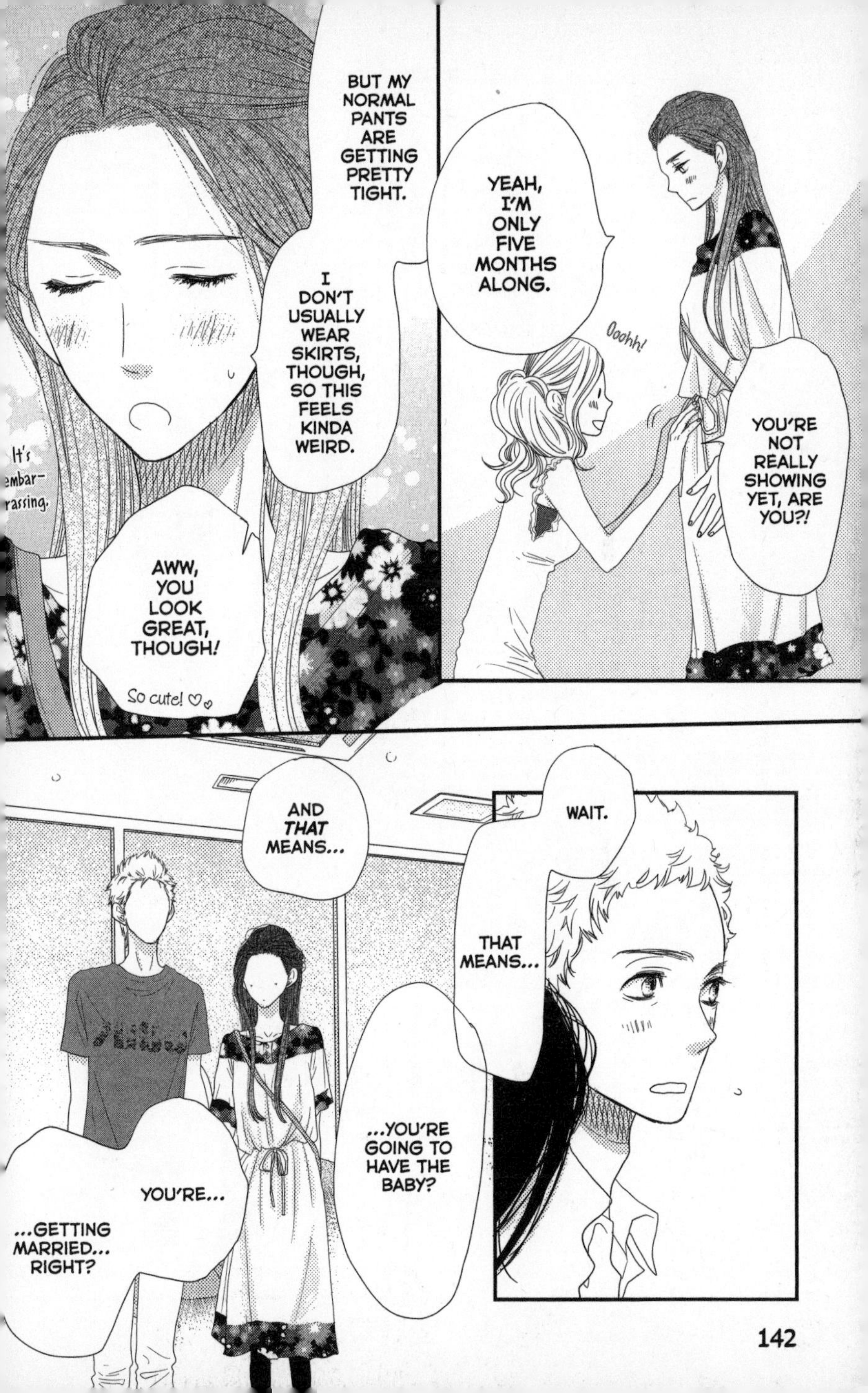
Ooohh!
YOU'RE NOT REALLY SHOWING YET, ARE YOU?!
YEAH, I'M ONLY FIVE MONTHS ALONG.
BUT MY NORMAL PANTS ARE GETTING PRETTY TIGHT.
I DON'T USUALLY WEAR SKIRTS, THOUGH, SO THIS FEELS KINDA WEIRD.
It's embar- rassing.
AWW, YOU LOOK GREAT, THOUGH!
So cute! ♡♡
WAIT.
THAT MEANS...
...YOU'RE GOING TO HAVE THE BABY?
AND *THAT* MEANS...
YOU'RE...
...GETTING MARRIED... RIGHT?

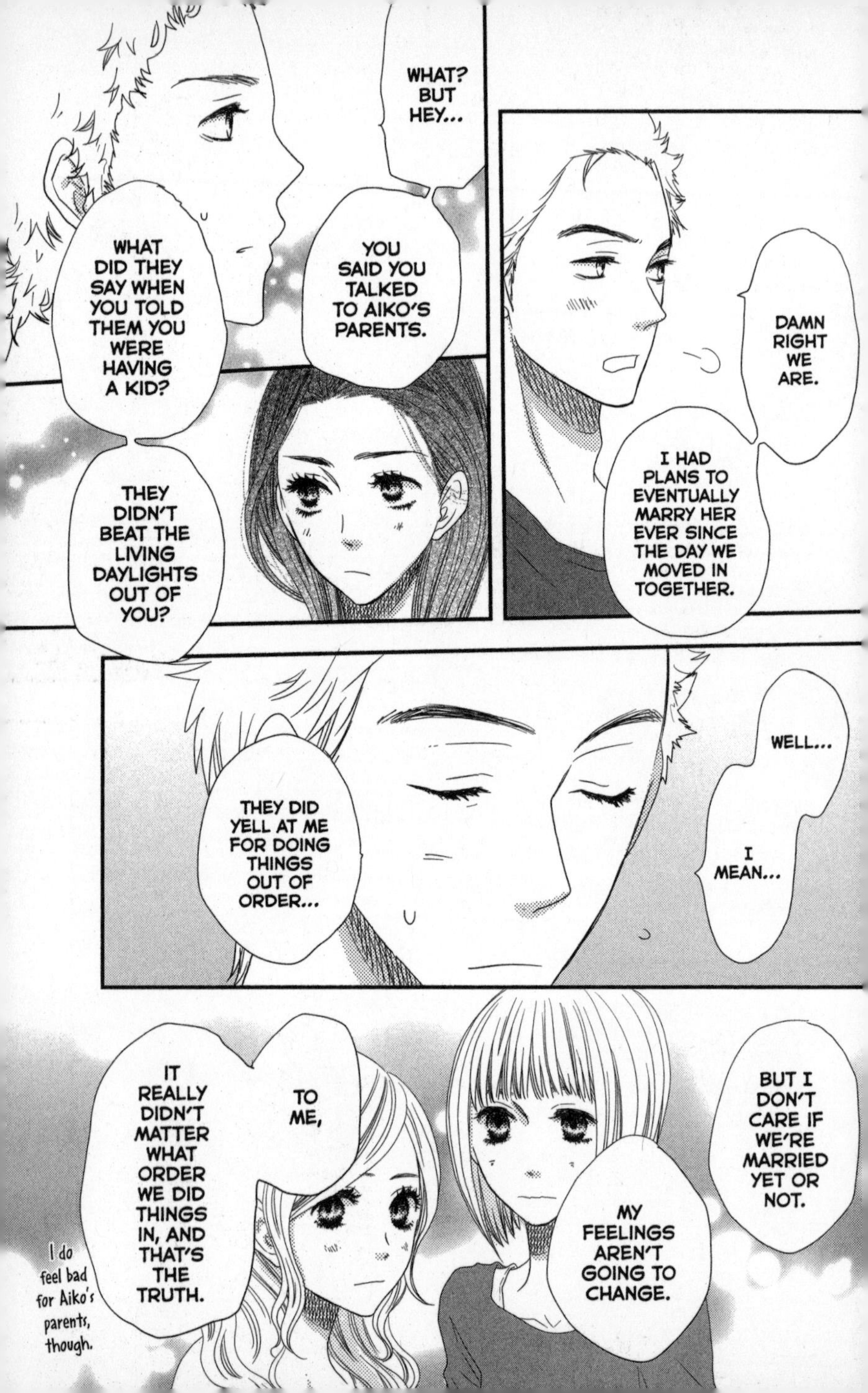
DAMN RIGHT WE ARE.
I HAD PLANS TO EVENTUALLY MARRY HER EVER SINCE THE DAY WE MOVED IN TOGETHER.
WHAT? BUT HEY...
YOU SAID YOU TALKED TO AIKO'S PARENTS.
WHAT DID THEY SAY WHEN YOU TOLD THEM YOU WERE HAVING A KID?
THEY DIDN'T BEAT THE LIVING DAYLIGHTS OUT OF YOU?
WELL...
I MEAN...
THEY DID YELL AT ME FOR DOING THINGS OUT OF ORDER...
BUT I DON'T CARE IF WE'RE MARRIED YET OR NOT.
MY FEELINGS AREN'T GOING TO CHANGE.
TO ME,
IT REALLY DIDN'T MATTER WHAT ORDER WE DID THINGS IN, AND THAT'S THE TRUTH.
I do feel bad for Aiko's parents, though.

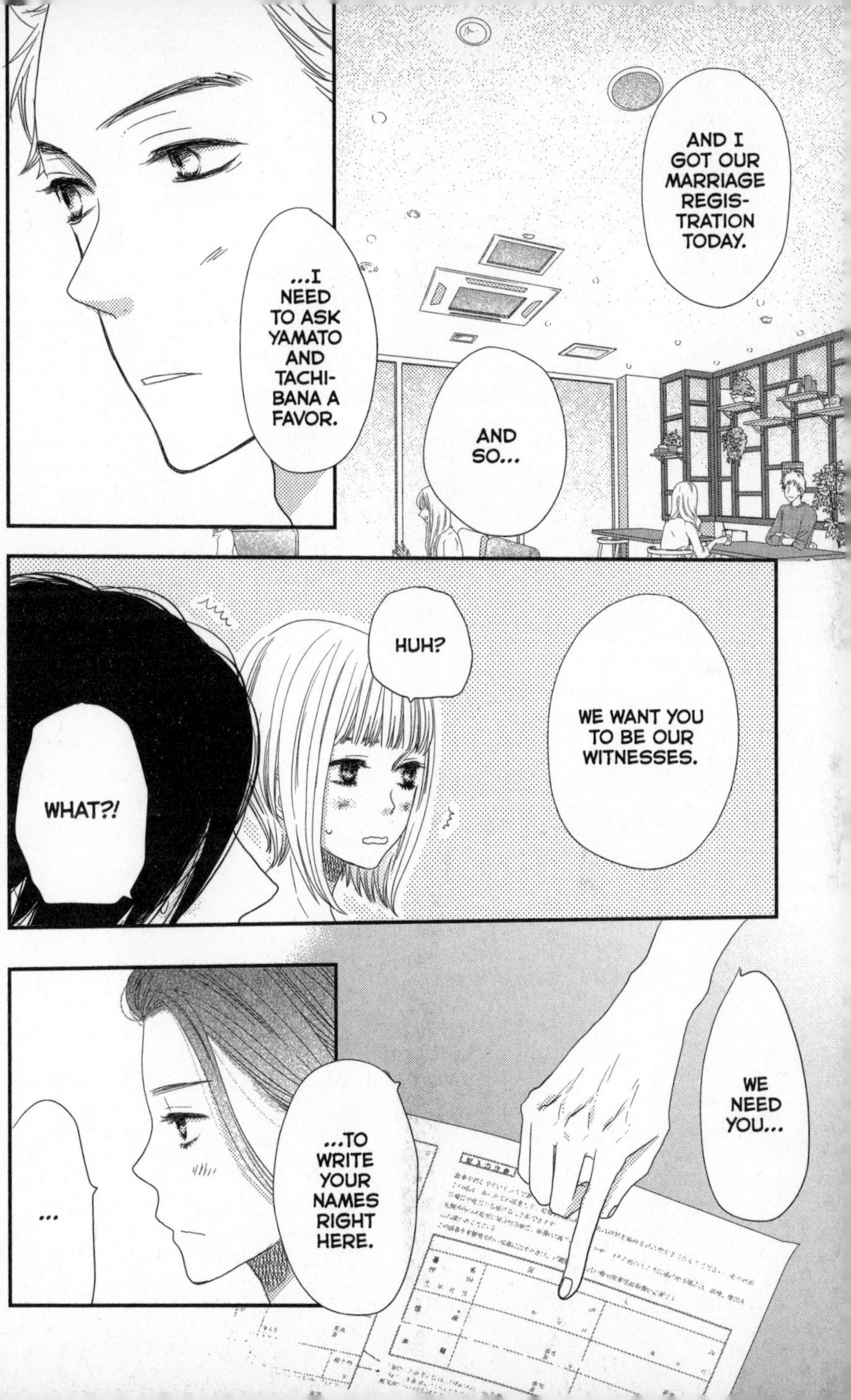
AND I GOT OUR MARRIAGE REGIS-TRATION TODAY.
AND SO...
...I NEED TO ASK YAMATO AND TACHI-BANA A FAVOR.
WE WANT YOU TO BE OUR WITNESSES.
HUH?
WHAT?!
WE NEED YOU...
...TO WRITE YOUR NAMES RIGHT HERE.
...

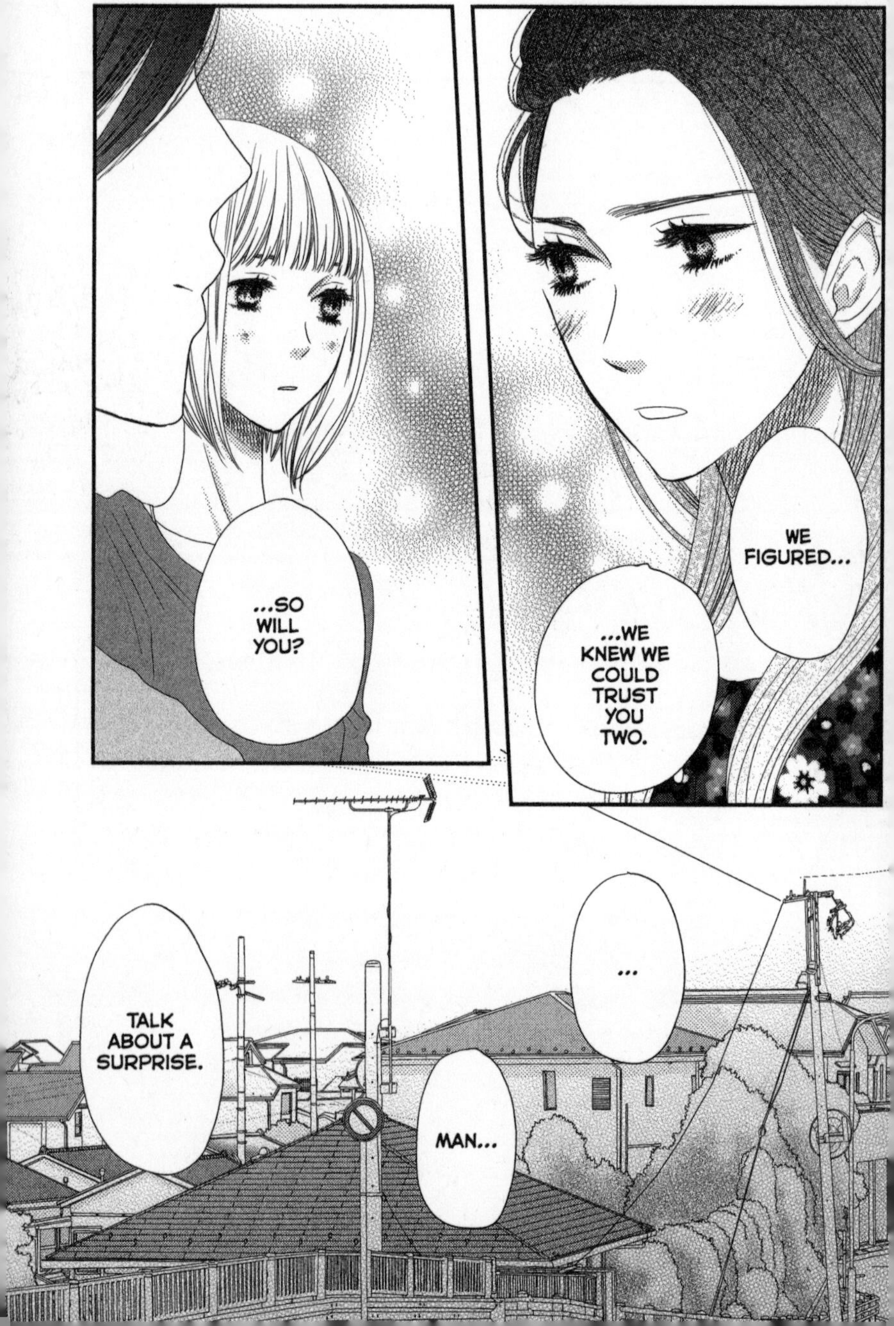
WE FIGURED...
...WE KNEW WE COULD TRUST YOU TWO.
...SO WILL YOU?
...
MAN...
TALK ABOUT A SURPRISE.

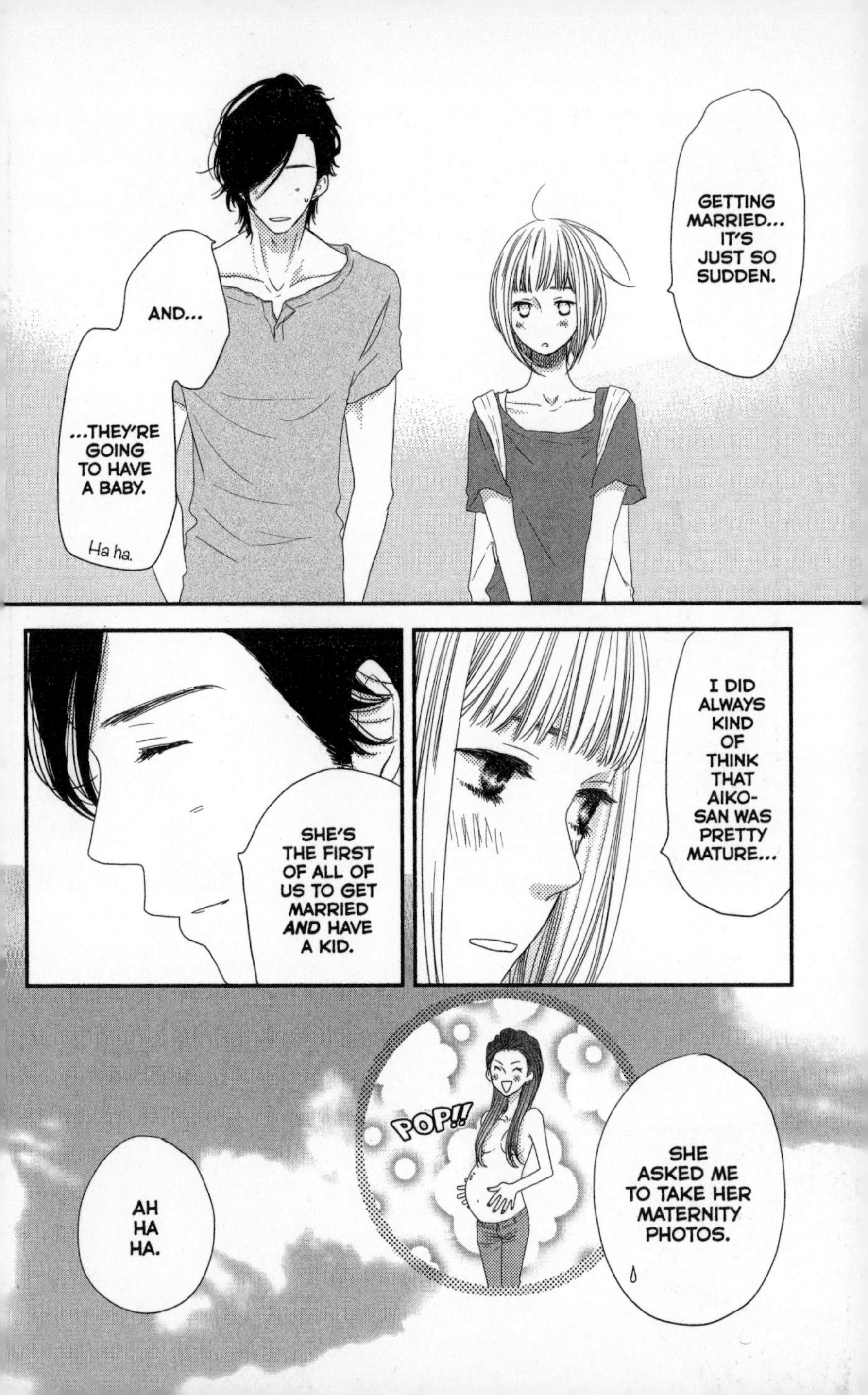
GETTING MARRIED... IT'S JUST SO SUDDEN.
AND...
...THEY'RE GOING TO HAVE A BABY.
Ha ha.
I DID ALWAYS KIND OF THINK THAT AIKO-SAN WAS PRETTY MATURE...
SHE'S THE FIRST OF ALL OF US TO GET MARRIED *AND* HAVE A KID.
SHE ASKED ME TO TAKE HER MATERNITY PHOTOS.
POP!!
AH HA HA.

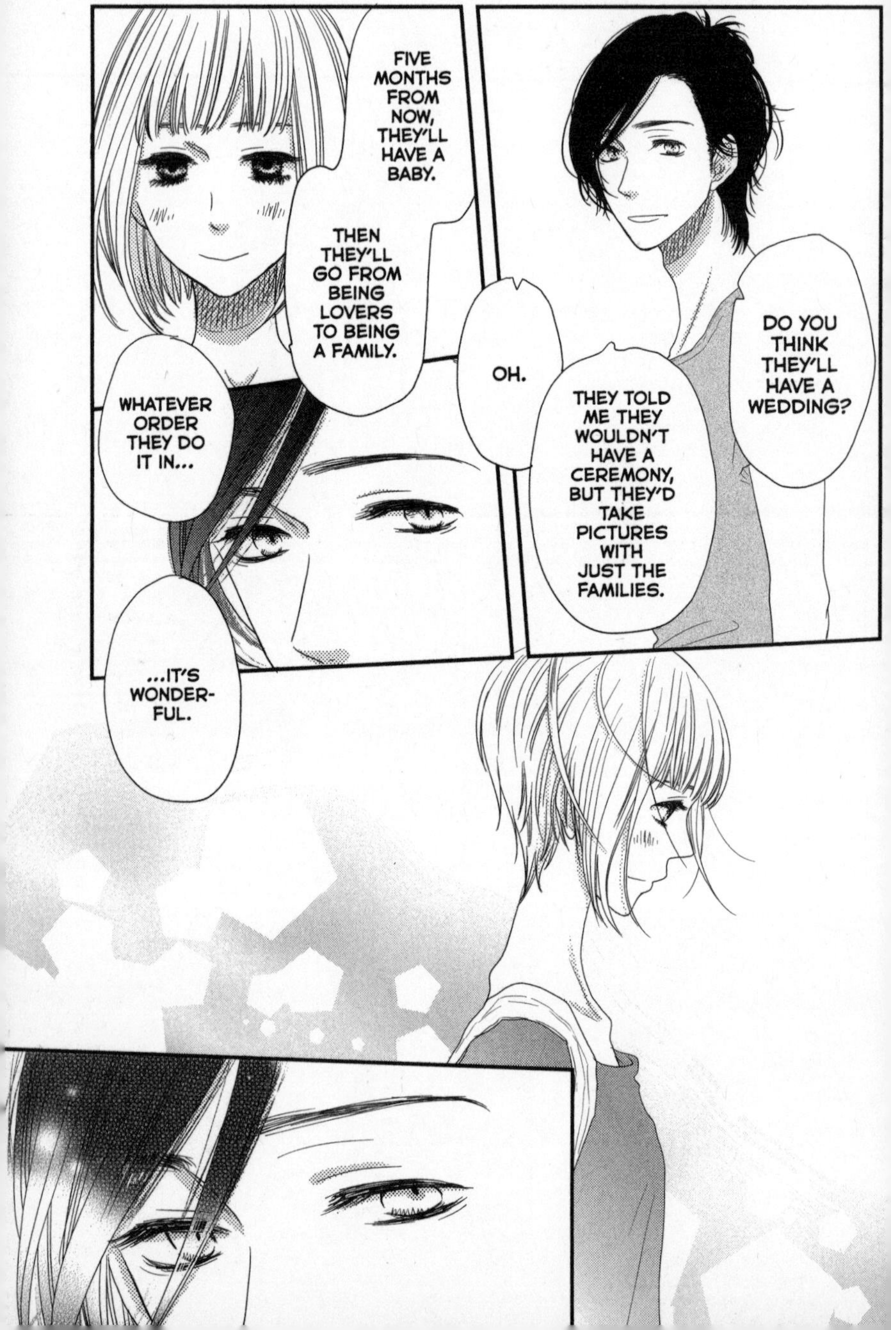
DO YOU THINK THEY'LL HAVE A WEDDING?
THEY TOLD ME THEY WOULDN'T HAVE A CEREMONY, BUT THEY'D TAKE PICTURES WITH JUST THE FAMILIES.
OH.
FIVE MONTHS FROM NOW, THEY'LL HAVE A BABY.
THEN THEY'LL GO FROM BEING LOVERS TO BEING A FAMILY.
WHATEVER ORDER THEY DO IT IN...
...IT'S WONDER-FUL.

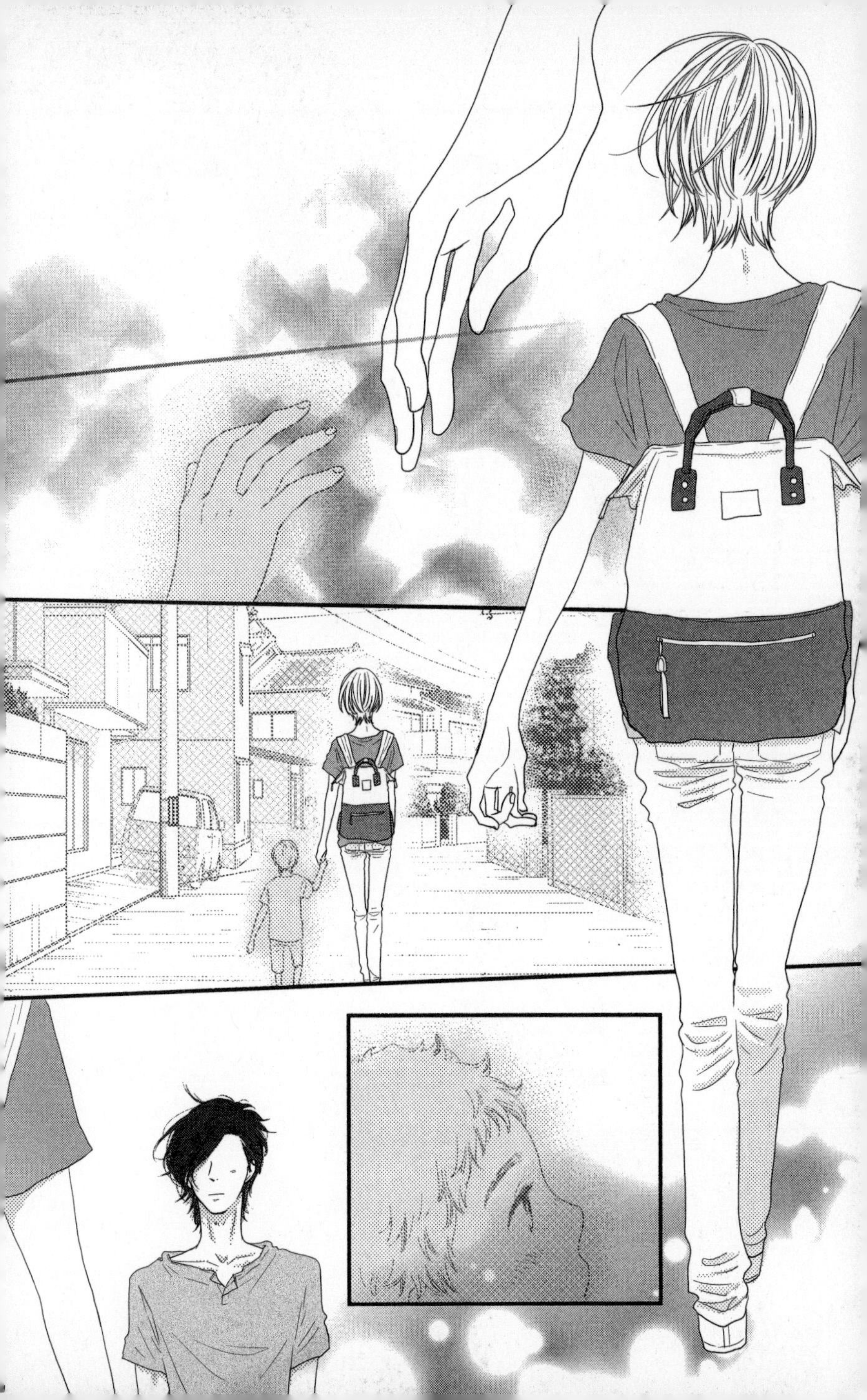

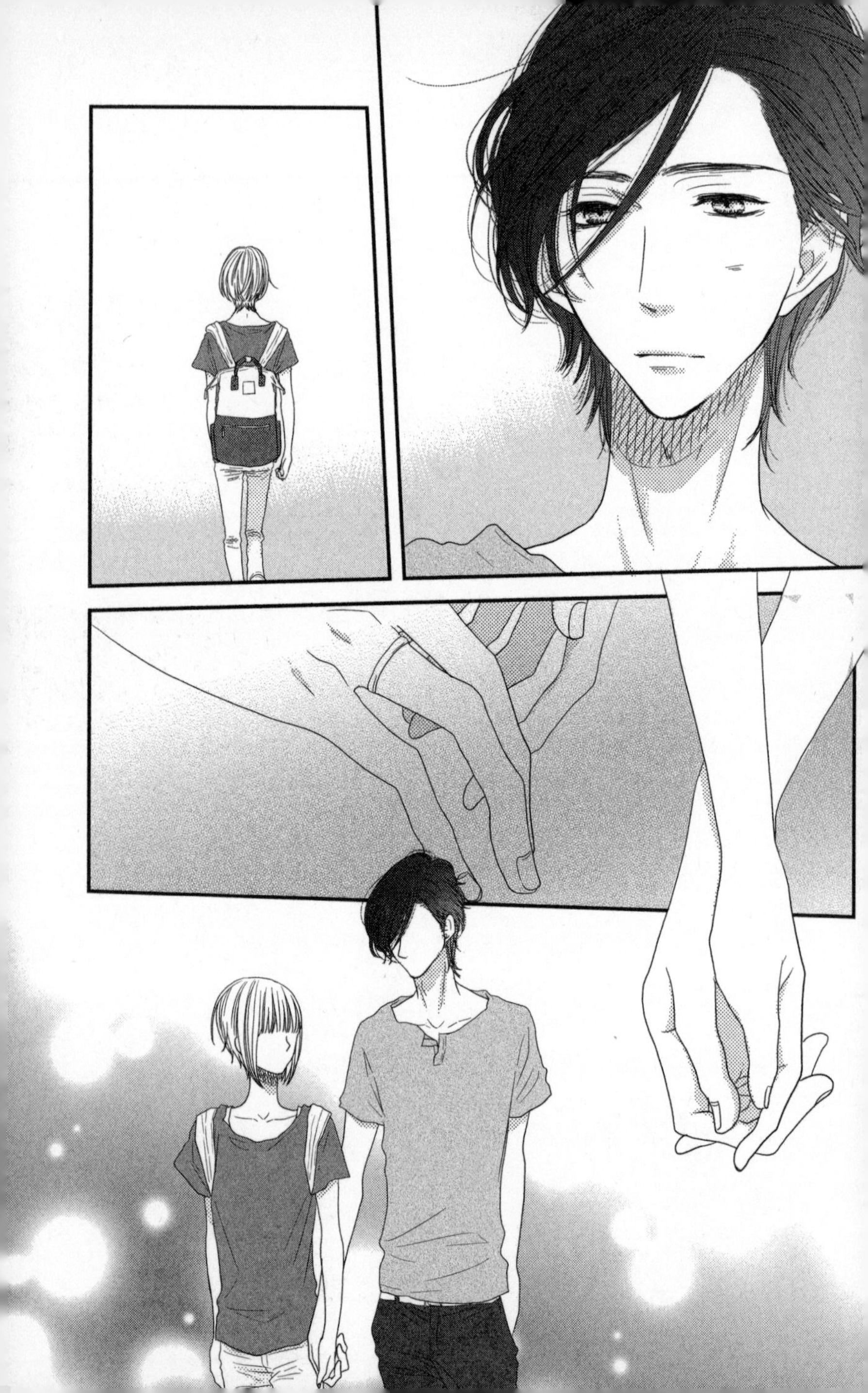

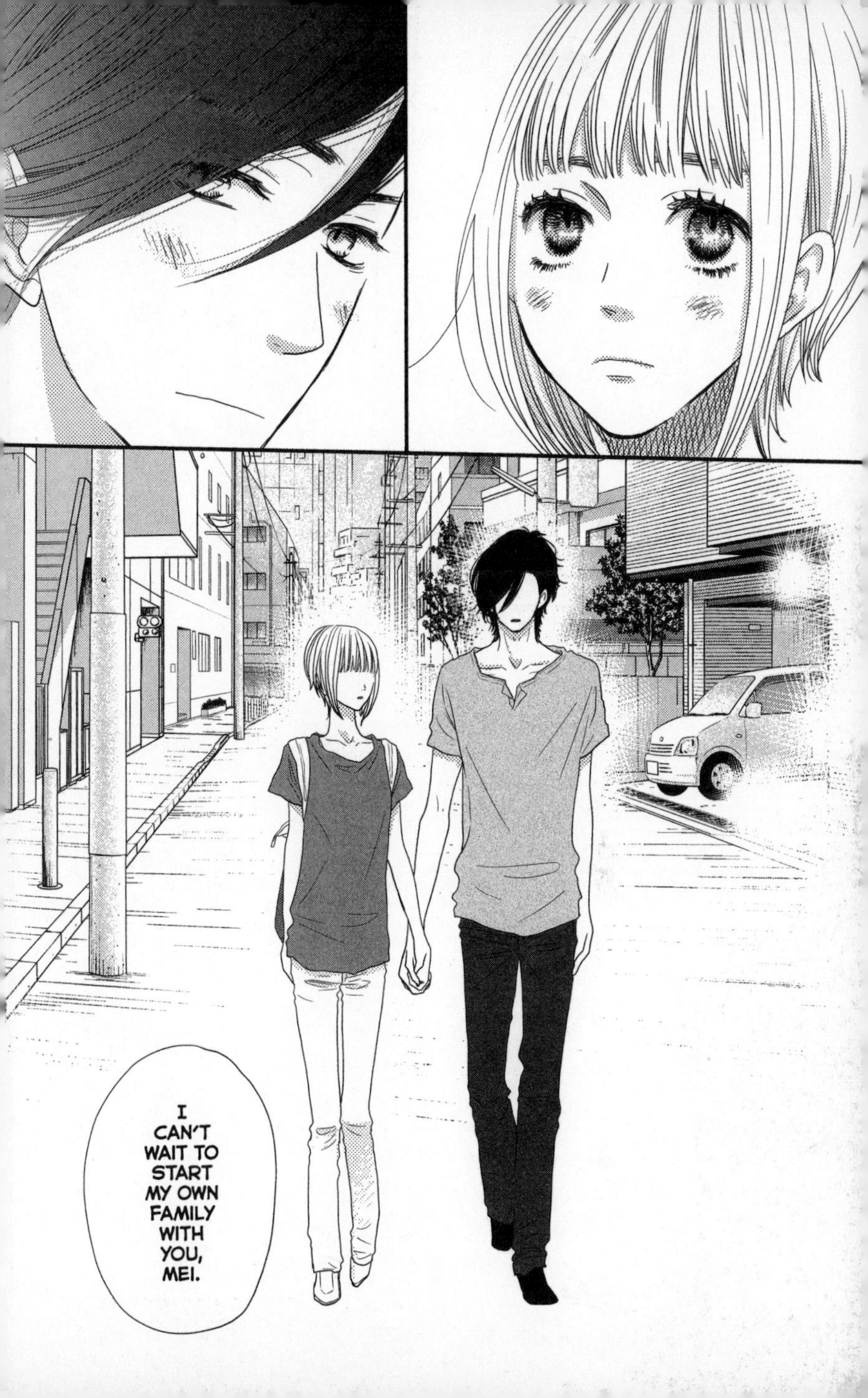
I CAN'T WAIT TO START MY OWN FAMILY WITH YOU, MEI.

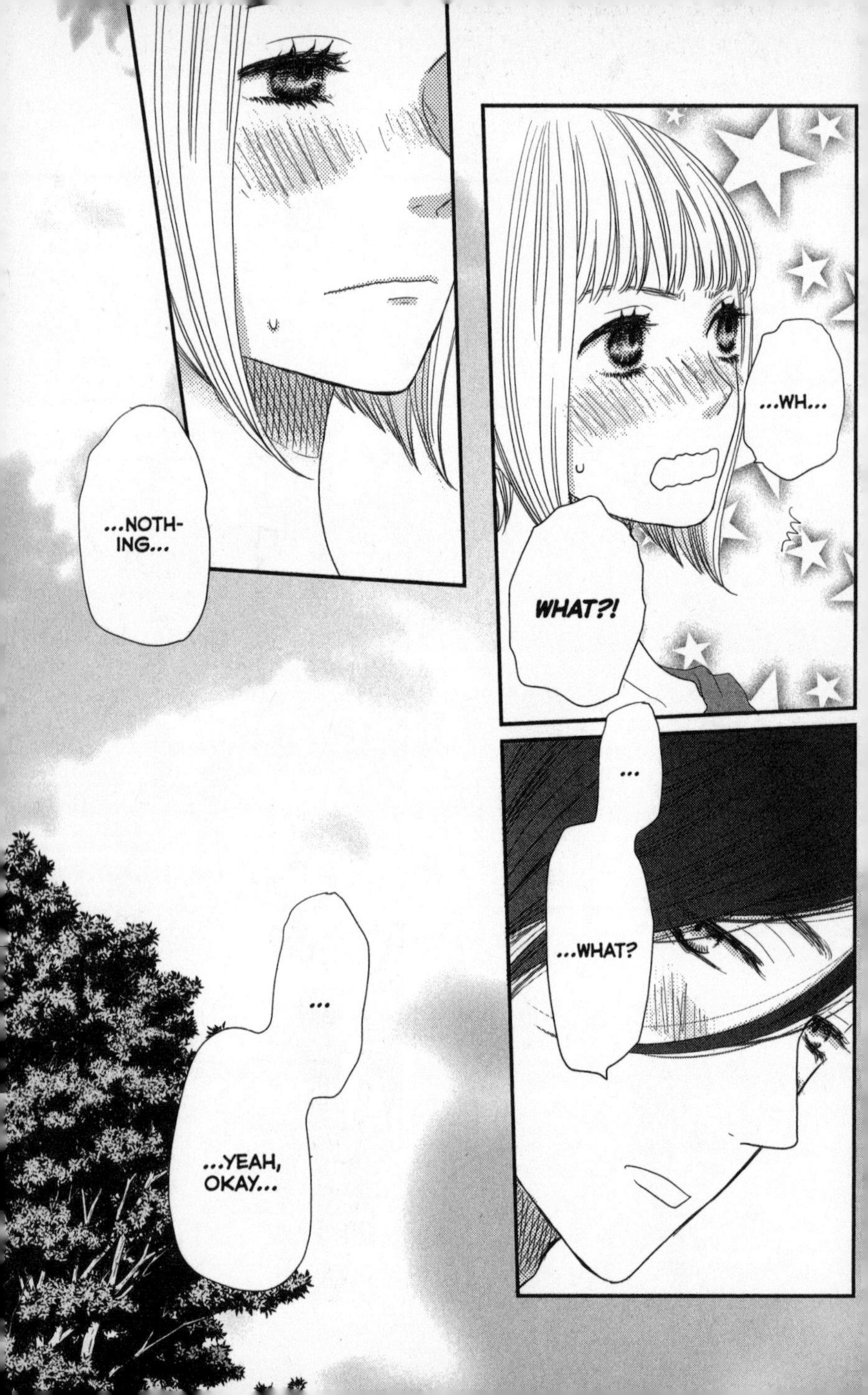
...WH...
WHAT?!
...NOTH-ING...
...
...WHAT?
...
...YEAH, OKAY...

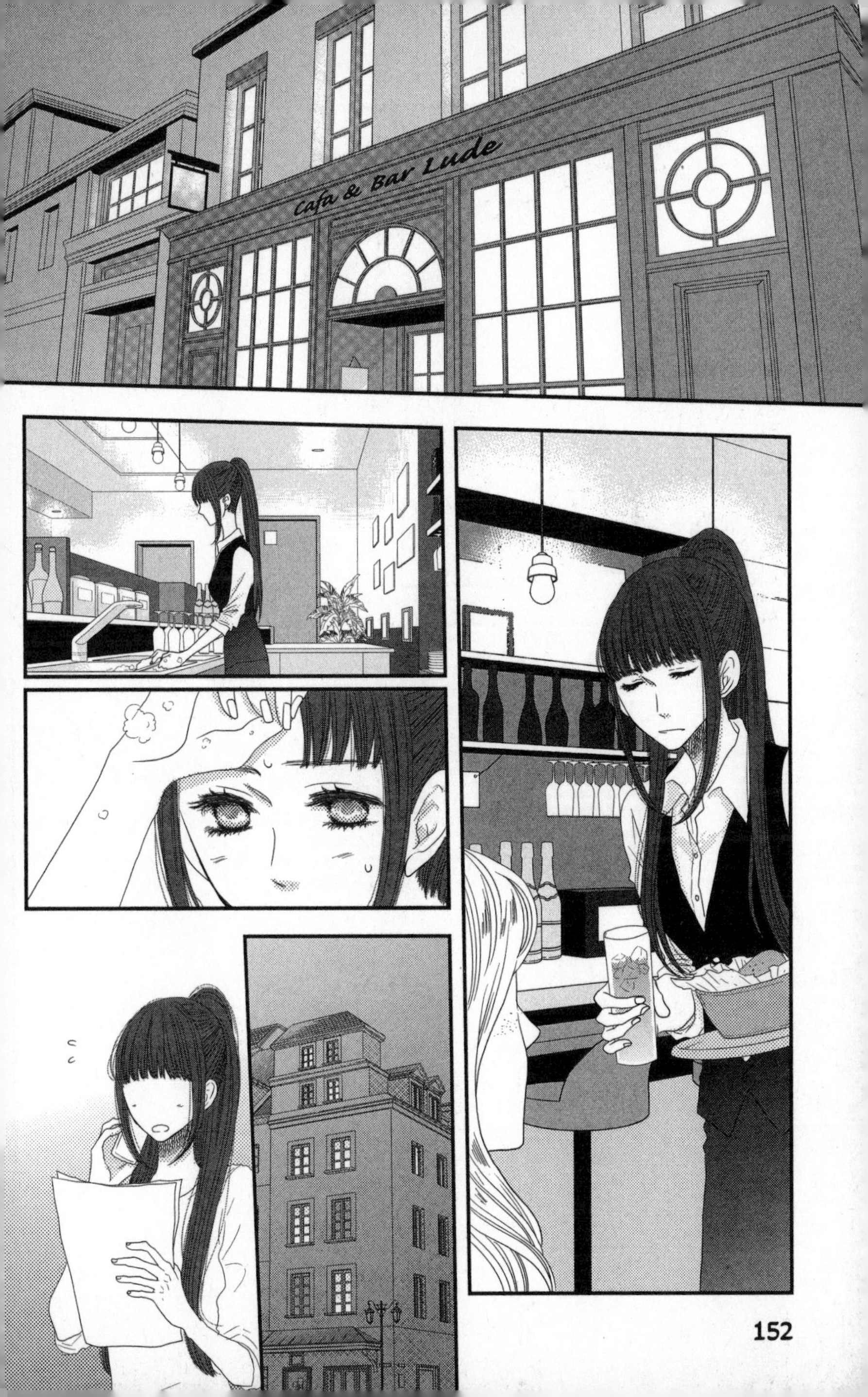
Cafa & Bar Lude

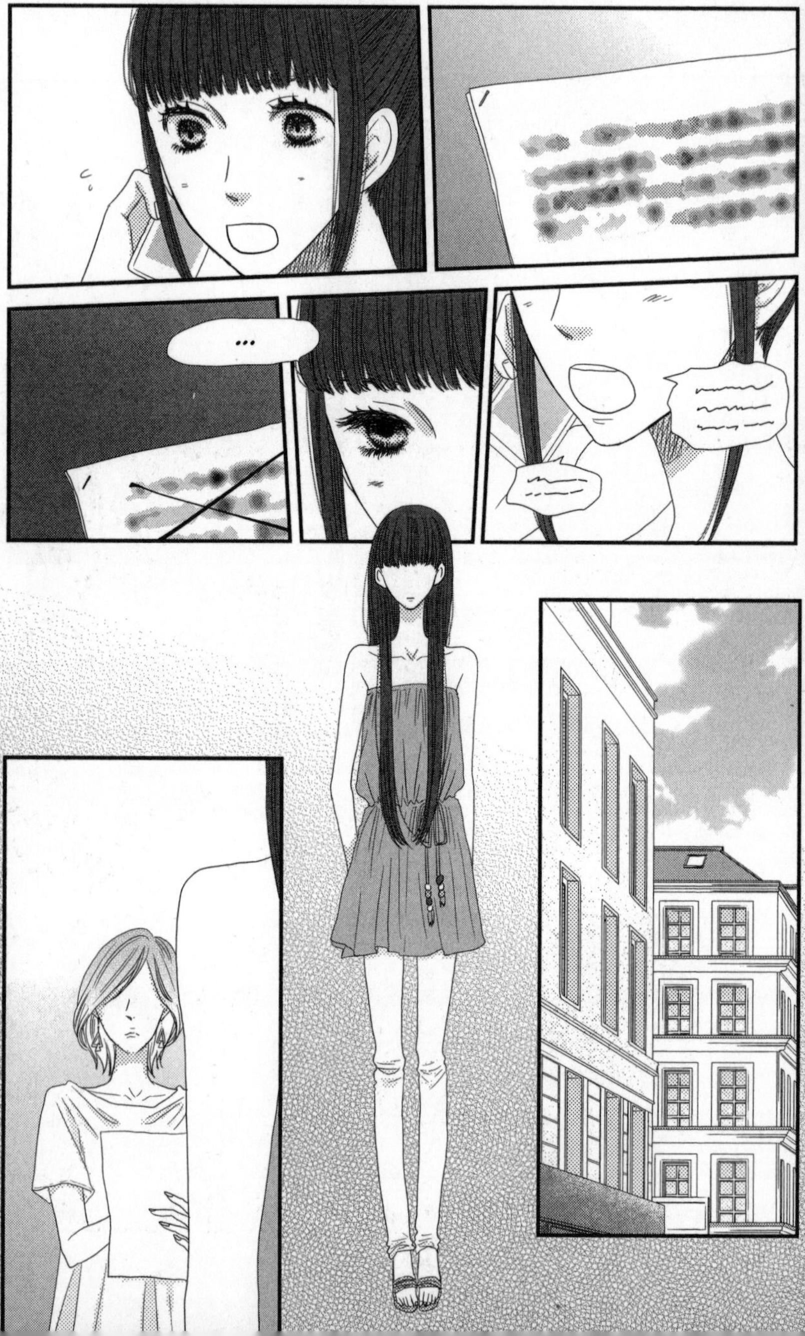
...

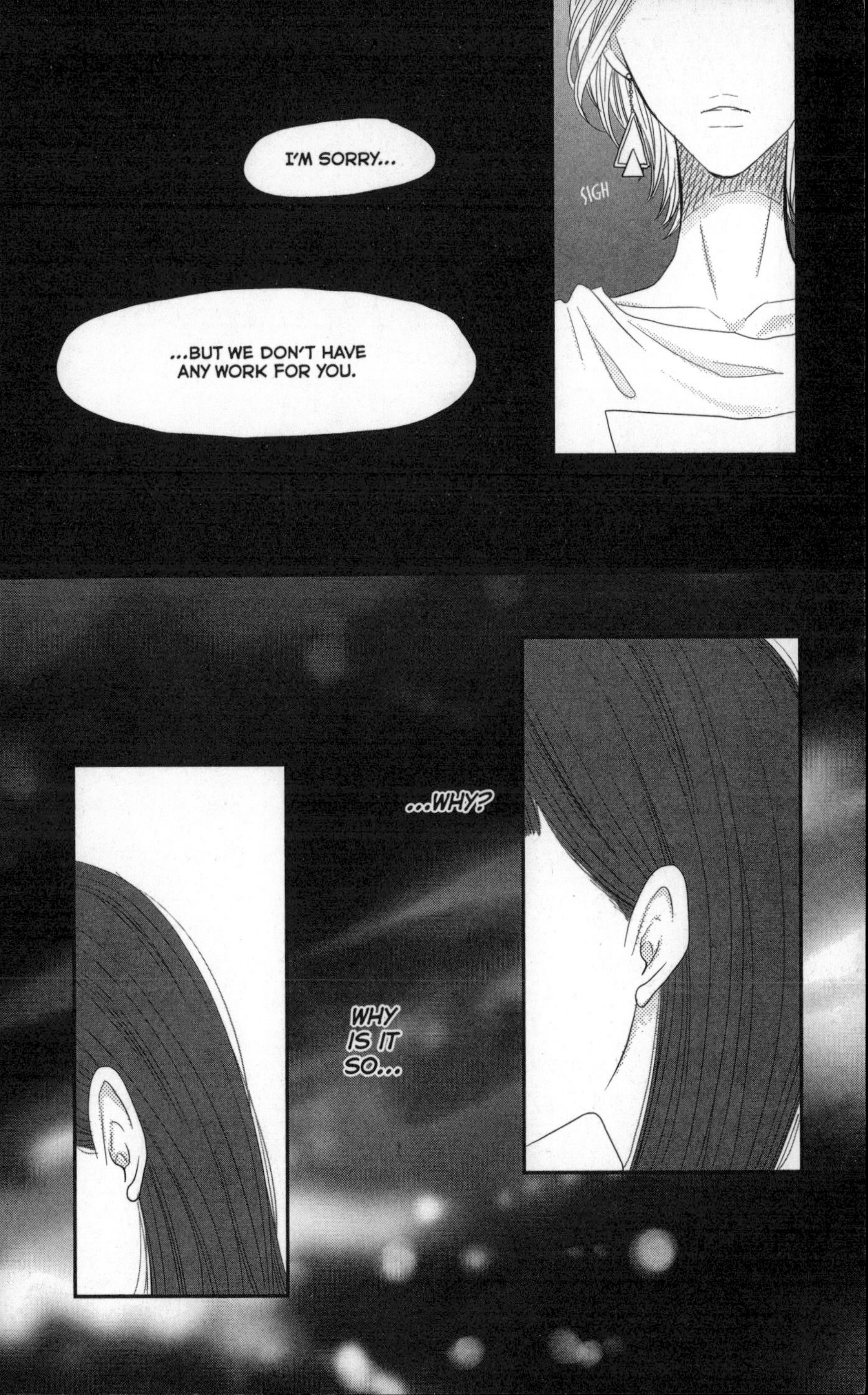
SIGH
I'M SORRY...
...BUT WE DON'T HAVE ANY WORK FOR YOU.
...WHY?
WHY IS IT SO...

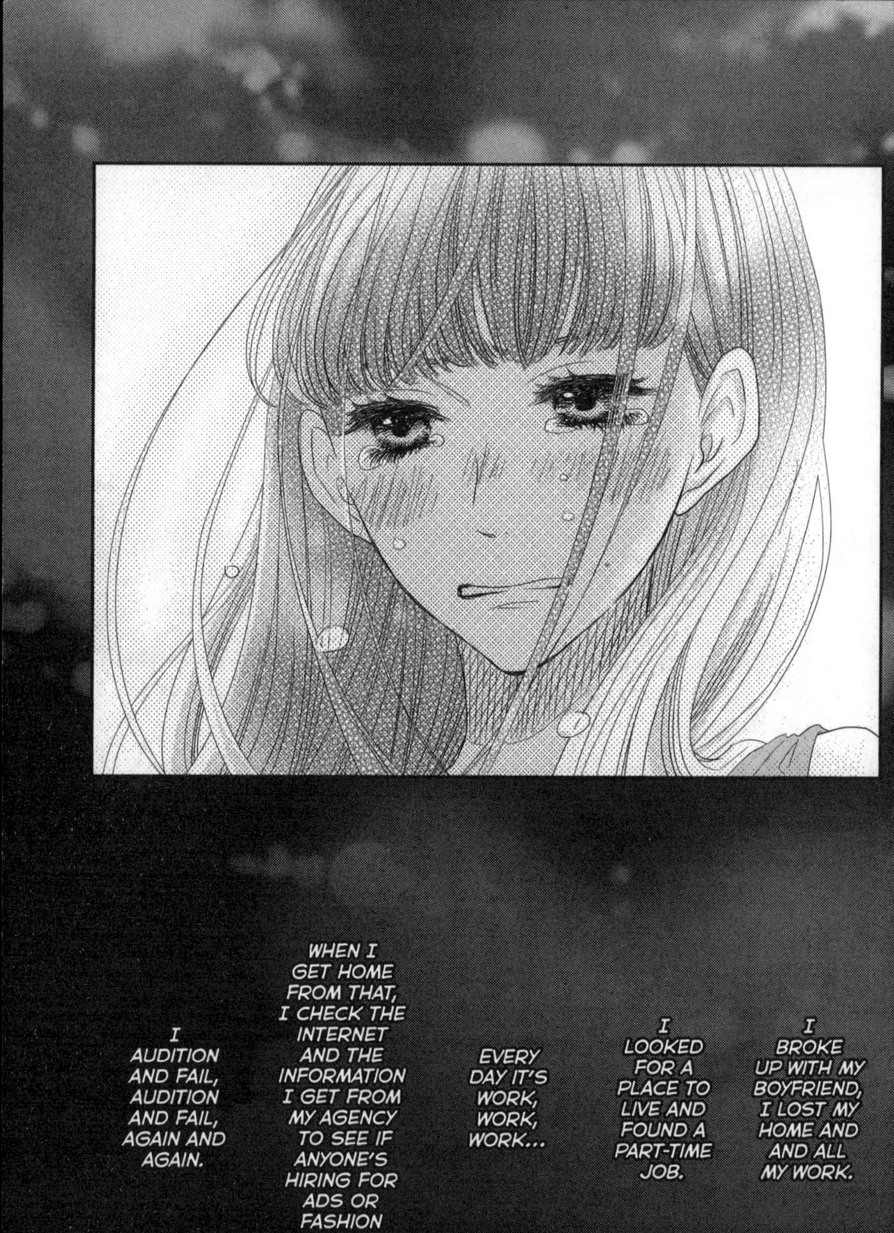
I BROKE UP WITH MY BOYFRIEND, I LOST MY HOME AND AND ALL MY WORK.
I LOOKED FOR A PLACE TO LIVE AND FOUND A PART-TIME JOB.
EVERY DAY IT'S WORK, WORK, WORK...
WHEN I GET HOME FROM THAT, I CHECK THE INTERNET AND THE INFORMATION I GET FROM MY AGENCY TO SEE IF ANYONE'S HIRING FOR ADS OR FASHION
I AUDITION AND FAIL, AUDITION AND FAIL, AGAIN AND AGAIN.

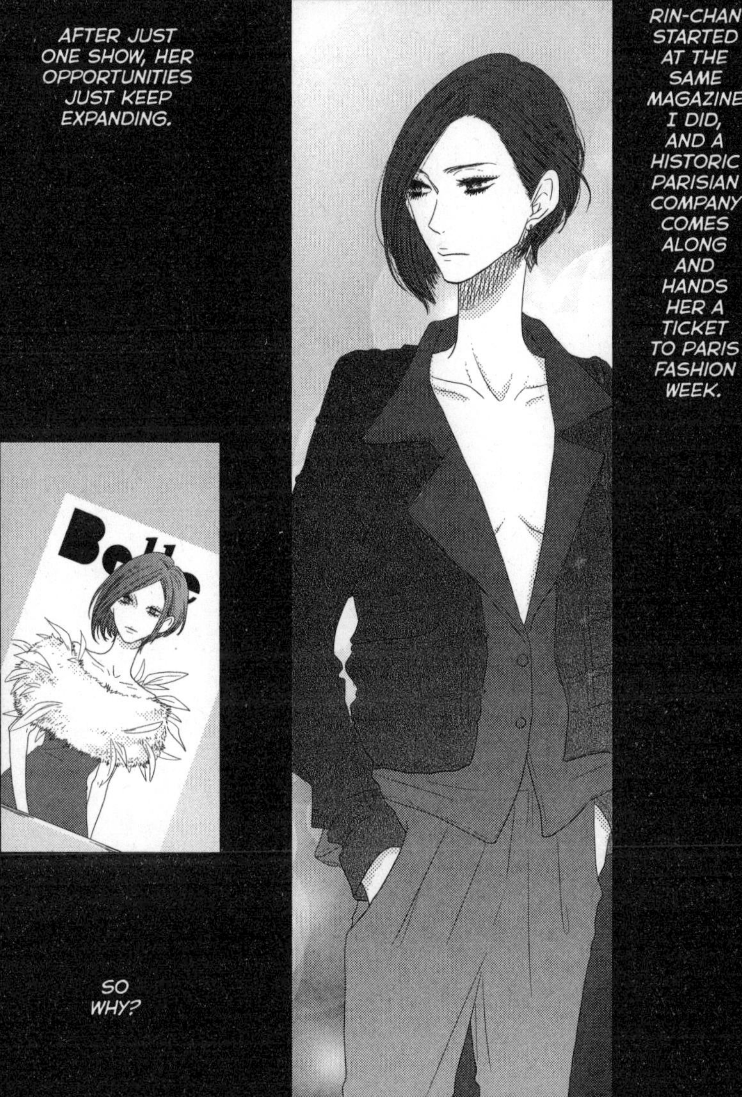
RIN-CHAN STARTED AT THE SAME MAGAZINE I DID, AND A HISTORIC PARISIAN COMPANY COMES ALONG AND HANDS HER A TICKET TO PARIS FASHION WEEK.
AFTER JUST ONE SHOW, HER OPPORTUNITIES JUST KEEP EXPANDING.
SO WHY?

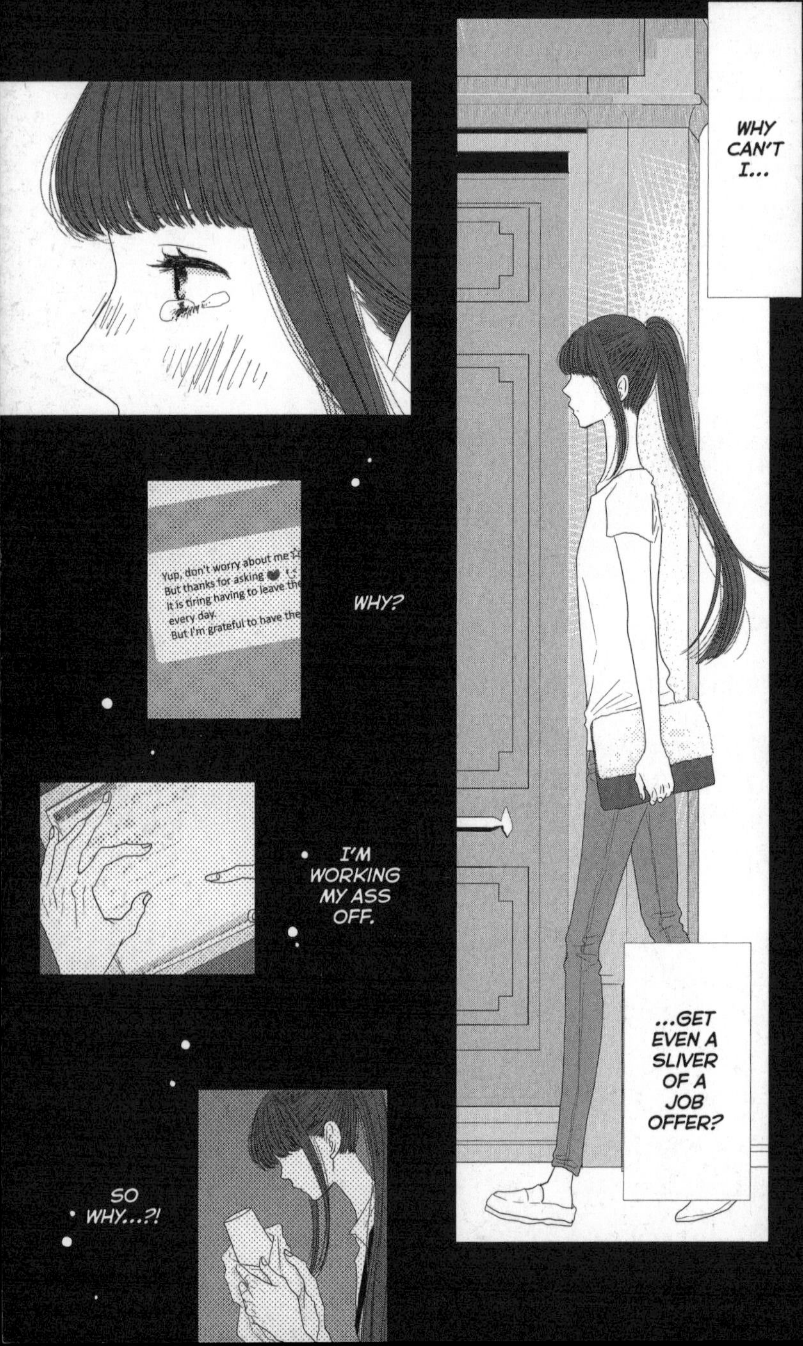
WHY CAN'T I...
...GET EVEN A SLIVER OF A JOB OFFER?
Yup, don't worry about me
But thanks for asking
It is tiring having to leave the
every day.
But I'm grateful to have the
WHY?
I'M WORKING MY ASS OFF.
SO WHY...?!

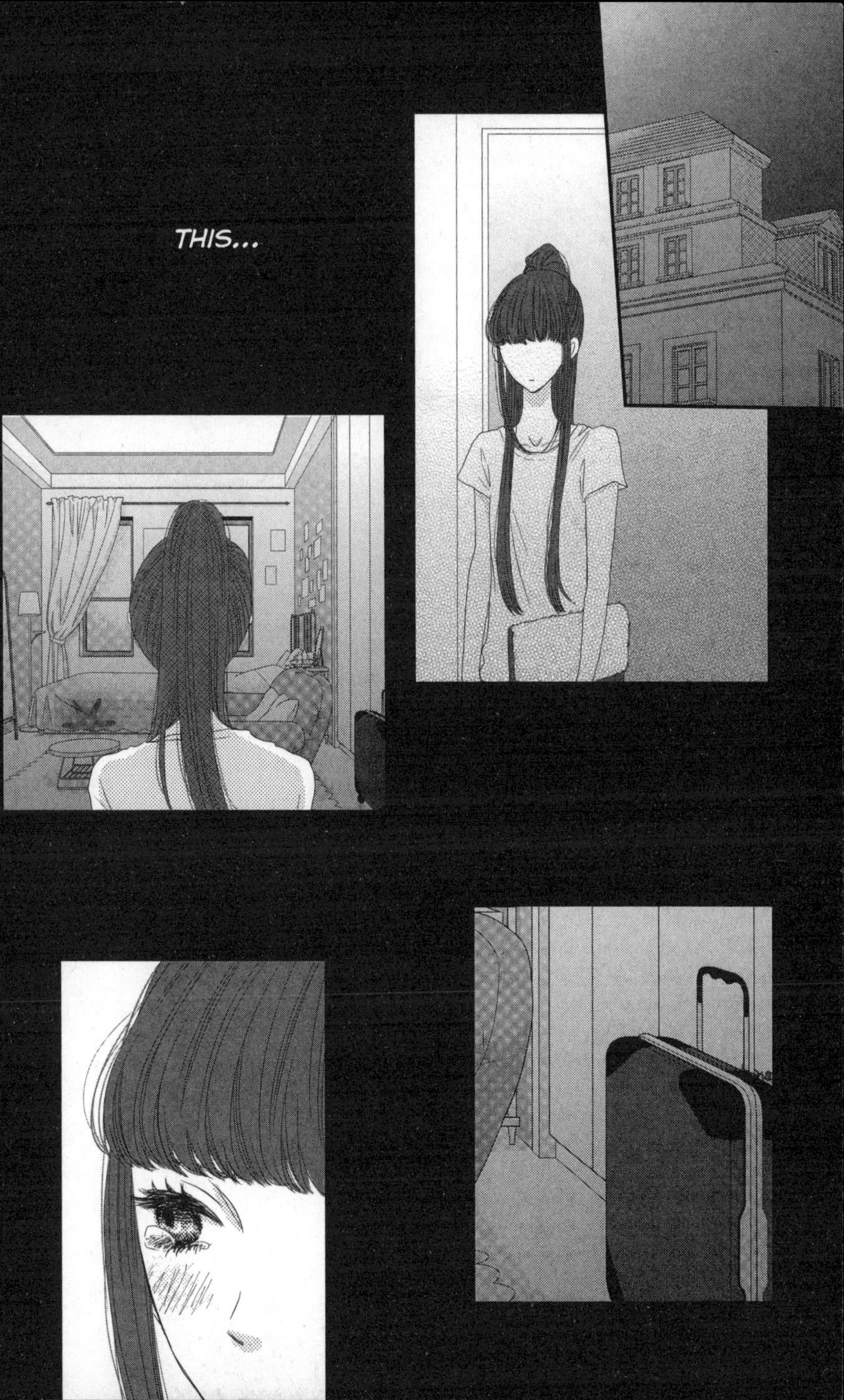
THIS...

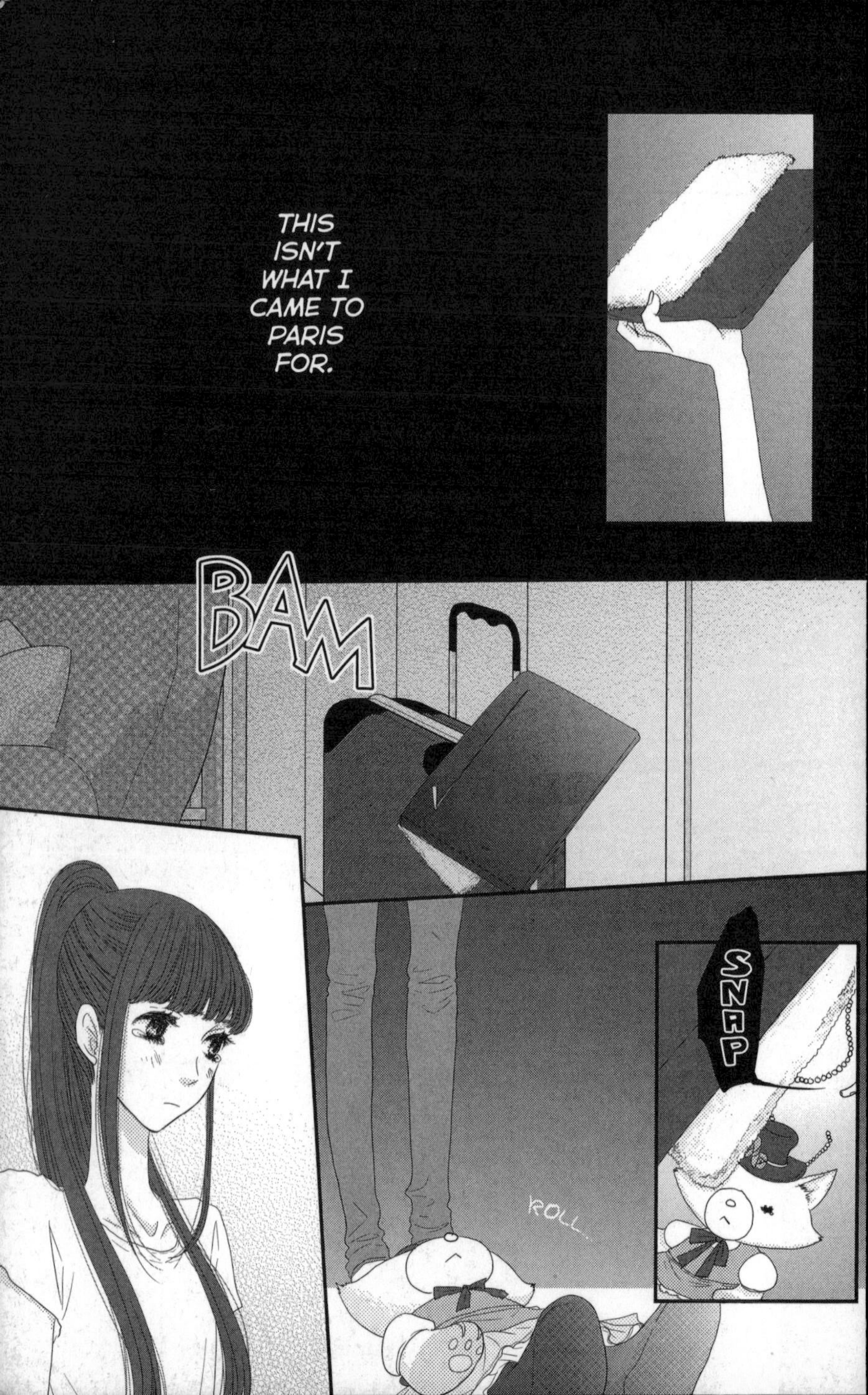
THIS ISN'T WHAT I CAME TO PARIS FOR.
BAM
SNAP
ROLL

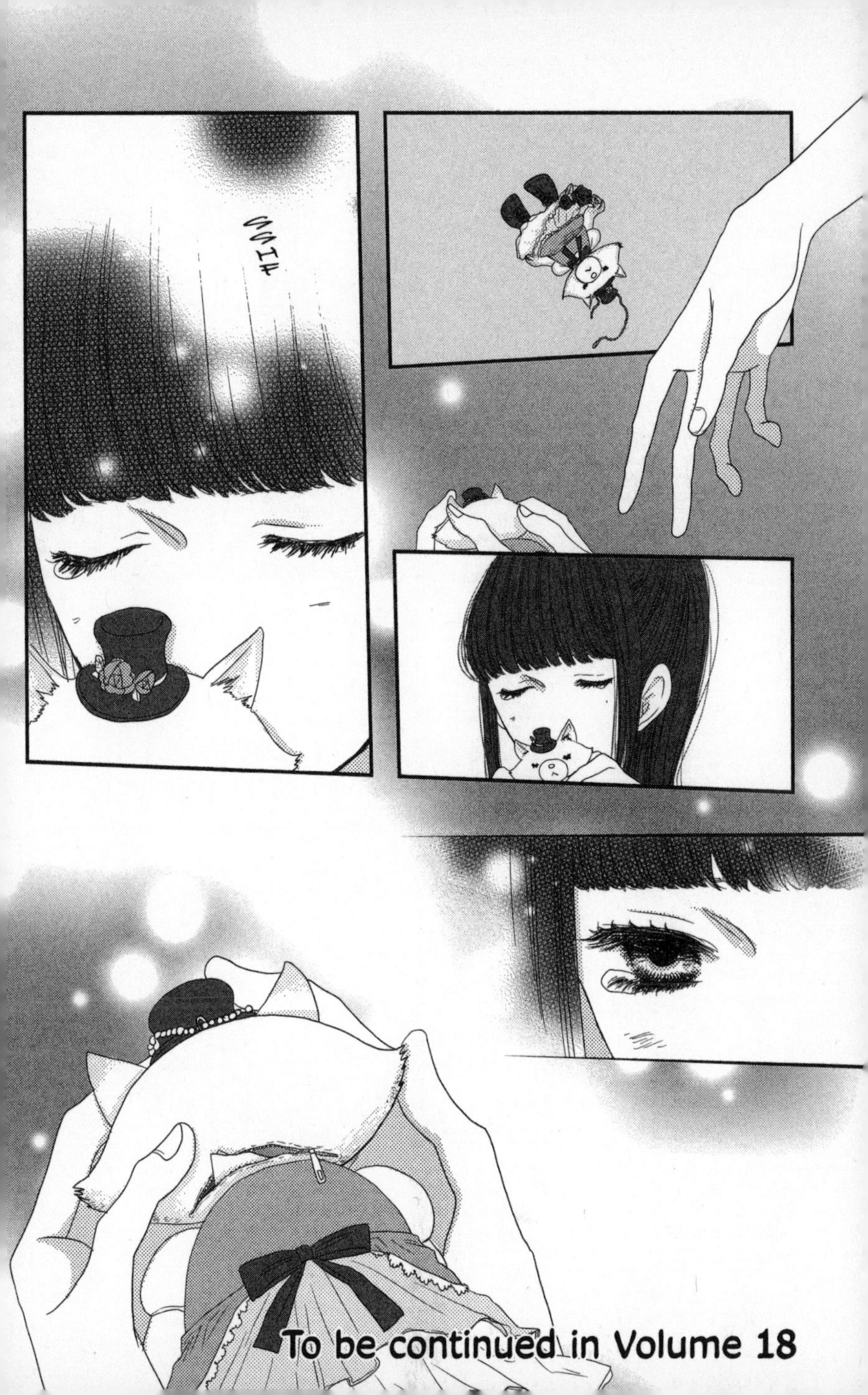
SNIF
To be continued in Volume 18

Say "I love you".

Hello, Kanae Hazuki here. This is volume 17.

The college arc started just last volume, but now they've already graduated and gone into the new beginnings arc.

Maybe some of you were surprised to read this volume.

After volume 16, I would get letters and messages from time to time, saying, "I'm really looking forward to seeing a new Mei and Yamato!"...so I'm sorry for moving the story along so quickly.

This is the way I imagined it developing from the time that I started drawing *Say I Love You*. The high school arc was the true essence of Mei and Yamato's story, or their starting point, so I took it especially slowly.

When it comes to manga, I've always thought that, more than presenting a story, I want the readers to see the characters and learn who they are, and *then* see the story.

You readers have all read up to this point...so I believe that you know what kind of people Mei and Yamato are.

How will they do things now that they're adults? I hope you'll all stick around to see it.

And I don't know if this is the right place to write about this, but... This is a personal matter, but as I'm writing this, there is a new life inside me.

If all goes well, it will have been delivered by the time this volume comes out.

It surprised me, too—I got pregnant at the same time Aiko did.

I never could have dreamed my series would have such a coincidence.

I don't know if I should write about this, either, but before this pregnancy, almost exactly a year ago, I experienced a pregnancy and miscarriage. It was my first pregnancy, and it was a big shock, so I was really nervous—every day I was scared that this one would miscarry, too. Every day.

And now I'm finally in my eighth month, and everything seems to be going well.

As I fumble through life, I'm still drawing manga, but because I'll likely have a hard time keeping this pace once the baby is born, my editor and editor-in-chief arranged for me to take a short break when this volume comes out [October 2016].

I tend to release graphic novels pretty slowly even without the delay, so I really want to apologize to those of you who were really looking forward to more.

I'm sorry for taking time off when we're so close to the end.

And for those of you who would say, "But I want it to keep going forever!", I have nothing but gratitude.

Actually, the ending had been decided quite a while ago, so unfortunately, I can't keep the story going that much longer, but I want to keep drawing the best I can, to the very last chapter.

I'll be taking a break for a while, but I hope you'll keep reading to the finale!

Let's meet again in the next and final volume.

Thank you for reading this far.

Kanae Hazuki

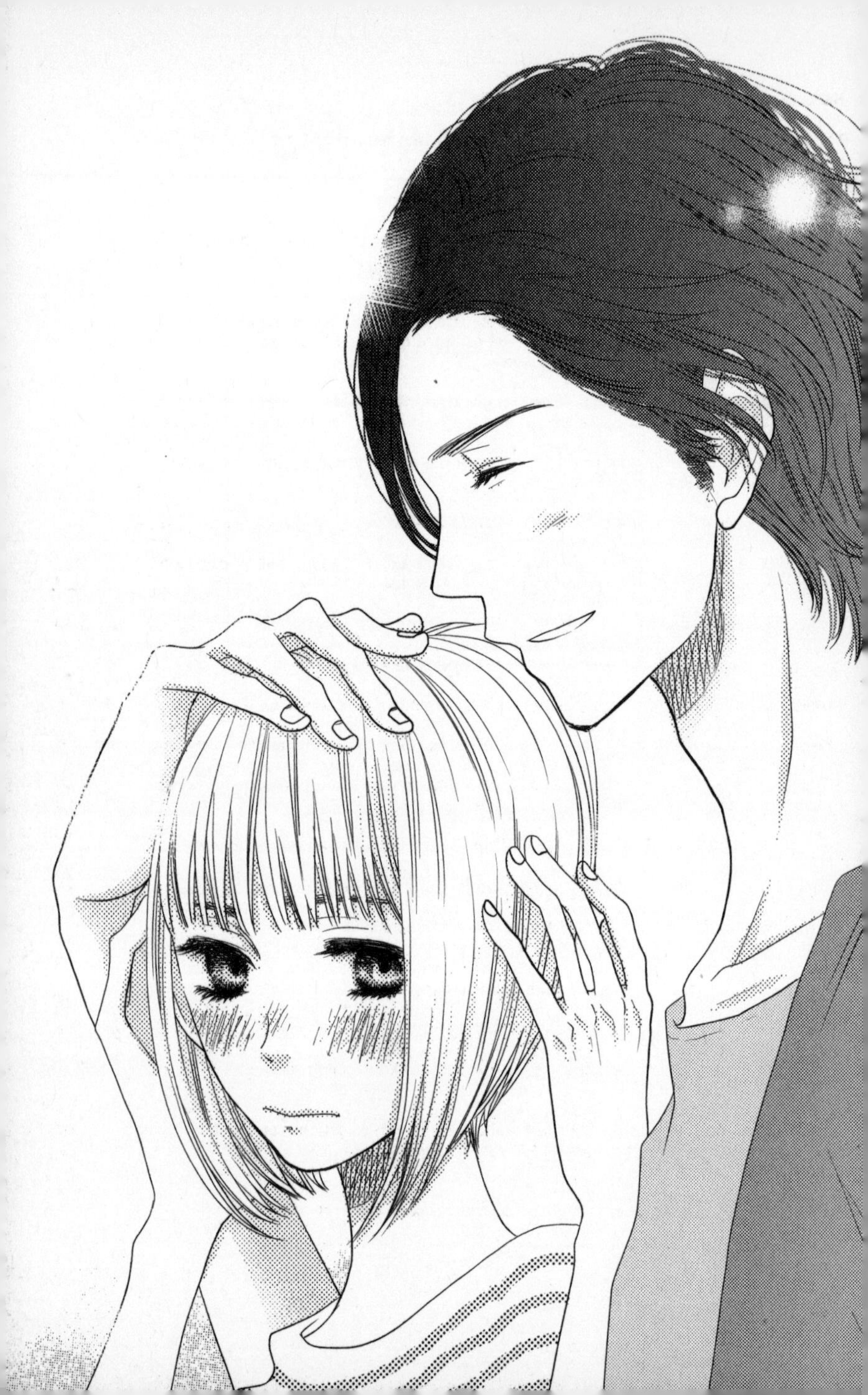

TRANSLATION NOTES

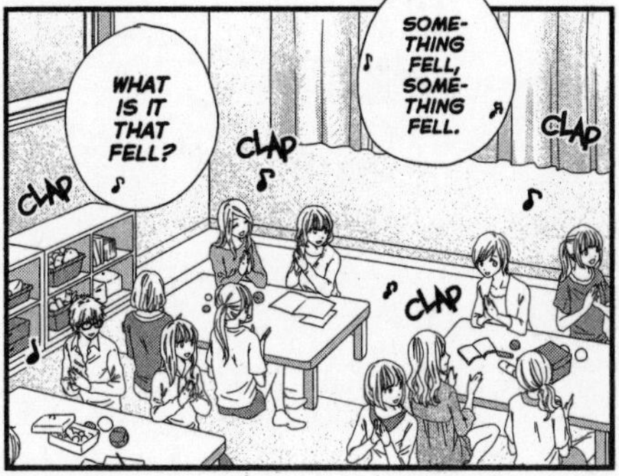
SOMETHING FELL, SOMETHING FELL.
WHAT IS IT THAT FELL?
CLAP
CLAP
CLAP
CLAP

Something fell, page 54

This is a sort of rhythmic children's game. First, the teacher sings that something fell, then the children ask what it was that fell. The teacher answers, and the children respond with an action. In the case of an apple falling, they move as if to catch the apple in front of them.

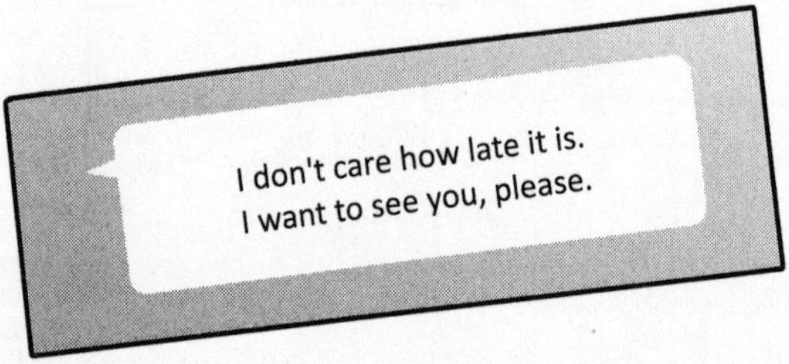
I don't care how late it is.
I want to see you, please.

I want to see you, please, page 71

It may be worth noting here that in her original Japanese message, Mei is using *teineigo*, or polite speech. Mei hasn't used polite speech when speaking to Yamato for years now, so her choice to use it now is an indication of the distance she feels between them, and may be part of why Yamato was so alarmed to read the message.

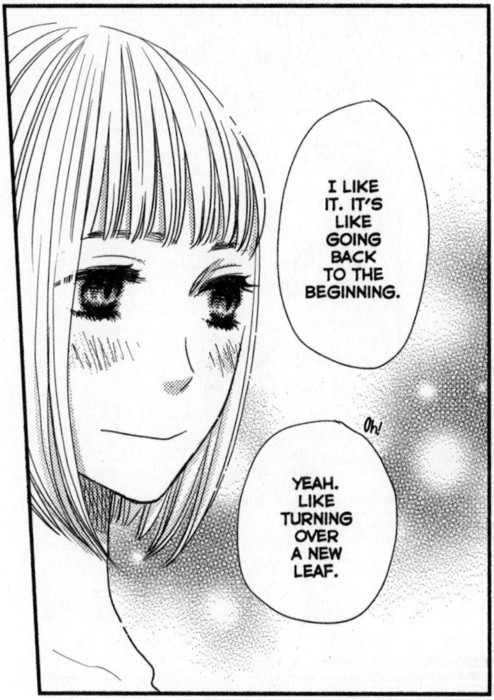
I LIKE IT. IT'S LIKE GOING BACK TO THE BEGINNING.
Oh!
YEAH. LIKE TURNING OVER A NEW LEAF.

Going back to the beginning, page 120

To be more precise, Yamato says it's like "returning to the heart of a beginner." This is a Japanese idiom that refers to the enthusiasm people tend to feel when they're just starting something new and exciting.

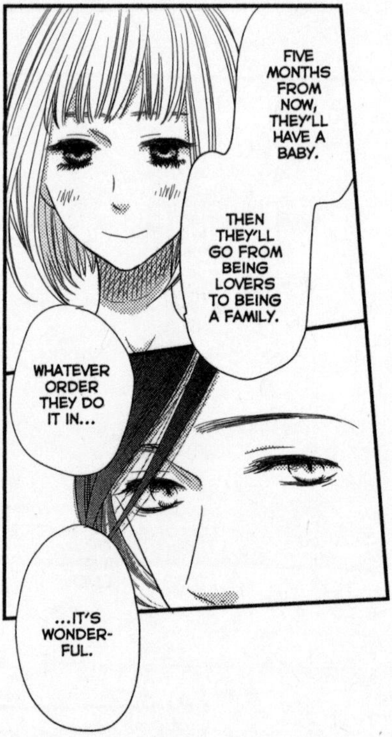
FIVE MONTHS FROM NOW, THEY'LL HAVE A BABY.
THEN THEY'LL GO FROM BEING LOVERS TO BEING A FAMILY.
WHATEVER ORDER THEY DO IT IN...
...IT'S WONDER-FUL.

Five months, page 147

It was previously mentioned that Aiko is already five months pregnant, and here, they are saying she has another five months to go, for a total of ten months. In most Western countries, a pregnancy is said to last forty weeks or nine months, but typically in Japan and some other East Asian countries, they say ten months. The exact reason isn't very clear, but the reason most often given is that countries like Japan used to be on a lunar calendar, in which forty weeks would amount to approximately ten months.

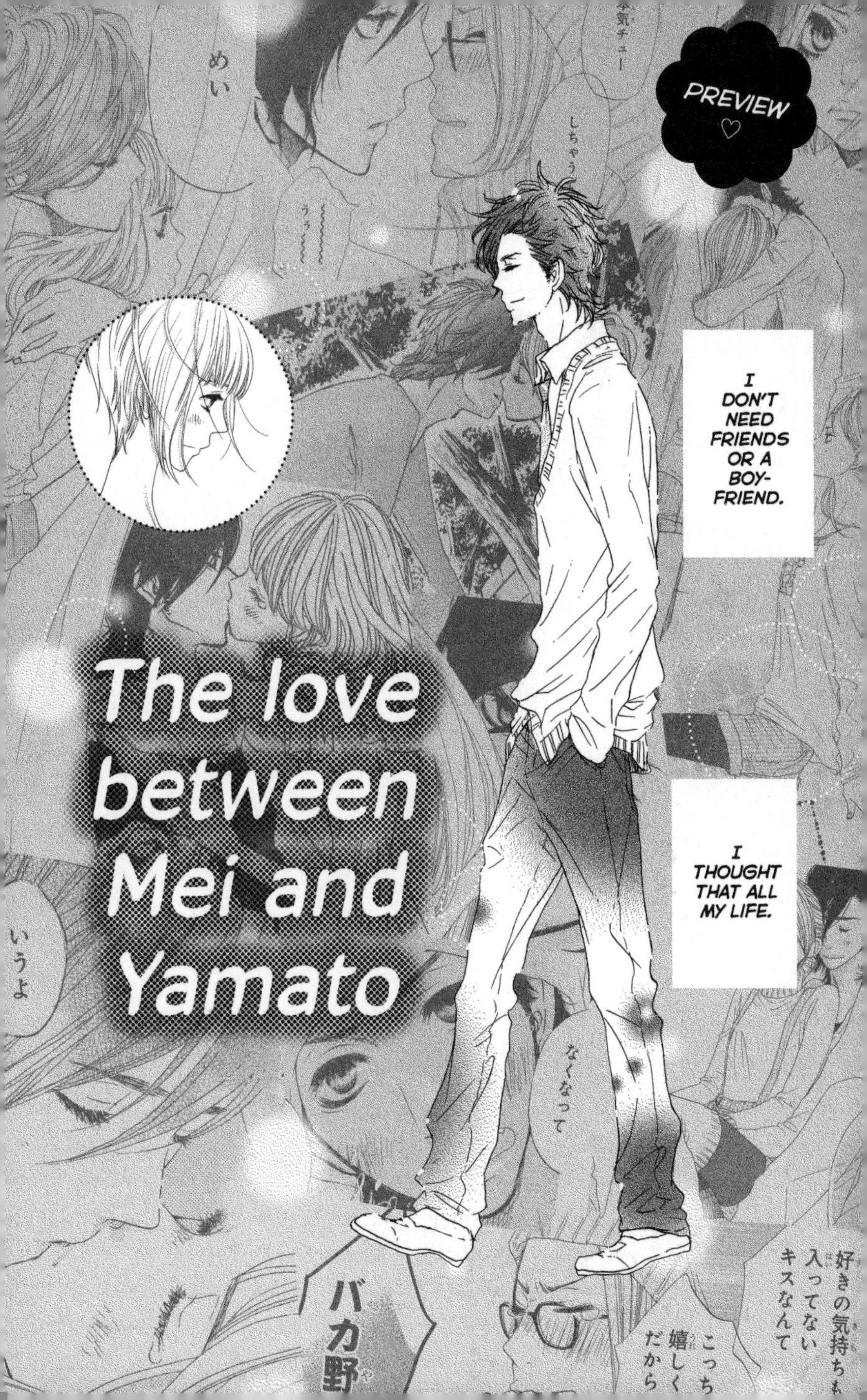
PREVIEW ♡
I DON'T NEED FRIENDS OR A BOY-FRIEND.
I THOUGHT THAT ALL MY LIFE.
The love between Mei and Yamato
しちゃう
めい
なくなって
いうよ

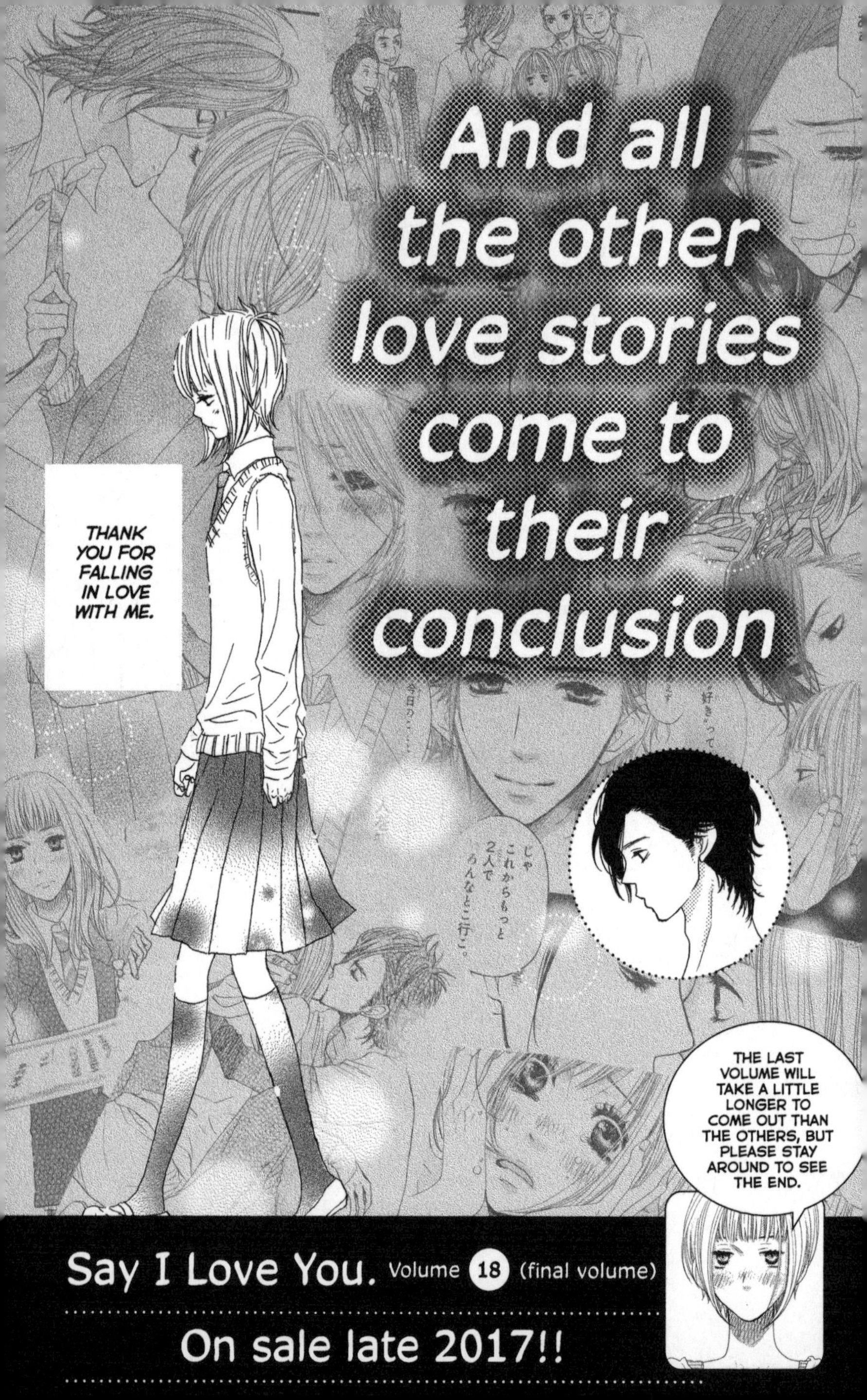
And all the other love stories come to their conclusion
THANK YOU FOR FALLING IN LOVE WITH ME.
THE LAST VOLUME WILL TAKE A LITTLE LONGER TO COME OUT THAN THE OTHERS, BUT PLEASE STAY AROUND TO SEE THE END.
Say I Love You. Volume 18 (final volume)
On sale late 2017!!

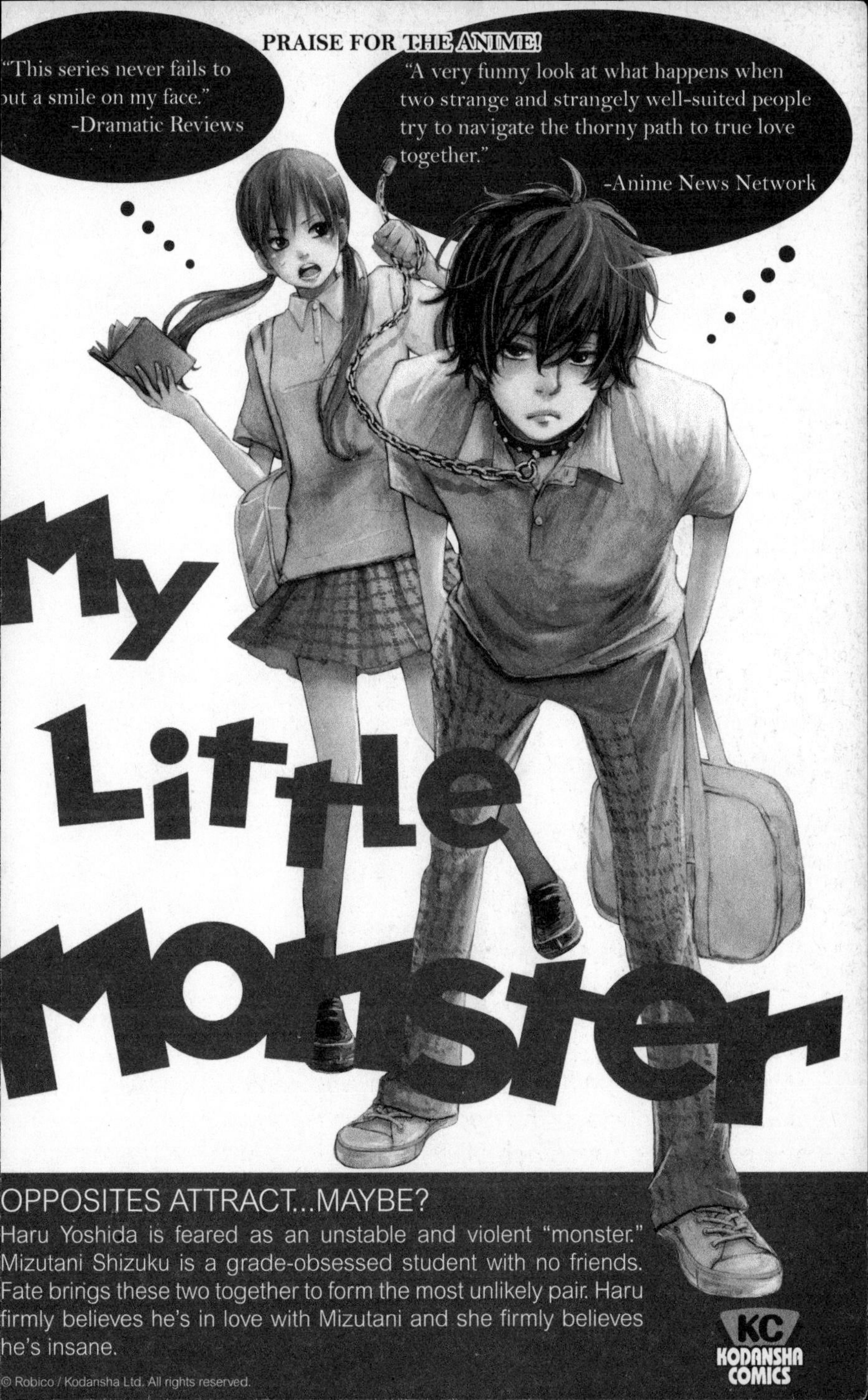
PRAISE FOR THE ANIME!
"This series never fails to put a smile on my face."
-Dramatic Reviews
"A very funny look at what happens when two strange and strangely well-suited people try to navigate the thorny path to true love together."
-Anime News Network
My Little Monster
OPPOSITES ATTRACT...MAYBE?
Haru Yoshida is feared as an unstable and violent "monster." Mizutani Shizuku is a grade-obsessed student with no friends. Fate brings these two together to form the most unlikely pair. Haru firmly believes he's in love with Mizutani and she firmly believes he's insane.
KC
KODANSHA COMICS
© Robico / Kodansha Ltd. All rights reserved.

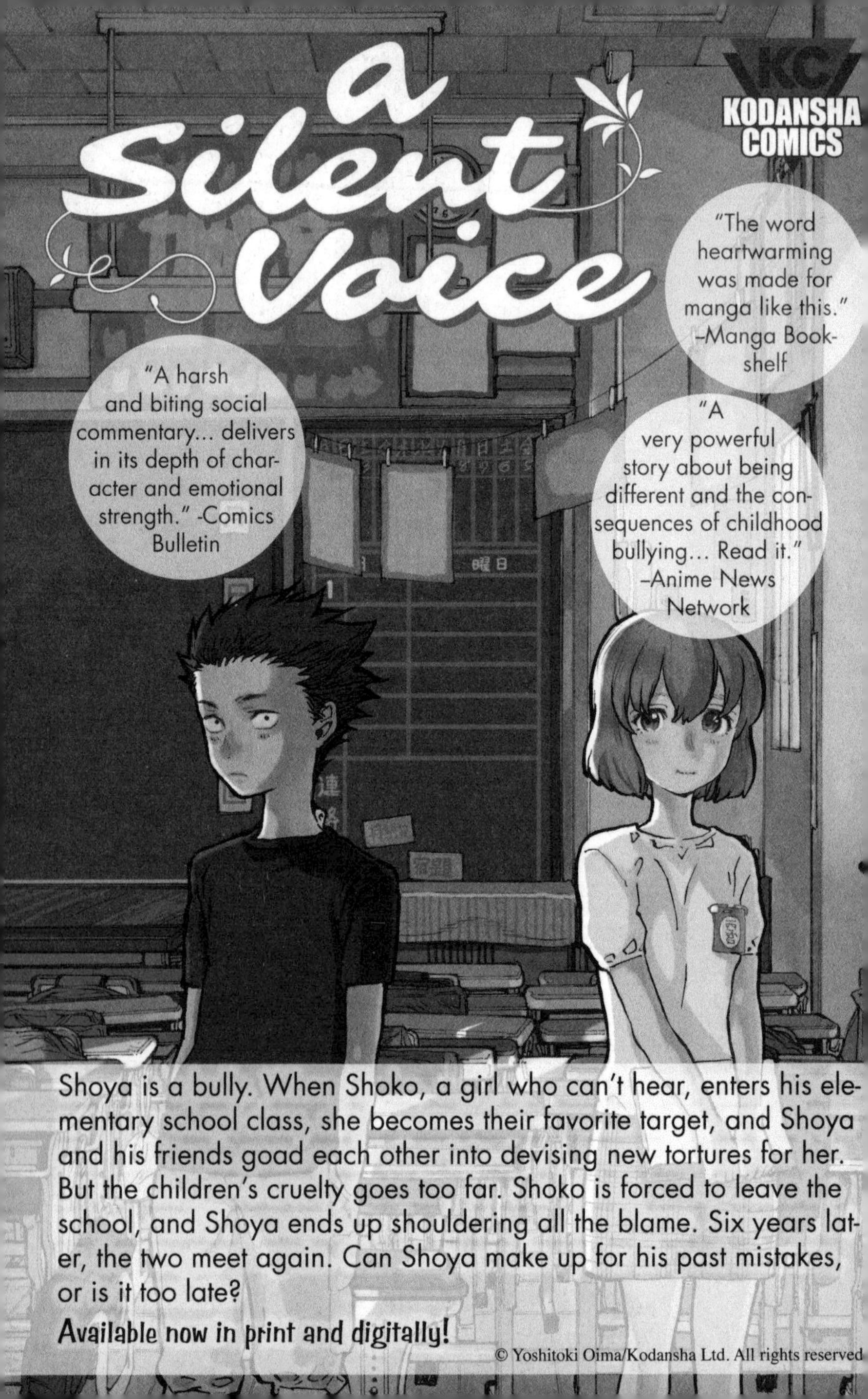
a Silent Voice
KC
KODANSHA COMICS
"The word heartwarming was made for manga like this." –Manga Bookshelf
"A harsh and biting social commentary... delivers in its depth of character and emotional strength." -Comics Bulletin
"A very powerful story about being different and the consequences of childhood bullying... Read it." –Anime News Network
Shoya is a bully. When Shoko, a girl who can't hear, enters his elementary school class, she becomes their favorite target, and Shoya and his friends goad each other into devising new tortures for her. But the children's cruelty goes too far. Shoko is forced to leave the school, and Shoya ends up shouldering all the blame. Six years later, the two meet again. Can Shoya make up for his past mistakes, or is it too late?
Available now in print and digitally!
© Yoshitoki Oima/Kodansha Ltd. All rights reserved

THE HEROIC LEGEND OF
ARSLAN

READ THE NEW SERIES FROM THE CREATOR OF FULLMETAL ALCHEMIST, HIROMU ARAKAWA! NOW A HIT TV SERIES!

> "Arakawa proves to be more than up to the task of adapting Tanaka's fantasy novels and fans of historical or epic fantasy will be quite pleased with the resulting book."
> -Anime News Network

ECBATANA IS BURNING!

Arslan is the young and curious prince of Pars who, despite his best efforts doesn't seem to have what it takes to be a proper king like his father. At the age of 14, Arslan goes to his first battle and loses everything as the blood-soaked mist of war gives way to scorching flames, bringing him to face the demise of his once glorious kingdom. However, it is Arslan's destiny to be a ruler, and despite the trials that face him, he must now embark on a journey

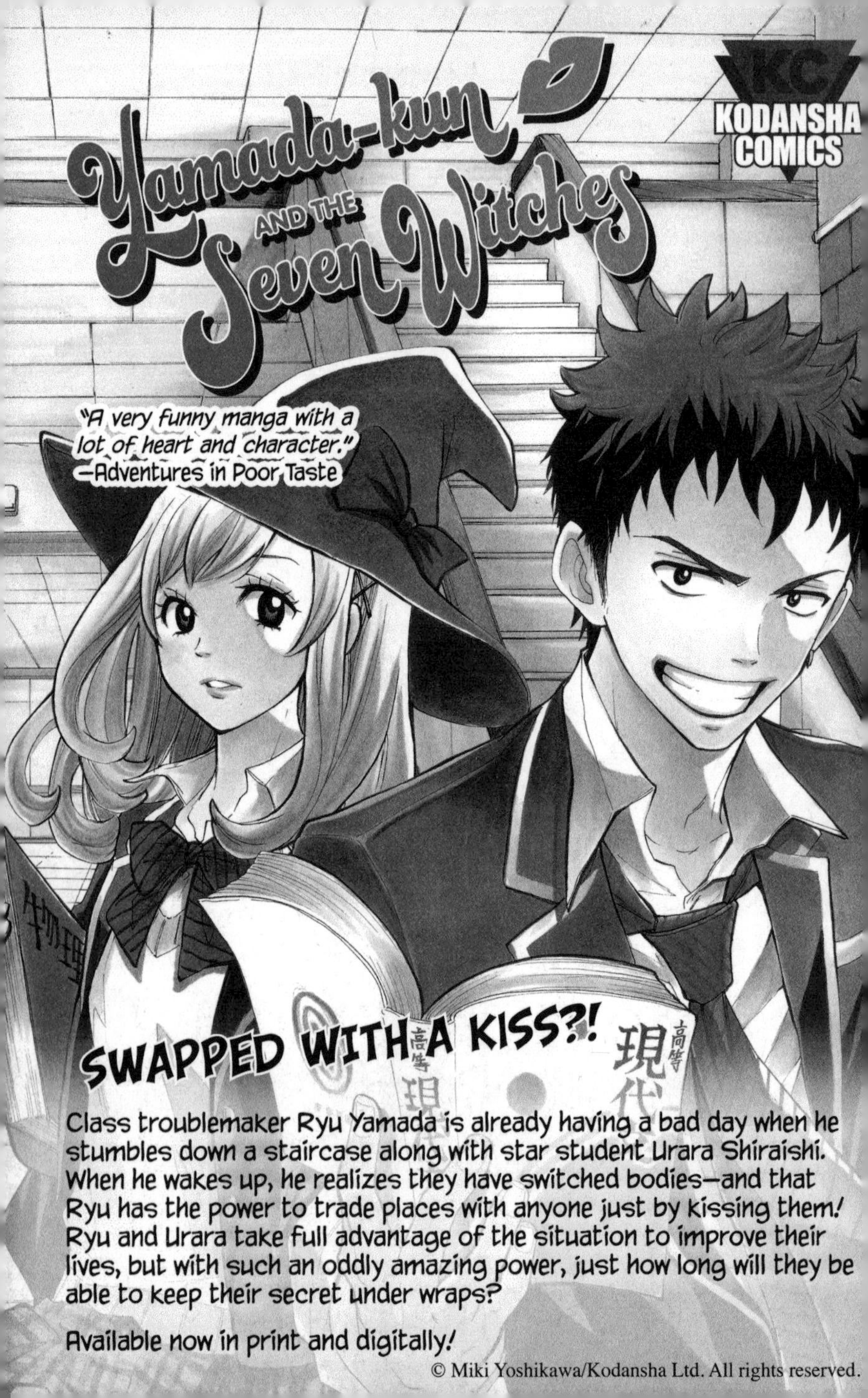
KODANSHA COMICS
Yamada-kun AND THE Seven Witches
"A very funny manga with a lot of heart and character." —Adventures in Poor Taste
SWAPPED WITH A KISS?!
Class troublemaker Ryu Yamada is already having a bad day when he stumbles down a staircase along with star student Urara Shiraishi. When he wakes up, he realizes they have switched bodies—and that Ryu has the power to trade places with anyone just by kissing them! Ryu and Urara take full advantage of the situation to improve their lives, but with such an oddly amazing power, just how long will they be able to keep their secret under wraps?
Available now in print and digitally!
© Miki Yoshikawa/Kodansha Ltd. All rights reserved.

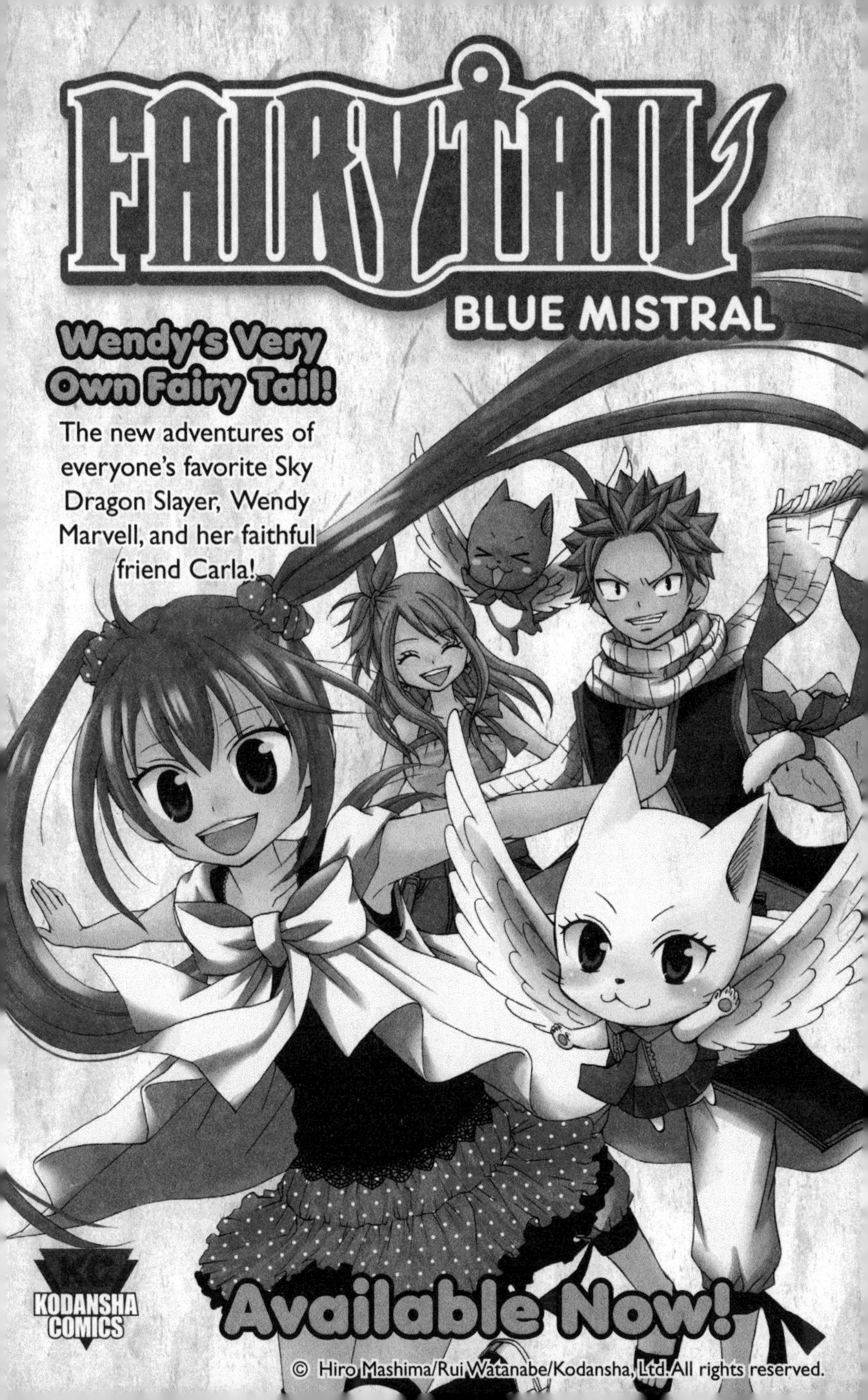
FAIRY TAIL
BLUE MISTRAL
Wendy's Very Own Fairy Tail!
The new adventures of everyone's favorite Sky Dragon Slayer, Wendy Marvell, and her faithful friend Carla!
KODANSHA COMICS
Available Now!
© Hiro Mashima/Rui Watanabe/Kodansha, Ltd. All rights reserved.

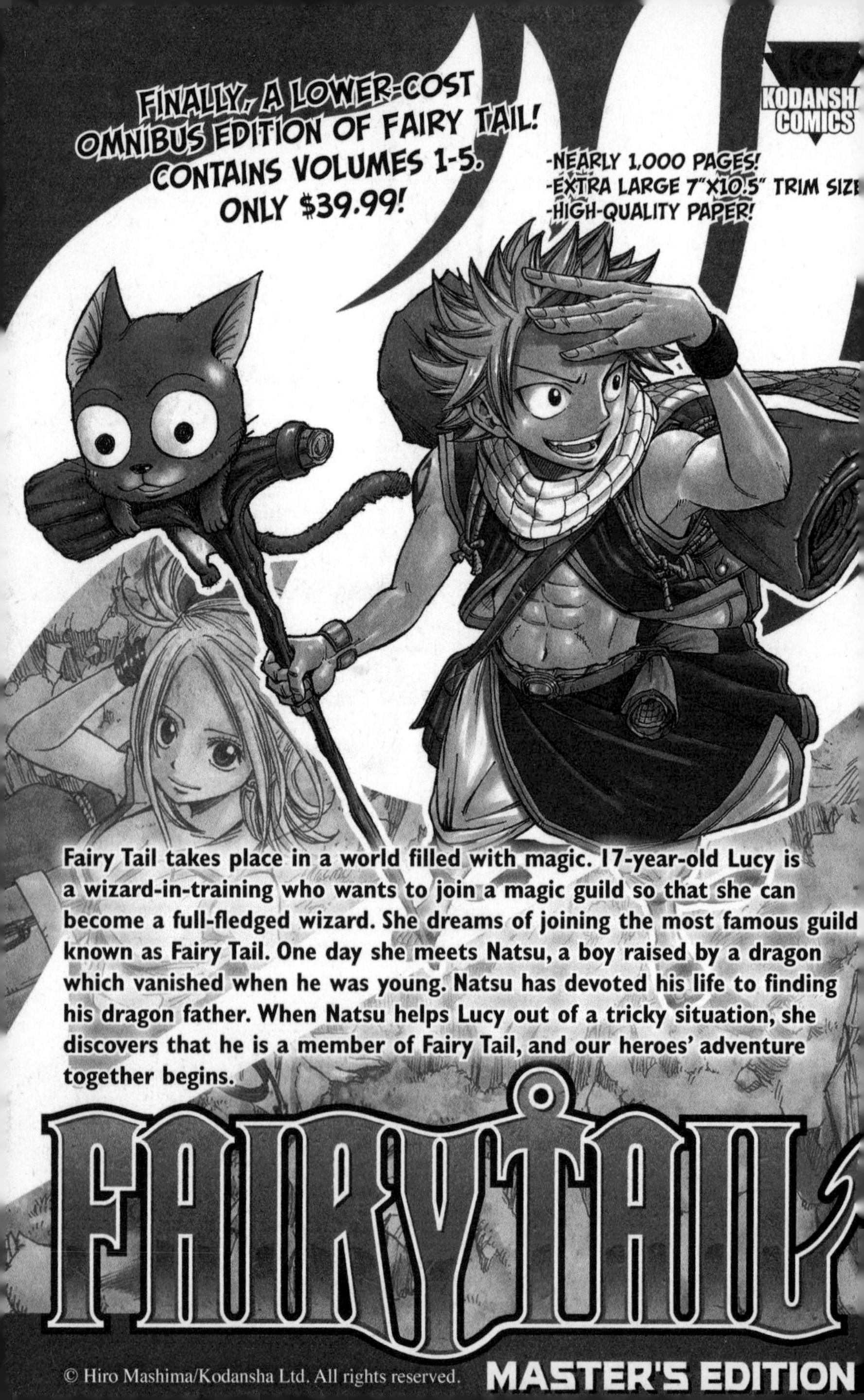
FINALLY, A LOWER-COST OMNIBUS EDITION OF FAIRY TAIL! CONTAINS VOLUMES 1-5. ONLY $39.99!
KODANSHA COMICS
-NEARLY 1,000 PAGES!
-EXTRA LARGE 7"X10.5" TRIM SIZE
-HIGH-QUALITY PAPER!
Fairy Tail takes place in a world filled with magic. 17-year-old Lucy is a wizard-in-training who wants to join a magic guild so that she can become a full-fledged wizard. She dreams of joining the most famous guild known as Fairy Tail. One day she meets Natsu, a boy raised by a dragon which vanished when he was young. Natsu has devoted his life to finding his dragon father. When Natsu helps Lucy out of a tricky situation, she discovers that he is a member of Fairy Tail, and our heroes' adventure together begins.
FAIRY TAIL
© Hiro Mashima/Kodansha Ltd. All rights reserved.
MASTER'S EDITION

A Kodansha Comics Trade Paperback Original
Say I Love You. volume 17 copyright © 2016 Kanae Hazuki
English translation copyright © 2017 Kanae Hazuki

All rights reserved.

Published in the United States by Kodansha Comics, an imprint of Kodansha USA Publishing, LLC, New York.

Publication rights for this English edition arranged through Kodansha Ltd, Tokyo.

First published in Japan in 2016 by Kodansha Ltd., Tokyo as *Sukitte iinayo.* volume 17.

ISBN 978-1-63236-303-9

Printed in the United States of America.

www.kodanshacomics.com

9 8 7 6 5 4 3 2 1
Translation: Alethea and Athena Nibley
Lettering: Jennifer Skarupa
Editing: Ajani Oloye
Kodansha Comics edition cover design: Phil Balsman